Contents

Thanks

Many people contributed their hard work, fresh ideas and sound advice to this book:

Niki Browne edited the book with sensitivity and thoroughness.
Liz Sharman supervised and guided the project from start to finish.
Hilary Fletcher was responsible for picture research and permission.
Sophie Dukan was responsible for text permission.
Oxprint Design designed the book.

James Richardson produced the recordings at Studio AVP, the engineer was Andy Taylor. More than 30 actors (too many to name individually) took part in the studio recordings.

Derek Mainwaring and Linda Thalman in France, Annette Blanche Ceccarelli and Hilary Isaacs in Italy, Zofia Bernacka-Wos and Joanna Burzynska in Poland and Derek Leverton and Jesús Marin in Spain gave us detailed comments on the previous edition of *Progress to First Certificate*. Almost 100 teachers from all over the world (too many to name) also gave us feedback on the previous edition through a questionnaire.

Annie Broadhead, Henrietta Burke, Anne Gutch, Jane Hann, Nick Kenny, Sean Power, Liz Tataraki and Clare West commented on sample and draft units.

To all the above: thank you very much!

From the second edition

No book of this kind can be produced by one person alone and in this case countless people have generously contributed their ideas and advice.

In particular, I'd just like to say how grateful I am to the following friends, colleagues and teachers:
Jeanne McCarten for guiding the New Edition through from start to finish and for her encouragement, perfectionism and good ideas; Jill Mountain and Kit Woods for their detailed comments on the first edition and for subsequently reading, evaluating and suggesting improvements to the first draft of this New Edition; Alison Silver for her editing expertise and sensible suggestions; Peter Taylor and Studio AVP for their professional skills in producing the recorded material; Peter Ducker for his meticulous work on the illustrations and design; Sue Gosling for her help and advice.

And thanks to the following teachers whose detailed comments on the first edition and helpful ideas led to many valuable changes in the New Edition:
Susan Barber, Lake School of English in Oxford; John Bradbury, FIAC Escola d'idiomes moderns in Sabadell, Catalonia, Spain; Susan Garvin, British Institute of Florence, Italy; Roger Johnson and Nick Kenny, British Council in Milan, Italy; Fern Judet, Swan School in Oxford; Lynne White, Godmer House School of English in Oxford.

And thanks to the following teachers who kindly wrote about their experiences of using the first edition, some of whom gave us their students' feedback:
H.G. Bernhardt, Tony Buckby and colleagues, J. Carvell, Emily Grammenou, Michael Hadgimichalis, Pearl Herrmann, Jill Jeavons, Katherine Karangianni, Marie Anne Küpper-Compes, Bryan Newman, Cathy Parker and colleagues, Véronique Rouanet, Claire Springett, Andrew Tymn, Robin Visel and J.T. Ward.

Finally, thanks to the numerous other teachers in many different countries (and their students) who have given us useful informal feedback on the first edition.

Thank you, everyone!

From the first edition

I'd like to express my thanks to Sue Gosling and Christine Cairns for all their encouragement and help during the planning, writing and rewriting of this book. Many thanks are also due
to all the teachers who used the pilot edition and made so many useful and perceptive comments. Thanks are due in particular to staff at the following schools and institutes: the British Centre in Venice, the British Institute in Paris, the British School in Florence, the Newnham Language Centre in Cambridge, the Studio School of English in Cambridge and the Université II in Lyons.

New
Progress
to First Certificate

Self-study Student's Book

Leo Jones

CAMBRIDGE
UNIVERSITY PRESS

PUBLISHED BY THE PRESS SYNDICATE OF THE UNIVERSITY OF CAMBRIDGE
The Pitt Building, Trumpington Street, Cambridge, United Kingdom

CAMBRIDGE UNIVERSITY PRESS
The Edinburgh Building, Cambridge CB2 2RU, UK
40 West 20th Street, New York, NY 10011–4211, USA
477 Williamstown Road, Port Melbourne, VIC 3207, Australia
Ruiz de Alarcón 13, 28014 Madrid, Spain
Dock House, The Waterfront, Cape Town 8001, South Africa

http://www.cambridge.org

First published 1997
Eighth printing 2003

Printed in the United Kingdom at the University Press, Cambridge

ISBN 0 521 49984 2 Student's Book
ISBN 0 521 49988 7 Self-study Student's Book
ISBN 0 521 49986 0 Teacher's Book
ISBN 0 521 49987 9 Class Cassette Set
ISBN 0 521 77426 8 Workbook
ISBN 0 521 77425 X Workbook with answers
ISBN 0 521 77424 1 Workbook Cassette

Acknowledgements

The author and publishers are grateful to the following for permission to reproduce copyright material. It has not always been possible to identify sources of all the material used and in such cases the publishers would welcome information from the copyright owners.

For permission to reproduce texts:

Reed Consumer Books Ltd for the extracts on page 12 and page 134 from *Conscientious Objections* by Neil Postman © 1988 by Neil Postman, reprinted by permission of Alfred A. Knopf Inc.; Dorling Kindersley for the extracts on page 23 from *Eyewitness Travel Guide To New York* (top) and *Eyewitness Travel Guide to London* (bottom); The Economist for the articles on pages 28, 50, 58, 68, 130 © The Economist; The Radio Times for the article on page 38; The Guardian for the articles on pages 41, 71, 139, 140, 146, 148, 149, 186, 188, 189, 191 (no. 1, no. 2 and no. 3) and the *How to Juggle* strip page 125 © The Guardian; The extracts from the leaflet *Safety on the Move* on pages 48, 201, 204 are Crown Copyright items reproduced with the permission of the Controller of HMSO; The Health and Education Authority for the extract on page 67 from the leaflet *Read this and know what to do about flu*; Blackwell Publishers for the extracts on page 137 from *Coping with Japan* (no. 1) and *Coping with America* (no. 2); Kuoni Travel Ltd for the text on page 74; Neal's Yard Bakery for the *Apple Crumble* recipe on pages 80, 81; Take Note Publishing for the *Somerset Cider Cake* recipe by Jacoba Gale and the *Dorset Apple Cake* recipe by Colette Louis on pages 80, 81; Penguin Books for the extract on page 90 from *The Captain and the Enemy* by Graham Greene; Toby Young for his review on page 98; The extracts on pages 106–107 are reprinted by permission of The Bodley Head, the Estate of F. Scott Fitzgerald, Harold Ober Associates Inc. and Scribner, a Division of Simon & Schuster, from *The Great Gatsby* (Authorised Text) by F. Scott Fitzgerald. Copyright 1925 by Charles Scribner's sons. Copyright renewed 1953 by Frances Scott Fitzgerald Lanahan. Copyright © 1991, 1992 by Eleanor Lanahan, Matthew J. Bruccoli and Samuel J. Lanahan as Trustees u/a dated 3/7/75 created by Frances Scott Fitzgerald Smith; The Midland Bank for the extract on page 116 from the leaflet *How to create a good impression at your first interview*; Sinclair Research Ltd for the advertisement on page 124; Dateline International for the advertisement on page 153; Curtis Brown Ltd for the reproduction of the extract on page 156 from *Mr Norris Changes Trains* by Christopher Isherwood, on behalf of the Estate of Christopher Isherwood © Christopher Isherwood; The Jorvik Viking Centre for the extract on page 161 from the *Jorvik* leaflet; Equinox Ltd for the extracts on pages 165–168 adapted from *Dreams for Sale*; Leeds Castle Enterprises Ltd for the text on page 168. The dictionary foreword on page 10 is taken from the *Cambridge International Dictionary of English*, Cambridge University Press, 1995.

For permission to reproduce photographs and other copyright artwork:

Roger Bamber for page 129 (top middle). The Anthony Blake photo Library/Gerrit Buntrock for pages 80 (top left, top right), 86, 87 (left), /Neville Kuypers for pages 80 (bottom right), 87 (right), /Charlie Stebbings for page 80 (bottom left). The Bridgeman Art Library/The British Library, London for page 145 (bottom right), /Giraudon/Wild Poppies, near Argenteuil 1873, Claude Monet © ADAGP, Paris and DACS, London 1996 for page 145 (middle left), /Lauros-Giraudon/Murnau with Church 11 1910, Wassily Kandinsky © ADAGP, Paris and DACS, London 1996 for page 145 (top left), /Lauros-Giraudon/The Wizard 1951, Rene Magritte © ADAGP, Paris and DACS, London 1996 for page 145 (top right), /Mauritshuis, The Hage for page 145 (bottom left), /Museum of Fine Arts Boston, Massachusetts for page 145 (middle middle), /National Gallery, London for page 145 (middle right). Bill Buchler/Travel Mal Catalogue for page 20 (top). Camera Press/Cecil Beaton for page 152 (right), /Karsh of Ottawa for page 152 (middle right), /Jerry Watson for page 152 (far left). Capital Pictures/Phil Loftus for page 152 (far right). Christo/Wolfgang Volz for page 150 (top left, top right). Colorific/Carlos Humberto for page 197 (bottom left). Compass Maps Ltd, Bath for page 54. Comstock for pages 29, 97 (right). Dateline International for page 153. Department of Transport for pages 48, 201 (top), 204. Dorling Kindersley Adult for page 42, /David Macaulay for pages 190 (bottom), 193 (bottom), 199 (bottom), 201 (bottom). Tim Dowling for page 46. Edifice/Darley for page 60 (top right), /Lewis for page 60 (top left, bottom left), /Jackson for page 60 (bottom right). Greg Evans International Photo Library for pages 16 (bottom right), 23 (top), /Greg Balfour Evans for page 58 (top left), /J. Flowerdew for page 88 (bottom left, bottom right). Mary Evans Picture Library for page 161 (top). First Choice Holidays/Ogilvy & Mather for pages 187 (top), 197 (top). The Ronald Grant Archive for pages 20 (bottom left), 96 (top right), /Columbia Tri-Star Films (UK) for page 98 (bottom left, bottom right). The Guardian Newspaper for page 129 (right), /Graham Turner for page 150 (bottom). Health Education Authority for page 67. Herts & Essex Newspapers for page 129 (left). Hulton Deutsch Collection for pages 186 (right), 196 (top right, top left). Robert Hunt for pages 50, 131. The Image Bank for page 23 (bottom), /Werner Bokelberg for page 64 (right), /Nancy Brown for page 24 (top left), /David Brownell for page 40 (left), /Andy Caulfield for page 75, /Flip Chalfant for page 88 (top right), /Giuliano Colliva for page 148 (top), /Paolo Curto for page 45 (top), /Steve Dunwell for page 16 (left), /Reinhard Eisele for page 40 (top right), /David Gould for page 163 (right), /Bill Hickey for page 57 (bottom left), /Janeart for page 24 (bottom left), /Janeart for page 16 (top right), /Don Klumpp for page 203 (middle right), /Chuck Kuhn for page 15 (bottom), /G&M David De Lossy for page 189 (left), /Cesar Lucas for page 74, /Peter Miller for page 40 (bottom right), /Benn Mitchell for page 195 (top right), /Donmata Pizzi for page 108 (bottom), /

Terje Rakke for page 144 (bottom left), /Schmid/Langsfeld for page 203 (top right), /Alvis Upitis for page 144 (top right), /Steven Burr Williams for page 64 (left). Impact Photos/Martin Black for page 49 (right), / Piers Cavendish for page 190 (left), /Mark Henley for page 49 (left), /Jon Hoffman for page 195 (bottom right), /Bruce Stephens for page 199 (top left). Leo Jones for pages 63, 148 (bottom). Jorvik Viking Centre, Coppergate, York for page 161 (bottom). The Kobal Collection for pages 31, 96 (top left, bottom left, bottom right). Leeds Castle Enterprises Ltd for page 168. Magnum Photos/Michael K. Nichols for page 187 (bottom left). The Metropolitan Museum of Art/Gift of Mrs William F. Milton 1923 for page 193 (top), /Wolfe Fund, 1907, Catherine Lorillard Wolfe Collection for page 191 (bottom). Midland Bank PLC for page 116. Mirror Syndication International for page 152 (left). Network /Paul Lowe for page 53 (left), /Jonathan Olley for page 53 (middle), /Homer Sykes for page 200 (top left). Philips Electronics UK Ltd for page 20 (bottom middle). Pictor International for pages 32 (left), 71 (left), 72 (top left, top middle, top right), 73 (bottom left), 140. Planet Earth Pictures/Brian Kenney for page 98 (top), /Herwarth Voigtmann for page 197 (bottom right). © The Post Office 1996. "The Post Office" is a registered trade mark of the Post Office. Reprinted with permission for pages 16 (middle), 203 (middle left). Quadrant Picture Library for pages 12, 53 (right). Rex Features for page 146 (top left), 152 (middle left), 203 (top left), /Peter Carrette/LGI for page 195 (middle right), /The Times for page 73 (top right). Peter Sanders for page 136 (top right, bottom left). Glyn Satterley for page 38. Science Photo Library for page 120 (top right). Scotland in Focus/RM047 for page 78 (middle), /R. Weir for page 78 (left, right). Sinclair Research Ltd for page 124. Frank Spooner Pictures/Gamma for page 187 (bottom right), /S. Morgan for page 129 (bottom middle). Sporting Pictures (UK) Ltd for page 32 (top right). Tony Stone Images for pages 32 (bottom right), 144 (bottom right), /Glen Allison for pages 58 (bottom right), 73 (top left), /Bruce Ayres for page 195 (top left), /Dan Bosler for page 24 (bottom right), /Bruce Forster for page 199 (top right), /Charles Gupton for page 136 (top left), /Graham Harris for page 73 (bottom right), /Ernst Hohne for page 73 (bottom middle), /Howard Grey for page 24 (top right), / Peter Newton for page 73 (top middle), /Lee Page for page 136 (bottom right), /Steven Peters for page 203 (bottom left), /Jon Riley for page 195 (middle left, bottom left), /Andy Sacks for page 203 (bottom right), /Andy Sotirou for page 142, /Arthur Tilley for page 88 (top left), /Bill Truslow for page 97 (left). Telegraph Colour Library for page 32 (top middle), /R. Jewell for page 57 (bottom right), /Chris Mellor for page 163 (left), /Peter Turnley/Black Star for page 189 (right). Topham Picturepoint for pages 90, 144 (top left), 186 (left), 200 (top right). Zefa Pictures Ltd for page 40 (middle), /J. Pfaff for page 190 (right), /The Stock Market for pages 65, 70 (left).

The following cartoons are used with permission of Punch: pages 6, 15, 22, 28, 55, 66, 76, 85, 95, 103, 110, 112, 117, 132, 135, 146 (bottom right), 151, 154, 169.

The following pictures were taken on commission for Cambridge University Press by Trevor Clifford: pages 8, 14, 20 (bottom middle/Kodak, bottom right/Beamish), 56, 57 (top left), 70 (right), 71 (right), 72 (bottom left, bottom right, bottom middle), 84, 91, 104, 108 (top, middle), 109, 120 (bottom left, bottom right, top left), 198, 207.

We would like to thank the following publishers for their assistance on pages 104, 108, 109: Bell College Saffron Walden, Harper Collins Publishers, Hodder Headline PLC, Penguin Books Ltd, Random House UK Ltd, Transworld Publishers Ltd. Sample answer sheets are reproduced by kind permission of the University of Cambridge Local Examinations Syndicate.

We have been unable to trace the copyright owner of the image on page 25 and would be grateful for any information to enable us to do so.

For permission to reproduce recorded material in Unit 2:

Mel Smith and Griff Rhys Jones for the *Firrips* radio advertisement; Courage Limited and The Special Artists Agency, Inc. for the Beamish Stout *Darkness Falls* radio advertisement; Hand Made Films for the *Life of Brian* radio advertisement © 1979 Paragon Entertainment Corporation.

Illustrations:

David Axtell, Heather Clarke, Edward McLachlan, Oxford Illustrators, Oxprint Design.

Typesetting by Oxprint Design Ltd, Oxford.
Cover design by Barnabas Haward.

Welcome!

This book will help you to prepare *progressively* for the Cambridge First Certificate in English examination (FCE). The exercises, tasks and activities will help you to learn more English and improve your language skills – they don't just test your knowledge, they help you to make *progress*. The nature of the exercises, tasks and activities changes gradually through the book until, by the time you reach Unit 20, you'll be answering questions that are just the same as the ones you'll have to answer in the exam itself.

The FCE exam consists of five papers:
Paper 1: Reading, Paper 2: Writing, Paper 3: Use of English, Paper 4: Listening and Paper 5: Speaking.

To help you to prepare for the exam, the sections in each unit focus on different skills that are needed for the exam:

- Some sections focus on the basic skills you need for individual papers in the exam: READING, WRITING, LISTENING and SPEAKING.
- Some sections focus on the important language points that you need to revise or learn for the Use of English and Writing papers: GRAMMAR REVIEW, VOCABULARY, WORD STUDY, VERBS AND IDIOMS and PREPOSITIONS.
- Some special sections focus on exam techniques for each paper in the exam. There are also plenty of exam hints, tips and advice scattered throughout the book.

Each unit is based on a different topic, covering all the topics that are included in the exam syllabus and which may come up in the exam. But, perhaps more important, they are all topics that will interest you and give you plenty to talk about.

In class, you'll be doing many exercises, tasks and activities in pairs or small groups. The purpose of this is to make sure that everyone gets plenty of practice in speaking English. Don't be surprised if your teacher decides to leave out some sections – the book is designed to be used selectively in this way.

Besides class work, there will also be quite a lot of homework for you to do:

- preparing reading passages that you'll be discussing later in class
- doing exercises that will be checked later in class
- and (of course!) doing written work to improve your writing skills.

On pages 170–185, you'll find the GRAMMAR REFERENCE sections, where the main problem areas of English grammar are explained and clear examples are given. You may need to refer to these sections before attempting the exercises in the GRAMMAR REVIEW sections.

On pages 186–207, there are 62 COMMUNICATION ACTIVITIES, where you and your partner are given different information that you must communicate to each other. There is an 'information gap' between you, and you must react spontaneously to what your partner says – just as in a real-life conversation.

Good luck during your exam preparation course – and enjoy using *New Progress to First Certificate*!

1 Communication

1.1 Ways of communicating
VOCABULARY AND SPEAKING

A   **Work in pairs**   **Look at the photos above and discuss these questions:**

- What is happening in each picture?
- What is the 'message' in each case?
- What might each person say instead of gesturing?
- Have you ever been in any similar situations? What happened?

B   **Fill the gaps in these sentences with a suitable word.**

1 *Man, woman, table* and *chair* are all concrete ....*nouns*.... and *speak, write, listen* and *read* are all ....*verbs*.... .

2 *Freedom, space* and *thirst* are a............ nouns, not concrete nouns like *man* and *woman*.

3 *Large, blue* and *red* are a............ and *happily, sadly* and *softly* are a............ .

4 *It, him, her* and *they* are all p............ .

5 *In, on, out of* and *about* are all p............ .

6 *But, although, while* and *after* are all c............ .

7 Nouns, verbs, adjectives and pronouns are all different p............ of speech.

8 *Run away, come back, fall in* and *fall out* are all p............ verbs.

9 *John, Monday, July* and *Britain* all begin with a c............ l............ .

10 *This whole sentence is printed in i*............ .

11 *Underneath, however, energy* and *instantly* all have three s............ .

12 *Pre-, in-, over-* and *un-* are all p............ . *-able, -less, -ment* and *-ful* are all s............ .

13 These words:/ɪŋglɪʃ/, /əmerɪkən/ and /welʃ/ are all printed in ph............ script.

14 Australians, Scots, Canadians and Indians all speak English with different a............ .

C 1   **Work in pairs**   **Your first impression of someone influences your relationship with them. Which of these things do you notice when you meet someone? Put them in order of importance:**

what they say   accent   body language   clothes   eyes   hair   hands
shoes   smile   voice   manners   personality

2   Everyone wants to be liked. Write down five adjectives to describe the impression you would like people to have of you and five adjectives to describe the impression you *don't* want them to have.

3   **Join another pair**   Compare your lists. Note down any useful words the others used which you'd like to remember.

Remembering vocabulary takes a bit of work. You need to keep notes for words you want to remember:

> new words you know will be useful
> new words you like the sound of
> words you already know, but which you'd like to use more often

but *not* unusual or technical words which you won't need to use yourself.

D **Work in groups** **Find out your partners' answers to the questions below about organising vocabulary notes.**

1 Where is the best place to keep your notes?

☐ an A4 ring binder ☐ a pocket-sized notebook

☐ a Filofax (personal organiser) ☐ a computer

2 How should the words be organised?

☐ by topics ☐ in the order that you learn them (by date)
☐ alphabetically

3 Which of this information should be included in your notes?

☐ translation ☐ part of speech ☐ definition
☐ example ☐ pronunciation ☐ drawing

4 What other useful advice can you suggest for remembering new words better?

1.2 **Signs** LISTENING

A **Work in pairs** What do you think these road signs mean?

B 🔊 You'll hear a talk about the signs that gypsies used to leave for each other in the past outside people's houses. Listen to the recording and *draw* the signs beside their meanings.

1 Beware of the dog △

2 Fierce dog ⊿

3 Friendly people

4 Friendly, generous people

5 Very friendly, generous people

6 Work to be had here

7 Gypsies not liked

8 Nothing to be had

9 Work available with good pay

10 These people will buy from you

11 This place has been robbed

C **Work in pairs** Here are some signs that teachers use when marking students' written work:

✓   ✓✓   X   XX   P   Sp   WO   G   V   !   ?

• What do you think they mean?

• If you make a spelling mistake, how can you avoid making the same mistake again?

1.3 Using a dictionary   WORD STUDY

A small bilingual pocket dictionary is handy if you're travelling. But it isn't much use if you want to learn new words. An English-to-English student's dictionary is a must.

A **Work in pairs** Discuss these questions:

- What are the advantages of having two or more different dictionaries in class to refer to?
- What are the advantages of a bilingual (translating) dictionary?
- What are the advantages of an English-to-English dictionary?

B **To do this exercise you need to refer to an English-to-English dictionary. Find the answers to these questions by referring to the dictionary.**

1 How is *mainland Greece* different from *Greece*?
2 What does the adjective *mainstream* mean? What is its opposite?
3 Can *mainstream* be used as a verb?
4 How many meanings does the verb *maintain* have?
5 How do you pronounce the verb *maintain* and the noun *maintenance*?
6 What could you describe as *majestic*?
7 Who would you address as *Your Majesty*?
8 What is another word for the adjective *major*?
9 What is an example of the adjective *major* in a sentence?
10 What does the noun *major* mean in the context of education?

C **1** **Work in pairs** Where does the text below come from? Why would someone read it?

2 🖉 Highlight the words you don't understand. Then use a dictionary to look them up.

Foreword

The *Cambridge International Dictionary of English (CIDE)* is one of the most recent developments from the oldest publisher in the world, Cambridge University Press. Strangely, Cambridge has never published mainstream monolingual dictionaries before, although it has in the last twenty years become a major contributor to the field of English Language Teaching. It is therefore appropriate that this first dictionary should be designed for the foreign learner of English in any part of the world. The fresh approach that we have taken should appeal to all those who appreciate good lexicography based on solid scholarly principles and using the latest computer techniques, many of them developed by our computer team. Our first concern in writing *CIDE* has been clarity and simplicity, that is the clearest presentation we could devise with the minimum of the fuss and clutter that are the usual feature of dictionaries. There are no cumbersome numbers, and a specific innovation of *CIDE* is that each entry is for one core meaning to which the reader is immediately directed by the GUIDE WORD, as in **bear** ANIMAL and **bear** CARRY or **bank** ORGANIZATION and **bank** RAISED GROUND.

Within each entry is a rich range of information: the definition is written in a controlled Defining Vocabulary; inflected forms are given, as are examples and usage, idioms, compounds, collocations, quotations, false friends and grammatical description. Grammar codes are kept deliberately simple, and every one is attached to an example sentence. This means that the learner always has a model of each pattern before its description, and helps to ensure that the learner *produces* the correct form.

---

3 **Work in pairs** Discuss these questions:

- What information did your dictionary give you?
- What type of information was most useful? Rearrange these in order of usefulness:

   pronunciation   definition   examples   cross-reference (to another entry)
   illustration (if any)   part of speech (noun, verb, adjective, etc.)   spelling

1.4 Present tenses GRAMMAR REVIEW

GRAMMAR REVIEW exercises will help you to *revise* grammar points you've probably studied before. You can check what you already know – and find out what you don't know.

A ● Look at the GRAMMAR REFERENCE section on Present tenses on pages 182–183. Study the examples there and highlight any points or examples you particularly want to remember.

B **Work in pairs** Which of the sentences on the right are *answers* to the questions on the left? Choose the answer that matches each question – and explain the reason for your choice.

1 What is she doing?
2 What does she do?

3 How long has she been writing?
4 How much has she written?

5 When are you having lunch?
6 When do you have lunch?

7 Where are you going for lunch?
8 Where do you go for lunch?

9 Does he speak Japanese or Chinese?
10 Is he speaking Japanese or Chinese?

About 200 words.
For about an hour.
Both, I think.
Finishing her homework.
It sounds like Chinese to me.
Later than usual today.
Probably the cafeteria today.
She's a student.
To the cafeteria most days.
Usually at one thirty.

C **Work in pairs** Five of these sentences contain errors. If a sentence is correct, put a tick ✓ beside it. If there are any mistakes in a sentence, underline them and write the correction alongside. Some lines have more than one mistake.

1 *I'm hoping you're feeling better today.*   I hope
2 *A dictionary isn't costing very much to buy.*
3 *She is living in London since she has been a child.*
4 *What time are you expecting her to arrive?*
5 *I am still waiting for her to answer my letter.*
6 *Are you understanding me if I am speaking very fast like this?*
7 *My sister's always annoying me.*
8 *I'm remembering his face but I'm forgetting his name.*

D **Complete the second sentence so that it has a similar meaning to the first sentence. Use the word in red and other words to complete each sentence. Don't change the word given.**

1 What's the difference between a colon and a semicolon?
know   Do .... you know .... the difference between a colon and a semicolon?

2 I'm always forgetting how to spell the word 'pronunciation'.
never   I .... how to spell the word 'pronunciation'.

3 Understanding every word isn't important.
matter   It .... if you don't understand every word.

4 I first began learning English when I was ten years old.
since   I .... I was ten years old.

5 Do you know when the rain started?
long   How .... raining?

6 I wish he didn't interrupt so much, it's so annoying!
always   He .... and it's very annoying!

7 She's a driving instructor.
people   She .... drive.

8 Oh dear, the rain hasn't stopped yet.
still   Oh dear, ... !

E **Work in pairs** Find out about each other's daily activities. How many different things does your partner usually do (or sometimes do) every weekday? Which of you has the busier life?

When do you wake up?

I usually wake up when my alarm clock rings at 6.55. What about you?

1.5 Good manners READING

A **Work in pairs**   The following quotes have been removed from this passage. Decide where each of them should be fitted in.

A 'How far is it to the next rest station?'   1

B 'I'm terribly sorry'

C 'Thank you'

D 'That's quite all right. Others frequently make the same mistake'

E 'The baby just threw up. Do you have a towel or something?'

F 'Well, it *was* awfully nice of you'

G 'You're welcome'

Etiquette

It is no secret that human beings have been replaced by baskets at toll-booth stations throughout the country. I, for one, am not at all sentimental about the substitution since in the first place, human money-collecting on highways is undignified and probably boring, and in the second place, baskets are much better suited to the job than human hands. Baskets are bigger and never clammy. A basket cannot make change, but that is only a temporary deficiency. With very little effort, baskets can be programmed to subtract 25 cents from anything up to a thousand-dollar bill. There would then remain only one problem for the basket. It cannot answer such questions as 'What exit do I take if I'm going to New Hyde Park?' or, ¹ .... Theoretically, a basket can be programmed to answer these and any other reasonable questions, although it is unlikely, even in theory, that a basket could ever respond intelligently to such a remark as ² .... Nevertheless, that problem can be solved by keeping one human being supplied abundantly with towels, in some sort of emergency booth.

This solves all of the problems from the basket's point of view. But there still remain several for the motorists, almost all of which concern their sensibilities. Each basket has an appendage that has been programmed to flash 'Thank you' after the motorist has performed her civic duty. Common courtesy, of course, compels the motorist to respond. In these circumstances, however, one feels quite silly saying ³ .... unless one has some sort of assurance that one's courtesy has been understood and perhaps appreciated. I know many motorists who refuse to say anything to the basket *only* because they assume the basket is indifferent to their responses. This is perfectly understandable, but it could be corrected if the basket were programmed to respond to a human's 'You're welcome' by flashing something like ⁴ ....

There still remains the problem of what one is to do or say when the coin has missed the basket. After you've retrieved the coin and thrown it in, the basket's appendage still says ⁵ .... but unquestionably the remark now has a sarcastic ring, which only adds to one's sheepishness. In such cases, the sensitive motorist will invariably say something like ⁶ .... to which the appendage could not, in all courtesy, reply, 'Well it *was* awfully nice of you.' That simply would not do. Perhaps the basket can be programmed to reply, ⁷ ....

Such a reply would make the motorist feel that her efforts are appreciated and she could proceed down the highway with that exhilarated air that comes to those who have exchanged cordialities with somebody or something.

B 1 Find these words in the first paragraph and <u>underline</u> them lightly in pencil:

baskets   toll-booth   sentimental   undignified   clammy   temporary   deficiency
subtract   abundantly

2 Look them up in a dictionary. Take your time to look at the examples of the words used in different contexts.

3 🖊 Highlight in the text any of those nine words you want to remember. If you think any of the words are *not* worth remembering, *don't* highlight them.

4 Go through the rest of the text looking for any words you don't understand. <u>Underline</u> them lightly in pencil. Then look them up in a dictionary, and notice the examples of the words in different contexts.

5 🖊 Highlight the words you want to remember, but *not* the ones that aren't worth remembering.

C 1 **Work in pairs**   Discuss these questions:

- Is the author British or American? What makes you think so?
- Do toll-booths in your country have baskets or people to collect the money?
- What is meant by 'exchanged cordialities' in the last sentence? Why is it pleasant to exchange cordialities with people?
- Why is politeness important when dealing with people?

2 **Work in groups**   Look at the illustrations below and discuss these points:

- Can you notice anything that might be considered good or bad manners in your country?
- Which do you think is the worst thing shown here?

1.6 **Remembering prepositions**   PREPOSITIONS

With prepositions, it isn't usually the prepositions themselves that are difficult, it's when to use them. This exercise tests your knowledge of the uses of some common prepositions.

A 1 Fill the gaps in the sentences below with a suitable preposition from this list. In some cases there may be more than one possible answer:

about   at   by   for   in   of   on   to   with

1 A is ......*for*...... apple.
2 Chris is a very good friend ......*of*...... mine.
3 We both share a love .... music.
4 It's warm .... the time of year.

5 I've been waiting .... an hour.

6 I'm looking for a book .... animals.

7 *Hamlet* was written .... Shakespeare.

8 She's read all the works .... Shakespeare.

9 He's interested .... sport and literature.

10 When does the train .... London leave?

11 Part-time workers are paid .... the hour.

12 How long has she been .... hospital?

13 The shops are closed .... Sundays.

14 The bill must be paid .... Monday.

15 He was wearing a coat .... a torn sleeve.

16 I opened the can .... a can-opener.

17 This pullover is a bargain .... £13.99.

18 Liverpool won .... three goals .... nil.

19 Harrods is a famous store .... London.

20 Ships are made .... steel.

21 Cambridge is 100 km north .... London.

22 My brother is very good .... maths.

23 The total cost is .... £100.

24 I bought it .... £3 in a second-hand shop.

2 Work in pairs When you've finished, compare your answers. Look carefully at the questions you got wrong.

B ● To help you to remember prepositions, try *highlighting* them in context in the reading texts in this book – and in other English texts you read. Look at the text about good manners in 1.5 and highlight the prepositions in it.

When you come across a new use of a preposition in a written text, use a highlighter to highlight the preposition *and* the word before and the word after. If, when you're listening, you hear a new use of a preposition, make a note of it in your vocabulary notebook. And add an example to help you to remember a context it may be used in.

interested in – I'm not interested in learning Latin.
a friend of mine – Mary is an old friend of mine.

1.7 Giving your opinions   LISTENING

Sally   Bill   Anthony   Tom   Julie

A 1 🔊 You'll hear five people giving their opinions about learning languages. Choose a sentence from the list which summarises what they each say. Match the name of the speaker to the appropriate sentence. There is one sentence which you do not need to use.

1 Most people can't learn a language in the country where it's spoken.

2 You can't learn a language without living in the country where it's spoken.

3 Learning Latin or Ancient Greek is a waste of time.

4 You never stop learning a language.

5 Some languages are more difficult than others.

6 It's hard to learn a foreign language in your own country.

Sally

Bill

Anthony

Tom

Julie

2 Which of the speakers sounded most unpleasant? Why did he sound unpleasant?

B 🔊 **Listen to the recording again. This time note down the phrases the speakers use to introduce their opinions.**

1 ...*It seems to me*... that some languages are easier to learn than others.
2 .... as an English speaker I could learn to speak Japanese as easily I could learn Italian.
3 .... learning it would be useful and relevant.
4 .... learning a dead language is a bit of a waste of time?
5 .... there's any practical value at all in learning classical languages.
6 .... if you learn a foreign language in your own country, it's quite difficult to appreciate the relevance of *any* language.
7 .... most people have to continue their studies, or earn a living.

C **Work in pairs** **Tell your partner what your opinion is on these topics, beginning with the phrases you noted down in B above:**

shopping   making new friends   hobbies   recycling   drinking and driving
living in a city   keeping fit   holidays abroad   eating out   examinations
going to the cinema   reading   unemployment   computers
the big story in the news today

1.8 What are your strengths and weaknesses?   WRITING

What are your strengths and weaknesses in writing in English? This exercise will help you and your teacher to find out.

A 🖋 **Choose *one* of these topics. Write about 150 words beginning with the words given. Make some notes before you start.**

1 A story beginning: 'It was a dark and stormy night . . . '

2 An account beginning: 'I first started learning English when I was . . . '

3 An article beginning: 'These days it's becoming more and more important to know English . . . '

B 1 **Work in pairs** **Read each other's compositions and look at each other's notes. How well do you think your partner dealt with the task? Is the composition interesting and readable?**

2 Hand in your composition *and* the notes you made to your teacher.

C **When you get the marked work back, pay special attention to the comments as well as the mistakes that have been marked. What aspect of your written English needs improving most?**

Highlighting the words you want to remember in this book will help you to remember them more easily. Before you start a new unit, look back at the previous unit. If you've highlighted the new words, they are all immediately noticeable. When you turn the page, you can't help noticing more words you want to remember. You're creating your own personalised revision aid!

"We were shattered to learn he was dyslexic.
We thought he was learning Bulgarian."

2

At your service!

2.1 Can I help you?   VOCABULARY AND LISTENING

A 1 Work in pairs   Imagine that a foreign visitor wants to know about shopping in your town or city. What information would you give? Discuss these questions:

- What time do the shops, department stores, supermarkets, banks and post offices open?
- When is the busiest time to shop? And the quietest?
- Which are the best local shops for music, clothes, books, shoes and groceries?
- Which is the best street market? And the best department store?

2 Work in pairs   Role-play a conversation between a resident and a foreign visitor who has a lot of questions about shopping in your town or city.

3 Work in groups   Discuss these questions:

- What is your favourite day of the week for shopping? Why?
- What is your favourite store? Why?
- Imagine that you have £100 to spend. Which shop(s) will you go to and what will you buy?
- What do you do if the shop hasn't got the things you want in stock?

B 1 🔊 You'll hear four conversations. Fill in the missing information in this table.

	Where are they?	What does the customer want?	What will the customer say next?
1			
2			
3			
4			

2 Work in pairs   Compare your answers and, if necessary, listen to the conversations again.

C Fill the gaps in these sentences with a suitable word.

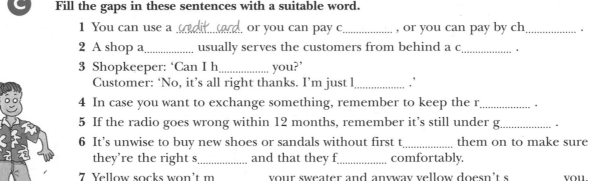

1 You can use a _credit card_ or you can pay c_____ , or you can pay by ch_____ .
2 A shop a_____ usually serves the customers from behind a c_____ .
3 Shopkeeper: 'Can I h_____ you?'
   Customer: 'No, it's all right thanks. I'm just l_____ .'
4 In case you want to exchange something, remember to keep the r_____ .
5 If the radio goes wrong within 12 months, remember it's still under g_____ .
6 It's unwise to buy new shoes or sandals without first t_____ them on to make sure
   they're the right s_____ and that they f_____ comfortably.
7 Yellow socks won't m_____ your sweater and anyway yellow doesn't s_____ you.
8 To find out how to wash a garment, look at the instructions on the l_____ .
9 In a bank or post office you may have to q_____ while you wait to be served.
10 These orange trousers were a real b_____ . I got them for half price in the s_____ .

D **Work in pairs** Imagine that you have to do some shopping, but there isn't a convenience store, department store or supermarket. What sort of shops can you buy these items in?

1 a kilo of tomatoes – and a knife to cut them with
   greengrocer's – ironmonger's, hardware store or kitchen shop
2 some sausages – and a frying-pan to cook them in
3 a personal stereo – and some cassettes to play on it
4 a loaf of bread – and some butter to spread on it
5 a notebook – and a pen to write in it with
6 a tube of toothpaste – and a new toothbrush
7 a postcard – and a stamp to stick on it

E 1 **Work in groups** Each member of the group should look at two members of another group. Then, *with your eyes closed*, take it in turns to describe from memory each person's clothes.

2 Discuss these questions:
   • Can you remember what each member of your group was wearing in the previous lesson? Describe each item of clothing and its colour or pattern.
   • What would you be wearing if it was much colder today? Or much hotter?
   • What do you wear if you want to look extra smart?

2.2 **Abbreviations and numbers** WORD STUDY

A **Work in pairs** What do these common abbreviations mean? Look up the ones you don't know in a dictionary – or ask another pair.

approx. _approximately_

c/o e.g. etc. FCE GMT incl. info. intro. max. min. misc.

No. N, S, E & W PTO Rd. RSVP St. VAT VIP vocab. Xmas 1st, 2nd & 3rd

B 1 Say these numbers and sums aloud:

333 _three hundred and thirty-three_

144 113 227 850,000 5.75 1,992 $^7/_8$ $1\frac{1}{4} + 2\frac{2}{3} = 3.9167$ $4\frac{3}{4} - 2\frac{1}{2} = 2.25$

2 Write the numbers out in full. When you've finished, compare your answers with a partner.

C **1** 🔊 Listen to the recording and write down the numbers you hear, in figures not in words. Examples 1–6 are telephone and fax numbers, 7–12 are just numbers, 13–16 are times and 17–20 are prices. The first one is: 5180477

2 Compare your answers with a partner. If necessary, listen again to check your answers.

D 👥 **Work in pairs** One of you should look at Activity *1* (on page 186), the other at *29* (on page 196). You'll have some names, addresses and numbers to dictate to your partner.

2.3 Spelling and punctuation WRITING

A Everyone makes spelling mistakes some of the time. But many spelling mistakes can often be avoided by checking your work carefully before you hand it in. There are 16 mistakes in these students' sentences. Underline the errors and correct them.

1 *Please let me know your <u>adress</u>.* address
2 *My brother is nineteen years old.*
3 *One day he's hopping to go to Amerika.*
4 *It was a realy wonderfull meal!*
5 *I recieved you letter this morning.*
6 *He want to improve his knoledge of english.*
7 *Concorde flys across the Atlantic in four ours.*
8 *Some people find speling especialy dificult.*

B **1** **Work in pairs** Another problem is punctuation, but probably only a few punctuation marks are used differently in English and your language. Take it in turns to say these punctuation marks aloud:

! ? . , ; : ' ' ' " " - – ( )

2 Here are some more examples of students' work. Find and correct the punctuation mistakes.

London's

Harrods is <u>Londons</u>' most famous department store. You can buy almost anything there and its one of the landmark's of London? people come to eat at it's restaurants and look round its' 214 departments But not everyone comes to buy many of the people who go there just enjoy looking at the enormous range of goods on display – and at the other customers

3 **Work in pairs** This paragraph has no punctuation at all! Add the necessary punctuation.

Every Tuesday Friday and Saturday in our part of the city theres an open-air market in the main square which everyone goes to Farmers come in from the countryside to sell their fresh vegetables and fruit Other stalls sell all kinds of things cheese jeans fish and even second-hand furniture Its almost impossible to carry on a conversation above the noise and shouting as customers push their way to the front trying to attract the stall-holders attention and demanding the ripest freshest fruit or the lowest prices

Most spelling errors can be avoided if you use a dictionary to look up any words you're unsure of – and if you check your written work through carefully. Many spelling mistakes are slips of the pen.

4 You'll find a corrected version of this paragraph in Activity *54*.

2.4 Questions and question tags GRAMMAR REVIEW

A **1** **Work in pairs** Imagine you're going to interview your favourite actor or singer. Write down eight questions you'd like to ask, beginning with each of these words:

Do . . . ? When . . . ? Where . . . ? How long . . . ?
How much . . . ? Who . . . ? What . . . ? Why . . . ?

2 **Join another pair** Check each other's work and make sure there are no grammatical mistakes. Then decide which are the five most interesting questions.

B **1** An indirect question is sometimes more polite than a direct question. Complete these direct and indirect questions.

See the Grammar
Reference section
on pages 183–184.

1	Age	How _____old are you_____ ?
		May I ask _____how old you are_____ ?
2	Date of birth	When _____ ?
		Could you tell me _____ ?
3	Place of birth	Where _____ ?
		Can you also tell me _____ ?
4	Address	Where _____ ?
		I'd like to know _____ .
5	Phone	What _____ ?
		Would you mind telling me _____ ?
6	British prime minister	Who _____ ?
		Do you know _____ ?
7	Population of UK	How many _____ ?
		Do you happen to know _____ ?

2 **Work in pairs**   One of you should look at Activity *13*, the other at *40*. Ask each other questions to find out as much as possible about your partner's pictures.

C **1** You'll hear some people using question tags. If you think the person is fairly sure they're right, put a tick ✓. If you think they're unsure, put a question mark ? Listen to the examples first. The first person is unsure and the second person is sure.

1 ? 　 2 ✓ 　 3 ☐ 　 4 ☐ 　 5 ☐ 　 6 ☐ 　 7 ☐ 　 8 ☐ 　 9 ☐ 　 10 ☐

2 Complete these sentences.

1 Shopping isn't always fun, _____is it_____ ?
2 Don't spend all your money, _____will you_____ ?
3 Going to town can be expensive, _____ ?
4 People shouldn't spend all their money on clothes, _____ ?
5 There's no point in saving money, _____ ?
6 Two for the price of one! That was a bargain, _____ ?
7 Banks must be pretty boring places to work in, _____ ?
8 They had to queue for a long time, _____ ?
9 We've nearly finished, _____ ?
10 Let's stop now, _____ ?

3 **Work in groups**   Ask questions to find out this information about each other. Don't make notes – rely on your memory.

Favourite: colour　food　drink　school subject　sport　film star　singer
Numbers: date of birth　phone　flat or house　post code
Names: mother's first name　their full name　street where they live
plus: *five* pieces of information about their family

4 Continue talking to the same partners. Use question tags to check that you remember all the information correctly.

> Your favourite colour's blue, isn't it?　　　You like eating pasta, don't you?

If you're fairly sure you'll say:

> It's blue, isn't it?　　　You like it, don't you?

But if you're not sure you'll say:

> It's blue, isn't it?　　　You like it, don't you?

2.5 Advertisements and commercials SPEAKING AND LISTENING

A **Work in pairs** Imagine that you want to describe this product to a friend who hasn't seen it. What would you say about it?

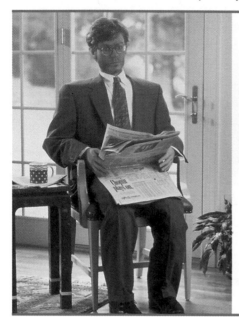

Safe-T-Man: Your personal bodyguard.

Designed as a visual deterrent, Safe-T-Man is a life size simulated male that appears to be 180 lbs. and 6′ tall, to give others the impression that you have the protection of a male guardian with you while at home alone or driving in your car. This unique security product looks incredibly real, with movable latex head and hands, and air-brushed facial highlights. Made of soft fabric polyfiber, he weighs less than 10 lbs. Dress him according to your own personal style (clothing not included): the optional button-on legs complete a total visual effect, if desired. Safe-T-Man can be stored and easily transported in the optional tote bag.

#4851913	Light Skin/Blonde Hair Man	$99.95
#4851907	Light Skin/Gray Hair Man	$99.95
#4852178	Dark Skin/Dark Hair Man	$99.95
#4852194	Button-on Legs (Specify Light or Dark)	$19.95
#4840017	Optional Zippered Carrying Tote	$34.95

Safe-T-Man keeps intruders away.

B **Work in pairs** One of you should look at Activity *4*, the other at *32*. You'll each see an advertisement that you will have to describe to your partner.

C **1** You'll hear four radio commercials. Match the commercials to the pictures a–d below.

a

b

c **PHILIPS**

d

2 Listen again and fill the gaps in these sentences, which summarise the four commercials.

1 The first commercial is for a brand of .... The customer is a (an) .... person and the sales assistant pretends that the products are made in .... At the end of the sketch the customer sees a .... that he likes the look of. 'The VR .... – video you can .... From Firrips.'

2 The second commercial is for a brand of .... When Eddie looks in his glass he imagines he can see a .... 'Beamish Stout just ....'

3 The third commercial is for a .... The speaker is John Cleese's ...., who lives in a home for .... She says she is .... years old.

4 The fourth commercial is for a brand of .... We are asked to imagine that we can actually .... colours. 'For a .... of colour we have the clicknology.'

3 **Work in pairs** Compare your answers. Which commercial did you think was the best? Why?

D **1** **Work in pairs** These are phrases we use when agreeing or disagreeing. Can you think of more?

> Yes, that's right!
> That's just what I think too.
> That's a good point.

> I don't really agree.
> Yes, I see what you mean, but...
> That's true, but...

2 **Work in groups** Look at the advertisements that you've brought to class:

- Which is the most attractive and the least attractive? Why?
- Which is the most amusing? Why?
- Which is the most effective and the least effective? Why?
- Do you have any favourite TV commercials? Tell your partners about them.
- What do you like and dislike about commercials on television?

2.6 Position and direction

PREPOSITIONS

A **1** Look at the box below and add the letters in the places described, using a pencil.

A is one centimetre from the bottom left-hand corner.
B is half-way between **A** and the right-hand edge.
C is half-way between **A** and **B**.
D is about one centimetre above **C**.
E is just inside the box, above **B**.
F is underneath **B**.

A   B

2 Your teacher will tell you where to put letters G to L.

3 **Work in pairs** One of you should explain where to add letters M to S in pencil, the other should explain where to add letters T to Z. You can put your letters anywhere on this page.

B **Work in pairs** One of you should look at Activity 7, the other at 35. You'll each have to explain the 'route' your partner's pencil should take *between*, *past*, *above* and *below* the letters and numbers in this box to draw the diagram or picture in your activity.
Begin like this:

First of all draw a round spot beside the top right-hand part of R. Now draw another spot just above and to the left of S. Now start drawing a continuous line from . . .

A	B	C	D	E	F	G	H
I	J	K	L	M	N	O	P
Q	R	S	T	U	V	W	X
Y	Z	1	2	3	4	5	6
7	8	9	10	11	12	13	14
15	16	17	18	19	20	21	22

2.7 Department stores READING

A 1 Work in pairs You're going to read about department stores in London and New York. Before you look at the texts, note down *three* things a visitor to the two cities would need to know about shopping.

2 Read the texts opposite and see if your questions are answered.

B 1 Find the answers to these questions in the texts and note them down. In some cases there are two or more correct answers.

Which store:

1 is the largest in the world?
2 is famous for its food?
3 has a men's store opposite?
4 will do your shopping for you?
5 will sell you tickets?

6 do most tourists visit?
7 is open late two nights a week?
8 adds tax on top of the price on the tag?
9 only sells goods carrying its own label?

2 When you've finished, compare your answers with a partner. If you disagree about any of the answers, look again at the texts to check who is right.

3 🖑 Read through the texts again, highlighting the words you would like to remember.

C Work in groups Discuss these questions:

• What are the *advantages* and *disadvantages* of shopping in a department store? Make a list, considering the following points:

price   choice   service   quality   convenience

• What products would you personally *never* buy in a department store? Why?
• What products can you *not* buy in department stores in your town or city? Where would you buy these items instead?

"Will you be paying by cheque, credit card, money, or are you shoplifting?"

2.8 Describing a place WRITING

A Work in pairs Discuss these questions and *make notes* of the main points:

• What is the best-known store in your town or city (or the place where you're studying)?
• What facts do you know about it? Why is it well-known? What does it sell? When is it open? How old is it?
• What do you like and dislike about it?
• What kind of people work there and shop there?
• What is it like to be there? What kind of atmosphere does it have?
• Is it a place that foreign tourists should visit? Why?

B 🖋 Write a description of the shop or store you have discussed. Imagine that this is going to be part of a handout for foreign visitors to your country.

1 Rearrange your notes and, if necessary, decide what information to leave out.

2 Write your description (about 150 words).

3 Look through your work and correct any *spelling* or *punctuation* mistakes.

4 Work in pairs Show your work to another student and ask for comments. Make any changes you think are necessary before handing your work in to your teacher.

SHOPPING IN NEW YORK

ANY VISITOR to New York will inevitably include shopping in their plan of action. The city is the consumer capital of the world: a shopper's paradise which is a constant source of entertainment, with dazzling window displays and a staggering display of goods.

Whether you have $50,000 or $5, New York is the place to spend it.

OPENING HOURS

Most shops in New York are normally open from 10am to 6pm, Monday to Saturday. Many department stores, though, are open all day Sunday and until 9pm at least two nights a week. The best time to avoid crowds is weekday mornings. The most crowded times are lunch hours (noon to 2.30pm), Saturday mornings, sales and holidays.

TAXES

The New York city sales tax, 8.25%, is added to the price when you pay. But you may still be asked to pay duty on goods at customs if you exceed the allowance. If the goods are sent direct, you won't have to pay sales tax.

DEPARTMENT STORES

Most of New York's large department stores are in midtown Manhattan. Allow plenty of time to explore as all these stores tend to be enormous, with an amazing range of goods. Prices are often high, but you can get bargains during the sales.

Stores such as Saks Fifth Avenue, Bloomingdale's and Macy's provide a diverse and extraordinary range of shopping services, including doing the shopping for you. But then you would miss out on what may be the shopping experience of a lifetime.

Abraham & Strauss, more familiarly known as A&S, is a bustling store which carries reasonably-priced ready-to-wear fashions for adults and children. It is the centrepiece of an Art Deco-style mall, the largest in Manhattan.

Barney's New York is a favourite among the young professional New Yorkers. It specializes in excellent, but expensive, designer clothes. A branch for men is located in the glittering World Financial Centre.

Bergdorf Goodman is luxurious, very elegant and understated. It carries top-quality contemporary fashions at high prices, specializing in European designers. The men's store is right across the street.

Almost every visitor to New York includes **Bloomingdale's** on their sight-seeing list. "Bloomies" is the Hollywood film star of the department stores, with many eyecatching displays and seductive goods. Its ambience is of a luxurious Middle Eastern bazaar, filled with wealthy, immaculately dressed New Yorkers seeking out the newest trendiest fashions. Bloomingdale's also has a high reputation for household goods and gourmet food – it has a shop devoted entirely to caviar. Extensive shopping services and amenities include a noted restaurant, Le Train Bleu, and a theatre ticket discount agency.

Lord & Taylor is renowned for its classic and much more conservative fashions for men and women. The store places an emphasis on US designers. You need a strong pair of legs, comfy shoes and lots of spare time to wander around.

Macy's, the self-proclaimed largest store in the world, manages to sprawl over an entire city block. It has ten floors, and sells everything imaginable from tiny tin openers to massive TVs.

Saks Fifth Avenue is synonymous with style and elegance. It has long been considered one of the city's top-quality department stores, with service to match. It sells stunning designer clothes for men, women and children.

SHOPS AND MARKETS IN LONDON

LONDON IS STILL one of the most lively shopping cities in the world. Within just a few minutes' walk you can find both vast department stores, with glittering window displays, and tiny, cluttered rooms where one customer almost fills the entire shop. Many of the most famous London shops are in Knightsbridge or Regent Street, where prices can be steep, but Oxford Street, which is packed with a huge number of shops offering quality goods at a range of prices, is also worth a visit. All over London, there are plenty of places tucked away down side-streets – and don't forget to try the markets for antiques, crafts, household goods, food and clothing.

WHEN TO SHOP

In Central London, most shops open somewhere between 9am and 10am and close between 5pm and 6pm on weekdays; some earlier on Saturdays. The 'late night' shopping (until 7pm or 8pm) is on Thursdays in Oxford Street and the rest of the West End, and on Wednesdays in Knightsbridge and Chelsea; some shops in tourist areas, such as Covent Garden and the Trocadero, are open until 7pm or later every day, including Sundays. A few street markets and a slowly growing number of other shops are also open on Sundays.

BEST OF THE DEPARTMENT STORES

The King of London's department stores, by tradition, is **Harrod's**, with its 300 departments and staff of 4,000. Prices are not always as high as you may well expect. The spectacular food hall, decorated with Edwardian tiles, has splendid displays of fish, cheese, fruit and vegetables; other specialities include fashions for all ages, china and glass, electronics and kitchenware. Though Harrod's is still just as popular, especially with well-heeled visitors, Londoners often head instead for nearby **Harvey Nichols**, which aims to stock

the best of everything with the price tags to match. Clothes are particularly strong, with the emphasis firmly on very high fashion, with many talented British, European and American names represented. There is also an impressive menswear section. The food hall, opened in 1992, is one of the most stylish in London.

Selfridge's vast building on Oxford Street houses everything from Gucci bags and Hermès scarves to household gadgets and bed-linen. **Miss Selfridge**, the popular high street fashion chain, also has a branch in the store.

The original **John Lewis** was a draper and his shop still has a gorgeous selection of fabrics and haberdashery. Its china, glass and household items make John Lewis, and its well-known Sloane Square partner, Peter Jones, equally popular with Londoners.

Liberty, the last privately owned department store in London, still sells the hand-blocked silks and other oriental goods it was famed for when it opened in 1875. Look out for the famous scarf department.

Fortnum and Mason's ground floor provisions department is so engrossing that the upper floors of classic fashion remain peaceful. The food section stocks everything from baked beans to the beautifully prepared hampers.

MARKS AND SPENCER

Marks and Spencer has come a long way since 1882 when Russian emigré Michael Marks had a stall in Leeds's Kirkgate market under the sign, 'Don't ask the price - it's a penny!' It now has over 680 stores worldwide and everything in them is 'own label'. It stocks reliable versions of more expensive clothes – Marks and Spencer's underwear in particular is a staple of the British wardrobe. The food department concentrates entirely on upmarket convenience foods. The main Oxford Street branches at the Pantheon (near Oxford Circus) and Marble Arch are the most interesting and well stocked.

3 Friends and relations

3.1 Relationships

VOCABULARY AND SPEAKING

A **Work in pairs**   Look at the photos above and discuss these questions:

- What's happening in each situation?
- What is the relationship between the people?
- What do you think they are saying to each other?

B Fill the gaps in these paragraphs with a suitable word from the lists on the right.

Before Maria went to live in the city, she felt very ¹　　　. For the first few weeks she felt ²　　　, but it didn't take long to find people she got ³　　　 with, and to ⁴　　　 new friends.

1 absent-minded   anxious   eager   nervy
2 abandoned   alone   lonely   single   unmarried
3 off   on   out   up
4 become   have   introduce   make

Sarah has been going ⁵　　　 with Bob for five years. When they first met at college they fell in love at first ⁶　　　 Although they've been ⁷　　　 for nearly two years they still haven't fixed a date for the ⁸　　　

5 back   in   out   up
6 glimpse   look   sight   view
7 promised   engaged   fiancés   intended
8 funeral   honeymoon   marriage   wedding

Their friends Anna and Tony ⁹　　　 last April – on the same date as Anna's parents' 25th wedding ¹⁰　　　. Bob was Tony's ¹¹　　　. They invited all of their friends and ¹²　　　 but not all of them could make it. Still there were over 60 ¹³　　　 and the ¹⁴　　　 afterwards went on till the small hours.

9 got married   became married   married each other   married themselves
10 anniversary   birthday   celebration   jubilee
11 best man   bridegroom   bridesmaid   eye-witness   godfather
12 next of kin   in-laws   parents   relations
13 guests   hosts   invitations   visitors
14 ceremony   procedure   reception   service

C 1 Work in pairs Look at this family tree and complete the sentences below.

1 Norman is Gerry's ....*son*.... .

2 Oliver is Ian's ....

3 Quentin is Diana's ....

4 Michelle is Ken's ....

5 Fiona is Eric's ....

6 Gerry is Ken's ....

7 Diana is Julie's ....

8 Julie is Paula's ....

9 Sandra is Norman's ....

10 Beatrice is Rosie's ....

2 Work in pairs Draw your own family tree, leaving three blanks. Explain it to your partner.

3 Join another pair Show the others your partner's family tree and explain it to them – they should ask questions to find out about the three blanks. Your partner should explain your family tree to them in the same way.

D 1 📼 You'll hear four people talking about their friends and what friendship means to them. Match each idea on the left to the person who expressed the idea. There are two ideas you do not need to use. First we hear from Charles.

1 Friends are people to have fun with.

2 Friends are people who have the same interests.

3 Friends don't take each other seriously.

4 Friends have no secrets from each other.

5 Friends tolerate each other's moods and faults.

6 It's a bad idea to have friends who are too close.

7 It's better if a friend has different interests.

8 You can't be a close friend with someone in your own family.

9 You should try to get on well with everyone, not just friends.

Charles

Sarah

Lenny

Anna

2 Work in groups Discuss these questions:

• Which of the people you heard do you think you'd get on with best? Why?

• What are the advantages of being an only child – and of having brothers and sisters?

• How is your relationship to each of these people different?

a friend   a class-mate   a brother   a sister
a relative   a teacher   your boss

• What are the qualities *you* expect in a friend?

3.2 **The past – 1** GRAMMAR REVIEW

A Eight of these sentences contain errors. If a sentence is correct, put a tick ✓ beside it. If there are any mistakes in a sentence, <u>underline</u> them and write the correction alongside.

1 When <u>have you left</u> school?   *did you leave*

2 The weather were lovely yesterday and the sun has been shining all day.

3 I have gone to the zoo last weekend.

4 Where you went on holiday last year?

5 They got married two years ago.

6 She has been born in 1980.

7 Our family was used to living in a smaller flat when I am younger.

8 Our broken window still wasn't mended yet.

9 I've been here for two years but I've only made a few friends.

10 The rain started during they played tennis.

See the Grammar Reference section on pages 180–181.

B 1 Fill the gaps in this story with *one* or *two* words.

A friend of mine ¹   *was walking*   home the other day when he
² _____ a hand-written sign on the windscreen of a beautiful red
sports car. The sign ³ _____ 'For sale – £10'. While he
⁴ _____ at the car, a woman ⁵ _____ out of a
house and ⁶ _____, 'Are you interested?' My friend
⁷ _____ that he was interested but he ⁸ _____ that
there must be a catch. But then the woman ⁹ _____ to show
him some more things which ¹⁰ _____ for sale inside the house.
   So he ¹¹ _____ inside the house with her. She
¹² _____ him into the lounge and there he ¹³ _____
a set of golf clubs, a Macintosh computer, some expensive suits and a hi-fi –
and they all ¹⁴ _____ brand new.
   The woman ¹⁵ _____ him he ¹⁶ _____ have
them all for £10. By this time my friend ¹⁷ _____ very suspicious.
So he ¹⁸ _____ her what ¹⁹ _____ on. The
woman said, '…

2 Can you guess how the story ended? Write down what you think the woman said.

C Complete the second sentence so that it has a similar meaning to the first sentence. Use the word in **red** and other words to complete each sentence. Don't change the word given.

1 The rain began to fall during my country walk.

it While <u>I was walking in the country it began</u> to rain.

2 We don't have a dog any more.

used We _____ a dog.

3 Is this your first visit to this country?

here _____ before?

4 Now we're studying Unit 3 in this book.

two We _____ units in this book so far.

5 During your absence we have done very little work.

away While you _____ much work.

6 I phoned you last night – why didn't you answer?

when What _____ last night?

7 Despite their argument yesterday, they are still friends.

row Although they _____ stopped being friends.

3.3   **Telling stories**   LISTENING AND SPEAKING

A   **1**   Before you listen to the recording, look at these pictures and see if you can guess what happened to the men in the two stories.

2   [▣] Listen to the stories and number the pictures to show the correct order of each story.

3   **Work in groups**   Discuss these questions:

- Were the speakers you heard both 'good story-tellers'? Why do you think so?
- Why are some people better at telling stories than others?
- What kinds of stories do you enjoy listening to or reading?
- Which of these things should a story-teller do?
  - get the events in the right sequence
  - add personal feelings and reactions
  - add dialogue
  - think of the audience

B   **1**   Most people aren't brilliant story-tellers – they need encouragement and help. Look at these phrases you can use to encourage and prompt a story-teller:

> What happened then?
> How did you/she feel?
> What did you/he do next?
> What did he say to you?
> What did you say to him?
> What was his/your reaction?

> Why did he/you do that?
> That's amazing!
> Wow!
> How strange!
> How funny!

2   **Work in pairs**   Take it in turns to retell each story in A in your own words. The listener should encourage and prompt the story-teller.

C   **1**   👥 **Work in groups of four (pairs of pairs)**   Two of you should look at Activity *24*, the others at *31*. You'll each have a cartoon strip to look at. Later you'll have to tell the story in your own words.

2   **Join a different partner**   Tell each other your stories.

3.4 Special occasions   READING

A **Work in groups**   Discuss these questions:

- How do you feel if a friend or a relation forgets your birthday (or name day)?
- How many people do you send birthday cards to? Or do you prefer to phone people on their birthday (or name day)?
- Who do you send postcards to when you're on holiday?

B **1** **Read the article below and find the answers to these questions.**

1 What is meant by the term *occasions* in the article?
2 How many of the greetings cards sent in the USA are Hallmark cards?
3 How many of the cards sold in the USA are non-occasion cards?
4 What do you think is the strangest type of non-occasion card mentioned?

From someone who loves you

MID-WAY between Father's Day (June 16th) and Halloween (October 31st) is the worst of times for American publishers of greeting cards. Despite their success in filling the calendar with 'occasions' (Mother-in-law's Day is October 27th), people send fewer cards than at any other time of the year. Hallmark Cards, the leader with a 44% share of a market worth almost $5 billion a year, is trying to change that by reviving an old habit.

Just as illiterate people in some countries still pay scribes to write letters for them, Hallmark is trying to persuade today's too-busy-to-write Americans to let it express their sentiments for them. That is how this private company, based in Kansas City with 15,000 employees, is getting people to send cards even on days when there is no 'occasion'. This latest marketing idea is designed to boost sales in a market that threatens to stop growing for the first time since 1945.

Some industry insiders trace the birth of Hallmark's so-called 'non-occasion' cards to a death-of-a-pet card the firm's 700-strong creative staff produced in 1984. Examples of non-occasion cards include a new line of adult-to-child cards, called 'To Kids With Love', which Hallmark introduced in January 1989. The number of cards in this series has grown to 125. They are supposed to help children aged 7 to 14 (and their parents) cope with growing up. Such cards include 'Would a hug help?'; 'Divorce won't change a thing between us'; 'Sorry I made you feel bad'; and 'You're perfectly wonderful – it's your room that's a mess.'

Hallmark is so encouraged by the success of these cards that it has produced a series of 520 non-occasion cards for adults. Some seek to deepen friendships ('You're more than a friend, you're just like family') or simply to keep in touch ('Do you realise we've been friends for more than half our lives'). Others address almost every imaginable calamity, from loss of a job to mental illness.

Hallmark's two biggest competitors – American Greetings with 30% of the market and Gibson Greetings with 8% – have followed Hallmark's lead. Non-occasion cards now account for more than 10% of the 7.3 billion greeting cards sold in America each year. Nobody knows how big non-occasion cards can become. But they too will eventually reach saturation. Perhaps the industry's next marketing frontier will be to get customers to send cards to themselves.

---

2 **Read the article again and decide if these statements are true ✓ or false ✗, according to the text. <u>Underline</u> the phrases in the text that provide the answers for the true statements.**

1 Halloween is the last day in October. ✓
2 Americans send fewer cards in summer.
3 Hallmark would prefer people to write each other letters, rather than send cards.
4 The market for cards has grown continuously from 1945 till now.
5 There are cards for people to send a friend whose dog has died.
6 There are cards to help a woman to make a date with a man.
7 There are cards to send people who have suffered any personal disaster you can imagine.
8 The last sentence is intended to be taken seriously.

"It's my first epidemic."

3 🔊 Highlight the words or phrases in the article which mean the same as these phrases.
(¶ shows the paragraph number.)

¶1 bringing back to life
¶2 who can't read or write   professional letter-writers   feelings
¶3 deal with a difficult situation
¶4 remain in contact   disaster
¶5 form a total of   a point where no more can be added

C 1 Work in pairs   Note down three questions you could
ask about the photo on the right.

2 Join another pair   Ask each other your questions.
Then discuss these questions:

- What do you enjoy most about birthdays and
  other special occasions?
- What happened on your last birthday?
- What gift do you hope you'll receive next
  birthday (or at Christmas)?
- Why do you think it's important to remember
  birthdays?

3.5   **Using prefixes – 1**   WORD STUDY

A   **Work in pairs**   Prefixes can be used with words to alter
their meaning. Look at the verbs in green. What are the
differences in meaning?

1 I arranged all these papers tidily on my desk, now
  someone has rearranged them all.

2 She told him she never wanted to see him again. She
  expected him to react sensibly, but he threw himself
  on the ground and started crying. He overreacted as
  usual.

3 I estimated the work would take five minutes, but I
  underestimated how difficult it would be.

4 Which is worse: pre-holiday tension or post-holiday
  depression?

B   Add more examples to the lists below, using these root words:

appear   build   charge   consider   crowded   dinner   excited   lunch   marry   pay✓
prepared   print   read   war

re	rearrange rename _repay_ ....
pre-	pre-Christmas pre-school ....
post-	post-war post-Christmas ....
over	overdone overpriced ....
under	underdone underestimate ....

C   Use the words in red at the end of each line to form new words to fit in the spaces.

1 We were late because we _underestimated_ how long the bus would take.   **estimate**

2 Many buildings had to be .... after the earthquake in 1980.   **build**

3 Most candidates suffer from .... nerves, but some are ....   **exam   confident**

4 I queued for ages at the checkout – that supermarket really is ....   **staff**

5 Most employees feel that they are .... and ....   **pay   value**

6 People who .... often become ....   **eat   weight**

7 I .... the letter because the first draft was full of mistakes.   **write**

8 He arrived late for work because he ....   **sleep**

3.6 Looking and seeing   VERBS AND IDIOMS

Look at the GRAMMAR REFERENCE section on page 181 for explanations, examples and rules on using *phrasal verbs* and *verbs + prepositions*.

A Fill the gaps in the sentences below with suitable forms of the verbs listed. In some cases there may be more than one possible answer:

gaze   look   notice   recognise   observe   see   stare   watch

1 It's amusing to *observe* the behaviour of people while they think nobody can see them.
2 We .... the boys playing football.
3 He .... at her admiringly.
4 I waved at you, but you didn't .... me.
5 I didn't .... you in your new glasses.
6 Don't you know it's rude to .... at people?
7 I usually .... TV on Fridays.
8 Have you been to .... that new film yet?
9 I'll .... what I can do to help you.
10 This exercise .... difficult.
11 Do you .... what I mean?
12 He tried to get to his seat without being ....

B 1 **Work in pairs**   Although you may not be able to work out the meaning of a phrasal verb from its parts, the *context* can sometimes help you to *guess* possible meanings. What do you think the missing idea is in these sentences?

1 He looked up to his grandfather as a role model.
2 When you check your written work, look out for spelling mistakes.
3 She looked through her homework carefully before handing it in.
4 I'm looking forward to meeting my old friend again.
5 Would you like me to look after your dog while you're away?

2 Look at Activity *33* to see what the missing phrases are.

3 Replace the words in green with a phrasal verb with *look* or *see*, using the words on the right.

1 Their aunt cared for them after their mother's death. *looked after*	**after**
2 They said goodbye to me at the airport. *saw me off*	**off**
3 Be careful! There's a car coming.	**out**
4 Most of the pupils respect their teacher.	**up to**
5 Leave it to me! I'll take care of all the arrangements.	**to**
6 The police are investigating a case of shoplifting.	**into**
7 He said he was innocent but they didn't believe his story.	**through**
8 If you don't know the meaning, find the word in a dictionary.	**up**
9 Next time you're in town, why don't you pay us a call and say hello?	**in**
10 I'm thinking about the holidays with pleasure	**forward to**

You can't always guess the meaning of an idiomatic phrasal verb – you'll have to learn some of them by heart. Another problem is that many phrasal verbs have more than one meaning. In the Verbs and Idioms exercises in this book you'll only meet the more common, useful meanings.

3.7 Writing a story   WRITING

A **Work in groups** Look at this story and decide together how it can be improved.

- What is the worst thing about the way it's written (the style)?
- What needs to be changed to make it more interesting?
- What extra information would you add to make it more interesting?

I'll never forget the night our car broke down. We were 9.5km from home and we had to walk home. It was 12.45 and it started to rain. We arrived home at 2.05. We couldn't unlock the door of our house because we had left the front door key in the car. We broke a window but a policeman came and we had to explain the situation to him. We went to bed at three o'clock.

B 1 Work alone Now decide how this story could be improved. What needs to be added and what needs to be changed to make it more interesting to the reader?

CASABLANCA

STARRING

Humphrey Bogart and Ingrid Bergman (1943)

An American called Rick owned a night club in Casablanca in Morocco in the war. Ilsa and her husband, Victor Laszlo, arrived there. Rick and Ilsa were in love in Paris before the war. Victor, a resistance leader, was in danger and wanted to escape to Lisbon by plane but he had no visa. Rick had two visas – for himself and Ilsa. In the end he gave them to Victor so that he and Ilsa could fly off to freedom. Rick and Renault, the chief of police, stayed at the airport.

The End.

> One of the choices in Paper 2 of the exam may be a story-writing question. When writing a story, try to imagine how the reader will react to your story. Will your reader find the story amusing or exciting – or boring?
>
> Most stories are told or written in the past tense, but the plot of a film or book is usually told in the present tense.

2 Work in pairs Compare your improvements.

C 1 ✎ Write a composition on one of these topics:

1 Tell the story of a favourite or memorable film.
2 Write a story about your own imaginary (or real) experiences beginning: 'I'll never forget the night . . . ' or 'I'll never forget the day . . . '

2 Work in pairs Before handing your stories in to be corrected, look at your partner's story. How could it be improved?

- Is the story interesting? Is there too little detail and dialogue, or too much? In general, is it a good idea to include a lot of dialogue in a story?
- Which of your partner's ideas could you use in your own written work?

4

Time off

4.1 **What do you enjoy?**   VOCABULARY

A **Work in groups**   **Look at the photos above and discuss these questions:**

- Which of the sports shown in the pictures do/would you enjoy? Why?
- What kinds of sport do you enjoy playing? And watching?
- How much free time do you have? How do you spend it?
- If you weren't here in class, what would you like to be doing?

B **Fill the gaps in these sentences with a suitable word.**

1. His _hobbies_ are c_____ stamps and t_____ photographs. What are yours?

2. Do you like to be a_____ in your spare time, or do you put your feet up and r_____ ?

3. Do you think an athlete should be a p_____ (paid) or an a_____ (unpaid)?

4. Which football t_____ do you s_____ ? Manchester United or Liverpool?

5. It was a really exciting m_____ . When the r_____ blew the final w_____ , there was a loud c_____ from the c_____ . The result was a d_____ – the final s_____ was 4–4 (four all) – so there'll have to be a replay next week.

6. Tennis is played on a tennis c_____ and golf is played on a golf c_____ . Where is your favourite sport played?

7. The winner of the tournament received a silver c_____ and a p_____ of $300.

8. The winner of the l_____ won £15 million. She says she'll give it all to c_____ .

C **1** **Work in pairs**   **Find out about each other's favourite *summer* and *winter* sport. Use a fresh page in your notebook and, with a dictionary, write down the words you need to describe:**

- the NAME of each sport
- the PLACE each sport is played (*in a stadium, on a pitch, in a pool*, etc.)
- the EQUIPMENT needed (*goals, a racket, skates*, etc.)
- the PEOPLE involved in each game (*players, referee, linesmen*, etc.)
- the SYSTEM OF SCORING, if any (*3–nil, 15–love*, etc.)

2 **Work in groups**   **Find out *why* your partners enjoy each of their favourite sports. Which sports do they *not* like? Why?**

4.2 Leisure activities

READING

A Before you read this newspaper article, look at these sentences and see if you can guess the missing words. Then find the answers to the questions in the text below.

1 The most popular sporting activity in Britain is ....

2 The second most popular sporting activity in Britain is ....

3 Over the past 20 years, 1,500 private .... have been built in Britain.

4 Over the past 20 years .... public leisure centres have been built in Britain.

How it shapes up

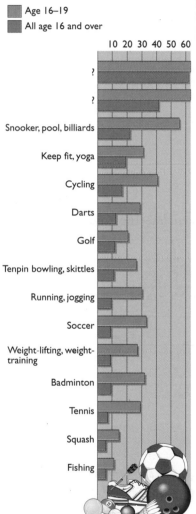

Participation in sport

Percentage of population participating in last 12 months

- Age 16–19
- All age 16 and over

10 20 30 40 50 60

- ?
- ?
- Snooker, pool, billiards
- Keep fit, yoga
- Cycling
- Darts
- Golf
- Tenpin bowling, skittles
- Running, jogging
- Soccer
- Weight-lifting, weight-training
- Badminton
- Tennis
- Squash
- Fishing

fitness or FUN?

■ WE BRITISH as a nation do all kinds of things in our spare time: we go shopping or jogging, we play darts or football, we collect records or stamps, we go to church or to the pub. The average working person has 40 hours of free time a week, sleeps for 49 hours, spends 45 hours at work or travelling to and from work. The remaining hours are spent on 'essential activities' (food shopping, housework, child care, cooking, etc.). Of course, some of our free time activities, like visiting relatives or taking driving lessons, may not be fun, but whatever we do, the way we spend our free time is probably providing other people with work. Leisure is our fastest growing industry.

■ ACCORDING TO the latest figures, during the past year, the most popular activity of all was walking: 35 million British people regularly walked two miles or more. More energetically, ten million people went to keep fit classes or took part in aerobics or yoga and half as many did

some kind of weight training in a gym. Not only did nine million people go cycling but four million went jogging and the same number played football and played golf. Other popular sports were bowling (six million), badminton (five million), tennis (four million) and squash (three million). Less actively, twelve million people played snooker or pool, seven million played darts and three million went fishing.

■ WATCHING OTHER people playing is also a popular leisure activity: the favourite sports among TV viewers are football, horse-racing, snooker, cricket and tennis. But although millions watch the matches on TV, not so many regularly go to watch football matches. 'New' television sports like American football, basketball and even darts are attracting loyal armchair experts.

■ THE FITNESS boom of the eighties led to a big rise in the numbers of people participating in sports. To cater for this boom and

provide the up-to-date facilities people want, over 1,500 private health and fitness clubs and the same number of public leisure centres have been built during the past twenty years. These modern centres, with their swimming pools (22 million people went swimming last year), squash courts, gyms and indoor courts for tennis and other sports, are competing with clubs, pubs and cinemas as places for people to go to spend their leisure time – and their money. Now practically every town has a leisure pool, often with a wave machine, water slides and tropical plants. Families can even spend their holidays at huge indoor water parks, where they can play or relax all day long in warmth and comfort without worrying about the weather outside. But this may not be helping us to get fitter: we may be becoming a nation of splashers, but not a nation of swimmers. The big question fitness experts are asking is: should sport be taken seriously or should it just be fun?

B Fill the gaps in this chart with information from the article.

Number of people who took part in sports and leisure activities in the last year:

walking	35 million	darts	....	weight training	....
swimming	....	golf	....	badminton	....
snooker and pool	....	bowling	....	squash	....
cycling	....	running and jogging	....	tennis	....
keep fit, aerobics and yoga	....	football	....	fishing	....

C   **Work in pairs**   Look again at the last paragraph of the text on page 33, which is about 200 words long. Where could you split it into three shorter paragraphs?

D   **Work in groups**   Find out your partners' views on these topics:

- What are your country's national sports? Why are they popular?
- Which of the leisure activities mentioned in the article are *not* popular in your country?
- What *non-sporting* leisure activities are most popular among your own friends and the people you know?
- Should sport be taken seriously – or should it be fun? Can it be both?

4.3   **Sorry to interrupt, but . . .**   SPEAKING

A   You'll hear a conversation about gambling. Match these opinions to the person who expresses them. There are two opinions which you do not need to use. The first speaker is Amanda.

1 Betting on horses requires skill and knowledge.
2 There's nothing wrong with buying a lottery ticket.
3 Sports should be enjoyed for their own sake.   Amanda
4 Gambling is like a drug.
5 Gambling provides harmless enjoyment.   Tony
6 The National Lottery gives a lot of money to good causes.
7 Horse racing is exciting if you've put money on a horse.   Debbie
8 Gamblers' wives and children suffer.
9 No one goes to the cinema any more.

B   Listen to the conversation again and notice how the speakers interrupted each other politely. Tick ✓ the expressions they used.

> I'm sorry to interrupt.   Just a minute.   By the way . . .
>
> Could I just say something?   I'm sorry but . . .   Er . . .
>
> I see what you mean, but . .   That reminds me . . .
>
> Yes, but . . .

C   **Work in groups**   Begin a discussion about the points listed here, experimenting with the phrases in B during your conversation. One member of the group should be an 'observer' who will simply listen to the discussion and give feedback later on how effective you were at interrupting – and how polite you sounded. Take it in turns to be the observer.

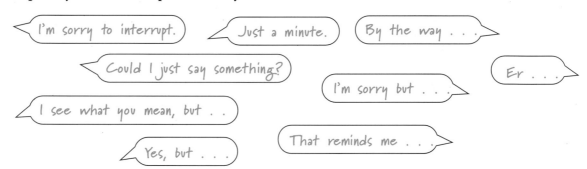

– sport and drugs   – sport and violence
– sport and money   – sport and snobbery

– competitive v. non-competitive sports
– watching sport on TV v. going to watch sport v. playing sports

hobbies and spare time interests:
– keeping busy v. doing nothing or relaxing
– hobbies v. listening to music v. watching TV v. reading
– going out v. staying at home

English proverbs: " All work and no play makes Jack a dull boy."
" Work hard and play hard."

4.4 Using prefixes – 2 WORD STUDY

A Work in pairs Prefixes can be used with words to alter their meaning. Look at the words in green. What do they mean?

1 Sometimes it's a bit rude to interrupt someone in mid-sentence.

2 An optimist would say the glass was half-full, a pessimist would say it's half-empty.

3 My grandfather is semi-retired, but he still works part-time. He can choose his own working hours because he's self-employed

B Add more examples to the lists below, using these root words:

afraid   air   asleep   automatic   circle   defence   finished   morning   pity
respect   twenties

half-	half-open half-eaten ....
semi-	semi-permanent semi-detached ....
mid-	mid-way mid-week ....
self-	self-confident self-taught ....

C Use the words in red at the end of each line to form new words to fit in the spaces.

1 It's amazing she can swim so fast – you'd never know that she was *self–taught* .   **teach**

2 Although he's in his .... he still plays football.   **fifty**

3 These trainers were a real bargain, they were ....   **price**

4 It's very cold in the mountains in ....   **winter**

5 A cafeteria is a .... restaurant.   **service**

6 If she wins this match, she'll be in the ....   **final**

7 A .... is just over 21 kilometres.   **marathon**

8 Is it time for our .... break yet?   **afternoon**

4.5 *Make* and *do* VERBS AND IDIOMS

A Decide which of the endings on the right go with the beginnings on the left:

Bill made . . .   Shirley laugh   Bill a favour   the washing-up   his/her duty
a cake   a noise   a mistake   an arrangement   the shopping

Shirley did . . .   a comment   a decision   an exercise   her/his homework
a good job   badly in the test   a good impression   me an offer
a promise   a statement   her/his best   very well   nothing at all

B Fill the gaps with suitable forms of the phrasal verbs below:

do up   do without   do with ✓   make up   make for   make up for
make out   make off with

1 This exercise is really difficult – I could *do with* some help.

2 Are you telling the truth or are you .... that story .... ?

3 They've just finished .... their flat and it looks really nice now.

4 I can't quite .... if that's your brother or you in this photo.

5 As you've arrived late, you'll have to .... the time you have lost.

6 We were .... the station when the thunderstorm broke.

7 A dog picked up my sandwich in its mouth and .... it.

8 He had to .... sugar in his coffee because he was on a diet.

4.6 **The past – 2** GRAMMAR REVIEW

See the Grammar Reference section on pages 180–181.

A 1 Look at these pairs of sentences and decide which ones are correct.

1 *How long have you been studying English?* ✓
2 *How long are you studying English?* ✗

3 *How long had you been playing tennis before it started to rain?*
4 *How long did you play tennis before it started to rain?*

5 *She asked me if I had finished my work yet.*
6 *She asked me if I finished my work yet.*

7 *They are already playing for an hour.*
8 *They have already played for an hour.*

2 Underline the mistakes in this paragraph and correct them.

was raining

It <u>rained</u> when we have arrived at the coast but by midday it had been stopping. We thought the rain lasted all day and we have been very glad it hadn't because we were wanting to go swimming. We found a café where we could eat outside and were having a nice meal. By the time we had finished lunch the sun shone brightly and the temperature rose to 30 degrees. We were all running down to the beach and, after we were changing into our swimming things, we dived in the sea.

B 1 Fill the gaps in this story with *one word* only.

I ¹ met my old school friend Vera the other day. We ² _____ not ³ _____ each other since we ⁴ _____ at school together. We ⁵ _____ at the sports centre where I ⁶ _____ just ⁷ _____ swimming and she ⁸ _____ just ⁹ _____ her aerobics class. It ¹⁰ _____ wonderful to talk about old times and we ¹¹ _____ able to catch up on each other's news. She ¹² _____ me that she ¹³ _____ kept in touch with several of our class-mates, but I ¹⁴ _____ sorry to hear that she ¹⁵ _____ lost touch with Anna, who ¹⁶ _____ to be my best friend. We ¹⁷ _____ on talking for an hour or more before it ¹⁸ _____ time for us both to go. It was a pity we ¹⁹ _____ not ²⁰ _____ more time. But we ²¹ _____ to meet again the same time next week.

2 Now do the same with this story.

We ¹ were sure that our team ² _____ going to win the match. But by half-time the other side ³ _____ scored three goals, and it looked as if the match ⁴ _____ as good as lost. After the interval, when the two teams ⁵ _____ back onto the field, we ⁶ _____ playing badly and the goalkeeper let in yet another goal. Then, with 30 minutes still to play, two substitutes ⁷ _____ on and then, suddenly, the team ⁸ _____ playing brilliantly. Within ten minutes we ⁹ _____ scored three goals! We ¹⁰ _____ still one goal down but in the last minute of the game there ¹¹ _____ a penalty and we ¹² _____ the equaliser. The final score ¹³ _____ four-all. It ¹⁴ _____ one of the most exciting matches I ¹⁵ _____ ever seen.

C 1 **Work in pairs** Help each other to remember everything you did last weekend, including what people said to you and what you said to them. Think about different times of day:

• Where were you at the time?
• Who were you with?
• What did you talk about?

2 **Join another pair** Find out about the other students' weekend activities by asking questions.

Where . . . ? When . . . ? How long . . . ? Who . . . ?
What did . . . say? What did . . . reply?

4.7 Safety at sea   LISTENING

A You'll hear part of a radio broadcast. Before you listen to the recording, look at questions 1–4 in B and try to predict what the answers might be.

B 🔊 Listen to the recording and answer the questions by matching the pictures to the meanings in 1 and completing the sentences in 2–4. There is one picture which you do not need to use.

1 Match the signals illustrated above to the meanings below. There is one extra signal which you do not need to use.

a) 'I am OK.' ☐

b) 'I need assistance.' ☐

c) 'I have a diver down. Keep clear and proceed slowly.' ☐

d) 'Faster!' ☐

e) 'Slower!' ☐

f) 'Speed OK.' ☐

g) 'Back to jetty.' ☐

2 Instead of using the Faster signal, you can ....

3 Instead of using the Slower signal, you can ....

4 Advice to the water skier:

a) There should be two people in the boat: one to .... and the other to ....

b) Before starting, your ski-tips must be ....

c) Give a clear signal to the helmsman of the boat when you're ready to ....

d) If you're falling forwards, you should ....

e) If you fall sideways, you should ....

f) If you fall, recover the skis at once because ....

Don't be dismayed if you can't answer every one of the questions on your first listening. Just answer the questions you can. Then, when you hear the recording again, you can concentrate on the ones you missed. In the exam or in a practice test, don't worry if there are still some questions you can't answer after two listenings. Not everyone can get 100% in a test.

C 🔊 **Work in pairs** Compare your answers. Listen to the recording again to settle any disagreements and answer the questions neither of you got the first time.

Stimulating and satisfying   READING

A **1** **Work in pairs**   Before you read the article, discuss these questions:
- What might be enjoyable for the people in the photograph?
- What would not be enjoyable?

2 The article describes a TV programme. Read it through and decide whether you would like to watch it. Why/Why not?

3 **Work in pairs**   Share your opinions.

IT'S TOUGH AT THE TOP

John Ridgway, the ex-Paratrooper famous for rowing the Atlantic, sailing twice around the world and canoeing down the Amazon, runs the most gruelling survival course in Britain. Perched halfway up a mountain in northern Scotland, overlooking a black lake, the Ardmore Adventure School is cold, bleak and forbidding. In this week's *Cutting Edge* programme, *Exposure*, it serves as a temporary home for 24 business managers from a multinational company – all in search of their real selves. The group are not super-fit athletes but very average 28–50-year-olds, ranging from the completely inactive to the modestly sporty. The film follows the men and women as they attempt abseiling, rock climbing, canoeing, orienteering, sea swimming and raft-building in the Scottish wilderness. It's only on the third day that they see their first glimpse of Ardmore House itself, with its relative comfort of bunk beds and cold showers. Their agony and resentment is clear at the beginning of the course, but, as the days go by, the exhilaration starts to show through. As one participant says, 'It was hell, but it was worth it.' It's a feeling Ridgway understands. 'I decided to create a small corner of the world where people could experience the confrontation with the elements that I find so stimulating and satisfying.'

B **1** Decide whether these statements are true or false, according to the article.

1 John Ridgway has a lot of experience with boats in extreme conditions.
2 The participants are students who have volunteered to take part.
3 The participants receive special training before the course.
4 On the first few days of the course they feel stimulated and satisfied.
5 As the course progresses they feel worse and worse.
6 John Ridgway wants people to feel the way he does about facing cold and wet weather.

2 Highlight the words in the article which mean the same as these words and phrases:

difficult and tiring   very fit   slightly   pain   anger and dislike   excitement   see and feel   bad weather   exciting

C **Work in pairs**   Decide where you would split the passage, which is about 200 words long, to make *five* shorter paragraphs.

4.9 Paragraphs   WRITING

In the exam you'll have to write two compositions of 120–180 words. These should be divided into paragraphs, but the question is 'Where?'

A new paragraph may signal a new direction or a new aspect of the topic. Or it may just be a way of making a long passage more readable.

Long, uninterrupted texts are harder to read and don't look interesting. The last 200-word paragraph of *Fitness or fun?* in 4.2 provides an example.

A 1 Work in pairs   Look again at *From someone who loves you* in 3.4. Why does each paragraph start in the place it does?

2 Look again at the last paragraph of *Fitness or fun?* in 4.2, which you split into three shorter paragraphs. Why did you decide to start each one in the place you did?

3 Look again at 4.8 C. Why did you decide to start each paragraph of *It's tough at the top* in the places you did?

B 1 Work in pairs   Plan a story (about 150 words) beginning with the words below. Decide what will go in each paragraph.

> There was a public transport strike, so we all had a day off last Wednesday.
> Although unfortunately it was a dull, rainy day, . . .

If you leave two or three blank lines between each paragraph, you'll have enough room to add an extra sentence later, if you think of an extra idea you want to include. And don't forget to leave enough room for your teacher to write in corrections, comments and suggestions.

2 Write your story, putting the very last paragraph on a *separate* sheet of paper.

3 Join a different partner   Show each other the main parts of your stories. Try to guess what happened in the last paragraph. Look at the last paragraph to see if you were right. Then discuss these questions:

- How many paragraphs are there in your stories? Should each story be divided into *more* paragraphs? If so, where?
- Or should there be *fewer* paragraphs? If so, which short paragraphs should be combined?
- In general, if in doubt, is it better to have more short paragraphs or fewer longer ones?

5

The world around us

5.1 **Nature**   VOCABULARY AND LISTENING

A   **Work in pairs**   Look at the photos above and discuss these questions:

- What is your favourite time of year? Why?
- What do you like most about each season? And what do you dislike?
- In your country, what's the weather like at different times of the year?

B 1 Work in pairs   Add *three* more items to each list. Use a dictionary if necessary.

Fruit:	grape, pear, peach, ...
Vegetables:	spinach, carrot, potato, ...
Trees:	pine, olive, oak, ...
Flowers:	rose, daisy, carnation, ...
Wild mammals:	rabbit, tiger, dolphin, ...
Birds:	sparrow, eagle, pigeon, ...
Domestic animals:	turkey, camel, goat, ...
Insects:	butterfly, wasp, ant, ...
Sea creatures:	shark, oyster, crab, ...

2 Join another pair   Compare your lists.

C 1 📼 **You'll hear three short conversations. Match the opinions below to the speakers. There are two opinions that no one mentions. The first speaker is Claire.**

1 Dogs don't get lonely.
2 People shouldn't keep dogs in apartments.
3 Dogs keep people company.   Claire

4 Some 'recycled' waste is actually buried, not recycled.
5 Recycling saves energy and unrenewable resources.   Steve
6 Recycling is cheaper.

7 Killing animals to eat their meat is cruel.   Emma
8 Everyone should stop eating meat.
9 Many people are eating less meat than they used to.

2 Work in groups   Find out your partners' views on the topics discussed.

5.2 The weather   READING AND LISTENING

A **1 Work in pairs** Where do you think are the best and worst places to be in a thunderstorm?

2 Read this article and decide which of these headlines would be best for it:

Avoiding that unlucky strike

Thunder and lightning

Dos and don'ts in a storm

FORTUNATELY we suffer relatively few lightning casualties in the UK, but the story in America is a lot more serious. More than 200 people a year are killed there on average by lightning, and surveys of the casualty figures upset a few cherished beliefs.

One revelation is that houses are by no means safe. Most indoor lightning casualties occur while talking on the telephone, particularly in rural areas, because outdoor cables can catch a lightning strike and send the electrical current surging down into the telephone itself. The next most dangerous indoor situation is in a kitchen, because of the metal pipes, taps and sink units which can pass current. Watching television carries the hazard that lightning strikes the aerial on the roof. And, of course, open windows and doors are an open invitation to a direct lightning strike.

There are even cases of deaths and injuries of people inside moving cars and, in one case, the rear window was smashed by lightning and the driver injured. Another case was more indirect: lightning knocked over a tree which knocked over a high voltage power line, electrocuting the driver. A number of people have been temporarily blinded by a lightning flash, causing accidents and injuries.

But direct strikes are much more frequent in open locations and three times as many males as females are killed in total because more men do outdoor work or recreation. One surprise is that twice as many anglers are killed than golfers by lightning, although golfers are more likely to suffer non-fatal injuries.

The advice to avoid lightning is clear. Stay away from metal fixtures in the home or outdoors. Avoid exposed shelters, open fields, open boats, lone trees and large trees in woods. Get off golf carts, bikes, horses and take cover. Do not swim.

3 Which of these activities are dangerous in a thunderstorm, according to the article? Tick the ones that are mentioned or implied:

talking on the phone	climbing stairs	sheltering under an isolated tree
washing up	working outdoors	sheltering in a building
watching television	climbing a ladder	sailing
sitting near a closed window	fishing	cycling
looking out of an open door	playing golf	swimming

4 Work in pairs Compare your answers. Which of the activities is the most dangerous? What does the article *not* tell you that you would like to know?

B You'll hear a weather forecast for the North (N), South (S), East (E) and West (W) of the country. Write the appropriate letter in the spaces as necessary. Not all the spaces need filling.

	Today	Tomorrow
heavy rain	S + E	W
dry and warm		
cloudy		
hazy sunshine		
temperatures above 25°		
thunderstorms		
scattered showers		
gale-force winds		
light breeze		
temperatures below freezing and frost		

C 1 Work in groups Here are the opening words of five stories. Discuss how each sentence could continue and then suggest how the story might develop.

1 It had been a stormy night . . .

2 One sunny morning in spring . . .

3 It was a cold, rainy morning . . .

4 Snow started falling during the night. By breakfast time . . .

5 The fog was so thick that morning . . .

2 Write the first *two* sentences of *three* stories, each beginning with a description of the weather in these pictures:

5.3 Global warming READING

A Work in pairs Before you read the article, look at these diagrams. Can you work out how the greenhouse effect works?

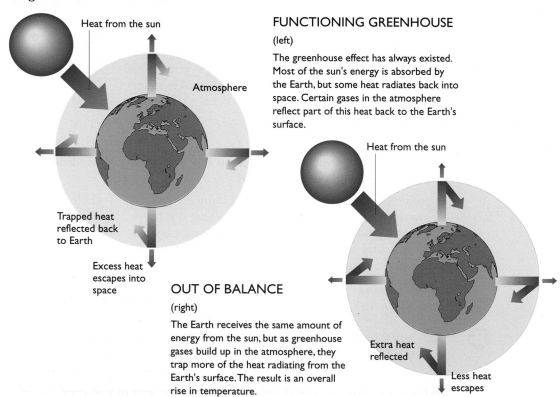

FUNCTIONING GREENHOUSE

(left)

The greenhouse effect has always existed. Most of the sun's energy is absorbed by the Earth, but some heat radiates back into space. Certain gases in the atmosphere reflect part of this heat back to the Earth's surface.

OUT OF BALANCE

(right)

The Earth receives the same amount of energy from the sun, but as greenhouse gases build up in the atmosphere, they trap more of the heat radiating from the Earth's surface. The result is an overall rise in temperature.

B Six sentences have been removed from the article opposite. Choose from the sentences A–G below the one which fits each gap 1–6. There's one extra sentence you don't need to use.

A Until recently all of this was absorbed by trees and plants, which converted it back into oxygen.

B So the amount of CO_2 in the atmosphere is increasing all the time.

C Some areas may actually benefit: the higher temperatures may allow a longer growing season, for example.

D At the time his predictions were regarded as science fiction.

E But it certainly looks as if inhabitants of this planet will have to get used to living in a warmer world.

F Consequently, the temperature rises.

G Surprisingly, the amount of CO_2 in the atmosphere has continued to fall.

GLOBAL WARMING
The Greenhouse Effect

As long ago as the 1960s Professor Bert Bolin predicted that the 'global warming', caused by an increase in the amount of carbon dioxide (CO_2) in the atmosphere, would lead to significant changes in the Earth's climate. [1]...
But most experts now agree that the amount of carbon dioxide in the atmosphere will double from 0.03% to 0.06% in the next 50 years and that temperatures worldwide will rise by 2° Celsius.

Although a temperature rise of 2° may not seem significant, the local effects may be much greater: by 2025 a rise of 10° is possible in polar regions and 4° in Northern Europe. Indeed the first effects will be felt by the end of the century – perhaps they are already being felt...

But how does the Greenhouse Effect operate and why should such a tiny proportion of CO_2 have such a harmful effect?

When living creatures breathe out and when things are burned, CO_2 enters the atmosphere. [2]... But the balance of nature has been disturbed. In power stations, in factories and in cars, we are burning more and more fossil fuels (coal, oil and natural gas). 18 billion tons of CO_2 enter the atmosphere every year. And the destruction of forests means that there are fewer trees to convert the CO_2 into oxygen. [3]...

As sunlight enters the atmosphere, the surface of the earth is warmed. Some of this heat escapes back into space, but the rest is trapped by CO_2, which acts rather like the glass in a greenhouse, allowing sunshine and heat to pass in but not out again. [4]...

As the temperature rises, the amount of water vapour in the air will increase and this too will absorb more of the Earth's heat. The oceans too will become warmer and store more heat, so that they increase the warming effect.

According to some scientists, the polar icecaps will start to melt and the oceans will expand as more snow and ice melts. Because the exposed ground, formerly covered in snow, won't reflect the heat so well it will absorb more sunlight and this will lead to even more snow melting.

Scientists predict that the level of the sea will have risen by ½ to 1½ metres by 2050. This will affect many low-lying areas of the world – millions of people today live less than one metre above sea level. [5]... For Northern Europeans, the extra warmth may be welcome – but there is also likely to be increased rainfall.

But many areas may suffer: the southern states of the USA can expect hotter summers and less rainfall, leading to worse conditions for agriculture, and the Mediterranean region may well be much drier and hotter than now.

Many experts believe that the Greenhouse Effect will bring significant changes to the Earth's climate, though they don't all agree how long this will take, or what form it will take. [6]...

C **Work in pairs** One of you should look at Activity *6*, the other at *34*. You'll see some more information about global warming to read and discuss.

5.4 Compound prepositions   PREPOSITIONS

A Which of these phrases could you use *instead of* the ones in green in the sentences below? There are two phrases which cannot be used:

as well as   because of   except for   in common with   in place of   owing to

1 Due to unforeseen circumstances, the film *Nostradamus* will not open until January.

2 Thanks to the good weather, most of my friends have left the city for the weekend.

3 Apart from dogs and cats, fish are Britain's favourite pets.

4 Together with most of my friends, I love spending time in the country.

B Fill the gaps in the sentences below with a suitable compound preposition from this list. In some cases there may be more than one possible answer:

according to   apart from   as well as   because of   except for   instead of
on behalf of   owing to

1 Our flight was cancelled _because of_ the fog.

2 Hello. I'm phoning .... Mr Brown. He asked me to give you a message.

3 Tropical forests are being destroyed .... the demand for hardwood for furniture.

4 People should protect the trees .... cutting them down.

5 They have two cats .... four pet rabbits.

6 Last week we had marvellous weather every day .... Sunday.

7 I love dogs .... those very fierce brown and black ones.

8 .... the weather forecast, it's going to snow.

5.5 Articles and quantifiers – 1 GRAMMAR REVIEW

(A) 1 **Which of these nouns are countable and which are uncountable – and which could be either, depending on their meaning?**

food   blood   glass   fire   milk   salt   money   mathematics   health   disease

2 **The nouns in the list on the left are uncountable. Which countable noun from the list on the right could you use to refer to a *single* item or example of each?**

Examples: accommodation – a room   advice – a suggestion

See the Grammar
Reference section
on pages 171–172.

accommodation advice bread	an animal a car a dollar a drop
education furniture information	an exercise a fact a lesson a report
homework luggage medicine money	a room a slice a sofa a storm
news traffic vocabulary water	a suggestion a suitcase a tablet
weather wild life	a word

(B) **Each of these sentences contains two or three errors. Find the mistakes and correct them.**

1 *I'm looking for an accommodation with a English family.*

I'm looking for (some) accommodation with an English family.

2 *More men are involved in the politics than women in every country in world.*

3 *If there were less cars in the city, there wouldn't be so much problems with the pollution.*

4 *To get to the leisure centre, go along the Coronation Avenue and take first right.*

5 *The education is compulsory – all the children have go to the school.*

6 *Anyone can have a look at church even if they don't go to the church on Sundays.*

7 *The pollution is very great problem in the world today.*

8 *The few people realise that using the sun's energy is better than burning the fossil fuels.*

(C) **Complete the second sentence so that it has a similar meaning to the first sentence. Use the word in red and other words to complete each sentence. Don't change the word given.**

cars
1 The traffic was so heavy that we couldn't cross the road.
There were so many cars that we were unable to cross the road.

information
2 There were so many facts to learn that my work took me all night.
My work took me all night _____ to learn.

how
3 Fifty to one hundred plants and animals become extinct every day – did you know that?
Do you know _____ become extinct every day? Fifty to one hundred!

clouds
4 It's so cloudy that it's sure to rain sooner or later.
There _____ that there's sure to be some rain eventually.

advice
5 I'm not sure what to do. Any suggestions?
Could _____ please?

never
6 No vegetarians are meat-eaters, but some are fish-eaters.
Vegetarians _____ fish.

(D) **Work in pairs** **What do you think is the story behind each of these newspaper headlines? Rewrite each one as a complete sentence.**

1 Tiger escapes from zoo   A tiger has escaped from the zoo.

2 Tiger found in wood after week-long search

3 Family anger as £60,000 is left to cat

4 Man bites dog

5 Dad loses £200,000 lottery ticket

6 Mum reunited with daughter after 20 years

7 Town missing from phone book

8 Golfer struck by lightning survives

5.6 Talking for a minute   SPEAKING

In the exam you'll have to talk for about one minute about two pictures. This doesn't just mean 'describe the pictures' – you'll be expected to compare them and explain what your reactions to them are. There is no 'correct way' of doing this. The purpose of the task is to give you an opportunity to keep talking without help from the examiner and without being interrupted by the other candidate. It's a test of how well you can express your ideas. Talking for this long takes practice.

A 1 Work in pairs   Look at these pictures. What kinds of things would you say about them if you were asked to compare them and explain your reactions to them?

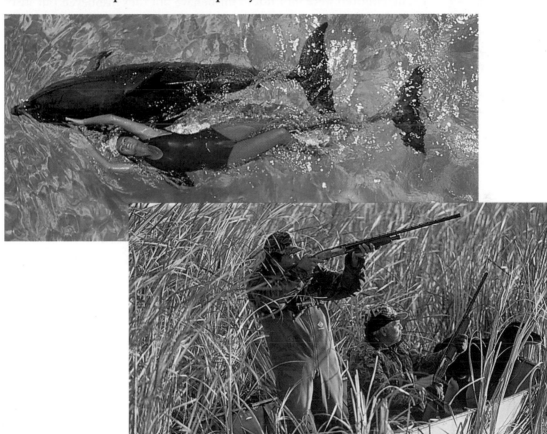

2   You'll hear two people talking about these photos in an examination situation. What aspects of the theme did they *not* mention which they could have done?

B 1   No one can speak for a minute without hesitating. But you can 'disguise' your hesitation by using words or phrases like these:

Well . . .	Now, it seems to me . . .	. . . um . . .
you see . . .	actually . . .	. . . er . . .
I mean . . .	. . . you know . . .	kind of

2   Listen to the recording again and tick ✓ the phrases above that the speakers used. What other 'hesitation techniques' did they both use?

3   Look again at the ways of introducing opinions you practised in 1.7. These phrases are also useful ways of 'playing for time' while you decide what to say next!

4 Work in pairs   Take it in turns to talk about the two pictures above for one minute each.

C 1   **Work in groups of four (pairs of pairs)**   Two of you should look at Activity *10*, the others at *38*. Each pair has two more pictures to discuss. Prepare what you'll say about them.

2 Join a different partner   Talk for a minute to your new partner about your photos. You can *encourage* each other (by saying: 'I see . . .' 'Yes . . .' 'OK . . .' 'Oh . . .', etc.), but *don't interrupt*. Then comment on each other's talks. How could your partner improve his or her one-minute talk?

5.7 Using prefixes – 3 · WORD STUDY

A **Work in pairs** Prefixes can be used with words to change their meaning. Look at the words in green. What do they mean?

1 Is 'the' the indefinite article or the definite article?

2 You'll certainly lose marks in the exam if your handwriting is illegible. And untidy work may also lose marks.

3 Make sure the information you give is relevant to the question. Again, irrelevant information may lose you marks.

4 The children were told not to misbehave but they disobeyed our instructions.

5 The students at the university called for a non-violent demonstration to express their disapproval of the government's education policy.

6 It took us ever such a long time to wrap your present nicely but you've unwrapped it without even admiring the paper.

B Add more examples to the lists below using these root words:

able   accurate   active   agree   button   comfortable   convenient   credible   direct
experienced   fair   fold   formal   fortunate   hear   like   necessary   pack
patient   pleasant   possible   pronounce   spell   tolerant   usual   willing

adjectives

un- unjust unkind unsatisfactory ....
....

in- inappropriate insincere ....
....

il- illegible illegal illiterate

ir- irregular irrelevant irresponsible

im- immature improbable immoral ....

verbs

un- unscrew undo untie ....

dis- disappear disqualify ....

mis- misunderstand misread ....

C Use the words in red at the end of each line to form new words to fit in the spaces.

1 Don't depend on him, he is a very unreliable person.   **rely**

2 I'd lost my key, so I couldn't .... the door when I got home.   **lock**

3 Don't be so .... , we've only been waiting a few minutes.   **patient**

4 Seven o'clock on Saturday is a rather .... time for an appointment.   **convenient**

5 Please don't be so .... , I can't do all the work by myself.   **reason**

6 The staff are always making mistakes because they are so ....   **efficient**

7 Sorry about the mistake. I .... the instructions you gave me.   **understand**

8 They've .... my name on this form – the first letter is L not R.   **spell**

9 An athlete who fails a drugs test is sure to be ....   **qualify**

10 Every year thousands of species of plants and insects ....   **appear**

If you find it hard to remember which prefix goes with which word, trust your feelings. Pick the one that sounds right to you – or avoid the word. Instead of 'He sounded insincere', you can say or write 'He didn't sound very sincere'.

"Well if it's all the same to you, I'd prefer one that has been tested on animals."

5.8 Making notes   WRITING

A

There are many ways of making notes. Which of these styles do you prefer, and why?

The key to writing better compositions is deciding what to write before you put pen to paper – by making notes before you start. Notes help you to organise your thoughts *before* you begin writing. And they help you to remember your ideas *while* you're writing a composition.

Making notes before you start takes a few minutes but these notes can save you time later. And if your mind goes blank while you're writing, you can refer back to the notes. But most importantly, your reader will find it easier to follow your ideas if they are well organised.

1

RECYCLING

1 Advantages:
  a) saving energy
  b) less need to use oil, gas and coal
  c) re-using resources

2 Examples:
  a) paper – save energy + save trees – but forests replanted on 'tree farms'
  b) glass – save energy by making new bottles out of old glass, but better to re-use bottles.
  c) metal – aluminium cans can be recycled, mining is expensive

3 Drawbacks:
  a) may be expensive
  b) may require high technology
  c) may use more energy than it saves

2

RECYCLING

paper   save energy, save trees – but forests replanted on 'tree farms'

bottles   new bottles from old glass – but better to re-use bottles.

metal   aluminium cans can be recycled – mining is expensive

FOR
energy saving
less oil, gas & coal
re-using resources

AGAINST
expensive?
high tech?
use more energy?

3

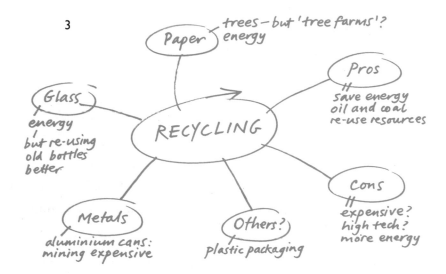

Paper — trees – but 'tree farms'? / energy

Glass — energy / but re-using old bottles better

RECYCLING

Pros — save energy / oil and coal / re-use resources

Cons — expensive? / high tech? / more energy

Metals — aluminium cans: mining expensive

Others? — plastic packaging

B 1 Work in pairs   Make notes in one of the styles shown above, summarising your views for and against *one* of these topics:

Factory farms   Medical experiments on animals   Hunting and fishing

2 Use the notes to write two paragraphs (about 50 words each) explaining your views.

3 Work in pairs   Read each other's work. How clearly have you expressed your ideas? How much did your notes help you while you were writing? Did you decide to leave some points out – if so, why?

C

✒ Write an article for an international student magazine (about 150 words) giving your views on *one* of these topics, as it relates to your own country and experience. Make notes before you start:

Zoos   Pollution in cities   Protecting the environment

6

Going places

A 1 **Work in pairs**   Look at the text below and discuss these questions:

- What are your reactions to the picture and to the slogan?
- What is the main message of the text?
- What advice about road safety do pedestrians, cyclists and drivers in your country need reminding about most? Note down *two* pieces of advice for each type of road user.

In a crash at 30 mph, an adult back seat passenger is thrown forward with a force of 3.5 tons, equal to the weight of an elephant.

Without a seat belt, this could result in death or serious injury to the passenger and to other people in the vehicle.

Never forget

Wherever you sit

Clunk Click

every trip.

2 The slogan of the text tells you what to remember. What information and advice would be given with these slogans, do you think?

Sorry mate
I didn't
see you.

Kill your speed not a child

3 👥 One of you should look at Activity *43*, the other at *51*, where you will see the complete texts that go with the slogans.

B **Work in pairs**   Fill the gaps in these sentences with a suitable word.

1 We put our luggage in the ___*boot*___ , got in the car and *fastened* our s_____ .

2 After you've passed your driving t_____ you'll get your driving l_____ .

3 An a_____ may happen if a driver forgets to look in the driving m_____ before o_____ another vehicle.

4 At a r_____ in Britain you have to give w_____ to traffic from the r_____ .

5 If you're going to turn left at the traffic l_____ , get into the left-hand l_____ .

6 If you can't find a parking s_____ in the street, you'll have to pay to park in a car p_____ or at a parking m_____ .

7 If you're caught speeding, you may have to pay a f_____ or you may even be d_____ from driving.

8 It's dangerous for p_____ to walk in the road. They should stay on the p_____ .

C Fill the gaps in the sentences below with one of the words listed. In some cases more than one word fits, and some words have to be used in several different sentences:

crossing   cruise   excursion   flight   journey   outing   tour   transport
travel   trip

1 When someone arrives you can ask them, 'Did you have a good .... ?' or 'How was your .... ?'

2 The .... from London to Tokyo takes about 12 hours.

3 It was a very rough .... and all the passengers were seasick.

4 The hotel runs various .... to see places of interest.

5 The weather's nice, let's take a(n) .... out of the city this afternoon.

6 The idea of a round-the-world .... sounds really exciting.

7 The guide will make sure you don't get lost if you go on a(n) ....

8 .... broadens the mind, they say.

9 There's no point in driving into the city, public .... is much more convenient.

10 When someone is leaving you can say to them, 'Have a nice ....', 'Have a good ....' or 'Have a safe .... !'

D **1** Choose the best alternative to fill the gaps in these sentences.

1 The quickest way to get from London to Manchester is to take the ....
   by-pass   highway   main road   main street   motorway   ring road

2 It's quicker and cheaper to cross London by .... than to take a taxi.
   bus   car   foot   metro   subway   tube

3 It costs less to travel a long distance by .... than to take the train.
   coach   hearse   limousine   plane   pullman   taxi

4 Go straight down the hill and take the third .... on the left. You can't miss it.
   bend   branch   corner   crossroads   junction   roundabout   turning

5 If you want to stop the car, you have to put your foot on the .... pedal.
   accelerator   brake   break   choke   clutch   handbrake   gas

6 If you're travelling by train, you have to buy a single or return ....
   ticket   card   fare   reservation   passage

2 Look again at the words which were *wrong* in D1. Check that you know what they all mean, and *why* they didn't fit in the gaps.

E **1** **Work in pairs**   Note down five questions about each of these pictures, and about the topics they bring to mind. (Choose questions that will provoke discussion, not Yes/No questions.)

2 **Join another pair**   Ask each other your questions and use follow-up questions to encourage your partners to say more. Tell them your own views too.

Why do you think that?
What makes you say that?
Can you give an example to show what you mean?
I don't quite understand what you mean by . . .

6.2 Cars in cities   READING

A Work in pairs   Before you read the article, discuss these questions:
- What will happen when the roads are so busy that there is no room for cars?
- What's it like driving or being driven in the rush hour in your city?
- How easy is it to find a parking space in your city? How expensive is it?

B 1 Five sentences have been removed from the article below. Choose from sentences A–F the one which fits each gap 1–5. There's one extra sentence you don't need to use.

  A But parking a car in Japan is expensive.
  B But the driving test in Japan is extremely difficult to pass.
  C For less experienced drivers, an ambulance is on standby.
  D In order to register a car in Japan, the owner must have somewhere to park it.
  E These allow two cars to share the same parking space.
  F This provides buyers of four-wheel-drive vehicles somewhere to get their tyres dirty.

EVER wondered what the car industry will do when roads become so congested there is no longer enough room to squeeze in any more cars? That is what is starting to happen in Japan, where car makers are moving into the car-parking business and building special driving courses where motorists can go to escape the country's traffic jams.

The impetus has come from tough new parking rules, backed up by hefty fines, that came into force this summer. 1................................... The new rules require a sticker to be displayed to prove the owner has a parking space at home or near the office. 2................................... Spaces in some residential areas in Tokyo can cost as much as ¥230,000 ($1,700) a month.

To help persuade households to buy a second car, some of Japan's car makers have moved into the business of selling machines which make double-tier parking possible. 3................................... They work like a lift. The driver parks his first car on a platform, then flicks a switch which raises the platform to allow a second car to be parked underneath. Toyota now sells six such devices, costing between ¥1.3m and ¥1.7m each. Honda not only sells home-parking equipment, but also manages car parks and provides information on the availability of parking spaces for car buyers.

Nissan even offers a home-parking machine that lowers cars into a pit below ground. Nissan has also opened a 'mobility park' 140 kilometres outside Tokyo. 4................................... The park provides instructors and a variety of off-road courses, ranging from a beginner's trail to an advanced course for more experienced off-roaders. 5...................................

HUNT.

2 Choose one of these headlines for the article:

Safer motoring in Japan

Running out of road

Keeping cars off the roads

3 Highlight any words or phrases in the article which you'd like to remember, and which you'd like to use yourself.

4 Work in pairs   Compare the words you've highlighted. Then discuss these questions:
- Which of the ideas in the article do you think is the best?
- Which ideas would work and not work in your country?
- Speaking as a pedestrian or cyclist, what changes would you like to see to traffic management in your city or town?

6.3 I don't get it! **VERBS AND IDIOMS**

Ⓐ **Work in pairs** What other words or phrases could you use in place of *get* in these sentences?

1 How many cards did you get for your birthday?
2 He got really upset when I told him he'd got to walk.
3 When I got home I realised I hadn't got my wallet with me.
4 You have to get your ticket before you get the train.

Ⓑ Fill the gaps in the sentences below with suitable forms of these phrases:

get better   get dark   get an expert to   get a headache   get lost   get ready
get rid of ✓   get the joke   get the sack   get to sleep   get started   get into trouble

1 I still haven't *got rid of* my cold.
2 I hope you soon ....
3 Right, everyone's here, so let's ....
4 I sometimes .... if I've been studying too long.
5 We ought to go home, it's ....
6 He didn't laugh because he didn't ....
7 I need plenty of time to .... before I go out.
8 If you haven't got a ticket, you'll .... if an inspector gets on the bus.
9 I was so excited that I couldn't ....
10 If you can't do it yourself, you'll have to .... do it for you.
11 She .... because her work was unsatisfactory.
12 Ask someone for directions if you ....

Ⓒ Fill the gaps in the sentences below with suitable forms of these phrasal verbs and verbs + prepositions:

get (a)round   get (a)round to   get at   get down   get off   get on with ✓
get on with   get on with   get out of   get over   get through   get together

1 Please *get on with* your work – I didn't mean to interrupt you.
2 They managed to .... doing the work by pretending to be busy.
3 I tried to explain what he'd done wrong but he didn't seem to see what I was ....
4 He got very upset about failing his driving test, but he soon .... it.
5 However difficult a problem is, there's usually a way to .... it.
6 .... the bus when you get to the stop by the railway station.
7 How are you .... this exercise?
8 She doesn't .... her younger brother, they're always quarrelling.
9 I hope I'll be able to .... answering the letters this evening.
10 I've tried ringing her several times, but I haven't been able to ....
11 They decided to .... later in the week for an informal meeting.
12 This dull weather is so depressing – it's .... me ....

| 6.4 | **Articles and quantifiers – 2** | GRAMMAR REVIEW |

A 1 Work in pairs Note down two more of each of the following. Write *the* where necessary.

Countries in Europe: .the Netherlands. ....
Countries in Asia: .Japan. ....
Countries in South America: ....

Oceans: .the Atlantic. ....   Cities in North America: ....
Seas: .the Baltic. ....   Rivers: ....
Mountain ranges: ....   Groups of islands: ....
Mountains: ....   Lakes: ....
Famous public buildings: ....   Famous streets: ....
Languages: ....   Planets: ....

See the Grammar
Reference section
on pages 171–172.

2 Join another pair Compare your notes and pool your ideas.

B 1 Work in pairs Fill the gaps in this extract from an article about driving in the USA with *a*, *an*, *the* or a zero article Ø. In some cases there may be more than one possible answer.

Because of [1] *the* inadequacy of [2] *Ø* public transport systems in [3] *the*
USA, [4] most areas have [5] special school buses (which take [6]
children to and from [7] school once [8] day, five days [9] week,
and do nothing at all for [10] most of [11] rest of [12] time). These are
usually painted yellow. When they stop to discharge [13] children, they display
[14] flashing red lights, and it is then illegal to pass [15] bus, even if you
are going in [16] opposite direction on [17] other side of [18] road.
All [19] traffic must stop.
[20] USA has [21] very few roundabouts. It does, though, have [22]
institution known as [23] 'four-way stop'. As you approach [24] crossroads,
you may see [25] stop sign with [26] words '4 WAY' underneath. This means
that all [27] four of [28] roads involved have [29] stop signs on
them. Priority goes to [30] vehicle that has arrived and stopped at [31]
crossroads first. If [32] two drivers stop at exactly [33] same time, one
driver supposedly gives way to [34] vehicle on his right. (This ought to mean that
if [35] four vehicles stop at [36] crossroads at precisely [37] same
time, they would all have to stay there indefinitely, but this does not seem to happen.)

2 Work alone Check your answers to B1 before filling the gaps in this second extract with *a*, *an*, *the* or a zero article Ø.

There seem to be [1] more parking restrictions in [2] USA than there are
in [3] Europe. Most Americans appear to get [4] parking tickets. If you
get one and feel like paying it, in many places [5] system is that [6]
envelope is left on your car so that you can post your fine to [7] appropriate
place. Some states swap [8] parking-ticket information, while others don't. If
your parking ticket is issued in [9] state [10] long way from [11] one
in which your car is registered, you probably need not bother to pay it.
  You must not park in front of [12] fire-hydrant. It is important to remember
this because there will be no signs anywhere to tell you. Fire-hydrants are easily
recognised: they are [13] large metal kerbside objects, perhaps fifty centimetres,
high, with [14] parking spaces in front of them.
  You must park in [15] direction of [16] traffic flow, even in [17]
daytime. Combined with [18] 'no U-turns in [19] business districts' rule,
this means that there is no way you can get to [20] parking space on [21]
other side of [22] road unless you go round [23] block and come back.

3 Work in pairs Bearing in mind the advice for non-Americans in B1 and 2, what advice
would you give to an American who intends to drive in *your* country? Write your own 'Tips for
American motorists'.

6.5 Boring in the Alps LISTENING

A **Work in pairs** Before you listen to the recording, discuss these questions:
- What do you know about Switzerland?
- What is it famous for? Note down three things.
- What do you think this map shows?

B 🔊 **You'll hear a broadcast about a project to bore new rail tunnels through the Alps. Complete these notes using a word, figure or short phrase.**

1 By Swissmetro, the journey time from Geneva to Zürich will be ....

2 The journey time from Basle to Bellinzona will be ....

3 The top speed of the Swissmetro trains will be ....

4 The total length of tunnels will be ....

5 The first part of the scheme will link the airports of Basle and ....

6 The first part of the scheme will cost SFr ....

7 Work on boring the Swissmetro network will start ....

8 The whole project will cost SFr ....

9 The cost of the feasibility study is SFr ....

10 The main advantage of the scheme is to keep ....

C **Work in groups** Find out about your partners' experiences of travelling by land, sea and air. Discuss these questions:

- If you had to travel across Switzerland in the future, would you choose to go by Swissmetro, train or car? Give your reasons.
- If you had to travel from Paris to London, would you go by sea, air or through the Channel Tunnel? Why?
  Have you been on a ferry? Tell your partners about it.
- If you had to travel between the two major cities in your country, how would you go? Would you fly, drive or go by train or coach? Why?
- What do you (or would you) like and dislike about flying?
  If you've flown, tell your partners about your most recent experience.
  When did you last meet someone at an airport? Tell your partners about it.

- What is the most *unusual* journey you've ever experienced?
- What is the *worst* journey by land, sea or air that you've ever experienced?

Can you tell me the way to . . . ?

LISTENING AND SPEAKING

A You'll hear a telephone call. Look at this street plan and draw a line to show the route that's explained.

Copyright Compass Maps Ltd. 1996 All rights reserved.

B 👥 **Work in pairs** One of you should look at Activity 9, the other at 36. You will take turns to explain more routes on the map above.

> Take the first left.
> You'll see . . . opposite you.
> When you reach . . . turn right.
> Cross the road and then . . .
> Take the second right.

> It's just to the left of . . .
> Go past the . . . and then . . .
> You can't miss it.
> Go straight on until . . .

Personal letters

WRITING

A **1** 🖊 In the two letters opposite, Jan is writing to Alex, a friend from abroad who is coming to stay for a few days. Alex has never visited Jan's country before. Highlight the parts of each letter which are most helpful for the reader. Choose the best features of each letter.

2 **Work in pairs** Compare the parts you've highlighted. Which parts of each letter are *unhelpful*? And why are they less helpful?

3 🖊 Highlight three examples of informal style and underline three examples of formal style. For example: 'I'm sorry I won't be able to' is appropriate in an informal personal letter, while 'I regret that I will be unable to' is more appropriate in a formal business letter.

4 Join another pair Compare the parts you've highlighted and underlined.

1

Dear Alex,

I'm sorry I won't be able to meet you. Here's a quick note on how to get here from the airport. There are three alternatives:

1 TAXI: This would be very expensive, so unless you have a lot of luggage it's not advisable.
2 BUS: There's a direct bus (number 108), which is cheap, but slow. Ask the driver to tell you when he gets to Greenwood Park Station.
3 UNDERGROUND: This is quick but you'd have to change twice, which could be tricky if you have loads of luggage.

Looking forward to seeing you,

Jan

P.S. I've drawn a little map to help you find your way to our flat in Greenwood.

2

Dear Alex,

I regret that I will be unable to meet you when you arrive at the airport because I will be at work. Unfortunately, there is no easy way of getting here apart from taking a taxi, which would be very expensive.

Therefore, if you do not have too much luggage, I would suggest taking the underground. You will have to change twice to reach the nearest station (GREENWOOD PARK). When you come out of the station, turn left and walk along the main road past Tesco supermarket and take the first left (South Road). Pine Road is on the right and 12A is on the first floor. My mother will be there to welcome you!

However, if you have time for a slower journey there is a direct bus (No 108) which will take you all the way from the airport and there is a stop opposite Greenwood Park Station. Ask the driver to tell you when to get off.

Looking forward to seeing you on Friday evening.

Jan

P.S. If you get lost or if you are delayed, phone me at work (0171 4418 extension 679).

B **1** **Work in pairs** How do you get from the nearest international airport to *your* home without taking a taxi? Work out the quickest route – and the cheapest route.

2 🖋 Your friend from abroad is coming to visit you for the first time. Unfortunately you can't meet your friend at the airport. Write a letter (120–180 words) explaining how to get to your home from your local airport. Your friend is a student and probably can't afford a taxi.

3 **Work in pairs** Show your completed letter to another student and ask for comments on the style and the content. How could the instructions be made clearer or more helpful?

"Excuse me, those seats are taken."

7

There's no place like home

7.1 Make yourself at home!   VOCABULARY

A   **Work in groups**   **Look at the pictures above and discuss these questions:**

- Describe the two rooms. What kind of person lives in each one, do you think?
- In your own home, where do you work or study? What furniture is in this room?
- How do you prefer to work: in complete silence, listening to music, or with the TV on? Do you need snacks and drinks while you're working? Give your reasons.
- What is the most important thing for you about a home?

B   **Fill the gaps in these sentences with a suitable word. There may be several possibilities.**

The Clarks live in a tiny ¹ apartment on the top ² f_____ of a ³ b_____ of flats in the city centre. It has ⁴ c_____ h_____ so it is very warm in the winter. It doesn't have ⁵ a_____ c_____ because the summers are never very hot. They were lucky to find it because ⁶ a_____ is very scarce in the city and it's easier to find a flat in a new estate on the ⁷ o_____ of the city or in the ⁸ s_____.

   Their dream is to ⁹ m_____ to the country and live in an old ¹⁰ c_____ in a little ¹¹ v_____. Where they live now, their ¹² n_____-d_____ n_____ are always ¹³ c_____ about the noise when Jane plays her trumpet, and they haven't got ¹⁴ r_____ for all their things: there aren't enough ¹⁵ s_____ in the ¹⁶ l_____ for all the children's books and the ¹⁷ _____ in the bedroom aren't big enough for all Tom's clothes.

   But if they did find a place in the country, they'd have to buy it and pay the ¹⁸ m_____ every month – more than the ¹⁹ r_____ they pay to their ²⁰ l_____ at the moment. Still, they wouldn't mind this if they could live somewhere that was more ²¹ _____

C   **Choose the best alternative to fill the gaps in these sentences.**

1   Some buildings have a basement room where things are stored called a(n) _____ .
   attic   cave   cellar   grave   loft

2   Some rooms don't have curtains at the windows, they have _____ instead.
   blinds   carpets   glass   stores   wallpaper

3   We haven't got a garage, so we leave our car outside the flat in the _____ .
   drive   garden   parking   patio   pavement   porch

4   He keeps all his tools and do-it-yourself equipment in a _____ in the back garden.
   barn   bungalow   hut   shack   shed   stable

5   In your own garden, you can sunbathe on the _____ in the summer.
   field   flowerbed   lawn   meadow   pasture

D 1 Work in pairs Imagine that you can design your ideal home. Draw a floor plan showing what furniture and equipment you'd have in each room. What about the garden?

2 Join another pair Describe your dream houses to each other.

7.2 Town or country?   LISTENING AND SPEAKING

A 1 Work in pairs Before you listen to the recording, list the advantages and disadvantages of living in a city and living in the country.

2 🎞 You'll hear three friends discussing where they'd prefer to live. Tick the boxes according to who says what. There are two points which no one mentions.

	John	Sarah	Terry
1 New York is a dangerous place.	☐	☐	☐
2 New York is safe if you avoid going to certain districts.	☐	☐	☐
3 There is always plenty to do in a city.	☐	☐	☐
4 People in villages tend to be older than people in cities.	☐	☐	☐
5 All cities are impersonal places.	☐	☐	☐
6 Some cities are friendly places.	☐	☐	☐
7 Life is more expensive in a city than in a village.	☐	☐	☐
8 In a city you don't have to be sociable unless you want to be.	☐	☐	☐
9 Underground trains are quick and convenient.	☐	☐	☐
10 It's lovely to live in a village.	☐	☐	☐

B 1 If you're talking about what you'd prefer, here are some useful phrases you can use:

> I think I'd prefer to . . . rather than . . .   As far as I'm concerned, it's better to . . .
> It would be better to . . . because . . .   It seems to me that . . . is better, because . . .
> I'd rather . . . because . . .   The reason why . . . is better is that . . .

2 Work in pairs Talk about your preferences by making up sentences about these topics, using the phrases above:

village – city   flat – house
suburbs – city centre   big city – small town
rent – buy   garden – swimming pool
modern building – old building

C 1 Work in pairs Look at the photos above and write down *five* questions you could ask about them and the topics they bring to mind.

> What would it be like to live in each place?
> How is the place you live in different from these places?

2 Join another pair Ask each other your questions and discuss your preferences.

7.3 Two cities   READING

A **1** **Work in pairs**   Name two major cities in four countries. What do you know about them?

2 Read the article below and choose a suitable heading for it:

Two cities: Madrid and Barcelona

Inter-city rivalry

A tale of two cities

Not as different as they look

A VISITOR from Barcelona arrives at a Madrid government office in mid-afternoon, and is surprised to find only the cleaning lady there. "Don't they work in the afternoons?" he asks. "No," she replies, "they don't work in the mornings. In the afternoons they don't come."

2 Lazy Madrid, busy Barcelona: it is just one of many stereotypes about Spain's great rivals. Mostly, the stereotypes are born of Barcelona's bitterness at its second-class status. Barcelona is the capital of Catalonia, a proudly autonomous region, but Madrid is the capital of Spain. This causes resentment. It makes Barcelona the largest city in Western Europe not to be a national capital. Worse, Barcelona (Catalonia's capital since the ninth century) regards Madrid (a creation of Philip II in the 16th century) as an upstart. Catalans rarely miss a chance to have a dig at the folks from Castille.

3 And, after being bossed about for so long, who can blame them? Over the years governments in Madrid did their best to strip Barcelona of political power. They tried to squash the Catalan language. They even decided what the modern city should look like: in 1860 an order from Madrid overruled Barcelona's choice of plan for its big expansion, and opted for a grid layout.

"We are more liberal, and that explains almost everything," says

4 Miquel Roca who, as parliamentary leader of the Catalan Nationalists, spends much of his time shuttling between the two cities. Barcelona has the liberalism that often characterises port cities. As Catalans see it, while Madrid bathes in bureaucracy, Barcelona gets on with business. An old-fashioned seriousness in Madrid, isolated high up on Spain's central plateau, contrasts with the light-heartedness of Barcelona, open to Europe and aggressively avant-garde.

5 Up to a point, these old caricatures still hold true. No visitor to government buildings in the two cities can fail to be struck by the contrast between them. In Madrid, there are creaky/ancient wooden floors, antique furniture and walls covered with paintings by Spanish old masters. In Barcelona, the city of Gaudí and Miró, designer chairs and tables are evidence of the place's obsession with modernism. Meetings of the Catalan cabinet are held in a room with a large, modern painting by Antoni Tàpies.

6 And yet, these days, the similarities between the two cities are at least as striking as the contrasts. Madrid is hardly lazy any more. Visitors find it hard to keep up with the pace of the place. Nor is it old-fashioned. Indeed, it has become almost outrageously modern. To judge by the local cuisine, you would think the place was a port: although far from the sea, seafood is a miraculous

Madrid speciality. In recent years once-isolationist Madrid has become every bit as fanatical about "Europe" as Barcelona.

7 As banks and businesses have been drawn to Madrid, it has become as much a commercial and industrial centre as an administrative one. Barcelona, meanwhile, in Spain's traditional industrial heartland, has been experiencing a rise in bureaucracy.

8 The rivalry between Madrid and Barcelona is bound to remain fierce, not least on the soccer field, where Real Madrid and Barcelona compete for Spanish supremacy. Barcelona will continue to press for yet more power to be devolved to it from Madrid: it is calling for the Senate, Spain's upper house of parliament, to be moved to the Catalan capital. But with a lot of local autonomy restored, and with the success of the 1992 Olympics behind it, the chip on Barcelona's shoulder is becoming ever harder to detect.

B   **Choose the best alternative according to the article.**

1 According to the old Catalan joke, Madrid people are lazy ....

in the afternoon   at the office   at home   in government offices

2 Historically, Barcelonans regard Madrid as ....

superior   inferior   a newcomer   less efficient

3 In the past Madrid made decisions that ....

didn't affect Barcelona   took power away from Barcelona   ignored Barcelona

4 Compared to Barcelona, Madrid was thought to be ....
   sensible   sensitive   old-fashioned   cultured

5 Government buildings in the two cities today look ....
   similar   different   modern   old-fashioned

6 The pace of life in Madrid today is .... than Barcelona.
   faster   sleepier   less crazy   more pleasant

7 Madrid is now much more important as a ....
   business centre   tourist centre   banking centre   government centre

8 Nowadays people in Barcelona don't feel so .... Madrid as they used to.
   afraid of   competitive with   envious of   resentful of

C 🖊 **Highlight the words or phrases in the article with similar meanings to these:**

¶2 independent   criticise   ¶5 stereotyped images   excessive interest
¶3 told what to do   destroy   ¶6 speed   cooking   madly interested
¶4 travelling   high plain   ¶8 feeling of resentment

D **1 Work in groups** Think of two major cities that you know about – not Barcelona and Madrid. Discuss the similarities and differences between the cities and the people who live there. Make notes on the main points.

2 🖋 Write an article of about 150 words comparing two cities in your country. Imagine that you're writing this article for an international magazine.

7.4 *Have and give*   VERBS AND IDIOMS

A **Which of the endings below go with these beginnings? Some of them go with more than one of the beginnings, sometimes with a different meaning:**

   Alex had …   Barry was having …   Charlie gave us …   Carol gave …

   a quarrel with Carol   an order   a sigh   no time to finish   permission to leave
   a good performance   a meal   a drink   his/her opinion   a headache
   his/her hair cut   a chance   a look   an interview   a good idea   the information
   an accident   a rest   a swim   the details   no imagination   better be careful

B **Fill the gaps in the sentences below with suitable forms of these phrasal verbs:**

   give away ✓   give back   give in   give out   give up   give up   give up
   have round   have on   have back

give

1 This information is secret, don't ...give... it ...away... to anyone.
2 When I'd read the books I .... them .... to her.
3 Smoking again? You told me you .... smoking.
4 A man was standing on the corner .... leaflets to everyone.
5 The criminal .... himself .... to the police.
6 You must check your work through before .... it .... at the end of the exam.
7 I tried to persuade him to join me, but in the end I ....

have

8 He .... his best suit .... for the interview.
9 When you've finished with the cassette, I'd like to .... it .... again.
10 It's been very nice .... you .... Do come and see us again!

A nice place to stay

A **1 Work in pairs** Imagine that you and your partner are going to stay for a few months in Greenwood, a medium-sized town on the coast of England. You don't want to stay with a family, but would prefer to share a flat together. You have asked your friends Bob and Louise to find out about suitable places to rent.

Read the advertisements below from the *Greenwood Evening Echo*, which your friends have faxed to you. Then discuss these questions:

- Which of the flats sounds the best? And which sounds the worst? Why?
- What is not mentioned in the ads that you could only find out by viewing them?

13A Balmoral Way

Superb 2-bedroom apartment, overlooking Queen's Park. 3 mins Greenwood Station. Newly decorated living room and bedrooms. Compact modern kitchen. Bathroom with shower. Extensive views over nearby countryside.

7B Windsor Avenue

Charming ground-floor flat with secluded garden. Living room. 1 bedroom. Spacious kitchen. Shower room. Available July to September.

44C Sandringham Gardens

Delightful south-facing living room with balcony. 1 good-sized bedroom. Kitchen and bathroom.

2 You'll hear two telephone messages from your friends about the flats, which they have now been to see. Write notes on the main points they make about each one.

3 Work in pairs Decide which of the three flats you would prefer. Note down three more pieces of information you need to know about it before you can make up your mind.

B ✎ Write a letter to the owner of the flat, asking for the extra information you require.

7.6 Modal verbs – 1 ·GRAMMAR REVIEW

A **Work in pairs** Match the sentences on the left to the ones on the right closest in meaning.

1 I can't help you to find accommodation. It's not my responsibility to help you.
2 I don't have to help you to find accommodation. I'm unwilling to help you.
3 I won't help you to find accommodation. I'm unable to help you.

4 She can't be joking. I'm sure she is.
5 She can't tell jokes. I'm sure she isn't.
6 She must be joking. She isn't allowed to.
7 She mustn't tell jokes. She's no good at it.

8 You can't leave now. It's not a good idea to go.
9 You could leave now. I won't let you go.
10 You don't have to leave now. It's unnecessary to go.
11 You needn't leave now. It would be possible to go.
12 You shouldn't leave now.

See the Grammar Reference section on pages 178–179.

B Each of these sentences contains at least one error. Underline the errors and correct them.

1 *May you tell me where I may catch a bus into town?*

  Could you tell me where I can catch a bus into town?

2 *I checked the timetable so I mustn't be wrong about the departure time!*

3 *You needn't to worry if I miss the last bus because I can get a taxi.*

4 *Do I ought to phone for a taxi, or may I pick one up in the street?*

5 *I could get a taxi but I must waiting for five minutes for one to arrive.*

6 *Don't be silly, you ought not to show your passport if you will buy a rail ticket!*

7 *You mustn't write anything down unless you want to.*

8 *You need spend as much time as you can on your homework.*

C **Work in pairs** Compare your lives now with your lives when you were ten years old by discussing the following points. Then write sentences about each point.

• two things you can do now

  I can travel alone on a bus and I can speak English quite well.
  When I was ten I couldn't do either of those things.

• two things you still can't do
• two things you don't have to do now
• two things you still have to do
• two things you may do one day soon
• two things you know you shouldn't do

D **1** **Work in pairs** Imagine that two friends are coming to stay with you in your home and attend lessons with you – one is from America and the other from a tiny, isolated village in your country. Your friends are very nervous about their visit . . .

   Put yourself in their position. What will be *strange* for them both? What advice would you give them about the customs, rules and habits they will have to get used to in your country, in your city, in your home and in your school or college? Make notes.

2 **Work in groups** Decide who's going to play each role and then role-play the situation. Imagine that you are sitting together after dinner on the visitors' first evening in your home.

Will I be able to . . . ?
Can I . . . ?
Will I have to . . . ?

You won't have to . . .
There's no need to . . .
You'll have to . . .
You ought to . . .
You won't be able to . . .
You can't . . .

7.7 Spelling and pronunciation – 1: Vowels   WORD STUDY

A One of the main difficulties of English spelling is that some words are pronounced the same, but are spelt differently and have different meanings. Can you think of words pronounced the same as each of these, but spelt differently?

guessed _guest_   warn ....   meet ....   won ....   threw ....

B 1 Work in pairs   Match the words on the right to the examples on the left, according to the vowel sound they share in common. Say them aloud to help you to decide.

Note that in American English and in regional accents of British English, several of these 'rules' of pronunciation and spelling don't apply. For example, *caught* and *court* are pronounced differently in many accents, and *cough* is pronounced /kɑːf/ in American English.

pure vowels

/æ/	bad	damage	apple		blood	tongue	country	thorough
/e/	bed	pleasure	leisure	lent/leant	blue/blew	root/route	new/knew
/ɑː/	calm	heart			weak/week	seize/seas	wheel/we'll
/ɔː/	saw	bored/board	caught/court		cushion	butcher	pull
/ɜː/	bird	worm			guilty	witch/which	mist/missed
/iː/	sheep	piece/peace			laugh	castle	half
/ɪ/	ship	sink	mystery		not/knot	knowledge	quality
/ɒ/	pot	what	yacht	cough	scandal	flat
/uː/	boot	truly	threw/through		bury/berry	weather/whether	check/cheque
/ʊ/	put	should	wood/would		turn	firm
/ʌ/	cut	worry	money	rough	wore/war	source/sauce	raw/roar

2 Add these words to the appropriate group above, according to their vowel sounds:

business   guard   marry   merry   push   receive   soup   walk
wander   wonder   work

3 You'll hear the answers to B1 and B2.

C Find the mistakes in each of these sentences and correct them.

1 *I am quite shore that this weak is going too be wonderful.*
2 *We are truely sorry that you had to weight so long four the delivery.*
3 *He has dredful manners — he paws tomato source on all his food.*
4 *They couldn't get thier new armchare threw the door.*
5 *Witch of these too alternatives is the write one?*
6 *He lent the ladder agenst the wall and climed onto the roof.*
7 *The cieling and walls of this room need peinting ergently.*

7.8 Starting and ending well   WRITING

A A good piece of writing requires an *opening sentence* that will catch the reader's attention. Which of these sentences would be the best opening sentence for the passage opposite?

1 G__ is a village I know very well.
2 The village of G__ lies at the mouth of a river.
3 The other day, I was talking with some friends about a little place I know called G__.
4 I'll never forget the day that I first went to G__.
5 G__ is a delightfully unspoilt village surrounded by fields and woods at the mouth of a river.
6 I'm going to tell you something about a place I know, called G__.

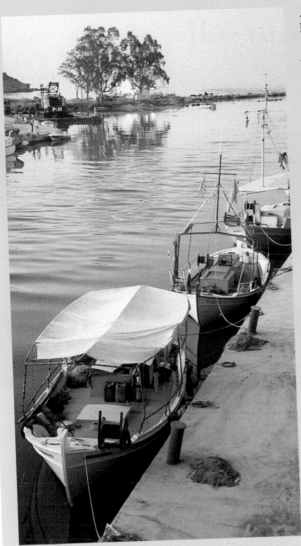

.... It's only an hour's bus ride from the busy city of H__.

The countryside around the village is incredibly green, with fertile fields, olive groves and orange trees. The river is wide and crystal clear – you can even see little turtles swimming in it or sunning themselves on the banks.

In the centre of G__ is the village square, dominated by tall trees which shade it from the hot sun. Around the square there are a few restaurants, a couple of cafés and one or two little shops. There you'll find the locals and visitors sitting for hours over their drinks in the cafés, chatting and watching nothing much happen. Right in the centre of the square is a small kiosk run by an old lady, who sells everything from razor blades to chewing gum and fresh fruit.

From the square a track leads you down to the main beach. This is a magnificent stretch of pale yellow sand, overlooked by bamboos and stretching away to the horizon. There are just a couple of bars down there, which serve drinks and snacks.

The local people are farmers or fishermen, though now everyone has built extra rooms on their property, which they let to visitors in the summer. In the season there are plenty of visitors around, but there are no large hotels in the village itself and the place seems to have avoided the worst effects of mass tourism and kept its character and charm.

If you're looking for peace and quiet and a lovely rural environment, then G__ is the place to escape to. ....
....

B A good piece of writing depends on an ending which will leave the reader feeling satisfied. Which of these sentences would be the best *closing sentence*?

1 I can't think of anything else to write.

2 Looking forward to seeing you there.

3 You can catch a bus back to the city from the village square.

4 Go there before everyone else discovers it!

5 It is quite different from other places you may have visited.

6 So I hope you'll be able to come there with me soon.

C **1** **Work in pairs** Look back through the previous reading passages in Units 1–6. Pick your two favourite opening sentences and your two favourite closing sentences.

2 Look at your own recent compositions. Can you and your partner improve on the opening and closing sentences you both wrote? Rewrite some of them.

D Imagine that you're writing to a foreign friend. You want your friend to come and visit you. Write a description (120–180 words) of the district, town or village you live in, making it sound as attractive and interesting as possible.

• Make notes before you start writing.

• Decide what your opening and closing sentences will be.

• Check your work through afterwards.

8

Looking after yourself

8.1 How are you feeling?   VOCABULARY

A **Work in pairs** **Look at the pictures above and discuss these questions:**
- How do you look after your health and keep fit?
- What do you do which is bad for your health?
- Which of these people would you *least* like to be? Put them in order of preference:

    dentist   doctor   lifeguard   nurse   patient   physiotherapist   psychiatrist

B **Choose the best alternative to fill the gaps in these sentences.**

1 If someone is seriously ill, they may need to go to hospital to have a(n) ....
operation ✓   plaster   filling   drug

2 If you want antibiotics, you'll have to ask the doctor for a ....
medicine   note   prescription   receipt   recipe

3 She was in terrible pain, so the nurse gave her a(n) ....
injection   scratch   stab   vaccine   wound

4 If you've got measles, your skin is covered in ....
blots   dots   freckles   spots   stains

5 He didn't feel like going to the party because he had a terrible ....
disease   headache   homesickness   infection   nostalgia

6 Her mother sent her to bed because she had quite a high ....
cough   fever   temperature   blood pressure

7 If you have hayfever, you can't stop ....
being sick   choking   blinking   sneezing   hesitating

8 If you're overweight, you'd better go on a(n) ....
bus   cure   diet   holiday   regime

C **In these sentences *three* alternatives are correct and *two* are wrong. Choose the best three.**

1 If you've got a bad cold, it's no wonder you're ....
on top of the world   off your food   out of order   out of sorts   under the weather

2 I've got a .... on my forehead because I fell out of bed last night.
black eye   bruise   bump   cut   hurt

3 You're less likely to become ill if you are ....

   hygenic   physically fit   living a healthy life   in good shape   running

4 Doctors say that drinking alcohol and smoking can .... your health.

   affect   damage   improve   ruin   wound

5 As I haven't had anything to eat today, I'm feeling a bit ....

   dizzy   faint   funny   silly   unconscious

D **1** **Work in pairs**   Complete these sentences.

1 She's got a *headache/toothache* .   5 She's got a pain in her ....

2 He's broken his ....   6 He's hurt his ....

3 She's cut her ....   7 Her .... aches.

4 He's bruised his ....   8 He .... his head on the cupboard door.

2 **Work in pairs**   Draw a rough sketch of a human body in the centre of a blank page. Label the parts, starting at the toes or at the fingers. Use a dictionary if necessary.

3 **Join another pair**   When you've finished, compare your labels.

8.2 Sleep and dreams   LISTENING AND WRITING

A **1** **Work in pairs**   Before you listen to the recording, look at the sentences below. Can you guess what some of the missing words are?

2 🔊 You'll hear an interview with a doctor. Complete these notes summarising what he says.

1 REM stands for '...............'.

2 To restore our brains during the night, we require ....

3 Dreams occur during ....

4 A dream usually lasts for ....

5 In dreams of falling or being chased, the dreamer is not usually ....

6 Dreams can help sleepers to .... in their waking lives.

7 Everyone dreams but not everyone can ....

8 If you sleep for an hour at midday, you need .... sleep at night.

9 There are no physical benefits from having a ....

10 The only cure for snoring is ....

B **1** **Work in groups**   Carry out a survey by interviewing your partners using this questionnaire. Make notes on their answers.

SLEEP SURVEY

1 How much sleep do you need? When do you go to bed? How long does it take you to get to sleep?

2 When do you get up? How easy is it for you to wake up in the morning?

3 How do you feel if you have less sleep than normal?

4 Are you a light sleeper? What kinds of things wake you up?

5 Do you ever suffer from insomnia? What do you do to help you to get to sleep?

6 Do you remember your dreams? If so, tell us about one of them.

2 Report to the rest of the class on the results of your survey. Do your findings confirm or contradict the information given in the recording?

3 🖉 The principal of your school has heard that students have been falling asleep in class. Write a report on your research (about 150 words) for the principal. Look at Activity *58* for guidelines and discuss them with a partner before you begin writing.

8.3 **Modal verbs – 2** GRAMMAR REVIEW

 A Some modal verbs have different implications, especially when referring to past events. Match the sentences on the left to the *implied* meanings on the right.

1 I should have given her my phone number.
2 I had to give her my phone number.
3 I didn't have to give her my phone number.
4 She wouldn't let me give her my phone number.

I gave her the number.
I didn't give her the number.

5 He can't have gone to hospital.
6 He couldn't go to hospital.
7 He must have gone to hospital.
8 He needn't have gone to hospital.
9 He shouldn't have gone to hospital.

I'm convinced he has gone.
I'm sure he didn't go.
He didn't go, because he wasn't able to.
He went, but it was a mistake to do so.
He went, but it was unnecessary to.

B Imagine that these sentences are what the doctor said to you when you went to see her. Rewrite each one as reported speech.

1 'I wish you had come to see me earlier.'
The doctor told me that *I should have gone to see* her earlier.

2 'You must take these tablets three times a day.'
The doctor told me that .... the tablets three times a day.

3 'You can stop taking them when you feel better.'
She told me that .... better.

4 'You may feel better in a few days.'
She told me that .... in a few days.

5 'You can't expect to get better if you don't follow my advice.'
She told me that .... her advice.

6 'You have to take some exercise every day.'
She told me that .... some exercise every day.

7 'You mustn't sit around doing nothing.'
She told me that .... sit around doing nothing.

8 'You need to eat less.'
She told me that .... eat less.

See the Grammar
Reference section
on pages 178–179.

C Complete the second sentence so that it has a similar meaning to the first sentence. Use the word given in red and other words *including a modal verb* to complete each sentence. Don't change the word given.

1 I wish I'd looked after my teeth better when I was a child.
regularly I *should have cleaned my teeth regularly* when I was a child.

2 Surely he doesn't need an injection before he travels to America.
possibly He .... going to America.

3 You aren't supposed to take aspirins if there's nothing wrong with you.
perfectly You .... all right.

4 Is it absolutely necessary for me to take more exercise?
really Do .... take more exercise?

5 Could you tell me how long I must sit in the waiting room?
wait I wonder how long I'll .... ?

6 The nurse wouldn't let him get out of bed.
stay He .... in bed.

7 It was silly of you to go to the doctor because you were coughing.
with You .... a cough.

8 I'm sure that the doctor wasn't able to give you anything to make your cough better.
cured The doctor .... your cough.

"If diseases were easier to pronounce, Mrs Jarvis, everyone would have them."

8.4 What to do about flu   READING

A 1 Read these sentences. Which of them do you agree with?

1 One symptom of flu is an aching back.
2 Antibiotics can help you to get better from flu.
3 If you have flu, it's essential to eat three times a day.
4 Flu is not a serious illness for anyone.
5 Flu is infectious – other people can catch it from you.
6 If you have flu badly, you should lie in a darkened room.
7 One vaccination gives several years' protection against flu.
8 The worst time of year for flu is the autumn.
9 Wash up very thoroughly if someone in your family has flu.
10 You should go and see the doctor if your flu goes on for longer than a week.

2 Read the leaflet and find out if you were right, according to the text. Tick ✓ the sentences which are true and put a cross ✗ by those which are false.

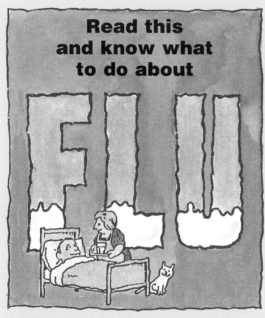

Read this and know what to do about FLU

FLU VACCINATION Flu vaccine is usually only given to people who are especially at risk because of their health and to people who cannot miss work, like nurses, doctors, firemen or policemen. These people may be offered flu vaccination once a year, generally in the autumn before winter epidemics. But even vaccination cannot give complete protection against flu.

REMEMBER Keep flu to yourself. Stay away from other people. Make sure handkerchiefs and also plates, knives, forks etc., are always well washed.

Look after yourself by resting in bed and having lots of cool drinks.

There's no need for the doctor unless the flu persists for more than a few days or gets suddenly worse.

You've got your own defence system – here's how to make it work.

You're feeling rotten – weak, shivery, with an aching head, back and limbs. Your temperature's up over 38°C (100°F). Probably you're sweating a lot, you've lost your appetite and you feel sick. You've got flu.

So what do you do?

There's no quick cure. Flu – influenza – is caused by a virus. And viruses can't be killed with antibiotics. Only the body's own defence system can get rid of them. So for most of us there's no point in seeing the doctor when we've got flu. But while a bout of flu lasts, which may be anything from 24 hours to several days,

Here's what you should do:

 Stay indoors, keep warm, and keep away from other people as much as possible so you don't pass on the infection.

 Have plenty of cool drinks – water, fruit drinks, milky drinks. About 2–3 litres a day.

If you feel shivery or feverish, with a temperature over 38°C (100°F) or aches or pains, try taking soluble aspirin every 4 hours during the day. And rest in bed if you can.

Try to have 3 light meals a day. But don't force yourself to eat if you've lost your appetite.

But if you are elderly and in poor health, or if you suffer from a severe chest condition like bronchitis or asthma, then flu can become a more serious illness.

So remember:
* When there's flu about, try to avoid crowded places and keep away from anyone who's got flu.
* If you think you've caught flu, get in touch with your doctor. Then he can at least keep an eye on you.
* In the autumn, ask your doctor if he thinks you should be vaccinated against flu.

B 1 Work in pairs   Imagine that a friend of yours feels unwell and may have flu. Write down *five* questions that you would ask to find out if he or she really does have flu. What advice would you give if you think it probably is flu?

2 Note down some expressions you can use when giving advice.

If I were you, I'd . . .   The best thing to do is to . . .

3 Role-play the conversation, with one of you playing the role of the sick friend. Try to use the expressions you've noted down. When you've finished, change roles. Now imagine that the friend is suffering from *insomnia*. What advice would you give? Role-play the conversation.

8.5 Smoke-free zones   READING

A **1** **Work in pairs** Find out about each other's attitudes to smoking. Why do people smoke? Why do people quit smoking? How does your government discourage smoking?

2 Read this article. Note down the ways in which laws in *your* country are different from New York.

IF THE air in New York seems a little less grimy this spring, thank Rudolph Giuliani. On January 10th, after months of burning debate, the city's non-smoking mayor signed the Smoke-Free Air Act. From April 10th smoking will be stubbed out in restaurants catering for more than 35 people, a move that will hit about half the city's 11,000 eating places. Nicotine addicts will also be smoked out at work, except in ventilated smoking rooms or offices occupied by no more than three consenting adults. More radically, outdoor seating areas will also become smokeless zones. Come the new baseball season, fans at Yankee Stadium will be breaking the law if they light up.

New York joins well over 100 American cities – and four states – that have passed laws banning smoking in public places. Some are harsher than the Big Apple's. In Los Angeles and San Francisco, along with the whole of Vermont, smoking is banned in all restaurants, regardless of their size. More than a third of American companies now forbid smoking in the workplace, up from a mere 20% in 1986. And the tobacco industry, which in America alone has annual sales of close to $50 billion, is watching its profits go up in smoke.

The industry may never recover. Polls suggest that nine out of ten Americans are irritated by cigarette smoke. With good reason. In 1993 the Environmental Protection Agency (EPA) classified "second-hand" smoke as a health hazard – one that, according to the EPA, caused 3,000 non-smokers to die from lung cancer each year.

New Yorkers must now wait and see if the pro-smoking lobby's alarming predictions of citywide economic collapse come true. (After all, who will want to dine in a smoke-free restaurant?) Tobacco company, Philip Morris, may show the way. Last year it threatened to move its 2,000 head-office employees (about two-thirds of them non-smokers) out of the city if the smoking ban became law. It also hinted that its hefty sponsorship of New York's arts might suffer, too. The firm is apparently still considering whether to kick the city for kicking the habit.

B Choose the best alternative, according to the text.

1 When does the Smoke-Free Air Act become law?

   a) January 10   b) April 1   c) April 10 ✓   d) next year

2 In how many restaurants in New York is smoking allowed?

   a) none   b) 35   c) 5,500   d) 11,000

3 At work, where will smoking be allowed?

   a) nowhere   c) in offices where no one minds
   b) in special smoking rooms   d) in the corridor

4 How many American companies allow smoking at work?

   a) a third   b) a half   c) two-thirds   d) three-quarters

5 Why are American cigarette companies worried?

   a) because their image is suffering   c) because their profits are falling
   b) because their sales are $50 billion   d) because their profits aren't rising so fast

6 What did the EPA report in 1993?

   a) that non-smokers are at risk from smokers   c) that smoking causes cancer
   b) that smokers are selfish   d) that smoking is anti-social

7 What do the people who are in favour of smoking predict?

   a) that New York's economy will suffer   c) that New Yorkers will obey the new law
   b) that the nation's economy will suffer   d) that the mayor will repeal the Act

8 How has the tobacco company Philip Morris reacted to the new law?

   a) by withdrawing its arts sponsorship   c) by saying it will set up its offices elsewhere
   b) by urging smokers to break the law   d) by moving its offices to New Jersey

C 🖊 Highlight the words or phrases in the article which have similar meanings to the following:

¶1 dirty   people who don't mind smoking   ¶3 surveys   danger

¶2 more severe   not allowed   ¶4 suggested   very large   quitting smoking

D **Work in groups**   Discuss your reactions to the article. Then look at the table below. Some of the information is missing – can you guess what the missing numbers are?

Number of cigarettes and litres of alcohol consumed per person per year			
	Cigarettes	**Litres of beer**	**Litres of wine**
Argentina	1,300	19	58
Belgium	1,700	125	24
Brazil	1,200		1
Czech Republic		130	12
France	1,700	40	70
Germany	2,000		23
Greece		24	24
Hungary	2,500	100	21
Italy	1,600	23	
Japan	2,500	44	1
Poland	2,600	29	8
Spain	2,200	73	
Switzerland	1,900	73	47
UK	1,700	110	12
USA	2,100	90	9

8.6 **Spelling and pronunciation – 2: Diphthongs**   WORD STUDY

A Can you think of words which are pronounced the same as each of these, but spelt differently?

their ...*there*...   allowed ....   brake ....   whole ....   right ....

B 1 Work in pairs   Match the words on the right to the examples on the left, according to the diphthong sound they share in common. Say them aloud to help you to decide.

/aɪ/	bite	height	guide	eye/I		destroy	employer
/aʊ/	now	crowd	loud			climate	by/buy/bye	thigh
/ɔɪ/	boy	join	poison			cleared	atmosphere
/eə/	scarce	where/wear				folk	nose/knows
/ɪə/	steer	here/hear	fear			wait/weight	male/mail	waste/waist
/eɪ/	make	sale/sail	great			proud	found
/əʊ/	note	joke	oval			stares/stairs	fare/fair	pair/pear

2 Add these words to the appropriate group above:

frown   paint   point   share   sincere   soap   time

3 ▣ Listen to the answers to B1 and B2.

C 1 ▣ Listen to the recording and write down the missing words in these sentences.

1 The part of your leg above the knees is your ....*thigh*.... .

2 What is your .... measurement in centimetres?

3 What is your .... in kilos?

4 What is your .... in metres?

5 If you jump out of this window, you'll .... your leg.

6 The .... of New York is against smoking.

7 Smoking isn't .... in restaurants in Los Angeles.

8 .... to .... keeps me fit.

2 Write down three more sentences, using words from B above. Then join another student and dictate your sentences to each other.

8.7 *At . . .* PREPOSITIONS

1 Fill the gaps in the sentences below with a suitable phrase from this list. There are two phrases which you *don't* need to use:

at all   at first ✓   at first sight   at last   at least   at a loss   at the moment   at once
at peace   at a profit   at any rate   at a time   at the same time   at war

1 I thought *at first* that I had flu, but then I realised it was only a cold.

2 Sorry to keep you waiting so long, I've finished .... !

3 .... it looked like a new car, and I didn't realise it was second-hand.

4 A business sells its products .... and not ....

5 The two countries used to be .... but now they are ....

6 The receptionist only allows one patient to see the doctor ....

7 You can't lose weight just by taking exercise, ... I don't think so.

8 When you receive the report, please pass it on to me ....

9 The twins always speak .... as each other.

10 He's so lazy – he doesn't take any exercise ....

2 Write two more sentences using the phrases you *didn't* use in the exercise.

8.8 How to stay healthy SPEAKING AND WRITING

In the Speaking part of exam, the examiner will say something like this:

> Here are two pictures. I'd like you to compare the types of activity shown and say which you prefer.

A **1** **Work in pairs** Look at these two photos and decide what you could say about them if you had to speak about them for one minute.

2 Speak about the photos for one minute each. Ask your partner for feedback on these points:

- Fluency – Did I 'disguise' my hesitation in an English-sounding way?
- Vocabulary – Did I use very basic words, or a wider vocabulary?
- Communication – Did I manage to communicate my ideas well?

3 Now do the same with these two pictures.

 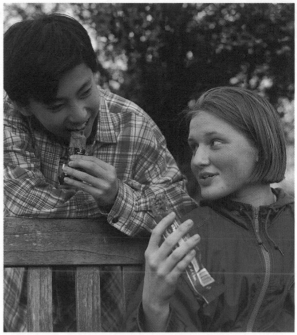

B **1** **Work in pairs**   Read this information and then discuss the questions below it.

> What some activities do for you
>
> The Health Education Authority defines fitness as a combination of three elements:
>   Suppleness – being able to bend, stretch and turn through a full range of movements.
>   Strength   – being able to exert force for pushing, pulling and lifting.
>   Stamina   – being able to keep going without getting tired quickly.
> All exercise helps improve fitness – but some activities are better for each of the three elements.

- What do you think are the benefits of these activities?

walking	racket sports	exercise classes/dance/yoga	cycling
jogging and running	swimming	weight-training	team games

- And what do you think are the disadvantages?

2 👥 When you've discussed this, one of you should look at Activity *16*, the other at *42*. You'll find more information on these activities to share with your partner.

C **1** 👉 This is the end of a letter that a friend of yours has written you. What are your friend's problems? Highlight the main points in the letter.

> and I get out of breath when I climb the stairs. I seem to get headaches a lot too, which makes it hard to study. And when I'm looking forward to a plate of chips, I can't even open the top of a new ketchup bottle! So I decided to play a game of tennis on Saturday, but I felt so stiff the next day that I could hardly move! I don't really think sport is the answer for me.
> Anyway, enough of my problems! Hope you're fit and well!
> Write to me soon,
>
> Best wishes, Jo

2 ✍ Write a letter to Jo (about 150 words) advising him or her what to do. Use *some* of the information from B and Activities *16* and *42*, together with your own ideas. Make notes. Before you start writing, decide on your opening sentence (after 'Dear Jo, Thank you for your letter') and your closing sentence (before 'Best wishes').

3 **Work in pairs**   Show your letter to your partner and ask for his or her reactions. Would he or she like to have received this letter? Why/Why not? Look at each other's use of vocabulary: have you used very simple words, or a wider vocabulary?

9

Having a great time!

9.1 Holidays

VOCABULARY AND SPEAKING

A 📼 You'll hear three people talking about their holidays. Match the photos above to the person who went there – and note down how long each person's holiday lasted. The first speaker is Susanna and the second speaker is James.

Susanna

James

Joan

B **1** Choose the best alternative to complete the gaps in this story. Be careful because some of the alternatives are only slightly wrong!

Many people go on a ¹ _____ holiday and book it at a travel ² _____ . But we decided to make our own ³ _____ . We sent off for dozens of ⁴ _____ and read lots of ⁵ _____ books before we decided which ⁶ _____ to go to.

We all enjoy ⁷ _____ , so we chose a place with a long sandy ⁸ _____ and some interesting places nearby to visit if we wanted to go on any ⁹ _____ .

Instead of staying in a hotel, we wanted to save money so we booked a ¹⁰ _____ apartment with a ¹¹ _____ of the sea and its own ¹² _____ .

In the photo the place looked ¹³ _____ , and the owners sounded really nice on the phone. But imagine our dismay when we arrived there to discover that . . .

1 charter   package   packed   packet
2 agency   bureau   office   service
3 arrangements   flights   excursions   travel
4 brochures   handouts   tickets   prospectuses
5 companion   guide   leader   phrase
6 marina   resort   spa   youth hostel
7 getting sunburnt   getting sunstroke   having a bath   sunbathing
8 beach   coast   seaside   shore
9 excursions   expeditions   pilgrimages   sightseeings
10 do-it-yourself   self-catering   self-study   survival
11 look   scenery   sight   view
12 balcony   box   gallery   porch
13 delicious   delighted   delightful   discouraging

Don't forget to check through the wrong answers: there's useful vocabulary among them.

2 **Work in pairs**   How do you think the story continued? What *did* they discover?

C In these sentences *three* alternatives are correct and *two* are wrong. Choose the best three alternatives for each.

1 In the summer, this little mountain village is full of ....

beachcombers   day-trippers   globetrotters   holiday-makers   sightseers

2 We stayed in a charming little guest house where we paid £25 a night for ....

bed and breakfast   breakfast and bed   full board   half board   a pension

3 Some people like to be .... when they're on holiday.

active   busy   energetic   strenuous   tiring

4 Others prefer a .... holiday.

dull   lazy   relaxing   restful   tedious

5 Most people like to have a .... of things to do when they're away from home.

confusion   choice   muddle   range   variety

6 We brought home a beautiful pottery vase as a ....

gift   present   reminder   souvenir   trophy

D **1** **Work in pairs**   Look at the pictures below and write down *five* questions you could ask about them to encourage someone to relate them to their own experiences.

What would it be like to be there?
Which of the places would you most like to be in? Why?

2 **Join a different partner**   Ask each other your questions and encourage each other to say more by asking follow-up questions.

E **Work in groups**   Look at each other's holiday photos (*or* photos of a weekend away or a day out). Find out all about them.

9.2 Brazilian Contrasts   READING

A 1 Read the page from a holiday brochure below and pick out the *two* places you'd most like to visit.

2 Work in pairs   Find out which places your partner selected – and why.

3 In which places, according to the text, could you find the following?

1 a taste of old Brazil   *Salvador*
2 historic buildings
3 a rapidly growing city
4 a statue of Christ
5 a fantastic view

6 a cable-car ride
7 unusual architecture
8 a samba show
9 a magnificent waterfall
10 wonderful costumes

Brazil from £590

BRAZIL
Salvador
Brasilia
Rio de Janeiro
São Paulo
Iguaçu
Atlantic Ocean

Brazilian Contrasts

Rio de Janeiro: 5 nights
Brasilia: 1 night
Salvador: 3 nights
São Paulo: 1 night
Iguaçu: 2 nights
plus extension weeks in Rio

Day 1 Wed London/Rio

Evening departure from Heathrow by scheduled service of Varig Brazilian Airlines to Rio.

Day 2 Thu Rio

Early morning arrival in Rio and transfer to your hotel. In the afternoon an optional tour of the city including cable-car ride up Sugar Loaf mountain, one of this exciting city's most famous landmarks.

Day 3 Fri Rio/Brasilia

Afternoon departure to Brasilia. This futuristic city was purpose built to become Brazil's new capital in 1960 and its unusual architecture and design sets it apart from all others.

Day 4 Sat Brasilia/Salvador

Late afternoon flight to Salvador. Contrast the unusual designs of Brasilia, with the colour and tradition of Salvador, one of Brazil's oldest cities.

Day 5 Sun and Day 6 Mon Salvador

Two full days to explore this intriguing old city. Rickety old buildings interspersed by narrow, cobbled streets wind up and down the hills on which Salvador was built, providing a fascinating glimpse of the taste and atmosphere of old Brazil.

Day 7 Tue Salvador/São Paulo

Early morning departure for São Paulo. A million new citizens are added every year to this vibrant city, a plane lands every minute, a new building goes up every hour and there are more daily newspapers, radio and TV stations than any other city in the world.

Day 8 Wed São Paulo/Iguaçu

Morning flight to Iguaçu. The distant roar of the Falls increases to a deafening crescendo as you approach, announcing your arrival at one of the natural wonders of the world.

Day 9 Thu Iguaçu

Full day at leisure to explore this incredible natural phenomenon. Niagara and Victoria Falls pale into insignificance as 275 separate cataracts and falls empty a million gallons of water every second into the foaming Parana river.

Day 10 Fri Iguaçu/Rio

An afternoon flight to Rio and transfer to the Continental hotel, which is located just 50 yards from Avenida Atlantica and legendary Copacabana Beach.

Day 11 Sat to Day 13 Mon Rio

Three full days at leisure in this exciting city. Visit the statue of Christ the Redeemer on top of Corcovado and enjoy one of the most famous views in the world. In the evening, take the optional Carioca night tour; see the city lights, enjoy dinner at a

speciality churrascaria restaurant and then finally on to a samba show, where you'll see some of those fabulous carnival costumes.

Day 14 Tue Rio/London

Final day at leisure before an evening departure by scheduled Varig flight to Heathrow, arriving in the UK early on Wednesday afternoon. Alternatively, why not extend your stay in Rio and return one week later.

LUXOR CONTINENTAL, RIO

Facts: Rooms: 290. Type of building: high rise. Lifts: four.

Location: Some 50 yards from the Avenida Atlantica and legendary Copacabana Beach, surrounded by cafés, shops, bars, night clubs and the exciting Samba shows.

Facilities: Restaurant, bar and small lounge.

Accommodation: Rooms vary in size and location but all have modern furnishings, central air conditioning, telephone, colour TV, radio, fridge, mini-bar and bathroom with shower only.

Entertainment: It's all around you so go outside your hotel and discover the night life of the world's most exciting city.

Opinion: An efficiently run hotel. Combining modern accommodation and friendly service with a superb location near Copacabana Beach – excellent value for money.

B 1 Now answer these more detailed questions and underline the phrases in the text that led you to choose each answer.

1 Would your flight from London be a charter flight?   *No*

2 What time of day would you arrive in Rio on your first day?

3 What are the two optional tours of Rio that you could go on?

4 What is the capital city of Brazil?

5 Are the streets in Salvador straight?

6 How quickly is the population of São Paulo growing?

7 How would you know that you were approaching Iguaçu Falls?

8 What time of day would you leave Rio on your last day?

2 Now find the answers to these questions about the hotel in Rio. Again underline the phrases in the text that provide the answers.

1 What is the name of the hotel?

2 Is it a large hotel?

3 Is the hotel on the beach?

4 Would you get a good view from your hotel room?

5 Would your room have a bath?

6 Is it an old-fashioned hotel?

C **Work in groups**   Discuss these questions:

• What would you enjoy most if you went on the *Brazilian Contrasts* holiday?

• What might be the drawbacks of some of the places mentioned (e.g. insects, heat, expense, etc.)?

• What problems have you (or friends or relations of yours) encountered on holiday?

9.3   By . . .   PREPOSITIONS

1 Fill the gaps in the sentence below with phrases from this list. There are three phrases you *don't* need to use:

by accident   by all means   by car   by chance   by day   by far   by hand   by heart
by mistake   by name   by night   by plane   by post   by ship   by sight ✓   by surprise
by the time   by train   by yourself

1 I know them both *by sight* but I don't know either of them ....

2 The Mediterranean is .... the most popular holiday area in Europe.

3 The only way to remember the words is to learn them ....

4 I didn't tread on your foot on purpose, it happened ....

5 It takes several days to cross Europe .... and even longer ....

6 The weather is very hot .... but it may be quite cool ....

7 The thunderstorm took us .... and we all got wet.

8 We didn't arrange to meet on the beach – we ran into each other ....

9 'Could you fill in this registration form?' 'Yes, ...'

10 There's no need to send the letter .... I can deliver it myself ....

11 .... we get to New York, you'll be fast asleep in bed in London.

12 It's very hard to put sun-cream on your back if you're ....

2 Write three more sentences using the phrases you *didn't* use in the exercise.

9.4 Spelling and pronunciation – 3: Consonants WORD STUDY

A 1 The consonant sounds of English can often be spelled in several ways. Look at these examples.

Apart from the sound /r/, most regional and national accents of English don't differ in the way consonants are pronounced. The differences are in the way some vowels and diphthongs are pronounced. For you, as a foreign speaker of English, it's perfectly acceptable in the exam (and in real life) to speak English with a foreign accent. The important thing is that people can understand you easily.

/p/ p *or* pp
stop stopped supposed ....
....

/b/ b *or* bb
bubble beach ....

/t/ t *or* tt
capital bottle little ....

/d/ d *or* dd
mud handled muddy ....
....

/k/ k *or* c *or* cc *or* ck *or* q *or* ch
king climate accommodation lucky
quantity chemist ....

/g/ g *or* gg *or* gu
garden struggle guard ....
....

/dʒ/ j *or* g *or* dg
jet jumping religion knowledge
....

/tʃ/ ch *or* ti *or* tu
church question nature ....
....

/l/ l *or* ll
skilful silly ....

/n/ n *or* nn *or* kn
run running knowledge ....
....

/m/ m *or* mm *or* mb
image accommodation thumb
....

/r/ r *or* rr *or* wr
right arrest wrist ....
....

/s/ s *or* ss *or* c *or* st
stone fussy circle castle ....

/z/ s *or* z
rise arrives zero ....

/ʃ/ sh *or* s *or* ti *or* c
shirt sure competition ocean
....

/ʒ/ s *or* g
leisure garage ....

/f/ f *or* ff *or* ph *or* gh
afraid affair photograph
apostrophe enough ....
....

/v/ v *or* f
vacation of ....

/ð/ and /θ/ th
this clothes thirsty truth
....

/w/ w *or* wh *or* u *or* o
weather/whether we'll/wheel
quite once ....

/j/ y *or* u *or* eu
yacht union Europe ....
....

2 🖭 Listen to the recording and add the words you hear to the appropriate lists above.

3 Check the correct spellings in Activity 5.

B Some consonants are written but not pronounced. Here are some examples of these 'silent letters'. Can you think of two more examples to add to each list?

gh sigh light caught fought ....
b lamb bomb climb combing ....
t castle Christmas listen ....
k knife knee ....
l half walk could ....
r beard word (*in some British accents only*) ....
h honest hourly ....
w wrist ....

C 👥 **Work in pairs** One of you should look at Activity *14* the other at *22*. You'll each have some more words to dictate to your partner.

"Why is it we never go on migration?"

Allan

9.5 *If . . . sentences – 1* GRAMMAR REVIEW

A **Work in pairs** What is the difference in meaning between these groups of sentences?

🖉 **Highlight the word or words in each sentence which show the differences in meaning.**

1 We can't go skiing until there's more snow on the mountains.
2 Unless there's more snow on the mountains, we can't go skiing.
3 We can't go skiing if there's more snow on the mountains.

4 In April, when the weather is warmer, I'll take a few days off.
5 I'll take a couple of days off if the weather is better in April.
6 If the weather were nicer in April, I'd take a short break.

7 You'd better take an overnight bag in case you have to stay the night.
8 If you have to stay the night, you'd better take an overnight bag.

9 I'll go to Rio for the Carnival if I can afford it.
10 If I could afford it, I'd go to Rio for the Carnival.
11 I might go to Rio at Carnival time if I had enough money.

See the Grammar Reference section on pages 174–175.

B **Most of these sentences contain errors. If a sentence is correct, put a tick ✓ beside it. If there are any mistakes in a sentence, underline them and write the correction alongside.**

1 *If I were rich, I would buy a villa in the Caribbean.* ✓
2 *If it's my birthday tomorrow, I'd invite my friends out for a meal.*
3 *If you will need any help, please let me know.*
4 *We'll enjoy our holiday unless it will rain all the time.*
5 *If the sun's shining tomorrow, we'll go swimming.*
6 *When I'm on holiday I'd like to relax rather than be active.*
7 *Let's go to the mountains if the spring comes.*
8 *I'll be arriving on Sunday until there's a change of plan.*

C **Complete the second sentence so that it has a similar meaning to the first sentence. Use the word given in red and other words to complete each sentence. Don't change the word given.**

1 My family have a holiday flat and that's why we always go to the same place.
own If my family *didn't own a holiday flat, we wouldn't* always go to the same place.

2 Go to Britain if you want to speak English all the time.
practise If you go to Britain, ... all the time.

3 You'll get sunburnt by sunbathing all day long.
sun If you .... sunburnt.

4 I can't go on holiday because I've got a holiday job this summer.
work If .... on holiday.

5 You won't find any accommodation if you don't book it in advance.
anywhere Unless you book ahead .... stay.

6 The evenings may be cool, so pack a jumper to wear after dark.
in case Pack a jumper to wear after dark .... cool.

7 Why don't you come on holiday with us – you'll certainly have a good time.
together If we .... yourself.

8 Suppose it was possible for you to travel anywhere in the world, where would you go?
country If .... travel to?

D **Work in pairs** If you were alone together on an isolated tropical island without hope of rescue . . .

• what would you do?
• how would you survive?
• what would you miss most (and least) about your present lives?

9.6 An excursion programme

A **Work in pairs** Look at the pictures above. What do you know about Scotland? What is Scotland most famous for?

B Imagine that you're in a hotel in Edinburgh having breakfast on the first day of your holiday in Scotland. You'll hear the tour leader announcing some changes to the excursion programme. Make any necessary alterations to the times and places shown on the programme, according to what the tour leader tells you.

Discover Scotland Holidays

Excursion programme

	Departure		Return
Sunday			
Monday	9:00	Braemar Castle and Aberdeen	17:30
Tuesday	8:30	Glencoe and Fort William	17:30
Wednesday	8:00	Inverness and Loch Ness	17:30
Thursday	14:00	Edinburgh City sightseeing tour	16:30
Friday	9:15	Galashiels and the Borders	16:00

C **1** **Work in pairs** If you had to organise a one-day coach tour around *your* area, what places would you visit? Make brief notes.

2 **Join another pair** Describe your excursion to them.

3 Write a description of your excursion for a tourist brochure about your area (about 150 words). Explain where the excursion will go and what attractions and sights will be visited. For some ideas on what to include, look at Activity *59*, where you'll see a written description of one of the Scottish excursions.

In the exam, leave enough room on the page for changes and corrections. Start writing on line three, not line one. Leave a blank line between paragraphs. Leave enough room at the end of each line to add an extra word, if necessary.

9.7 Use of English: Fill the gaps   EXAM TECHNIQUES

When you're doing a gap-fill exercise (in Part 2 of the Use of English paper) and you're not sure what the missing word is, try to decide what *kind* of word is required:

adjective   conjunction   verb   noun   pronoun   preposition   article   adverb

A 1 What *kind* of words are missing in each of these sentences?

1 If you have flu, you often have a bad headache.   *adjective*

2 I spent a sleepless night worrying about my problems.

3 It's safest to cross the street at a pedestrian crossing.

4 We finally arrived after a long journey and unpacked our cases.

5 A beach holiday is the most boring kind of holiday I can imagine.

6 I don't like spending nights in a hotel by myself.

2 Now suggest a word to fill each gap.

B 1 Choose the best alternative to fill each gap in the first part of this story.

> We were late as ¹   . Michael had
> insisted on doing his packing by
> ²   and when he discovered that
> he couldn't manage he'd asked me for
> help at the last ³   . So now we
> had an hour to get to the ⁴   .
> Luckily, there wasn't much traffic on the
> ⁵   and we were able to get there
> just in ⁶   .
> We checked in and went straight to the
> departure ⁷   to wait for our
> ⁸   to be called. We waited and
> waited but no announcement was
> ⁹   . We asked at the information
> ¹⁰   and the clerk there told us
> that the plane hadn't even arrived yet...

1 general   typical   usual   usually

2 hand   himself   night   mistake

3 hour   time   minute   opportunity

4 harbour   station   airport   take-off

5 runway   route   road   carriageway

6 moment   time   luck   particular

7 saloon   room   lounge   channel

8 journey   flight   take-off   numbers

9 announced   called   made   done

10 pack   desk   place   table

In the exam, if you can't think of the correct answers to fill some gaps, make a pencil mark beside them on your question paper and move on to the next section. Then, towards the end of the exam, have another go at the ones you marked. If you still aren't sure, have a guess. It's always better to write in something (even if it may be wrong) than to leave a blank.

2 Fill each gap in the second part of the story with one word only. If you aren't sure what the missing word is, try to decide what *kind* of word is missing.

> In the ¹¹ *end* there was another announcement telling us that passengers waiting for
> Flight LJ 108 could collect a ¹²   meal voucher. We reported to the desk and were
> told that the plane hadn't left Spain because of ¹³   problems. We thought this
> meant that it wasn't safe for the plane to ¹⁴   . We waited again for ¹⁵   . It
> was late in the evening before we were asked to report to the ¹⁶   desk again. They
> told us we would be spending the ¹⁷   in a hotel at the airline's ¹⁸   .
>   The next morning we reported back to the airport. Guess what had ¹⁹   while we
> were ²⁰   ? Our plane had arrived and taken off again leaving us ²¹   . All the
> other ²²   had been woken up in the night to catch the plane, but for some
> ²³   or other we had been forgotten. You can ²⁴   how we felt!

10

Food for thought

Mmm, this looks delicious!

A **Work in groups**   Ask your partners these questions:

- How many different kinds of desserts and cakes can you think of?
- What's your favourite fruit?
- What are the two typical desserts or cakes which are most popular in your country?
- Have you got a sweet tooth? Do you sprinkle sugar on your food?

B **The illustrations, ingredients and instructions for four recipes have been mixed up. Which ingredients (A–D) and instructions (1–4) go with each of these dishes? And which photo (a–d) illustrates each dish?**

Dorset Apple Cake ☐ ☐ ☐   Apple and Blackberry Pie ☐ ☐ ☐

Somerset Cider Cake ☐ ☐ ☐   Apple Crumble ☐ ☐ ☐

A

For the filling:	*For the pastry:*
500 g cooking apples	200 g plain flour
250 g washed blackberries	100 g butter
75 g sugar	a little cold water

C

225 g self-raising flour	100 g sugar
Pinch of salt	1½–2½ tablespoons of milk
100 g margarine	Grated zest of a lemon (optional)
350 g cooking apples, peeled and chopped into chunks	Brown sugar for sprinkling

B

675 g cooking apples	100 g butter
200 ml apple juice	50 ml honey
5 ml ground cinnamon	5 ml (1 teaspoon) grated lemon rind
225 g fine wholewheat flour	

D

700 g raisins	4 eggs, beaten
250 ml cider (or apple juice)	550 g self-raising flour or maybe a bit more if mixture needs it
700 g cooking apples, peeled, cored and chopped	
450 g sugar	2 level teaspoons coriander or mixed spice
350 g butter	

1

Soak the raisins in the cider overnight.

Pre-heat oven to 180°C.

Mix the butter and sugar until creamy, then add the beaten eggs gradually.

Mix the dry ingredients together and add to the creamy mixture with the chopped apple, raisins and cider, adding extra flour if needed.

Bake in a roasting tin 30 cm x 25 cm lined with greaseproof paper. Bake in the centre of the oven for 1¼ hrs at 180°C. This is a HUGE cake! If you halve the quantity, it will make a 23 cm cake.

2

Pre-heat the oven to 220°C.

First make the pastry and leave it to rest while you prepare the fruit. Peel and slice the apples and put them into the pie dish. Then add the blackberries and the sugar. Roll out the pastry and lay it over the dish to form a lid. Then press down the edges with a fork and make a hole in the centre for the steam to escape from.

Brush the pastry with milk and sprinkle some more sugar on the top. Put the pie into the oven and bake it for ten minutes at 220°C, then turn the heat down to 190°C and bake for another 30 minutes until the pastry is golden brown.

Serve the pie hot with cream or ice cream.

3

Sieve the flour and salt and rub in the margarine. Stir in the rind, sugar and apples. Add the milk and mix to a firm dough.

Place on a large greased baking sheet in an oval shape.

Bake in a preheated oven at 180°C for 50 minutes.

Best eaten immediately sprinkled with sugar and served with cream. Also delicious the next day cold. This cake will spread during cooking.

4

Heat the oven to 180°C.

Cut the apples into very small pieces. Put into an ovenproof dish.

Pour the apple juice and cinnamon into a mixing jug. Mix together and pour over the apples.

Put the flour in a mixing bowl. Gently rub in the butter with your fingertips.

Add the honey and grated lemon rind: stir in carefully with a metal spoon.

Pour the crumble topping over the apple and bake at the bottom of the oven for 45–50 minutes or until the topping is browned.

Serve immediately with whipped cream or yogurt.

C Highlight the words in A–D that mean the same as these phrases:

A the inside part   the outer crust

B made into a powder   brown flour containing all the grain

C with the outer skin removed   cut into small pieces   the outer layer of the rind

D a drink made from apples containing alcohol   with the middle part removed
flour containing an agent which makes cakes rise

D **Work in groups** Which of these would be considered good or bad table manners in your country? What could you put in the last box, to show another example of bad manners?

In Britain, a waiter or waitress (or your host or hostess) may say 'Enjoy your meal' at the start of a meal, and you'd reply 'Thank you'. But if your host or hostess doesn't say anything, it's good manners to say something like 'Mmm, this looks delicious!' before you start eating.

1

2

3

4

5

6

7

8

10 **10.2** **Cooking and eating** VOCABULARY

A **Work in pairs** Which of these cooking methods would you use for the ingredients below?

steam   boil   fry   roast   bake   grill   barbecue

I think I'd . . . it/them.   You could either . . . or . . . that/those.
It is possible to . . . them but I'd prefer to . . . them.

B **1** **Work in pairs** Make a list of things to eat that begin with each letter of the alphabet.

apples   bread   cheese   d . . .

2 **Join another pair** Compare your lists. Then discuss what you'd *do* with each item.

I'd put them in a pie.   I'd put them in a fruit salad.   I'd eat them raw.
I'd cut a slice, and then spread it with butter and honey.   I'd toast it and
eat it with butter and apricot jam.   I'd eat it with some bread as a snack.
I'd put it in a Greek salad with tomatoes and cucumber.

C Choose the best alternative to complete each sentence.

1 I love Thai food – but sometimes it's too .... for me.

  hot   peppery   sharp   warm

2 Japanese *sushi* (raw fish) is one of my favourite ....

  bowls   courses   dishes   plates   sauces

3 That was absolutely delicious. Can you give me the .... ?

  formula   instructions   prescription   receipt   recipe

4 How would you like your steak cooked? Well done, medium or ....

  bloody   blue   rare   raw   red

5 A lot of food you buy nowadays contains all sorts of artificial ....

  additions   additives   extras   spices   supplements

6 Waiter, could I see the .... , please?

  card of wines   list of wines   wine card   wine list   wine menu

7 The reason why he always eats so much is simply that he's very ....

  eager   greedy   hungry   starving

8 She liked the dessert so much that she asked for a second ....

  dish   go   helping   plate   serving   try

9 If you're on a diet, there are some foods you have to ....

  avoid   deny   escape   lack   stop

10 You forgot to put the milk in the fridge and now it has gone ....

  away   back   down   off   out

11 Would you prefer sparkling mineral water or .... ?

  still   fizzy   dull   gassy   flat

12 Every person can recognise only four tastes: sweet, salty, sour and ....

  savoury   sugary   rich   oily   bitter

D **Work in small groups** Ask each other questions to find out about each other's favourite foods – and the most delicious (and maybe most disgusting) things you've ever eaten.

10.3 *-ing* and *to . . .* – 1 GRAMMAR REVIEW

A **Work in pairs**   Some of these sentences contain errors. If a sentence is correct, put a tick ✓ beside it. If there are any mistakes, underline them and write the correction alongside.

1 *Eating all the time will* <u>*making*</u> *you fat.*   make
2 *I'm looking forward to go on holiday.*
3 *To smoke is not allowed in restaurants in New York.*
4 *It was kind of you inviting me joining you.*
5 *At night it's too dark to see without to use a flashlight.*
6 *Do you think that cooking for a family is easier than running a restaurant?*

See the Grammar
Reference section
on pages 175–176.

B **Complete the second sentence so that it has a similar meaning to the first sentence. Use the word in red and other words to complete each sentence. Don't change the word given.**

1 I'll be happy when I can have something to eat.
forward   I'm looking .... something to eat.
2 Boiling eggs is not difficult – poaching them is more difficult.
than   It is easier .... poach them.
3 If you want a table for twelve people, you must phone the restaurant.
essential   It's .... book a table for twelve.
4 They had stopped serving lunch by the time we arrived there.
late   We got there .... lunch.
5 Trying new dishes from other countries is something I like doing.
interested   I'm always .... new dishes from abroad.
6 It was disappointing that my favourite dish wasn't on the menu.
find   I was disappointed .... on the menu.
7 If I drink strong coffee at night, it keeps me awake.
prevents   .... strong coffee ....
8 You shouldn't eat so many sweets – it'll damage your teeth.
bad   Don't you realise .... teeth?

C **Fill each gap with *one* or *two* words, using the *to . . .* or *-ing* form of an appropriate verb.**

Last Sunday we drove into the country ¹ .... my grandparents. I always look forward to
² .... them and enjoy ³ .... the day with them.
  My grandmother never prepares a meal without ⁴ .... fresh vegetables and refuses
⁵ .... any ingredients which have artificial additives.
  When we arrived we decided ⁶ .... for a walk before ⁷ .... down to lunch.
  By the time we got back, the table was laid in the garden for lunch and we all began
⁸ .... and we went on ⁹ .... all afternoon! I'm not used to ¹⁰ .... so much, but
the food was so good that I just couldn't stop ¹¹ .... my plate with more!
  When we had all finished ¹² .... , we all stayed outside ¹³ .... round the table
and went on ¹⁴ .... till it was dark and too cold ¹⁵ .... outside.

D 1 **Work in pairs**   Note down some things you find *easy* to do – and some you find more *difficult*. Here are some examples to start you off.

riding a bike or driving a car   writing a letter – or a story

2 Join another pair   Use these expressions to compare and discuss your ideas:

Is it easier to . . . or to . . . ?   Is . . . -ing easier than . . . -ing?
It's easier to . . . than it is to . . . because . . .   . . . -ing is easier than . . . -ing because . . .
It's not as easy to . . . as it is to . . . because . . .   . . . -ing isn't as difficult as . . . -ing because . . .

3 Note down some more activities which are *interesting, expensive, tiring, dangerous* and *pleasant*. Compare them using the same phrases.

10.4 Eating out   LISTENING AND SPEAKING

A **1** Before you hear the recording, look at the questions in 2 below. Which of them can you already answer from your own knowledge of international food?

2 Now listen to the recording and fill the gaps.

1 Before the meal, Paul has .... to drink and Amanda has ....

2 A Greek salad is made of cucumber, ... , ... and cheese.

3 A Spanish omelette is made of eggs, ... and ....

4 *Wiener Schnitzel* is a thin piece of .... coated in egg and .... and pan-fried.

5 *Moules marinière* are mussels cooked in .... with onions and a little .... You can have them as a .... or as a ....

6 *Rösti* is .... potatoes, ... and onions fried together. You can have it with two .... on top as a main course.

7 *Lasagne al forno* is thin .... of .... and .... sauce with a creamy sauce, baked in the .... with .... on top.

8 Amanda orders .... as a starter and .... as a main course with a .... salad.

9 Paul orders .... as a starter and .... as main course.

10 With the meal, Amanda has .... to drink and Paul has ....

B **1** 🗣️ **Work in groups of three**   Imagine that the three of you are sitting together in a restaurant looking at this menu – the problem is that you don't understand some of the dishes. For more information, Student A should look at Activity *11*, B at *44* and C at *52*.

 Before you start, listen to the model conversation, which gives some ideas on how to begin.

Leo's Restaurant

Today's menu   *£11.99 for three courses, including VAT and service*

STARTERS   Avocado with prawns   Home-made paté   Melon and orange salad

MAIN COURSES   Lancashire hotpot with seasonal vegetables
Steak and kidney pie with new potatoes and vegetables
Cottage pie with seasonal vegetables
Chicken Madras with rice
Nut and mushroom roast with brown rice

DESSERTS   Pancakes served with lemon juice and brown sugar   Chocolate mousse
Apple crumble   Blackberry fool   Apple and blackberry pie

All our dishes are prepared using the freshest ingredients.   *ENJOY YOUR MEAL!*

2 Imagine that you're all very hungry and discuss what you're going to order.

> Could you tell me what . . . is?
> I'm not sure what . . . is.
> I'd like to know what . . . is.
> I'd like to have . . . to start with and . . . to follow.

10.5 Compound words – 1 WORD STUDY

The best way to learn compound words is to make a note of them when you read or hear them. Usually, the meaning of a compound word can be worked out from the meanings of the words it is made from.

A 1 What do the words in green mean?

1 She is a kind-hearted person. *she has a kind heart*
2 He uses a food processor. *a kitchen machine that processes food*
3 He is left-handed.
4 A blue-eyed, red-haired boy.
5 May I see the wine list?
6 Have you got a can opener?
7 I've got a new wristwatch.

2 Most compound *adjectives* are written with a hyphen. Many compound *nouns* are written as *two* words or as *one* word (with no hyphen). Add more examples to the lists, using these words:

-aged   -best   -class   -respect   -grown   -hand   -known   -level   -off   -speed
-produced   -discipline   -service   -sized   -pressure   floor   name   course   cousin

first	first cousin	first-class	....	....	....
second	second-class	second course	....	....	....
high	high speed	high-pressure	....	....	
low	low-level	....	....		
home	home-made	....	....		
middle	middle-class	middle name	....	....	
self	self-control	self-defence	....	....	....
well	well-done	well-informed	....	....	

3 🔊 Listen to the answers to A2 on the recording. Pay attention to the pronunciation.

B Fill each gap with a word that combines with the one given to make a suitable compound.

In the good old days everything you ate was ¹ home-made and prepared in the traditional, ² _____ way. Nowadays, ³ _____ is replacing the slow, careful preparation of fresh ⁴ _____ vegetables and other ingredients. All the modern cook needs is a ⁵ _____ and a ⁶ _____. It's not only in canteens and ⁷ _____ cafeterias – even many restaurants serve ⁸ _____ meals instead of individually prepared and cooked dishes for each customer. A steak or grilled fish is always freshly cooked. But it's unlikely that prawns in the prawn cocktail you had for your ⁹ _____ were fresh today: if you get ¹⁰ _____, they may be the cause. And if you suspect that the ¹¹ _____ isn't freshly squeezed, it may be safer to drink ¹²

1 made
2 old
3 food
4 home
5 tin
6 food
7 self
8 produced
9 course
10 food
11 fruit
12 water

If in doubt, write a compound adjective with a hyphen and a compound noun as two words.

"Don't go to any trouble on my account. I'll just have what everybody else is having."

1 Fill the gaps in the sentences below with suitable phrases from this list. There are three phrases you don't need to use:

on business   on duty   on purpose   on the other hand   on the house
on the telephone   on the whole   on holiday/vacation   on time   on your own
out of date   out of doors   out of order   out of reach   out of work

1 It's important to arrive .... if you're meeting someone ....

2 The lift is .... so we'll have to use the stairs.

3 When we're .... we always like to eat .... if the weather's nice.

4 Are you .... ? Would you like to join us at our table?

5 There was nothing to pay because Harry, the owner, said their meal was ....

6 Don't get angry, I didn't break the plate ....

7 Frozen food is certainly convenient but, ... , fresh food tastes much better.

8 The frying pan is on the top shelf, it's ....

9 A policeman can't join you for a drink if he's ....

10 .... I must say that I prefer eating at home to eating out.

2 Write sentences using the three phrases you *didn't* use in the exercise.

A **1** Before you hear the recording, look at the ingredients and instructions below. The instructions are in the wrong order. Can you decide what the correct order should be? There's one extra instruction which shouldn't be there – find it and cross it out!

Potatoes with Sesame Seeds

1 kilo potatoes
6 tablespoons vegetable oil
2 tablespoons sesame seeds
about ¼ teaspoon cayenne pepper or chilli powder
1 teaspoon salt
juice of half a lemon

A   Serve with any meat dish, or on their own.

B   Continue frying the potatoes till they are crisp and brown.

C   Cut the potatoes into 2 cm cubes and allow them to cool.

D   Drain the potatoes.

E   Fry the potatoes for five minutes, stirring all the time.

F   Heat the oil in a frying pan.

G   Peel the potatoes.

H   Boil or steam the potatoes in their skins for about ten minutes.

I   Then add the cayenne pepper, salt and lemon juice.

J   Add the onions and fry them for a few minutes.

K   When the oil is hot, throw in the sesame seeds.

L   When the seeds start to pop, add the potatoes.

2 Listen to the recording. Rearrange the instructions in the correct order. Remember that there is one extra instruction which is not given.

3 Compare your answers with a partner and, if necessary, listen again to settle any disagreements.

B 👥 **Work in pairs** The class is divided into an even number of pairs. Half the pairs should look at Activity *55*, the other half at *60*. You'll find out how to make two refreshing non-alcoholic drinks.

Lassi

Old-fashioned lemonade

C **Work in pairs** Where do you think each extract below comes from? Give your reasons.

a letter to a friend   a magazine article   a recipe book   a story

1 Peel the lemons thinly, removing only the rind, and squeeze the juice into a large bowl. Add the sugar and

2 This is a favourite drink in our family and it's easy to prepare. All you need is four lemons and some sugar. First of all you have to peel the lemons but very thinly, so that you remove only the rind – that's the outside part of the peel, not the white part. Then you have to squeeze the

3 He peeled the lemons thinly and squeezed the juice into a bowl. Then he opened the cupboard to look for some sugar, but there was none to be found. So he looked around for something

4 Unlike the commercial fizzy lemonade that is available in cans or bottles, home-made lemonade is pure, tasty and free from artificial additives. It contains only lemons and sugar and is simple to prepare. It is also considerably cheaper than commercial lemonade because

5 You asked me to send me my recipe for home-made lemonade. Well, it's quite easy to make: All you need is a few lemons, some sugar and fresh water. First of all, you take a sharpe knife and

D **1 Work in pairs** Imagine that a foreign friend has asked you for the recipe of a typical national dish which is a speciality of your country (or region), and which is fairly straightforward to prepare. Decide on a suitable (fairly simple) national or local dish. Then discuss the questions below. Make notes, using a dictionary if necessary.

• What ingredients are needed and are they obtainable abroad, do you think?
• How is it made, step by step?
• Why have you chosen this particular dish?

2 ✍ Write the letter to your friend (about 150 words). Explain why you have chosen this dish and how the dish can be prepared.

3 Work in pairs Show your completed composition to your partner and ask for comments. Refer to Activity *61* for guidance on giving feedback to each other.

11 You never stop learning

11.1 / Education   VOCABULARY

A **Work in groups**   Look at the photos above and discuss these questions:

• What do you think the people in each picture are studying? How are they feeling?
• Which class looks the most interesting?
• How would each scene look different in your country for pupils/students of the same age?
• What changes have there been in education in your country recently?

B **1** Fill the gaps in this text with a suitable word from the list on the right.

In Britain 95% of children attend ¹ _____ schools, rather than
private schools. Most schools in England and Wales are ² _____ ,
but some areas have single-sex schools. Children start ³ _____
school at the age of five, and move to a secondary school when they
are 11. (Some areas have selective secondary schools, but most schools
are ⁴ _____ schools.) The National ⁵ _____ defines what all
⁶ _____ have to learn, but the ⁷ _____ of each school organises
the ⁸ _____ and decides which members of ⁹ _____ teach each
class.

   At the age of 16 all children take their GCSE ¹⁰ _____ in a number
of different ¹¹ _____ . GCSE ¹² _____ begin in Year 10 – the
children choose which ones they will take two years before the exam.
Some subjects, like English and maths are ¹³ _____ but others like
art or history are ¹⁴ _____ . Some students leave school at 16, but
about 50% stay on in the ¹⁵ _____ or attend a college to do two or
three A levels. About 25% go on to ¹⁶ _____ education at a ¹⁷ _____
or college when they are ¹⁸ _____ or older.

co-educational
comprehensive
compulsory
courses
curriculum
eighteen
exams
head teacher
higher
optional
primary
pupils
sixth form
staff
state
subjects
timetable
university

2 **Work in pairs**   Discuss these questions:

• What were/are your favourite school subjects? Why?
• What are the differences between the British system and the system in your country?

11.2 *If . . .* sentences – 2   GRAMMAR REVIEW

A

Work in pairs   Explain the differences in meaning by adding either *yesterday*, *now* or *tomorrow* in the brackets.

1 I would have been able to do my homework (.................) if I hadn't had a headache (.................).
2 I would be able to do my homework (.................) if I didn't have a headache (.................).
3 I'll be able to do my homework (.................) if I don't have a headache (.................).
4 I'm not doing my homework (.................) because I've got a headache (.................).
5 I won't be able to do my homework (.................) unless my headache has gone (.................).
6 I would be able to do my homework (.................) if I hadn't missed the lesson (.................).

See the Grammar Reference section on pages 174–175.

B 1

Complete the second sentence so that it has a similar meaning to the first sentence. Use the word given in **red** and other words to complete each sentence. Don't change the word given.

fun
1 He didn't enjoy himself at school, so he played truant all the time.
   If *he'd had more fun at school, he wouldn't have played* truant all the time.

where
2 I couldn't get in touch with you because you didn't give me your address.
   If .... in touch with you.

higher
3 He didn't study hard enough, which is why he got a low mark.
   He .... harder.

badly
4 She did well in the test because she was lucky.
   If she .... in the test.

much
5 They had a lot of studying to do during the vacation so they couldn't go on holiday.
   If they .... on holiday.

2

Check your answers to B1 before doing the rest of this exercise.

remembered
6 I forgot to post the letter because I was so busy with my work.
   I .... so busy with my work.

sorry
7 She didn't do any work at school, and now she regrets it.
   If she .... now.

without
8 I'm glad you helped me – that's why I was able to finish the work on time.
   I .... help.

longer
9 He can't speak English very well because he's only been learning it for a few years.
   If he .... to speak it better.

C 1

Fill the gaps in this story with a word or short phrase.

If [1] *I'd been born* a genius, my life so far [2] .... very different. I [3] .... had to work hard at school and I [4] .... top of the class in every subject. I [5] .... all my exams with flying colours and I [6] .... had to do any revision. If I [7] .... a musical instrument, I [8] .... to play it perfectly, so that by now I [9] .... a famous musician.

On the other hand, being a genius [10] .... as wonderful as all that. If everything [11] .... easy, there [12] .... no satisfaction in achieving things. It [13] .... quite boring to know that I [14] .... 100% in every test – and other people [15] .... envious of me and they [16] .... me. I think it [17] .... hard to make friends with people if I [18] .... a genius. I'm glad I [19] .... normal.

2

Work in groups   Use your imagination as you discuss the questions below.

Just imagine if you'd been . . .

– born the child of a millionaire.
– born in an English-speaking country (and attended school there).
– born a boy rather than a girl – or a girl rather than a boy.
– born with an ability to see the future.

• How might your life have been different so far?
• How would your life be different now – and in the future?

A **1** Read this passage and answer the questions which follow. Underline the details in the text that relate to each question. Some of the wrong alternatives are only slightly wrong!

1   I am now in my twenty-second year and yet the only birthday which I can clearly distinguish among all the rest is my twelfth, for it was on that damp and misty day in September I met the Captain for the first time. I can still remember the wetness of the gravel under my gym shoes and how the blown leaves made the courtyard slippery as I ran recklessly to escape from my enemies between one class and the next. I slithered and came to an abrupt halt while my pursuers went whistling away, because there in the middle of the courtyard stood our formidable headmaster talking to a tall man in a bowler hat, a rare sight already at that date, so that he looked a little like an actor in costume – an impression not so far wrong, for I never saw him in a bowler hat again. He carried a walking-stick over his shoulder at the slope like a soldier with a rifle. I had no idea who he might be, nor, of course, did I know how he had won me the previous night, or so he was to claim, in a backgammon game with my father.

2   I slid so far that I landed on my knees at the two men's feet, and when I picked myself up the headmaster was glaring at me from under his heavy eyebrows. I heard him say, 'I think this is the one you want – Baxter Three. Are you Baxter Three?'

3   'Yes, sir,' I said.

4   The man, whom I would never come to know by any more permanent name than the Captain, said, 'What does Three indicate?'

5   'He is the youngest of three Baxters,' the headmaster said, 'but not one of them is related by blood.'

6   'That puts me in a bit of a quandary,' the Captain said. 'For which of them is the Baxter I want? The Christian name, unlikely as it may sound, is Victor. Victor Baxter – the names don't pair very well.'

7   'We have little occasion here for Christian names. Are you called Victor Baxter?' the headmaster inquired of me sharply.

8   'Yes sir,' I said after some hesitation, for I was reluctant to admit to a name which I had tried unsuccessfully to conceal from my fellows. I knew very well that Victor for some obscure reason was one of the unacceptable names, like Vincent or Marmaduke.

9   'Well then, I suppose that this is the Baxter you want, sir. Your face needs washing, boy.'

10 The stern morality of the school prevented me from telling the headmaster that it had been quite clean until my enemies had splashed it with ink. I saw the Captain regarding me with brown, friendly and what I came to learn later from hearsay, unreliable eyes. He had such deep black hair that it might well have been dyed and a long thin nose which reminded me of a pair of scissors left partly ajar, as though his nose was preparing to trim the military moustache just below it. I thought that he winked at me, but I could hardly believe it. In my experience grown-ups did not wink, except at each other.

1 How old was Victor (the narrator) when he first met the Captain?
   a) 11   b) 12   c) 21   d) 22

2 How old is Victor at the time of writing?
   a) 11   b) 12   c) 21   d) 22

3 Victor was running fast because
   a) he was playing with some other boys   c) he wanted to meet the Captain
   b) other boys were chasing him   d) the headmaster had called him

4 Victor is called Baxter Three because
   a) he has two elder brothers in the school
   b) he has two younger brothers in the school
   c) there are two older boys called Baxter in the school
   d) there are two younger boys called Baxter in the school

5 The Captain said later that Victor's father had
   a) asked the Captain to look after Victor   c) given Victor to him
   b) lost Victor to him in a gambling game   d) sold Victor to him

6 Victor's fellow-pupils
   a) did not know his first name   c) knew his first name
   b) liked the name Victor   d) were keen to find out his first name

7 Victor's face was dirty because
   a) he had had an accident with some ink   c) he hadn't washed that morning
   b) he was a careless boy   d) the other boys had made it dirty

8 The adults that Victor knew all seemed to him to be
   a) kind and generous   c) humorous and friendly
   b) strict and severe   d) unhappy and bad-tempered

2 Work in pairs Check your answers and, if you made any mistakes, make sure you understand *why* you were wrong. Did any of the questions seem 'unfair' to you?

B 🖊 Highlight the words or phrases in the passage that mean the same as these words or phrases. Don't use a dictionary – try to work out the meanings from the context.

   ¶1 stones   *gravel*   sports shoes   not worrying about the danger   slid   sudden
   ¶6 not knowing what to do
   ¶8 unwilling   keep secret   hard to understand
   ¶10 according to what other people said   half open   cut

C **Work in groups** Discuss these questions:
   • What kind of a person does Victor seem to be?
   • How happy were his days at the boarding school, do you think?

D 1 📼 You'll hear five people remembering their first day at school. Match the names of the speakers to the events they remember. There is one event that no one remembers.

Nick   Kate   Adam   Cecilia   Neil

1 He/she was frightened by the older pupils.

2 His/her mother was specially kind on that day.

3 He/she did the wrong thing on the bus to school.

4 His/her appetite for breakfast was spoiled by nervousness.

5 The teacher hurt him/her on the first day at school.

6 The teacher's behaviour changed after the first day.

Nick

Kate

Adam

Cecilia

Neil

2 Work in groups Find out what your partners remember about their first day at primary school, at secondary school and in this language class.

Compound words – 2 WORD STUDY

A **1** **Combine the words in these two lists to make compound nouns. These are compound nouns that are normally written as *two words*, with no hyphens.**

For example: air travel and civil servant

air	civil	coffee	computer	account	break	book	bread
exercise	further	general	high	coffee	computer	court	cup
higher	instant	intelligence		education	education	ground	
personal	railway	restaurant		knowledge	owner	program	
savings	school	sports	staff	professor	room	school	servant
story	tea	television	tennis	set	station	teacher	telling	test
university	wholemeal			travel			

2 **Combine the words in these two lists to make compound nouns. These are compound nouns that are normally written as *one word*, with no hyphens.**

For example: airport and boyfriend

air	boy	bread	chair	class	ache	ache	book	brush	crumbs
head	home	house	note	play	friend	girl	ground	keeping
post	school	tax	time	tooth	man	man	paste	payer	port
tooth	tooth				room	table	work	

3 **Combine the words in these two lists to make compound adjectives. Remember that most compound adjectives are normally written *with hyphens*.**

For example: absent-minded and accident-prone

absent	accident	blue	brand	behaved	eyed	fashioned	haired
curly	good	kind	last	narrow	handed	hearted	looking	minded
old	right	short	sun	well	minded	minute	new	prone
					sighted	tanned		

4 📼 **The correct answers to 1, 2 and 3 are recorded. Pay attention to the pronunciation.**

B **1** **Work in pairs** Write six sentences with one or two gaps which require a compound word from the exercises in A1–3.

My first .... was a very .... person.

2 **Exchange your six sentences with another pair. Fill the gaps in their sentences.**

In . . . PREPOSITIONS

Fill the gaps in the sentences below with suitable phrases from this list:

in a hurry   in a way ✓   in all   in common   in confidence   in general   in other words
in particular   in prison   in public   in private   in trouble   in tears

1 He said he agreed with me <u>in a way</u> . – .... , he didn't entirely agree.

2 They get on well with each other because they have so much ....

3 She must have been .... because she rushed past me without saying hello.

4 This book contains 208 pages ....

5 .... I like discussion lessons, but I didn't enjoy that particular one.

6 The story ended with the heroine .... because her husband was ....

7 I'm telling you this .... – I don't want anyone else to know.

8 Let me know if you're .... and I'll see if I can help you at all.

9 He seems sensitive and charming .... , but .... he's aggressive and disagreeable.

10 I liked most of my classes at school but I must say that I enjoyed chemistry ....

11.6 / Using your brain   LISTENING

A You'll hear part of a talk about the human brain. Answer the questions below. You'll probably need to hear the talk at least twice to get all the answers.

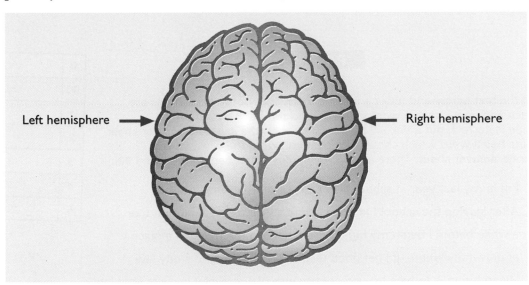

Left hemisphere →   ← Right hemisphere

1 The left-hand side of the brain normally controls the .... side of the body.

2 What functions do the two hemispheres of the brain control?

LEFT (rational side)	RIGHT (irrational side)
language	rhythm
....	....
linearity	....
analysis	....
....	space: three dimensions
....	seeing .... of things as a whole
sequencing	

3 In left-handed people, these priorities are often ....

4 The .... is the link between the two hemispheres. It is the key to ....

5 The first question the speaker suggests you ask in the experiment is: 'What is .... ?'

6 The second question is: 'What piece of furniture is .... ?'

7 While someone is trying to answer the first question they will .... to prevent themselves being distracted by ....

8 Unfortunately, the experiment will not be successful if they ....

9 As we get older our memories ....

10 You forget things more easily if your brain doesn't have enough .... or ....

11 Your brain can deteriorate if you don't get enough .... or if your .... is unhealthy.

12 The three Golden Rules of brain power are:
a) Use your senses and don't only think .... Imagine a problem ....
b) Use .... of your brain.
c) Don't say .... because your brain is .... as anyone else's.

In the exam, if you haven't got time to write each answer down during the first listening, just write the first letter and come back to it later. Otherwise you may miss the answer to the next question.

B **Work in groups**   Discuss these questions:
• Which hemisphere of your brain do you think is dominant?
• Are you left-handed or right-handed?
• How good are you at remembering information?
• Do you find it easier to remember numbers or words?
• If you want to remember a particular piece of information, what do you do to help yourself?
• How do you remember English vocabulary?

11.7 **Use of English: Correcting errors** EXAM TECHNIQUES

A Look at these questions from Part 4 of the Use of English paper. One of the answers given in questions 1–5 is wrong – which one is it?

PART 4

Read the text below and look carefully at each line. Some of the lines are correct, and some have a word which should not be there.
If a line is correct, put a tick (✓) by the number **on the separate answer sheet**.
If a line has a word which should **not** be there, write the word **on the separate answer sheet**. There are two examples at the beginning (**0** and **00**).

0	✓	
00	*the*	
1	*in*	
2	✓	
3	*of*	
4	*or*	
5	*to*	

0   I'm in my last year at school now and I take my exams in June.

00   After leaving the school I hope to spend a year travelling around for

1   a while before I begin my higher education. I hope to get in a place

2   at university where, if I get good results, I'm planning to study law.

3   My ambition is to be a lawyer, not because of successful lawyers earn lots

4   of money or but because I really enjoy working with people.

5   I'm looking forward much to my 'year out' because after taking my exams

B **1** **Work in pairs**   Look at this exam advice. Are there any points you don't follow, or which you disagree with?

In this part of the exam, the extra words are most likely to be *grammatical* words:
– articles: *a* or *the*
– pronouns: *she, it,* etc.
– prepositions: *in, on, with,* etc.
– other grammatical words: *so, much, some, down,* etc.
and not *content* words like *education, enjoy, continue,* etc.

Recommended procedure

1   Read the whole text through to get the gist before you start writing your answers.

2   Then read it again, line by line. In the question booklet (not the answer sheet) put a ring in pencil round the extra words and put ticks or question marks by the lines that seem OK. Copy your answers onto the answer sheet later.

3   If a line looks OK to you, don't put a tick immediately. Read it again (or come back to it later) before you commit yourself on the answer sheet. You can expect about ten lines to contain an extra word and five to be correct.

2 **Now do the rest of the exercise yourself, using a pencil. Write the answers in your notebook.**

6   at the end of the year I don't want to continue on studying even harder.

7   At the moment I'm not sure still what exactly I'm going to do, but

8   I'll certainly have to get a job for a few months at the least to earn

9   some money to pay for my travels. I'm trying to persuade a friend of

10   mine to join me because it's not much fun travelling on your own,

11   especially in a foreign country. The question is, however, where we to go?

12   We could travel around Europe for a couple of months – so you can get

13   a rail pass which it lets you travel anywhere you want for one whole month.

14   Or you can buy a bus pass with which you can go all over North America with.

15   What do you think we should to do?

11.8 Advantages and disadvantages — WRITING

A 1 Work in pairs Make notes on this topic. Begin by dividing up a page in your notebook as shown on the right.

Write an article for a school magazine on the advantages and disadvantages of taking a year out between school and higher education.

If you know a lot about a topic, you may be able to think of lots of pros and cons – more than you can fit into 120–180 words. In that case you'll have to select which points to include and which to leave out. Your essay shouldn't look like a shopping list, and this is why reasons or examples are necessary to back up your points.

2 One of you should write the first half of the article (about 70 words on the advantages) and the other the second half (about 70 words on the disadvantages). Write the concluding sentence together.

3 Join another pair Look at each other's notes and articles. What are the strong and weak points of each?

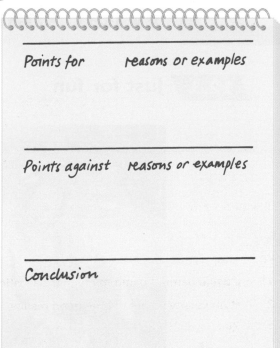

Points for — reasons or examples

Points against — reasons or examples

Conclusion

B 1 Work in pairs Make notes together (in the same style as before) for an article on this topic:

What are the advantages and disadvantages of working in pairs or groups in a language class?

2 Join another pair Compare your notes, adding further ideas if necessary. Decide which of the points for and against are important – and which can be left out if you haven't got room or time to cover them.

3 Work alone Write your essay (about 150 words).

C 1 Work in groups Look again at the guidelines for giving feedback in Activity 61.

2 Read each other's articles and comment on their strong and weak points.

"I often say, Mrs Dent, I'd rather have your little Christopher in my class than **all** the bright, clever ones!"

12 What shall we do this evening?

12.1 Just for fun

VOCABULARY AND LISTENING

A Work in groups   Look at the scenes above and discuss these questions:

- What do you think is happening in each scene?
- What kind of film do you think each one comes from?
- What kinds of films do you enjoy most?
- What kinds of films do you avoid, or hate seeing?

B **1** 🔲 You'll hear three people talking about the films they enjoy. Put a tick ✓ in the appropriate column to show the films they like or a cross ✗ to show the films they dislike.

	Joan	Chris	Bob	Your partner
action films				
old black and white films				
cartoons				
horror films				
romantic comedies				
thrillers				
westerns				
dubbed foreign films				
foreign-language films with subtitles				

2 Work in pairs Now find out the same information from your partner, and put ticks and crosses in the right-hand column.

C 🔊 You'll hear a recorded message telling you about the films showing this week. Below is the cinema's advertisement for *last* week. Cross out the times that are different this week and put the new times on the right, as in the examples.

Ritz Film Centre						
5 screens all with Dolby Stereo Surround Sound						
DUMB AND DUMBER 12	~~12:45~~	~~3:15~~	5:20	8:50	*12:30*	*3:30*
TIMECOP 12	1:05	3:25	5:40	8:20		
I LIKE IT LIKE THAT 15	1:15	3:55	6:05	8:50		
DISCLOSURE 18	1:20	3:35	5:55	8:10		
Movie Classics: SOME LIKE IT HOT U			6:20	8:55		
recorded information 774112		credit card bookings 774422				

D **1 Work in pairs** Everyone watches television, and most people say they are selective – but how selective are you? Do this questionnaire together.

TV VIEWING HABITS

1 Put these types of TV programmes into one of these categories:

A I usually enjoy watching …   **B** I never watch …   **C** I sometimes watch …

the news   documentaries   football   pop music   weather forecasts
educational programmes   other sports   classical music   crime series   feature films
game shows   soap operas   current affairs   nature programmes   comedies   talk shows

2 Which channel do you watch most?

3 How many hours do you watch TV per week?

---

2 Join another pair Compare your answers to the questionnaire.

E **Work in groups** Think of occasions when you went out with friends during the past month and discuss these questions:

- Where did you go? Why did you go there?
- What did you do? What did you enjoy most about the occasion?
- Who did you go with? Who did you meet?
- What's your favourite way of spending an afternoon or evening out?

Groundhog Day
(February 2nd)

Recognised in US popular tradition as the day when the groundhog, a small mammal, is supposed to appear from hibernation; it is said that if the groundhog sees its shadow, it goes back into hibernation for six more weeks, thereby indicating six weeks of winter weather to come.

A 1 **Read the first part of this film review and find the answers to these questions:**

1 What type of film is *Groundhog Day*?
2 In the film, what happens every morning to the main character?
3 What is his job and why does he have to travel to Punxsatawney every year?

A life in the day of . . .

Imagine having to live the same day of your life over and over again. Whatever you do on that day, you wake up the following morning to discover the same day beginning again. In some ways this is good: you can stop

TOBY YOUNG
is touched by a comedy about one man's nightmare 24 hours.

worrying about cholesterol, for a start. Concern for the future becomes a thing of the past. But if you're trying to make Andie MacDowell fall in love with you, it's not so good. No matter how much progress you make, the following day you'll have to start again.

This is Bill Murray's predicament in *Groundhog Day*, a romantic comedy directed by Harold Ramis. Murray plays a weatherman for a Pittsburgh television station who has to travel to the small town of Punxsatawney every year to cover a local festival, in which a groundhog is asked by the town elders whether they should expect six more weeks of winter or an early spring. This awful little town and its loathsome ritual represent everything Murray despises about his dead-end career. Yet he is forced to live the day of the groundhog festival until the end of time.

2 **Work in pairs** Note down *three more* things you'd like to find out about the film before you read the rest of the review.

B Read the rest of the review and find out if your questions are answered.

Groundhog Day is unusual in that its single idea is so ingenious 3 you're happy to sit back and watch as all its implications are worked out. It's also weirdly engrossing. As it dawns on Murray that he is stuck in the same day for eternity, you feel something close to panic.

Being destined to relive the same 24 hours for ever soon becomes a curse. Murray falls in 4 love with his producer, Andie MacDowell. He has barely spoken to her before the day of the festival, so he only has the remainder of the day to win her. Even if he succeeds it scarcely matters, because the next day he'll be back to square one.

Not that this stops him trying. The funniest sequence in the film occurs as Murray attempts to 5 impress MacDowell with clever conversation. Each time he fluffs it, he starts again the following day and corrects his mistake. When he proposes a toast to the groundhog, MacDowell says: 'I usually drink to world peace.' Next time round he gets it right. After months of practice, he finally gets the routine perfect, only to be rebuffed at the last minute. The prospect of starting all over again is appalling, but not as appalling as it is when she finally falls for him. As Murray says to her. 'The worst part is that tomorrow you'll have forgotten all about this, and you'll treat me like a jerk again.'

The horror of Murray's situation leaves you reeling. What is the point of living in a world in which nothing you do affects the future? Murray could forget about MacDowell and spend his time in the local library, studying Western philosophy, but what would be the 6 point if any work he produced would have to be written all over again the following day? He could rob a bank – come to think of it, he does rob a bank – but the money is gone the next morning, along with the house he bought with it. Murray, an ambitious man, finds himself in a world in which it is impossible to achieve anything.

Of course, the effect of all this is to teach Murray the true meaning of life, and in this respect *Groundhog Day* is 7 unremarkable. But it would be churlish to condemn it for its lapse into sentimentality. *Groundhog Day* is an ordinary comedy transformed into a dazzling piece of entertainment by an extraordinary idea.

C Decide whether these statements are true or false according to the review.

1 The viewer remains distant from the main character and his predicament.
2 Every morning Murray's producer starts out disliking him.
3 His producer never changes her attitude to him: she still dislikes him every evening.
4 Murray is able to benefit from the money he steals.
5 Murray enjoys most aspects of his situation.
6 The reviewer thinks the film is wonderful.

D Highlight the word or phrase in the review that means the same as each of the following:

¶2 difficult situation   revolting   job which is never going to improve
¶3 original and creative   realises
¶4 have to start again at the beginning
¶5 makes a mistake   rejected   idiot
¶6 shaken
¶7 rude and ungrateful   marvellous

E 1 Work in groups Discuss these questions:

- Who are your favourite international film stars?
- Who are your favourite directors?
- What were the last two films you saw?
- What was the best film you've ever seen? Why was it so good?
- What was the worst film you've ever seen? Why was it so bad?
- Which two recent films would you like to see? Why do you want to see them?

2 Work in pairs What influences you when deciding on a film or show to see? Rate these influences in order of importance from 1 to 5:

– stars   – director
– reviews   – personal recommendation
– advertisements or previews   – other influences

3 Join another pair Compare your ratings. What other influences are missing from the list?

12.3 **-ing and to . . . – 2** GRAMMAR REVIEW

Imagine having to live the same day of your life over and over again. Whatever you do on that day, you . . .

A ✎ Re-read the review of Groundhog Day in 12.2 and highlight all the examples of *-ing* forms and *to . . .* (but not the preposition *to*).

- Which verbs are followed by *-ing*?
- And which verbs are followed by *to . . .*?

B 1 Complete each sentence with suitable words.

1 Before I go out this evening I have to finish _doing this exercise_.

2 If someone has hayfever, they can't help ....

3 The couple behind us in the cinema were having a chat and they refused .... Despite our complaints they just went on .... all through the film.

4 The old lady couldn't carry all her groceries so I offered ....

5 My little brother couldn't understand his English homework so I helped him ....

6 He looks healthy, I'm sure he's just pretending ....

7 He's quite a shy person, but his friends encouraged him ....

8 We wanted to go out for a walk but it's just started ....

See the Grammar Reference section on pages 175–176.

2 **Work in pairs** Compare your sentences.

C Complete the second sentence so that it has a similar meaning to the first sentence. Use the word in **red** and other words to complete each sentence. Don't change the word given.

1 I'm happy to drive you home; it's no trouble.
mind I _don't mind driving_ you home.

2 I don't normally dress up when I go out for the evening.
used I'm .... when I go out for the evening.

3 We could go to the cinema or the theatre.
prefer Would .... to the cinema or theatre?

4 An expensive restaurant like that is out of my price range.
such I can't afford .... expensive restaurant.

5 They went on smoking all through the meal.
stop They didn't .... all through the meal.

6 It was such a tiring drive that we needed a break.
stopped The drive was so .... have a break.

7 I'll never forget the time I went to see Walt Disney's *Pinocchio* when I was little.
remember I'll always .... Walt Disney's *Pinocchio* when I was little.

8 Oh dear, I was supposed to phone my uncle but I forgot!
remember Oh no, I .... phone my uncle!

D **Work in groups** Find out about each other's likes and dislikes by asking questions about these *and other* activities:

– boxing, football, golf and other sports
– jazz, opera and other types of music
– walking, reading and other interests
– the news, quiz shows and other programmes
– pizza, steak, fish and other dishes
– dancing, eating out, cinema, etc.

Do you enjoy . . . ? Do you like . . . ? Would you like . . . ?
Do you prefer . . . ? Would you prefer . . . ?

Encourage each other to say more than just 'yes' or 'no', by adding an extra comment like this:

Yes, I love reading books — but I wouldn't like to read one now.
Yes, I like going for walks — but I don't feel like going for one today.
Normally, I hate watching quiz shows on TV — but I don't mind watching 'Mastermind'.
I enjoy watching boxing on TV — but I wouldn't like to be a boxer myself!

12.4 Rewriting sentences EXAM TECHNIQUES

 1 Look at these questions from Part 3 of the Use of English paper – and the *wrong* answers given by various candidates below.

PART 3

Complete the second sentence so that it has a similar meaning to the first sentence, using the word given. **Do not change the word given**. You must use between two and five words, including the word given. Write **only** the missing words **on the separate answer sheet**.

1 I don't want to go out this evening.
rather
I .... go out this evening.

would prefer to stay at home rather than – too many words
rather think it's a bad idea to – changes the meaning and too many words
I'd rather not go – the 'I' shouldn't be included
It's rather a bad idea to – ingenious but unacceptable and too many words

2 You'll have to book in advance if you want a ticket for the show.
impossible
You'll find .... get a ticket for the show unless you book in advance.

that it is completely impossible to – too many words
that it isn't possible to – word changed
that getting a ticket is impossible – repeats the information and too many words

3 I don't like films which are full of violence.
approve
I .... violent films.

disapprove of
will not give my approval to

4 People say that *Some Like It Hot* is a really funny film.
supposed
Some Like It Hot .... a really funny film.

is, I supposed,
is supposedly

2 What's wrong with the answers to Questions 3 and 4? What are the *right* answers?

B Now try the remaining six questions on your own. The meaning of the second sentence must be as close as possible to the first sentence. But the emphasis or style may be slightly different.

5 I haven't got much energy, so I don't feel like going out for a walk.
energetic
If I .... feel like going out for a walk.

6 We saw the film and then went to have a pizza.
over
When the film .... to have a pizza.

7 If we had arrived late, we would have had to queue.
early
We .... that we didn't have to queue.

8 Watching a film on video is very different from seeing it on a big screen.
between
There is a .... watching a film on video and at the cinema.

9 I decided not to see the film because I'd read what the critics had to say.
reviews
After .... the film I decided not to go and see it.

10 I think you really did like the show, because you laughed at all the jokes.
enjoyed
You laughed at all the jokes, ... the show.

5	
6	
7	
8	
9	
10	

Words + prepositions – 1   **PREPOSITIONS**

Fill the gaps in the sentences below with a suitable preposition from this list:

about   for   in   of   from   with   on

1 Everyone admires him .... his wisdom and common sense.

2 I agree .... you that it was an awful programme.

3 Dick apologised .... not sending us a thank-you letter.

4 I don't approve .... their bad behaviour.

5 We all started to argue .... him .... his political ideas.

6 I believe .... government support for the movie industry.

7 Everyone can benefit .... a better road system.

8 You can't blame me .... your own mistakes.

9 Peter's always boasting .... his own achievements.

10 Would you like to borrow a pen .... me?

11 Max is capable .... doing much better work than this.

12 We would like to congratulate you .... getting engaged.

13 Water consists .... hydrogen and oxygen.

14 There is no simple cure .... hayfever.

15 The salesman tried to convince me .... the advantages of buying the car.

Using suffixes – 1: Adjectives   **WORD STUDY**

A 1 Work in pairs What is the difference in meaning between the words in green?

1 Careful? Certainly not, she was really careless!

2 I thought the injection would be painless, but it was extremely painful.

3 He took swimming lessons because he knew that if he fell in the water he'd be completely helpless. The swimming teacher was really helpful.

4 It wasn't very tactful of you to mention her divorce. How could you be so tactless?

2 Which of these words can you add either of the suffixes -less or -ful to? And which can you only add one of the suffixes to?

delight   end   hope   power   rest   speech   success   thought   use

B 1 Add more examples to the lists below using these root words:

accident ✓   admire ✓   blood   cloud   comfort   dirt   education   emotion   enjoy   fashion
fool   geography   noise   old   philosophy   prefer   rain   sleep   small   tall   tradition
young

-able	acceptable	reliable	*admirable*	....	....	....
-al	regional	national	*accidental*	....	....	....
-ical	biological	historical	....	....		
-ish	childish	whitish	....	....	....	....
-y	draughty	foggy	....	....	....	....

Remember that these words end in -ible not -able:

(in)credible   (in)edible   (in)flexible   (im)possible   (ir)responsible   (in)visible
eligible   horrible   negligible   terrible

2 The answers are recorded. Pay attention to the pronunciation and practise it.

C Use the words in red at the end of each line to form new words that fit in the spaces.

1 It was very *careless* of you to break that coffee cup.   **care**

2 Thank you for your postcard, it was very .... of you to send it.   **thought**

3 She's quite .... : she plays the flute and the piano.   **music**

4 It was rather .... of him to cry when he did badly in the test.   **child**
5 We started our trip on a beautiful .... morning.   **sun**
6 I enjoyed the book so much because it was so ....   **read**
7 His .... knowledge is very poor – he thinks Venice is in Austria.   **geography**
8 Her hair is .... , not bright red.   **red**
9 A very old car is usually a(n) .... car.   **rely**
10 I'll always remember that film – it was ....   **forget**

12.7   Short sentences? Or long ones?   WRITING

Short sentences are easier to write than long, complex ones. Often short sentences are easier to read and understand too. But very short sentences may look too simple – even childish.

A   **Look at these paragraphs, which are part of a story. Which do you prefer and why?**

1 *She was engaged to marry a tall dark-haired man with attractive brown eyes, whose clothes were always smart and who always behaved charmingly even when people were not pleasant to him.*

2 She was going to marry a tall dark-haired man with attractive brown eyes. His clothes were always smart. He always behaved charmingly even when people were not pleasant to him.

3 She was going to marry a tall dark-haired man. He had attractive brown eyes. He always wore smart clothes. People weren't always nice to him. But he always behaved charmingly.

B 1   **Write two paragraphs (about 100 words altogether), incorporating all of these ideas, but not necessarily in this order. Add one more idea of your own.**

FOR AND AGAINST WATCHING TELEVISION

– difficult to turn off
– better to be selective
– most programmes terrible
– next day you can't remember what you saw the evening before

– temptation to watch everything
– some programmes interesting
– stops families communicating

2 **Work in pairs**   Look at each other's work, paying particular attention to the length of the sentences. What improvements can you suggest?

3 **Work in pairs**   Make notes for three separate paragraphs on the topics below. Then, in your pairs (or alone), write the three paragraphs.

1 Is it better for American or English films to have subtitles or be dubbed into your language? Explain your reasons.

2 What are the advantages and disadvantages of passive entertainment (films, TV, video games, etc.) and active leisure (sport, hobbies, etc.)?

3 Which do you prefer: seeing films at the cinema or on video or on TV? Why?

4 **Join another pair**   Look at the other pair's paragraphs and suggest improvements.

C   Write a review of a film or TV programme you have seen recently (about 150 words). Give a summary of the story and explain what you liked and disliked about it. Imagine that you're writing this for a school magazine whose readers are students like yourself.

13 Read any good books?

A good read   VOCABULARY

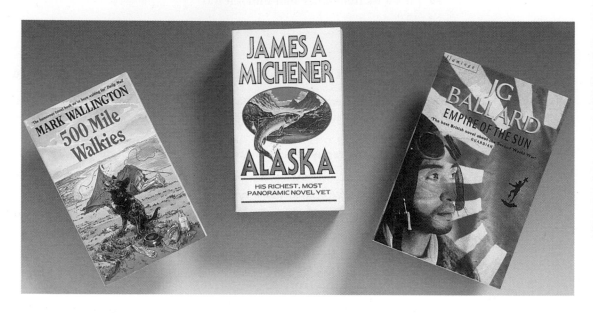

(A) **Work in groups**   Find out about the last book each of your partners has read and make notes on these points:

– Author and title
– Type of book and what it's about
– Reason for liking it
– Reason for recommending it to others

(B) **Work in pairs**   Choose the best alternative to complete these sentences.

1 *Oliver Twist* is a classic work of English ....
   literature   non-fiction   letters   editions

2 The plot of the novel was very exciting, but I didn't find the .... very interesting.
   persons   people   characters   figures

3 This book is a special edition for foreign readers, so there's a(n) .... at the back.
   appendix   glossary   introduction   preface   table of contents   supplement

4 A novel is usually divided into several ....
   chapters   units   sections   passages

5 If you need to find some information in a non-fiction book, look it up in the ....
   atlas   blurb   catalogue   diary   index   review

6 Cambridge University Press is the .... of the book you're reading.
   author   editor   printer   publisher

7 A great novel has a good plot and a strong ....
   communication   meaning   message   significance

8 The book was marvellously .... and it was a joy to read.
   stylistic   tedious   well-written   wonderful

9 Ernest Hemingway is one of my .... American writers.
   best   favourite   ideal   most popular

10 The thriller was so exciting that I couldn't ....
   let it down   look it up   pick it up   put it down

11 Even the .... characters in the book are really interesting.
   less   minor   small   tiny

12 I'd like to .... that book when you've read it.
   borrow   hire   lend   loan

C In these sentences *three* alternatives are correct and *two* are wrong. Choose the best three alternatives for each.

1 The .... character in the book is called Oliver.
   central   main   principal   principle   top

2 I enjoy her books because her style is so very ....
   dull   entertaining   readable   tedious   true-to-life

3 I found that the characters in the story were very ....
   amusing   believable   informative   likeable   thrilling

4 There were so many twists in the plot that I didn't really think it was ....
   accurate   authentic   convincing   realistic   true-to-life

5 She doesn't read any fiction because she prefers reading ....
   biographies   short stories   textbooks   non-fiction   science fiction

6 I can't .... books like those – they just send me to sleep.
   bear   carry   enjoy   stand   suffer

D Fill the gaps in these sentences with suitable words.

1 You can borrow books from a .... or buy them from a ....

2 A writer can also be called an ....

3 I can't afford to buy the book in hardback, so I'll wait till it comes out in ....

4 I can't remember the .... of the book, but I know it had a yellow ....

5 A book that tells somebody's life story is called a ....

E Work in groups   Discuss these questions:

- Which of the books on page 104 looks most interesting? What do you think you'd enjoy (and not enjoy) about each one?
- Who are the most famous writers in your country's literature?
- Imagine that you are recommending one of their books to a foreign person – what would you tell them about the book and its author?

Each year FCE candidates can choose to read one (or more) optional 'background reading texts' from a list of about five. You can write about one of these set books in Part 2 of the Writing paper. Most of the set books are simplified or abridged editions.

The question in Paper 2 may look something like this (although the titles change each year):

Background reading texts

Answer the following question based on your reading of **one** of these set books:

Brave New World   by Aldous Huxley
The Great Gatsby   by F. Scott Fitzgerald
From the Cradle to the Grave   edited by Clare West
Rebecca   by Daphne du Maurier
The Captain and the Enemy   by Graham Greene

Who do you think is the most unpleasant person in the book you have read? Give a brief **account** of the person's character and explain why you found him or her particularly unpleasant.

Write your account, giving enough details for another student who may not have read the book.

Reading a set text and answering a question about it is *optional*, and you don't have to answer the question about it unless you want to.

13.2 The Great Gatsby   READING

A Work in groups   Discuss these questions:

- What makes you decide to read a particular book: a friend's recommendation, reading the first page, reading reviews, reading the blurb on the cover – or something else?
- Which of these types of books do you enjoy (or not enjoy) reading? Give your reasons.

    spy stories   thrillers   detective stories   poetry   romantic novels
    history books   biographies   science fiction   classic works of literature

B **1** Read two different versions of an extract from the same novel: a 'simplified edition' and the original edition of *The Great Gatsby* by F. Scott Fitzgerald. *Note down* your answers to these questions:

- Which version of the story do you prefer? Why?
- What are the advantages and disadvantages of each version?
- What is *left out* in the simplified version? What is *added*? Underline an example of each.

2 Work in groups   Compare your notes and your answers to the questions.

Simplified
version

There was music from my neighbour's house through the summer nights. In his blue gardens men and girls came and went, floating among the whisperings and the champagne and the stars. In the afternoon by the shore I watched his guests swimming in the Sound, or lying in the sun on the hot sand, or water-skiing from his two motorboats.

At weekends his big open car became a bus, carrying groups of people to and from the city between nine in the morning and long past midnight, while his second car met all the trains at the station. And on Mondays eight servants, including an extra gardener, worked all day to repair the damage from the night before. Every Friday five boxes of oranges and lemons arrived from a fruit shop in New York – every Monday these same oranges and lemons left his back door in a pile of empty halves.

About once in two weeks there was a really big party. The trees were all covered in coloured lights and a dance floor was laid down on the lawn; a big group of musicians came down from New York to play music for dancing. Wonderful food arrived, with dozens of waiters to serve it, and in the main hall a bar was set up, serving every possible kind of alcoholic drink. I remember the sense of excitement at the beginning of the party.

By seven o'clock the last swimmers have come in from the beach and are dressing upstairs; cars from New York are drawing up every minute, and already the halls and sitting rooms are full of girls in bright dresses with the newest, strangest hairstyles. Trays of cocktails are floating through the garden outside, until the air is alive with talk and laughter.

The lights grow brighter as darkness falls, and now the musicians are playing cocktail music and the voices are higher and louder. Laughter is easier, minute by minute. The party has begun.

C Note down your answers to these questions, showing whether you found the answers in the simplified version, the original version or in both.

1 When did Gatsby's parties happen? *Every two weeks in summer – both versions*
2 What did Gatsby's guests do during the afternoon?
3 Which of Gatsby's cars ferried guests to and from New York?
4 How many people helped to clear up after the parties?
5 How was the orange juice made?
6 Where did the guests dance?
7 Where was the bar?
8 What kind of orchestra played at the parties?

Original version

There was music from my neighbor's house through the summer nights. In his blue gardens men and girls came and went like moths among the whisperings and the champagne and the stars. At high tide in the afternoon I watched his guests diving from the tower of his raft or taking the sun on the hot sand of his beach while his two motor-boats slit the waters of the Sound, drawing aquaplanes over cataracts of foam. On weekends his Rolls-Royce became an omnibus, bearing parties to and from the city, between nine in the morning and long past midnight, while his station wagon scampered like a brisk yellow bug to meet all trains. And on Mondays eight servants including an extra gardener toiled all day with mops and scrubbing brushes and hammers and garden-shears, repairing the ravages of the night before.

Every Friday five crates of oranges and lemons arrived from a fruiterer in New York – every Monday these same oranges and lemons left his back door in a pyramid of pulpless halves. There was a machine in the kitchen which could extract the juice of two hundred oranges in half an hour, if a little button was pressed two hundred times by a butler's thumb.

At least once a fortnight a corps of caterers came down with several hundred feet of canvas and enough colored lights to make a Christmas tree of Gatsby's enormous garden. On buffet tables, garnished with glistening hors d'oeuvre, spiced baked hams crowded against salads of harlequin designs and pastry pigs and turkeys bewitched to a dark gold. In the main hall a bar with a real brass rail was set up, and stocked with gins and liquors and with cordials so long forgotten that most of his female guests were too young to know one from another.

By seven o'clock the orchestra has arrived – no thin five piece affair but a whole pit full of oboes and trombones and saxophones and viols and cornets and piccolos and low and high drums. The last swimmers have come in from the beach now and are dressing upstairs; the cars from New York are parked five deep in the drive, and already the halls and salons and verandas are gaudy with primary colors and hair shorn in strange new ways and shawls beyond the dreams of Castile. The bar is in full swing, and floating rounds of cocktails permeate the garden outside until the air is alive with chatter and laughter and casual innuendo and introductions forgotten on the spot and enthusiastic meetings between women who never knew each other's names.

The lights grow brighter as the earth lurches away from the sun and now the orchestra is playing yellow cocktail music and the opera of voices pitches a key higher. Laughter is easier, minute by minute, spilled with prodigality, tipped out at a cheerful word. The groups change more swiftly, swell with new arrivals, dissolve and form in the same breath – already there are wanderers, confident girls who weave here and there among the stouter and more stable, become for a sharp, joyous moment the center of a group and then excited with triumph glide on through the sea-change of faces and voices and color under the constantly changing light.

Once you have read a simplified version of a story, it might be worth re-reading it in the original version – if you enjoyed it. Or if you've really enjoyed an English or American novel translated into your language, why not buy the original and read it again in English?

13.3 **Reading habits**   LISTENING

A **1** Before you hear the recording, look at the questions below and see if you can guess what some of the answers are.

2 Listen to the recording and fill the gaps with information from the broadcast.

1 According to recent research, ... percent of American adolescents can't read a printed page unless they have a background of ....

2 The main advantages of printed books over cassettes and computers is that they are relatively .... and very ....

3 To use a book, the only equipment you need is a ....

4 Many people only buy .... book(s) a year, which they read in the .... , on the .... and on the ....

5 Books by .... are selling more copies every year.

6 Five books are mentioned in the broadcast. Match these front covers to the back covers below.

a

In the shadowy recesses of Whitehall and Washington an unholy alliance operates between the intelligence community and the secret arms trade.

Jonathan Pine is taking refuge from his demons as a night manager in the luxury hotel trade until the day he agrees to stand up and be counted in the fight against this ultimate heart of darkness.

His mission takes him from the cliffs of West Cornwall, via northern Quebec and the Caribbean, to the jungles of post-Noriega Panama. His quarry is the worst man in the world.

b

Blessed with beauty and talent, Jazz Kilkullen is an internationally acclaimed photographer and the owner of DAZZLE, a fashionable studio in Venice Beach, California. Successful and sexy, she is pursued by three exciting yet vastly different men, who have one thing in common, a passion for Jazz.

But Jazz has enemies and, when her father dies suddenly on his vast estate in Orange County, she discovers a family plot to sell the land to developers who are determined to exploit its fabulous wealth.

Jazz realizes that she must fight with guts and determination to safeguard her heritage and to secure her future happiness.

c

Two Supreme Court Justices are dead. Their murders are connected only in one mind, and in one legal brief conceived by that mind.

Brilliant, beautiful and ambitious, New Orleans legal student Darby Shaw little realises that her speculative brief will penetrate to the highest levels of power in Washington and cause shockwaves there.

Shockwaves that will see her boyfriend atomised in a bomb blast, that will send hired killers chasing after her, that will propel her across the country to meet the one man, investigative reporter Gray Grantham, who is as near the truth as she is.

Together can they stay alive long enough to expose the startling truth behind The Pelican Brief?

d

On the forty-fifth floor of the Nakamoto Tower in downtown L.A., a grand opening celebration is in full swing at the new American headquarters of the immense Japanese conglomerate.

On the forty-sixth floor, in an empty conference room, the dead body of a beautiful young woman is discovered.

The investigation begins... and immediately becomes a headlong chase through a twisting maze of industrial intrigue... a no-holds-barred conflict in which control of a vital American technology is the fiercely coveted prize - and the Japanese saying 'business is war' takes on a terrifying reality...

e

'A real valentine from hell' – *Time Out*

When Sandor snatched little Joe from the path of a London tube train, he was quick to make clear the terms of the rescue. 'I saved your life', he told the homeless youngster, 'so your life belongs to me now.'

Sandor began to tell him a fairy-tale: an ageing prince, a kidnapped princess chained by one ankle, a missed rendezvous. But what did this mysterious story have to do with Sandor's preparations? Joe had only understood his own role. Sandor had taught him the new word. He was a *gallowglass*, the servant of a Chief ...

B **Work in groups** Discuss these questions:

- Are CD-ROMs and online information going to replace printed books, magazines and newspapers?
- What kinds of information do you prefer to get from a computer or from books?
- In the future, will students use computers instead of text books?
- If a book you want to read for pleasure is available both as a book and as a CD-ROM, which version would you buy? Why?

A Look at these sentences, all of which contain relative clauses, and add any missing commas. If no commas are missing, put a tick ✓.

1 The book I've just finished reading is by Agatha Christie. ✓
2 Agatha Christie who wrote detective stories died in 1976 when she was 86.
3 Her books some of which have been made into films have all been best sellers.
4 Hercule Poirot who is Belgian is Agatha Christie's most famous creation.
5 The person who committed the murder was the butler.
6 The knife which was used in the murder was taken from the kitchen.
7 The victim's elder brother who lived in Paris was an accountant.
8 His sister who lived in London worked in an office but his other sister was still at school.

See the Grammar Reference section on page 177.

B 1 Work in pairs Join these pairs of sentences, beginning with the words given. Each can be joined *in two different ways*. Make sure you use commas in the right places.

1 Hercule Poirot knows all the answers. He solved the mystery.
  Hercule Poirot, *who solved the mystery, knows all the answers.*
  Hercule Poirot, *who knows all the answers, solved the mystery.*

2 New York is a wonderful city. I'd love to go there one day.
  New York _____ .

3 Ms Fortune was a writer. She was found dead in the cellar.
  Ms Fortune _____ .

4 My friend is a great reader. He told me all about a book he'd just read.
  My friend _____ .

5 A car was stolen. It was found at the airport.
  The car _____ .

6 Science fiction is about the future and space travel. Some people love it, others hate it.
  Science fiction _____ .

7 You recommended the book to me. It was very good.
  The book _____ .

8 A simplified edition is easier to read than the original. It's shorter.
  A simplified edition _____ .

2 Join another pair Compare your sentences. Which of the two possibilities do you prefer?

C Choose the best alternative to complete the gaps in this summary.

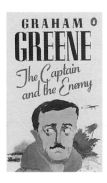

'The Captain and the Enemy' is a novel ¹_____ was written by Graham Greene in 1988. It is a story ²_____ a boy, Victor Baxter, ³_____ father (⁴_____ he calls 'the Devil') loses him in game of backgammon to a man ⁵_____ is only known as 'the Captain'. The Captain, ⁶_____ real name is never revealed, appears to be some sort of criminal. ⁷_____ the boy has been taken away from his boarding school, he is brought up by a woman called Lisa, ⁸_____ is the Captain's mistress. From time to time the Captain returns to visit them, ⁹_____ for months on end they are alone together. ¹⁰_____ this time a close relationship develops ¹¹_____ them, and Lisa treats Victor as if he is her son. Eventually, the Captain goes to live in Panama, ¹²_____ tells them that they cannot join him there ¹³_____ he has made enough money. ¹⁴_____ he is 18, Victor leaves Lisa and gets his own flat but ¹⁵_____ her death in a road accident, he flies to Panama to meet the Captain . . .

1	which	what	who	it
2	about	by	on	of
3	who	whose	his	without
4	which	who	whose	him
5	who	whom	whose	his
6	who	whom	whose	his
7	Before	After	Although	Now
8	she	who	because	that
9	because	but	when	so
10	Before	While	During	On
11	among	over	between	to
12	still	but	though	he
13	after	by	until	if
14	When	So	Then	Why
15	because	while	as	after

13.5 Using suffixes – 2: Actions and people

(A) **Work in pairs**   What is the meaning of the words in green in these sentences?

1 It was a deafening noise.

2 What's the difference between a psychologist and a psychiatrist?

3 Are you going to read the simplified edition or the original edition?

4 Who was the inventor of the Walkman?

5 Most national theatres and opera houses are subsidised by the government.

6 Do you think a photographer is an artist?

(B) 1 Add more examples to the lists below, using these root words. Write them down, because in some cases the spelling changes.

bright ✓   clear ✓   deaf   general   intense   loose   memory   personal   simple   straight
summary   weak

-ise/-ize	criticise	sympathise	subsidise	....
-en	sweeten	strengthen	harden	*brighten* ....
-ify	classify	horrify	terrify	*clarify* ....

Notice that these verbs don't have a suffix:

↑   raise   lift
    heat   warm   melt

↓   lower   drop
    cool   chill   freeze

2 🔊 The correct answers are recorded. Listen carefully to the pronunciation and practise it.

(C) 1 Add more examples to the lists, using these root words:

account   art   assist   collect   correspond   direct   drive   edit   guitar   inspect
novel   paint   piano   report   science   speak   supervise   violin   visit

-er	employer	photographer	reader	....
-or	author	inventor	conductor	....
-ant	participant	servant	....	
-ent	resident	student	....	
-ist	chemist	biologist	motorist	....

2 🔊 The correct answers are recorded. Listen carefully to the pronunciation.

(D) Use the words in red at the end of each line to form new words that fit the spaces.

1 The .... needed two .... to help with the experiment.   **science   assist**

2 After the road had been .... , every .... drove faster.   **wide   motor**

3 Who gave the better performance: the .... or the .... ?   **piano   violin**

4 The knife may need .... before it is used.   **sharp**

5 Can a horse .... travel faster than a .... ?   **ride   cycle**

6 Most of the .... of the USA are .... or their ....   **inhabit   immigrate descend**

7 The voice that tells a story is the .... , who isn't really the same as the ....   **narrate write**

8 Would you .... this book as a thriller or science fiction?   **class**

13.6 Words + prepositions – 2   PREPOSITIONS

Fill the gaps in these sentences with a suitable preposition.

1 Are you interested ....*in*.... local politics, by any chance? You are? Well, I'd like to introduce you .... George, who is involved .... politics: he's our local councillor. Now that George has been elected we all hope .... better things in the future. Many local people don't have much confidence .... politicians but George will change all that. For example, some people are upset about the lack .... a good library in our town, but George says he's going to deal .... that problem.

2 Bill was engaged .... Liz for two years and then got married .... Jane! I'll never forgive Bill .... the way he treated Liz.

3 There's no such thing as a perfect book – it all depends .... the individual. If you've bought a book, you can't exchange it .... a different one – but you can if you've borrowed it .... a library.

4 She said she could put up the bookshelves by herself, but he insisted .... helping her. In fact, he kept on interfering .... what she was trying to do.

13.7 Writing against the clock   EXAM TECHNIQUES

In the exam, you'll have to write two compositions in 1 hour 30 minutes – including the time you need to read the paper and decide which question in Part 2 to choose, making notes before you write and checking your work afterwards.

From now on, whenever you write a composition, time yourself. Try to finish every composition within 40 minutes, including time for thinking, planning and making notes – plus five minutes at the end for checking it through and making small changes. If you can't fit all this into 40 minutes yet, try to lose five minutes each time you do a composition until you can. But don't sacrifice too much planning time or time for checking.

1 ✍ **If you're reading one of the set books, look at Activity *19* for a special list of composition titles. If you aren't reading a set book, answer this question.**

Recommend a book by a writer from your country to an English-speaking friend. Write a letter (120–180 words) explaining what it's about and why your friend will enjoy it or find it interesting.

2 Work in groups   Before you begin, decide on a suitable book to write about.

3 Work alone   Time yourself. If you take a break between each step, stop the clock and restart it when you begin again.

1 Make notes before you start.

2 Write the letter, leaving enough space to make small changes and corrections later if necessary.

3 Count the number of words. (It's quicker to count the number of words in an average line and then multiply by the number of lines, than to count every single word.)

4 Check your work and make any changes and corrections that are necessary.

5 Stop the clock! How long did it take? Keep a record of your time.

In the exam, it may be best to make notes on *both* compositions at the beginning, in case your mind goes blank later. For Question 1, which is compulsory, make sure you include *all* the relevant information – it may be best to make notes for this by highlighting the main points on the question paper itself.

If you leave two or three blank lines between each paragraph, there will be room to add an extra sentence later. If your paragraphs are all squashed up together, you won't be able to do this. But remember that you'll be writing in the answer booklet so you may not have a huge amount of space.

14

All in a day's work

14.1 Earning a living   VOCABULARY

A **Work in groups**   Ask your partners these questions:

- What do you (plan to) do for a living?
- What do the other members of your family do for a living?

B **Choose the best alternative to complete these sentences.**

  1 A doctor is a member of a respected ....
occupation   profession   trade   work

  2 It's wise to think about choosing a .... before leaving school.
business   career   living   vocation

  3 You'll probably have to fill .... an application form.
down   in   on   through

  4 If you're a(n) .... , you have to do what your boss tells you.
employee   employer   director   manager

  5 It's difficult these days for anyone to find a well-paid .... job.
eternal   permanent   reliable   stable

  6 She was .... after three years with the company.
advanced   elevated   promoted   raised

  7 An apprentice is required to do several years' ....
coaching   education   formation   training

  8 A retired person is paid a ....
grant   pension   rent   scholarship

  9 If you are paid monthly, rather than weekly, you receive ....
revenue   a reward   a salary   wages

  10 Some of my work is quite interesting, but a lot of it is just ....
habit   practice   routine   tradition

C **In these sentences *three* alternatives are correct and *two* are wrong. Choose the three best alternatives for each.**

  1 She's looking for a better position with another ....
association   company   firm   organisation   society

  2 Ford is a multi-national corporation that .... motor vehicles.
constructs   fabricates   makes   manufactures   produces

  3 He was .... because he was an unreliable and lazy worker.
dismissed   dispatched   fired   left   sacked

  4 A good worker is usually someone with the right kind of ....
experience   experiences   experiment   personality   qualifications

  5 All the members of our .... are expected to work hard.
department   personal   personnel   staff   team

D **Work in groups**   Discuss these questions:

- What is the most *difficult* job you can imagine?
- What is the most *unpleasant* job you can imagine? And the most *pleasant*?
- If you could choose any job in the world, what would it be? Why?

"Yes, darling! Mummy has to keep her hands lovely in case she ever wants to go back to brain surgery."

Paper 5: Speaking EXAM TECHNIQUES

A **1** 🖉 **Highlight what you think are the most important points in this description of Paper 5.**

The Speaking paper is in four parts. There are two candidates and two examiners. One examiner will tell you what to do, ask you questions and sometimes join in the conversation. The other will sit silently listening to you, assessing the way you communicate in English.

In Parts 1 and 2, which last about eight minutes in total, you'll be talking mainly to the examiner, not to each other.

PART 1 The examiner asks you some personal questions about yourself, where you live, your interests, future plans, etc.

PART 2 You are each in turn given some pictures and you have to talk about them for about a minute, comparing and contrasting them. The examiner may ask you further questions and there may be a short discussion.

In Parts 3 and 4, which last about seven minutes in total, you'll be talking mainly to each other, but with the examiner helping to keep the discussion going.

PART 3 You and the other candidate are both given another picture or set of pictures. You take part in a problem-solving activity or discussion.

PART 4 The examiner then leads a discussion, encouraging you both to develop your opinions on the topic of the picture(s).

The examiners will be assessing these aspects of your spoken English: grammar, vocabulary, pronunciation, fluency, interactive communication and task achievement.

After taking part in the speaking activities and discussions in this book, this paper will not be difficult for you. The only problems may be:

- Nerves – Everyone feels nervous in exams. The examiners are aware of this and they know how to put you at your ease.
- The other candidate – It may be hard to have a discussion with a person you don't get on with, or whose English is much worse or better than yours. The examiners are aware of this problem, and the other candidate's performance will *not* affect your marks in any way. But you are expected to *communicate* with each other – so if you give the other candidate a chance to join in the discussion, you'll get better marks.

2 **Work in pairs** Compare the points you've highlighted. What points were new to you? Do you have any other questions about this paper?

B **Work in groups of four** You're going to take part in two mock exams. First, Students A and B are 'Candidates' and Students C and D are 'Examiners'.

1 👥 The two 'Examiners' should look at Activity *25*. Candidates: wait for your instructions. After the activity discuss what happened – and how the two Candidates could perform better.

2 👥 Swap roles. The two new 'Examiners' should look at Activity *47*. Candidates: wait for your instructions. After the activity discuss how the Candidates could perform better.

14.3 Joining sentences – 2: Conjunctions

A Match the beginnings on the left to the endings on the right.

See the Grammar Reference section on page 177.

1 She's been looking for work	after the interview had gone so badly.
2 She sent in her application	as soon as she saw the advertisement.
3 She felt very nervous	because she had such good qualifications.
4 She didn't do well in the interview	before she had even left the building.
5 She didn't think she'd get the job	before the interview.
6 The other candidates were well qualified	even though she is intelligent and charming.
7 She was amazed that they offered her the job	since leaving university.
8 She got the job	so she wasn't very optimistic.

B 1 Complete the second sentence so that it has a similar meaning to the first line, using the word given in red. Do not change the word given. You must use between two and five words, including the word given.

1 We went out for a walk in spite of the heavy rain.
although　We went out for a walk ~~although it was raining~~ hard.

2 My dictionary weighs a lot. Still, I've brought it with me.
even　I've brought my dictionary with me .... heavy.

3 I phoned the office. I wanted to tell them when I'd be arriving.
let　I phoned the office .... my time of arrival.

4 I was busy in the office. Meanwhile my friends were enjoying their day off.
fun　My friends were .... I was working.

5 I want to go for a swim at lunchtime. However, there may not be enough time.
have　If I .... go for a swim at lunchtime.

6 The bus drivers are on strike tomorrow. Nevertheless, I'm going to try to get to work.
despite　I'm going to try to get to work .... tomorrow.

2 Write a single, long sentence combining these short sentences, incorporating the words in red You may need to rearrange some of the ideas.

1 You could get a part-time job. It would help you to pay for your course. It would also give you useful experience.
besides　Getting ....

2 She hasn't finished her studies yet. She has no idea what kind of job she wants to do. She'll decide that when she gets her degree.
until　She can't ....

3 Some school subjects seem irrelevant to the world of work. Other subjects have a direct relevance. Languages are likely to be useful in work. History may not be so useful.
such as　Although ....

4 He has been offered a new job. It is in another city. It sounds really interesting. Living in another city would be interesting. Moving to another city would mean leaving his family. But he'll probably take the job.
even though　He's probably going to take ....

C **Work in pairs**　Write a single sentence to explain each headline. Don't use *and* or *but*. When you've finished join another pair and compare your sentences.

1 **FACTORY CLOSES – 500 lose jobs**
　500 workers have lost their jobs because a factory has been closed down.

2 **Kitten rescue – teacher rewarded**

3 **LINER SINKS – ALL SURVIVE**

4 **HEAVY RAIN IN MOUNTAINS – LANDSLIDE THREATENS VILLAGES**

5 **PRESIDENT PROMISES TAX CUTS – LANDSLIDE VICTORY PREDICTED IN ELECTION**

6 **Pound Down, Dollar Up – exports rise**

7 **Teachers to get pay rise – strike called off**

8 **NEW FACTORY OPENS – 500 new jobs created**

14.4 First jobs LISTENING

A You'll hear four people describing the first jobs they had. Decide which of the alternatives best completes each sentence. Read the questions before you listen to the recording.

1 **Jill** first worked in a studio as a ....
   a) designer   b) secretary   c) typist

2 She got into trouble when ....
   a) her boss returned from holiday   b) her boss was on holiday
   c) she returned from holiday

3 Some weeks later, when her boss wrote her a letter, ...
   a) the horrible woman was on holiday   b) Jill returned to the studio
   c) the horrible woman had left

4 **David** enjoyed himself in the library by ....
   a) giving people the wrong books   b) putting books on the wrong shelves
   c) guessing what books people were going to borrow

5 **Richard** found that the other postmen in Berlin used to ....
   a) arrive early for work   b) help him   c) think he was strange

6 His journey to work took about ....
   a) 30 minutes   b) one hour   c) 90 minutes

7 Compared with an English postman's work, a German postman's work seemed ....
   a) enjoyable   b) responsible   c) tiring

8 If **Joscelyn** didn't sell any encyclopedias, she ....
   a) didn't earn any money   b) didn't earn enough to live on
   c) earned just enough to live on

9 She found that the key to success in the job was ....
   a) having a sense of humour   b) not being shy   c) talking to people

10 She earned enough to pay for ....
   a) a new car   b) a holiday   c) her education

In the exam, you don't have to get *all* the answers right – just most of them. As you'll hear the recording twice, you'll always get a second chance to try to answer the difficult questions.

B **Work in groups or as a class** If anyone has worked (even only holiday work), get them to describe their first job. First, write down *four* questions you'd like to ask them about it.

14.5 Words + prepositions – 3 PREPOSITIONS

Fill the gaps in these sentences with suitable prepositions.

1 Eric quarrelled ....with.... Louise ...about... the preparations .... the party. I couldn't go because I was suffering .... flu. But I thanked them .... inviting me.

2 Sarah reminds me .... Julia Roberts, but they aren't related .... each other!

3 You can never rely .... Jim to provide you .... useful information. And I'm tired .... waiting .... him to make up his mind when he has to make a decision.

4 The store detective suspected the man .... stealing the goods .... the shop, but the receipt proved that they had been paid ....

5 I've got plenty of sandwiches. Would you like to share them .... me?

6 On behalf of the students and staff, I'd like to welcome you .... our school.

7 You can only succeed .... an exam if you revise carefully .... it.

8 Helen worked .... ACME plc, where she was responsible .... dealing with complaints .... customers. But the work was so unrewarding that she has just resigned .... the job.

14.6 How to create a good impression . . . READING

A **1** **Work in pairs** Before you read the article below, note down two things you think candidates *should* do at a job interview and two things they *shouldn't* do.

2 Read the first part of the article and then decide which of the points (1–10) are DOs and which are DON'Ts.

3 Read the next part of the article and decide which of the points (11–20) are DOs or DON'Ts.

HOW TO CREATE A GOOD IMPRESSION AT YOUR FIRST INTERVIEW

With unemployment so high, and often scores of applicants chasing every job, you have to count yourself lucky to be called for an interview. If it's your first, you're bound to be nervous. (In fact if you're not nervous, maybe your attitude is wrong!) But don't let the jitters side-track you from the main issue – which is getting this job. The only way you can do that is by creating a good impression on the person who is interviewing you.

1 Find out as much as you can about the job beforehand. Ask the job centre or employment agency for as much information as possible.
2 Walk into the interview chewing gum, sucking on a sweet or smoking.
3 Jot down your qualifications and experience and think about how they relate to the job. Why should the employer employ you and not somebody else?
4 Choose your interview clothing with care; no one is going to employ you if you look as though you've wandered out of a disco. Whether you like it or not, appearance counts.
5 Make sure you know where the interview office is and how to get there.
6 Be on time, or better, a few minutes early.

7 Bring with you any school certificates, samples of your work or letters of recommendation from your teachers or anyone else you might have worked part-time for.
8 Bring a pen; you will probably be asked to fill in an application form. Answer all the questions as best you can. And write neatly. The interviewer will be looking at the application during the interview; he or she must be able to read it.
9 Have a light meal to eat, and go to the toilet. If you don't, you may well be thinking about your insides during the interview.
10 Have a drink beforehand to give you courage.

The interview

The interview is designed to find out more about you and to see if you are suitable for the job. The interviewer will do this by asking you questions. The way you answer will show what kind of person you are and if your education, skills and experience match what they're looking for.

11 Forget to shake hands with the interviewer.
12 Make a real effort to answer every question the interviewer asks. Be clear and concise. Never answer 'Yes' or 'No' or shrug.
13 Smoke or sit down until you are invited to.
14 Give the interviewer a hard time by giggling, yawning, rambling on unnecessarily or appearing cocky or argumentative.
15 Admit it if you do not know something about the more technical aspects of the job. Stress that you are willing to learn.
16 Show some enthusiasm when the job is explained to you. Concentrate on what the interviewer is saying,

and if he or she asks if you have any questions, have at least one ready to show that you're interested and have done your homework.
17 Stress poor aspects of yourself, like your problem of getting up in the morning. Always show your best side: especially your keenness to work and your sense of responsibility.
18 Sell yourself. This doesn't mean exaggerating (you'll just get caught out) or making your experience or interests seem unimportant (if you sell yourself short, no one will employ you).
19 Ask questions at the close of the interview. For instance, about the pay, hours, holidays, or if there is a training programme.
20 After the interview, think about how you presented yourself: could you have done better? If so, and if you do not get the job, you can be better prepared when you are next called for an interview. Good luck!

B 1 🖉 Highlight these words and phrases in the first paragraph of the article. Then work out their meanings from their context – don't use a dictionary.

  1 scores of
     a) a few   b) a large number of   c) hardly any
  2 chasing
     a) escaping from   b) running after   c) applying for
  3 count yourself
     a) congratulate yourself for being   b) feel proud that you are
     c) consider yourself to be
  4 the jitters
     a) over-confidence   b) nervousness   c) lack of experience
  5 side-track
     a) distract   b) emphasise   c) interest
  6 issue
     a) argument   b) purpose   c) difficulty

2 🖉 Highlight these words and phrases among the DOs and DON'Ts. Then work out their meanings from their context without using a dictionary.

  1 giggling (in point 14)
     a) arguing   b) coughing   c) laughing in a silly way
  2 rambling on (14)
     a) talking for too long   b) going for a walk   c) hesitating
  3 cocky (14)
     a) nervous   b) proud   c) over-confident
  4 done your homework (16)
     a) practised being interviewed   b) worked hard at school
     c) found out as much information as possible about the company
  5 get caught out (18)
     a) be found to be lying   b) be in danger   c) be wasting your time
  6 sell yourself short (18)
     a) are too nervous   b) are too modest   c) don't talk enough

3 Now use a dictionary to look up the ones you couldn't guess from the context.

4 Discuss these questions:
  • What kind of people are the intended readers of this article?
  • Which do you think are the three most important points?
  • Can you add one more DO and one more DON'T to the list?

C Work in groups   Imagine that you're giving advice *not* to someone who's going to a job interview but to someone who hasn't taken part in an *oral examination* before. Which of the points in the article are in any way relevant to an FCE speaking exam?

"I'm basically a problem solver – as long as the problems are simple."

14.7 Using suffixes – 3: Abstract nouns

WORD STUDY

A 1 Add more examples of nouns formed from the verbs listed. Check the spelling changes in a dictionary.

accept ✓   achieve ✓   agree   approve   astonish   collect   create   decide   direct   employ   encourage   entertain   imagine   improve   insist   insure   prefer   produce   propose   protect   replace   resist   retire   survive

Nouns from verbs

-ment	arrangement argument development *achievement* ....
-ance	performance appearance entrance *acceptance* ....
-ence	reference interference pretence ....
-ion	prediction action education ....
-tion	description addition ....
-ation	pronunciation qualification explanation ....
-al	arrival refusal denial ....

2 📼 Listen to the correct answers in the recording and practise the pronunciation.

B 1 Add more examples of nouns formed from the adjectives listed. Use a dictionary to check your spelling, if necessary.

absent ✓   aware ✓   brilliant ✓   careless   efficient   fluent   formal   happy   important   lonely   nervous   patient   polite   popular   possible   present   private   proficient   real   rude   secure   selfish   significant   simple

Nouns from adjectives

-ness	kindness friendliness shyness *awareness* ....
-ance	arrogance reluctance relevance *brilliance* ....
-ence	violence confidence difference *absence* ....
-ity	ability curiosity generosity ....
-cy	accuracy frequency redundancy ....

2 📼 Listen to the correct answers in the recording and practise the pronunciation.

3 What *adjective* do you associate with each of these abstract nouns?

anxiety   freedom   strength   wisdom   boredom   pride   hunger   thirst

C Part 5 of the Use of English paper is a word-formation exercise. You may have to add a prefix or a suffix (or both!) to the root word. If the gap requires a verb, make sure the tense is right.

Read the text below. Use the word given in capitals at the end of each line to form a word that fits in the space in the same line.

One of the ¹ .... people have in their work these days is coming to terms with ² .... Technology is changing fast, and many of the skills we learn today may no longer be ³ .... in the future. We should all expect to be ⁴ .... several times during our working lives.

   The experience of ⁵ .... is typical: today computers are used in every business. Without a good working ⁶ .... of computers you can't expect to find ⁷ .... these days. It is also absolutely essential for employees to have an ⁸ .... of how various software applications work.

   Although computers are more user-friendly than they used to be, keyboard skills are still essential. Voice ⁹ .... technology is unlikely to provide a ¹⁰ .... for the keyboard – whose layout is exactly the same as an old-fashioned typewriter.

DIFFICULT
MODERNISE
USE
TRAIN
COMPUTERISE
KNOW
EMPLOY
AWARE

RECOGNISE
REPLACE

14.8 Including relevant information   WRITING

When writing a composition, include only ideas and information that are relevant – if you're writing a composition about 'my ideal job', there's no point in writing about all the jobs you would *hate* to do!

A **1 Work in pairs**   **Imagine that you or a friend wants to apply for the job below:**

* What information would be *relevant* in your letter? What information would be *irrelevant*?
* What questions would you ask to find out more about the job?

> We are looking for an intelligent, self-confident person who is fluent in at least one foreign language. The work involves answering correspondence, meeting visitors and clients from abroad in the office and talking to clients on the phone. The working week will be 20 hours per week Monday–Friday, mornings or afternoons only. Previous experience would be useful but not essential.
>
> Apply in writing to Ms Pat Brown, ACME Enterprises, 13 Armada Way, Brookfield BF2 7LJ

2 Look at these two letters. What important information is *missing* from each of them? What *irrelevant* information is included? Which of the letters do you prefer and why?

1

Dear Sir,

   After reading your advertisement in the Evening Chronicle, I wonder if I might be suitable for the part-time post advertised? I am studying at Brookfield University. My typing is quite good and I enjoy dealing with people.

   I am 1.73 metres tall, have dark brown curly hair and I wear glasses.

   Please let me know if you think I may be suitable for the post. I can come for an interview at any time convenient for you because if I have to miss any lectures, I can always get the notes from my friend Bob. They don't keep an attendance record at the University.

   I would also like to know what kind of salary you are offering. And how many hours' work there would be per week.

   Yours sincerely,

2

Dear Ms Brown,

   I am interested in applying for the post advertised at the top of page 13 of the Evening Chronicle on 1st April.

   I am 20 years of age and in my second year at Brookfield University, where I am studying business administration. As my lectures take place in the mornings and evenings, I would be available to work in the afternoons from about 1.30 or 2 pm.

   I speak and write fluent Italian and some German, as well as English. I have had some experience of office work in my own country. I am available for interview any afternoon during the next two weeks. I would also be pleased to discuss my suitability for the post on the telephone – my number is 173982.

   Looking forward to hearing from you.

   Yours sincerely,

B **Write a letter of 120–180 words applying for the job on the right. Remember to make notes before you start. Check your work through afterwards and correct any mistakes you notice.**

   Time how long it takes you to write this composition, and check the number of words.

If you took longer than 45 minutes, you'll need to improve your speed. If you took less than 30 minutes, you may not be spending enough time planning beforehand or checking afterwards. Or your composition may be too short.

If you write too many words in the exam, the examiner will only look closely at the first 180 words of your composition – you may not get any credit for good material after the first 180 words. So keep to the word limit.

SIX MONTHS IN THE CARIBBEAN

The Palm Beach Resort is looking for outgoing fun-loving people to work for the winter season (November to April) as Sports and Leisure Assistants at its new beach resort on St Lucia in the Caribbean.

Depending on skills and personality, assistants will help to run water sports activities or other land sports, assist in running our daily excursions by boat and help to organise evening activities.

No special sports or management qualifications are required – the emphasis is on encouraging our guests, joining in with them and helping to make sure everything is running smoothly.

Write to us, telling us about yourself, which area(s) you'd be best suited for and why you think you're the right kind of person to work for us for six months.

15 Can you explain?

15.1 | Science and technology   VOCABULARY

A **Work in groups** **Look at the photos above and discuss these questions:**
- What do you think the photos show?
- What does each of the things shown do? How do they work?
- What's your favourite gadget or piece of equipment?

B **Fill the gaps in these sentences with a suitable word.**

1 A _molecule_ of water (H_2O) consists of two atoms of h............... and one of o............... .

2 The three main branches of science are: ch............... (the study of the elements that make up the universe), ph............... (the study of matter and natural forces) and b............... (the study of living things).

3 Technology is the activity of using scientific knowledge for p............... purposes.

4 Scientists can find out if a theory is true by carrying out e............... in a l............... .

5 Your idea might work in theory, but I don't think it would work in p............... .

6 A computer, the mouse and the keyboard are known as the h............... . Your word processor and other applications are known as s..............., which are stored on a ....

7 You can use the remote control to .... the volume on the TV – all you have to do is press a .... If you are unsure how it works, you should read the ....

8 Equipment needs to be .... regularly, otherwise it may .... unexpectedly at any time and it may be expensive to have it ....

9 Some common tools used by a .... are a hammer, a saw and a ....

10 To make a piece of furniture you need some wood, ... and some ....

C **1** **Work in pairs** **Think of some gadgets or equipment that you use at home or at work (e.g. bicycle, hairdryer, electric shaver, cassette player, scissors, can opener, etc.). Without getting too technical (and without opening them up to find out what's inside!), list the important controls and parts of components. Use a dictionary if necessary.**

2 **Join another pair** **Tell your partners what you have found out.**

15.2 Using the passive GRAMMAR REVIEW

A Fill the gaps in this table, which shows the basic structures used in the passive.

See the Grammar Reference section on page 179.

Active		Passive
They often do it.	→	It _is often done_ .
They are doing it now.	→	It _is being done_ now.
They did it yesterday.	→	It .... yesterday.
They were doing it last week.	→	It .... last week.
They have already done it.	→	It ....
They will do it eventually.	→	It .... eventually.
They will have done it before long.	→	It .... before long.
They had done it earlier.	→	It .... earlier.
They had to do it at once.	→	It .... at once.
They may not have done it yet.	→	It .... yet.

B **Work in pairs**   What are the differences in emphasis between the sentences in each pair?

1 If something doesn't work properly, it should be repaired by an expert.
2 If something doesn't work work properly, it should be repaired.
3 In 1982 Sony marketed the first camcorders.
4 Camcorders were first marketed in 1982.
5 Smoking is not permitted in restaurants in New York.
6 The New York Police Department doesn't permit people to smoke in restaurants.

C Complete the second sentence so that it has a similar meaning to the first sentence, using the word given in red. Do not change the word given. You must use between two and five words, including the word given.

marketed
1 Post-it™ Notes first went on sale in 1980.
Post-it™ Notes _were first marketed_ in 1980.

without
2 You can only see these particles through a microscope.
These particles .... a microscope.

everywhere
3 People are using computers in all kinds of places these days.
Computers .... nowadays.

must
4 You have to keep dangerous chemicals in a secure place.
Dangerous .... in a secure place.

made
5 3M are the manufacturers of Scotch Tape and Post-it™ Notes
Both Scotch Tape and Post-it™ Notes ....

probably
6 We are unlikely to discover intelligent life on other planets.
Intelligent life .... on other planets.

yet
7 This room is still very dirty.
This room .... cleaned.

shot
8 The killer of President Kennedy is unknown.
No one is sure who .... by.

D **1** **Work in pairs**   Can you guess when each of these things was invented or discovered?

aeroplane   bicycle   camcorder   computer   compact disc   light bulb
margarine   Post-it™ Notes   telephone   television   thermometer

1593   1840   1869   1876   1878   1903   1926   1943   1980   1982   1982

When do you think planes were first invented?   *I guess that the first plane was invented in 1903.*

2 Write *five* sentences beginning with *If…* about the inventions and discoveries.

If planes hadn't been invented, we'd all have to travel by train or ship.

15.3 **Paper 4: Listening** EXAM TECHNIQUES

A 1 Read this information about the Listening paper. Highlight the most important points.

There are four parts in Paper 4. You hear each part twice. There is time for you to read the questions before you have to answer them. The whole test lasts up to 45 minutes.

PART 1 You will hear people talking in eight different situations. Each conversation or speech lasts about 30 seconds. There are eight questions. You have to choose the best answer from three. For example:

This person is explaining what is wrong with her car. She is talking to

A a friend
B her child
C a mechanic

| A | 1 |

PART 2 This part consists of a broadcast or discussion, lasting about three minutes, with ten note-taking, sentence completion or open question items. For example:

Many inventions were discovered | by accident | 9 |

PART 3 You will hear five short monologues or extracts from conversations, each about 30 seconds in length. You have to select the correct answer from a list. There are five questions, but six possible answers. You may, for example, have to put a letter in a numbered box like this:

| D | 19 |

PART 4 You will hear a conversation lasting about three minutes. There are seven items, which may be three-option multiple-choice or true/false questions, for example. You may have to put a letter in a numbered box like this:

| T | 24 |

2 Work in pairs Compare what you have highlighted. If you have any further questions, ask your teacher.

B In this section we'll practise Parts 1 and 2. Your teacher will play each recording twice. Read the questions before you listen to the recording.

PART 1

You will hear people talking in eight different situations. Choose the best answer, **A, B** or **C**.

1   Listen to this woman talking to a friend. Why was she angry?
    A She missed a TV programme she wanted to see.
    B She wasted a day waiting for the repairman.
    C She changed her mind about having her TV repaired.

2   You've taken your camera to a shop for repair. When is it going to be ready?
    A Monday
    B Tuesday
    C Wednesday

3   Listen to this woman talking to a colleague. Why is she upset?
    A Someone has taken her camcorder.
    B Someone borrowed her camcorder without permission.
    C The rain may have damaged her camcorder.

4   Listen to a man talking about a gadget. Why do the batteries need replacing?
  A They need recharging.
  B They are the wrong type.
  C They are the wrong size.

5   You're in the kitchen at a friend's flat. What does he want you to do?
  A carry something for him
  B open a can
  C open a packet

6   Listen to a man talking to a colleague. What is he talking about?
  A a keyboard
  B a fax machine
  C a photocopier

7   Listen to a woman talking to a man. She's an expert, but what is she an expert in?
  A computers
  B publishing
  C business

8   Listen to this man talking. Who is he talking to?
  A students at a lecture
  B some friends in an informal conversation
  C customers at a sales demonstration

PART 2

You'll hear part of a broadcast about some important discoveries which happened by accident. Complete the notes which summarise what the speaker says. Write a word or a short phrase in each box.

Penicillin was discovered when Alexander Fleming found some mould growing on a laboratory dish he had left beside the [window **0**]

Radar is now used by [**9**] and [**10**]

[**11**]

Radar was discovered while scientists were looking for a new type of [**12**]

Teflon was discovered while chemists were doing research on [**13**]

Artificial sweeteners were discovered when scientists tasted a [**14**]

Chewing gum was discovered while scientists were looking for a [**15**]

Post-it™ Notes were invented when a researcher found an adhesive that wouldn't [**16**] or [**17**]

Over time the adhesive didn't become [**16**] or [**17**]

On Sundays the 3M researcher [**18**]

C **1 Work in pairs**   Check your answers and then discuss these questions:

- What was hard about the two parts? What was easy?
- How can you do better next time?

2 Work in groups   Find out your partners' views on luck by discussing these questions:

- Do you believe in good luck and bad luck?
- What part has good luck played in your life?
- What lucky accidents have happened to you?
- Are some people born lucky and others born unlucky?

15.4 Effortless cycling   READING

 A Read this advertisement. Eight sentences have been removed from it. Choose from A–I the words which fit each gap 1–8. There is one answer which you don't need to use.

TAKE THE SLOG OUT OF CYCLING

THE NEW SINCLAIR **ZETA** TRANSFORMS <u>YOUR</u> BIKE FROM PEDAL POWER TO ELECTRIC POWER IN MINUTES TO GIVE YOU EFFORTLESS CYCLING. JUST £144.95 DELIVERED.

SIMPLE 'ON' / 'OFF' CONTROL

MAXIMUM SPEED: 14 mph.
RANGE: 10 - 30 MILES.
NO TAX, INSURANCE OR LICENCE REQUIRED.

ZETA

SIMPLE BATTERY RECHARGE

 Have you ever cycled up a hill and had to get off and walk? Or cycled into a stiff breeze getting nowhere fast? Have you ever wished someone would come up with an ingenious invention to take the effort out of pedalling when it gets too much?

1 .... Called The Sinclair ZETA, it's a world's first. The inventor is none other than Sir Clive Sinclair, originator of the pocket calculator.

2 .... A neat, electric power unit transforms your bike from pedal power to electric power, greatly reducing the amount of effort needed to pedal.

To use ZETA, simply touch the "on/off" switch on the handlebar.

ZETA is so well engineered that it's maintenance free and works well in all weathers. 3 ....

MAINTENANCE FREE

The battery pack and charger are included in the price, and the battery can be fully recharged for less than 1p.

Charging can be carried out in situ, or by removing the battery from the unit. 4 ....

Depending on how much use it gets, one battery can last anything between 3–10 years.

The distance you can travel on one battery will vary depending on how much effort you put in. 5 .... If you don't pedal at all and let ZETA do all the work for you, then you can expect to get about 10 miles.

SAFE IN ANY WEATHER

The beauty of ZETA is that it will go wherever your bike goes, making it ideal for relaxed cycling with the family at weekends, or going to and from work without effort. 6 .... It has a top speed of 14 mph and can be legally ridden by anyone over the age of 14.

LESS THAN 1p FOR A RECHARGE

7 .... So, fill in the coupon at the bottom of the page, or telephone your order on 0933 279 300.

8 .... Your money will be refunded in full if not totally satisfied.

ENVIRONMENTALLY FRIENDLY

A And just like your bicycle, ZETA requires no licence, tax or insurance.

B By reserving ZETA for gradients and headwinds you could get up to 30 miles.

C Each ZETA carries an unconditional one-year guarantee.

D Gradients disappear, headwinds vanish, cycling becomes enjoyable again.

E Like most brilliant inventions, ZETA is simplicity itself.

F The device you've been waiting for has just been invented.

G What's more, you can fit it to your existing bike in a matter of minutes.

H You can purchase a back-up battery to carry with you to extend your range.

I Priced at just £144.95 including VAT and delivery, ZETA is not available in the shops.

B **1** **Work in pairs** Discuss these questions and make notes:

- What are the advantages and disadvantages of the ZETA?
- What information does the advertisement *not* give you which you would need before deciding whether to buy one? What questions would you ask the manufacturers?

2 **Join another pair** Compare your notes.

3 Write a letter to Sinclair Research asking the questions that you noted down earlier.

15.5 **How do they do that?** LISTENING AND SPEAKING

A **1** You'll hear two people talking about how to juggle. Listen to the conversation and number the explanations below in the correct sequence (1–4). Then match the pictures (a–d) to the explanations.

How to juggle

You will need:
three bean bags, balls or any other small evenly-shaped objects of the same size

Facing a bare wall, imagine two spots about 30cms away, in front of your forehead. Keep concentrating on them at all times.

[ ] Practise tossing one ball from your right hand so that it passes through the imaginary spot on the left and is caught by your left hand.

[ ] Hold two balls in your right hand and one in your left. Begin as for two balls, but toss the third ball when the second one passes through the spot on the right as it makes its way to your right hand. Do not worry about catching the third ball at first. It is more important to learn when to toss it, aiming for the spot on the left when it leaves your right hand. Keep practising and you will improve.

[ ] With a ball in each hand, start as before. When the first ball reaches the spot on the left, toss the second ball. Repeat this until both balls move evenly and you catch them every time.

[ ] Then toss it back to the right hand, making sure it passes through the spot on the right. Repeat this until you can toss one ball in an even figure-of-eight.

a

b

c

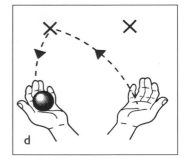
d

2 **Work in groups** Explain to your partners how to operate the gadget you have brought to class. The listeners should pretend to be ignorant rather than knowledgeable!

B **Work in small groups** Two of you should look at Activity *15*, the others at *39*. You'll see explanations of how two everyday devices work.

15.6 Opposites   WORD STUDY

A **1 Work in pairs** Write down the opposites of these adjectives, which are formed with a negative prefix (see 5.7):

accurate   comfortable   honest   kind   legal   lucky   mature   necessary   personal
pleasant   polite   regular   relevant   safe   true   visible   willing

inaccurate   uncomfortable

2 Many opposites are different words. Write down the opposites of these adjectives:

difficult   bright   arrogant   beautiful   cheap   cruel   dangerous   full   ill   nervous
noisy   old-fashioned   rude   soft   stale   tight   wide awake   wrong

easy   dull, dim

3 Write down the opposites of these verbs:

accept   oppose   find   raise   rise   tell the truth   win   mend   begin   turn on

reject   support

B Where a word has more than one meaning, there may be various opposites. Fill the gaps in this exercise.

1 I don't want a glass of *dry* wine, I want a glass of ....*sweet*.... wine.
2 The weather isn't going to be *dry*, it's sure to be ....
3 This isn't a *hard* exercise, it's ....
4 The bed wasn't *hard*, it was ....
5 A truck isn't a *light* vehicle, it's ....
6 At midnight it isn't *light*, it's ....
7 The sea wasn't *rough*, it was ....
8 A baby's skin isn't *rough*, it's ....
9 We won't *fail* the exam, we'll .... it.
10 She didn't *fail* to get the job, she .... in getting it.
11 I'm quite *poor* but a millionaire is very ....
12 His work was very *poor*, but hers was very ....
13 *Poor* Tom – he *lost* the match. .... Jim, he .... it!
14 I *lost* my pen yesterday, but now I've .... it.
15 He didn't *lose* weight, he .... it.

> If you can't think of the right word to express your idea, try thinking of the *opposite* – it may help you to remember the right word. If not, leave a gap in your composition and come back to it later.

15.7 Coming and going   VERBS AND IDIOMS

A Fill the gaps in these sentences with suitable forms of the verbs from the list below. In some cases there may be more than one possible answer.

bring   carry   come   deliver   fetch   go   take

1 Will you be able to .... and see us next weekend?
2 Will you be able to .... and see them in London?
3 I'm certainly going to .... a swimsuit with me when I go to the coast.
4 .... round to my house tonight and .... a friend with you if you like.
5 Don't forget to .... a pencil and a rubber to the exam with you.
6 The goods were .... to the shop in a van.
7 I'm just going to my room to .... my glasses – I'll be back in a minute.
8 It was very kind of you to .... my suitcase for me.

B Replace the words in green with a phrasal verb with *come* or *go* using the words on the right.

1 Bob has been Mary's boyfriend for a year.   **out with**

   Bob has been going out with Mary for a year.

2 While I was going through my drawers I found these old love letters.   **across**

3 You shouldn't wear those red socks, they don't match your grey suit.   **with**

4 The beach is washed clean by the sea when the tide rises, and you   **in**
  can see the rocks sticking out of the water when the tide falls.   **out**

5 The date on this yoghurt is 1 May: it must have gone bad by now.   **off**

6 A bomb has exploded and several people have been hurt.   **off**

7 She left at 7 a.m. and we never saw her again.   **off**

8 He entered the competition and won a Caribbean cruise.   **in for**

9 Hurry up! We have to be at the station in half an hour.   **on**

10 Before we continue, let's examine the correct answers to this exercise. **on**   **over**

15.8 / Describing a process   WRITING

A Decide what is 'good' and 'bad' about these paragraphs:

Anything you write is going to be read by another person – and you want to inform and interest that person. Always try to imagine how your reader will react. Put yourself in your reader's place as you write.

You can assume that the examiner knows something about the same subjects that you know – but he or she may not be an expert.

> A computer mouse has little wheels inside. When you move the mouse from left to right, the pointer on the screen moves. When you want to move the pointer up or down, you move the mouse towards you or away from you.

> A microwave oven is very useful for preparing food quickly and re-heating cooked food. To work it you press buttons on the control panel to set the time you want it to operate for and select the power setting you require. Then you place the food on a non-metallic plate and put it in the oven. Then the turntable starts to revolve and the microwaves go into the food, which contains water molecules. These molecules heat up by radiation and the heat is conducted to the surrounding food, making that hot too.

B ✍ Write an explanation of how another everyday process works – for example, a telephone, a compact disc, a cassette, etc. First of all, make notes of the main points you want to make in the composition. If possible, discuss your notes with another student before you start writing.

You may prefer to describe one of the processes shown in Activity *15* or *39* – but the information contained within the diagrams must be given in words. And the whole process should be in your own words, not copied word-for-word!

When you check your work afterwards, look systematically for mistakes you may have made in each of these areas:

– **Spelling** *What was the affect of this?*

– **Prepositions** *I'm interested for science.*

– **Verb forms and endings** *I was gave it.*   *If I would be rich …*   *She live in London.*

– **Articles** *I'm interested in the science.*

16

Keeping up to date

16.1 The press, politics and crime   VOCABULARY

A 1 Work in pairs   Complete this questionnaire for your partner.

NEWS QUESTIONNAIRE

1 Where do you find out about the news? Number these sources in order of importance:

☐ national newspaper   ☐ local newspaper   ☐ magazine   ☐ TV
☐ radio   ☐ other people

2 Which of these adjectives best describes what you think about the news? Number them in order. I think the news is:

☐ depressing   ☐ interesting   ☐ boring   ☐ annoying   ☐ amusing
☐ relevant   ☐ irrelevant

3 What event was the main news topic yesterday?

---

2 Join another pair   Compare your questionnaires. How different are your answers?

B   In these sentences *two* alternatives are correct and the others are wrong. Choose the two best alternatives for each.

1 I've only had time to read the .... in this morning's paper.

   columns   headings   headlines ✓   main story ✓

2 I read an interesting .... in the paper the other day.

   article   information   news   report

3 A newspaper's opinions are given in its ....

   cartoons   editorial   leader column   reports

4 The terrorists who hijacked the plane last night are still holding ten ....

   casualties   hostages   pedestrians   people   refugees   victims

5 According to the newspaper, a .... has started in Transylvania.

   civil service   civil war   return   revolution

6 Over 100 people are believed to have died in the ....

   earthquake   earthshake   explosion   bomb

7 Even in some democratic countries it is compulsory to vote in a(n) ....

   constituency   election   referendum   selection

8 In Britain the leader of the majority party in parliament is the ....

   chancellor   president   PM   prime minister   MP   sovereign

9 The police have .... the man who is suspected of committing the murder.

   arrested   captivated   caught   court   imprisoned   punished

10 Over £2 million was .... in the robbery.

   ceased   liberated   robbed   seized   stolen

11 The burglar was sentenced to 18 months in ....

   dock   gaol   goal   jail   jury   trial

12 He was .... of the crime and fined £500.

   convicted   found guilty   found innocent   responsible

C 1 Work in pairs   Think of the big news stories of the past seven days. Make a chart showing: the main news event each day, the country where it happened and your comment on it.

2 Join another pair   Compare your charts.

16.2   What happened?   WRITING

A 1 Work in groups   What do you think the story is behind these headlines?

    1 Woman left 'granny' in part-exchange for car

    2 Teenager's flat stripped bare after message misunderstood

    3 **Wash-day kitten comes out clean**

2   One of you should look at Activity 3, one at 8, and the other(s) at 12.

B 1 Work in pairs   Look at the photographs below and decide what's happening in each one. What happened before and what is likely to happen next?

2   Choose one of the pictures and imagine that you are one of the people in it. Work out a short story which either starts or ends with the event in the picture. Then do the same with a different picture.

C 1   Look at this announcement in an international magazine for students. Imagine you've decided to enter the competition with one of the stories you discussed in B.

> ► SHORT STORY COMPETITIO**N** ◄
>
> **FIRST PRIZE: Two weeks in London!**
>
> Write a 150-word story based on a photograph and send it with the photo to us. The ten best stories and photos will be published in our June issue. The one that our readers vote the best will win the first prize.

2   Write your story in 45 minutes, without using a dictionary. Make notes before you start. Remember to check your work through and correct any mistakes in spelling and grammar – especially verb forms and endings, prepositions and articles.

3 Work in groups   Vote for the best story.

Shoplifting in America   READING

A **1** **Read this article and then look at the questions below.**

Krazy Kirk meets Dr Shortage

'SHRINKAGE' was a hot topic of conversation at the annual congress of America's retailers in New York, which ended on January 16th. Given the fact that store groups are going bust all over the land, getting smaller seems to be the least of their worries. But shrinkage does not mean reducing a store's size. The term is the industry's euphemism for shoplifting, which is itself a euphemism for stealing. And thieves are threatening to send still more of America's shopkeepers to the bankruptcy courts.

America's shops lose 2% of their merchandise to thieves compared with 1.5% for Canada's shops and less than 1% for shops in Japan. Even the American figure may not sound like much, but in the low-margin business of retailing, where moving large volumes of goods quickly is the key to success, a 2% loss can wipe out a store's profits.

A recent survey of 160 big American retailers indicated that these chains spend a total of $365m a year, or 0.3% of sales, trying to stop thieves. And yet their average losses are still 1.9% of sales. Department stores, with a shrinkage rate of 2.2%, and drug stores, with 2.3%, do significantly worse.

Thirteen shoppers are caught thieving for every employee who is caught. But at $1,350, the value of merchandise recovered from employees is seven times greater. So retailers are policing workers as well as shoppers. Some of the methods now being employed by stores to combat shrinkage sound weird, but shopkeepers are in a mood to try almost anything.

Saks Fifth Avenue, a chain of high-class department stores, believes 'gimmicks, gimmicks and more gimmicks' are needed to keep staff conscious of security. A Saks manager who has forgotten to lock a door or close a cash register will find a helium balloon floating beside his desk the following morning. Saks gives a cash bonus to anyone

detecting a shoplifter. And the chain has installed two types of cameras in its stores: highly visible ones to deter thieves, and hidden ones to record those who try to snatch something. The company displays as many as six television monitors at employees' entrances.

Loehmann's, a New York-based chain specialising in ladies' clothes, believes in frequent stock checks. Where other chains physically count their stock once or twice a year, Loehmann's has always done a monthly check. If a store's shrinkage hits an unacceptable level, senior managers arrive to find out why. In the most persistent cases, the backgrounds of recently hired staff and cleaners are investigated. The company has also found that communal dressing rooms discourage shoplifters. And its 'no refunds' policy makes it harder for dishonest cashiers and customers to collude.

Carter Hawley Hale, a group that owns five department-store chains, cut its shrinkage to 2% in 1990 from 3.5% four years ago with a variety of stunts. At The Broadway, one of its stores, a mock radio station was set up called KSOS: the call letters stood for 'stop our shortage'. Shop assistants were encouraged to call the radio station's host, a store detective named Krazy Kirk, with questions about shortages and to compete for prizes in a radio quiz on loss prevention. The station also distributed comic books starring three superhero-DJs who oppose the evil plans of a sticky-fingered villain called Dr Shortage. Such methods sound silly, but they work.

More conventional has been a new generation of anti-theft technology. Security Tag Systems and Sensormatic, the companies which have stuck most of the clumsy plastic tags on goods across America, both now offer tags filled with ink. If an unauthorised person tries to remove the tag, it breaks and spills the dye on the about-to-be-stolen garment as well as the shoplifter. Once the clothes are stained they cannot be worn or sold, so thieves lose their motive to steal them. Preliminary experiments indicate that the tags work, though retailers are reluctant to attach them to leathers, furs and pricey designer clothes.

2 **These sentences summarise each paragaph of the article. Choose the most suitable summary from the list A–I for each paragraph 1–8 of the article. There's one extra sentence which you don't need to use.**

A Different kinds of stores lose different amounts from shoplifting.
B Goods are stolen by customers and employees.
C Many shops in America are facing financial difficulty.   *paragraph 1*
D One chain has its own radio station.
E One chain of stores checks its stock each month.
F Shops operate on a very low profit margin.
G Some chains have their own television stations.
H Some shops are willing to damage their own goods to discourage theft.
I Some staff are paid extra if they catch someone stealing goods.

B **Highlight the words or phrases in the article which mean the same as the following:**

¶1 bankrupt   a word used to avoid using an unpleasant word

¶4 goods on sale   watching carefully   strange

¶5 tricks to catch people's attention   extra money   steal

¶6 shared   work secretly together to cheat

¶7 tricks   pretend, not real   bad person who is always stealing

C 1 Work in groups Which of these goods do you think are most likely to be stolen from shops? Why?

Ladies' clothes · Men's clothes · Children's clothes · Health and beauty · Jewellery · Shoes · Fashion accessories · Toys, hobbies · Records, cassettes · Radios, stereos · Sporting goods

2 Look at Activity *56*, where you'll see the results of the survey mentioned in paragraph 3.

3 In most countries the following crimes are on the increase:

shoplifting   theft from parked cars   theft of cars: 'joyriding'
theft from empty apartments   bag-snatching   pickpocketing

- How do you think such crimes can be prevented?
- What are two other crimes which seem to be on the increase in your country?
- How should people who are convicted of each of the crimes be punished?

16.4 Paper 4: Listening   EXAM TECHNIQUES

A   This section practises Parts 3 and 4 of the Listening paper.

PART 3

You will hear five short news interviews. For Questions **19–23**, choose from the list **A–F** what each speaker is talking about. Use the letters only once. There is one extra letter which you do not need to use.

A A car was stolen.

B A man was robbed.

C A flat was robbed.

D A car was damaged.

E A rich criminal was not convicted.

F A robbery was prevented.

Speaker 1	**19**
Speaker 2	**20**
Speaker 3	**21**
Speaker 4	**22**
Speaker 5	**23**

PART 4

You will hear part of a radio discussion between three people: Tony Towers, Bill Brown and Mary Matthews. Answer Questions **24–30** by writing **TT**, **BB** or **MM** in the boxes.

24 Who says that everyone has a right to privacy?   **24**

25 Who says that everyone is interested in other people's lives?   **25**

26 Who says that famous people owe their living to the public?   **26**

27 Who says that the press should show respect for people?   **27**

28 Who says that no one is interested in reading about ordinary people?   **28**

29 Who says that the Minister should not have resigned?   **29**

30 Who says that famous people have no right to a private life?   **30**

B   **Work in groups**   Check your answers and then discuss these questions:

- What was unexpectedly easy? What were the hardest things about the two parts?
- What would you do *differently* if you were able to do the two parts again?

16.5 **The past – 3: Reported speech** GRAMMAR REVIEW

A **Work in pairs** Look at the sentences below. What were the *exact* words each person said?

1 They asked me how I was feeling. *'How are you feeling?'*

2 She asked me what the time was.

3 He wondered if I had had lunch yet.

4 They invited me to go for a walk with them.

5 He reminded me to make the phone call.

6 She told me that she'd just got back from holiday.

7 He wanted me to meet him there the next day.

8 She asked me very politely to help her with her work.

See the Grammar Reference section on pages 184–185.

B **1** Change these quotations into reported speech. First, here are some questions that a reporter asked a round-the-world sailor after her voyage.

1 'How long did the voyage take?'

He asked her how long the voyage had taken.

2 'When did you set off?'

3 'How do you feel now that you're home again?'

4 'What was the worst moment of your voyage?'

5 'Are you pleased to be home?'

6 'Would you like to sail round the world again?'

2 And here are her answers to the reporter's questions.

7 'The journey took seven months.'

She told him that the journey had taken seven months.

8 'I said goodbye to my family on 1 April and I haven't seen them again till today.'

9 'I feel very tired, but I'm proud of what I've achieved.'

10 'The worst moment was when the sails were torn in a storm.'

11 'I'm delighted to be back home – I've missed everyone terribly.'

12 'If I did it again, I'd take my family with me on the trip.'

3 Now here are some things that she said to her children after her return.

13 'Shall I take you with me if I go again?'

She offered to take them with her if she went again.

14 'If I were you, I wouldn't spend so long on your own as I've just done.'

15 'Please don't expect me to be the same person I used to be.'

16 'I'll take you to a fancy restaurant to celebrate my return.'

17 'Could you lend me some money? I'll pay you back tomorrow.'

18 'Open the champagne! Let's celebrate!'

If you write a story in the exam, try to include a mixture of direct and reported speech. Direct speech can help your story to sound more realistic and interesting – and you don't have to worry about changing tenses, as you do with reported speech.

'But make sure your punctuation is correct!' he said.

'And remember that a different speaker's words should begin a new line,' she added.

C **1** **Work in pairs** Imagine that one of you has done something newsworthy, and the other is a reporter. Role-play an interview.

2 **Join another pair** Tell your new partners what was said in the interview. If necessary, correct each other.

She told me that . . .   *That's not quite right. I think I said that . . .*

"Look, I'd sit down if I were you. Have you got a drink? Now, it's nothing to worry about, really it isn't . . ."

16.6 Pauses and stress   SPEAKING

A 1 📼 **You'll hear this news item read aloud. Why is this reading difficult to understand?**

A lawyer who arrived late for his case at Lewes Crown Court explained that he had been accidentally locked up with the prisoners.

2 📼 **Now you'll hear a better reading of the same item, followed by a reading of four more items. As you listen, mark the *pauses* that the reader makes using a vertical line (|). The first item is done for you as an example.**

Chíldren at Sóuthgáte School | in Énfield, Éssex, | have been tóld nót to táke their móbile phónes to cláss | because ín-cóming cálls have interrúpted léssons.

A woman in Ashford, Kent, persuaded her husband to drive fifteen miles to return a live crab to the sea after fighting gulls had dropped it in her back garden.

A robber armed with a knife stole a half-smoked cigarette from a man's mouth in Commercial Road, East London.

The British lost forty million pounds through holes in their pockets, down the backs of sofas and in other odd places last year. The Royal Mint said four hundred and fifty million coins disappeared from circulation, including twenty-five million one pound coins.

3 📼 **Now listen to the recording again. Mark the syllables that are stressed in each sentence. Look back at the first item. The stressed syllables have been marked for you as an example.**

4 Work in pairs   Compare your versions and then look at the 'marked-up' version of the news items in Activity *46*.

B 1 🗣️ **Work in pairs**   One of you should look at Activity *17*, the other at *20*. You'll each have some more news items to read out to your partner.

2 📼 **Now listen to the same news items on the cassette.**

Although you won't have to read aloud in the exam, your pronunciation will be assessed, including your rhythm, placing of stress, intonation patterns and how easy it is for people to understand you. Reading aloud may help you to focus on pronunciation, without having to worry about what to say and how to express your ideas.

16.7 *Put*   VERBS AND IDIOMS

Fill the gaps in the sentences below with suitable forms of the phrasal verbs listed:

put away   put back   put back   put down   put forward   put off   put off   put off
put on ✓   put on   put out/off   put through   put up   put up   put up with

1 It's getting dark, could you ......put...... the light ......on...... please?
2 Don't forget to .... the lights .... when you leave the room.
3 If you want to stay with us, we can .... you .... in our spare room.
4 I'm trying to concentrate but if you keep whistling you'll .... me ....
5 I'm afraid we'll have to .... our meeting .... till next month.
6 Since I last stayed at this hotel, they have .... their prices ....
7 He has .... a lot of weight since I last saw him.
8 You'll be able to remember the words if you .... them .... in your notebook.
9 If you've finished with the book, would you mind .... it .... on the shelf?
10 I .... the aspirins .... somewhere safe, but now I can't remember where.
11 At the start of Summer Time we .... the clocks .... and at the end we .... them ....
12 Mr Green is on the line. Shall I .... him .... or ask him to ring back?
13 If you've got a cold, you've just got to .... it.
14 They had planned to go out but they were .... by the bad weather.

16.8 Paper 1: Reading   EXAM TECHNIQUES

A 1 Read this information about the Reading paper, and look again at the exercises referred to.

The Reading paper lasts 1 hour and 15 minutes and is in four parts. You have to read a total of about 2,000 words and answer 35 questions.

PART 1   Six or seven multiple-matching questions on one text. You have to match headings to paragraphs, or summary sentences to paragraphs (as in 16.3).

PART 2   Seven or eight multiple-choice questions on one text (as in 11.3).

PART 3   Six or seven single sentences or whole paragraphs have been removed from the text (as in 15.4), and are printed below it. You have to decide where they belong.

PART 4   Thirteen to fifteen questions (mostly multiple-matching but one or two may be multiple choice) on one long text or several shorter texts. You have to find the answers to a list of questions by locating information in the text(s). This is similar to an exercise you did in 9.2.

2 Work in pairs   Which part seems the hardest? Which should you spend longest on? Do you have any further questions?

B 1 Do a complete practice test for Paper 1, using a sample FCE paper or *Cambridge Practice Tests for First Certificate*. Time yourself, keeping a record of how long you spend on each part of the paper, and how long you have to spare at the end.

2 Check your answers and add up your score. Then look again at the ones you got wrong and make sure you see why you were wrong in each case.

3 Work in groups   Discuss these questions:

- How long did each part take you?
- Which was the hardest part? And which was the easiest?
- Did you have *any* time to spare at the end? How could you use your time better?
- What were your two main problems – apart from understanding the texts?

If you are unsure of some answers, don't leave a blank – just guess because you may be lucky! Make a note of the questions you guessed. Then, if you have time at the end, you can come back to them and maybe change your mind about some of them.

Before you read each text, read the instructions carefully. They tell you where each text comes from and what exactly you have to do.

16.9 Giving your opinions   WRITING

A 1 Read these two quotations and then note down your own views on whether it's best to get your news from television or a newspaper.

> The whole problem with news on television comes down to this: all the words uttered in an hour of news coverage could be printed on one page of a newspaper. And the world cannot be understood in one page. Of course there is a compensation: television offers pictures, and the pictures move.
>
> Neil Postman (American writer)

> A newspaper can easily afford to print an item of possible interest to only a fraction of its readers. A television news programme must be put together with the assumption that each item will be of some interest to everyone that watches. Every time a newspaper includes a feature which will attract a specialised group it can assume it is adding at least a little bit to its circulation. If a television news programme includes an item of this sort, it must assume that its audience will diminish.
>
> Reuven Frank (NBC News Executive)

2 Work in pairs   Compare your notes. Have you got enough material to write about 150 words on the topic? If you have too much, what would you leave out?

B

The examiner will be looking at how well you have communicated and the variety of structures and vocabulary you have used. Short sentences and simple vocabulary may be more effective than wrongly-used complicated sentences and 'advanced' vocabulary.

When you're writing a composition that asks you to give your opinion about a topic, you'll probably need to *explain* what you mean and give your *reasons*. Choose *four* of these opening lines and write *two* more sentences for each, adding an explanation or reason.

1 I hardly ever read a newspaper because . . .

I find that I get a much better picture of what is going on in the world by watching the news on television. Television news is also much more up-to-date than a newspaper and only the most important items of news are reported.

2 People like reading human interest stories in the paper, not politics, because . . .

3 Nuclear power stations are a good/bad thing because . . .

4 The reasons why the government should change/not change the law on drugs are . . .

5 If a criminal has committed a very serious crime . . .

6 The only solution to terrorism is . . .

7 Exams are a good/bad thing because . . .

8 Parents can be really annoying because . . .

C

Work in pairs Look at these typical exam questions. Make notes of the points you could make if you wrote each of these articles.

1 An international magazine for young people is planning a special issue on pollution in different countries. Write a short article for this magazine, describing the situation in your country and what can be done to improve it.

2 An English-language newspaper in your country recently published a report about how few women take part in politics. Write an article for the newspaper, explaining why this is so and how the situation could be improved.

3 A college magazine recently published a report that marriage is out-of-date. Write an article for the magazine, giving your views on this topic, based on your own experience.

D 1 ✎ Write an article for a young people's magazine (120–180 words) beginning like this:

One of the most serious problems facing the world today is . . .

or One of the most serious problems facing my country today is . . .

Time yourself while you make notes and then write the article.

2 **Work in pairs** Read each other's articles. Refer to the guidelines for feedback in Activity *61*.

"Yes, but is there any news of the iceberg?"

17

It's a small world

17.1 Other countries   VOCABULARY

(A) 1 Work in pairs   Look at the photos above and discuss these questions:
- In which country do you think each photograph was taken? Give your reasons.
- How do you think life in those countries is different from life in your country?
- Which foreign countries have you visited?
- Which foreign countries would you most like to visit one day? Give your reasons.

2 Note down four *adjectives* you could use to describe each photograph.

3 Join another pair   Tell the others what adjectives you've written down for each picture, but without identifying the picture. Can they guess which one you're talking about?

(B) 1 Work in pairs   Can you identify these countries? In reality they are all different sizes. Which are the two largest and the two smallest countries?

2 Write down the nationality adjective for each of the countries.
For example: Portugal – *Portuguese*   Turkey – *Turkish*

3 What countries have a common border with your country (or what countries are nearest)?

C **1** This is part of the introduction to a book called *Coping with Japan*. Fill the gaps with suitable words from the list on the right.

The rest of the world has always baffled the Japanese. They realize that by turning inwards they miss much and perhaps get dangerously out of step. But the ability to accept the new and to adapt is a vitally ¹ .... part of the Japanese character. In the last century the Japanese accepted industrialization and parliamentary democracy. In this ² .... they quietly accepted sweeping changes after the last war.

The ³ .... of Japanese society as not one rock but a series of rocks that shift and change, but in the end remain rocks, has often been ⁴ .... Japan also has a very ⁵ .... image – beautiful shops, gleaming office ⁶ .... and excellent highways. In fact, Japanese people visiting European ⁷ .... think them very old and perhaps rather grey. But Japan's appearance should not delude the visitor into ⁸ .... that the country has westernized; rather it has ⁹ .... spectacularly modernized.

Visitors, ¹⁰ .... on business or pleasure, will be given excellent treatment in Japan, travelling in ease, comfort and ¹¹ .... , anywhere they will. On the practical level coping with Japan presents perhaps fewer ¹² .... than most countries, but if coping with the country includes ¹³ .... the way the society works and trying to work with it, then the visitor must be prepared for perpetual studenthood.

One thing is certain: if you have the ¹⁴ .... to go to Japan, take it. Its charm and attractions are ¹⁵ .... You will be left with enchanting memories.

1 essential   important   necessary   large

2 way   century   democracy   peace

3 stereotype   image   picture   landscape

4 excelled   employed   heard   taken

5 new   modern   late   strange

6 streets   blocks   houses   workers

7 offices   cities   people   hosts

8 realising   thinking   admiring   hearing

9 seemed   become   changed   risen

10 or   if   whether   weather

11 safety   trains   leisure   transport

12 chances   opportunities   interests   problems

13 understanding   ignoring   entering   joining

14 possibility   probability   chance   money

15 alone   unique   unfamiliar   once

2 This is part of the introduction to *Coping with America*. Fill the gaps with one suitable word.

This is not a guidebook in the normal sense of the word. It does not tell you ¹ .... to see, which places to visit, ² .... to stay or how much anything costs. ³ .... information of that sort other guidebooks can be consulted. What this book tries to do is to provide you ⁴ .... the sort of information that cannot be ⁵ .... in traditional guidebooks to the USA, which are mostly written ⁶ .... (and for) Americans, who have no way of knowing ⁷ .... aspects of life in their country can come ⁸ .... problems or surprises to the foreign visitor. I have tried to give the first-time foreign, and particularly European, visitor to the USA information ⁹ .... how to do things, what to say and ¹⁰ .... to expect in different situations. The USA is not a difficult ¹¹ .... to get along in, but in many ways it is not, as yet, geared to catering ¹² .... foreign visitors, though individual Americans are enormously helpful to people they recognize ¹³ .... foreign – so do ask for help if you ¹⁴ .... it. The USA is also a surprisingly foreign country even to, say, Britons and Australians, who speak the same ¹⁵ ....

3 Check your answers. Which words were the most difficult to guess?

4 **Work in pairs**   What would you tell a Japanese or an American visitor who was coming to *your* country for the first time? Note down the points you would make.

5 ✍ Write a description of your own country (about 150 words). Imagine that this is going to be the introduction to a book helping foreigners to cope with *your* country.

17.2 Comparing and contrasting GRAMMAR REVIEW

A **1 Work in pairs**   Look at the bar chart in the GRAMMAR REFERENCE section on page 173. Refer to the statistics about old people in different countries and the examples given.

- Write *four* sentences comparing 1950 with the present day.
- And *four* sentences comparing 2025 with the present day.

2 Join another pair   Compare your sentences. How old will you be in 2025?

B Look at these sentences about the World Weather Guide below. Underline the errors and correct them.

See the Grammar Reference section on page 173.

1 *July in Cairo is <u>far more dryer as</u> Buenos Aires.*   July in Cairo is much drier than Buenos Aires.

2 *The daytime temperature in Tokyo in July is the same than New York.*

3 *There are not much differences between the weather in New York and Warsaw.*

4 *The weather in Athens in July is more warmer than London.*

5 *New York is more cold in winter as London.*

6 *There are much less wet days in Tokyo than in Warsaw.*

WORLD WEATHER GUIDE

	AVERAGE TEMPERATURE				NUMBER OF RAINY DAYS	
	JULY		JANUARY		JULY	JANUARY
	day	night	day	night		
Athens	33°	23°	13°	6°	2	16
Buenos Aires	14°	6°	29°	17°	7	8
Cairo	36°	21°	18°	8°	0	1
London	22°	14°	6°	2°	12	15
New York	28°	19°	3°	−4°	12	12
Tokyo	28°	21°	8°	−2°	10	5
Warsaw	23°	12°	0°	−6°	16	15

C Complete the second sentence so that it has a similar meaning to the first sentence, using the word given in red. You must use between two and five words, including the word given. Do not change the word given.

1 Cairo is much hotter than London in July.

like   London isn't ...anything like as hot as... Cairo in July.

2 There are fewer rainy days in Buenos Aires than in New York.

much   There isn't .... Buenos Aires as in New York.

3 There is less rain in Tokyo than in Athens in January.

rain   More .... in Tokyo in January.

4 It isn't anything like as warm in Buenos Aires in July as it is in New York.

much   In July Buenos Aires .... New York.

5 London and New York have a similar number of rainy days.

falls   About the same amount .... as in New York.

6 Summer nights in Cairo are much warmer than in London.

hot   Summer nights in London are .... Cairo.

7 New York in winter isn't as cold as Warsaw.

place   Warsaw .... New York in winter.

8 In July New York and London are equally wet.

number   New York and London .... rainy days as each other.

D **1 Work in groups**   What are some of the similarities and differences between *your* country and Britain or the USA? (Think about what you've read about the UK or USA and films you've seen.) Consider the following aspects and make notes:

size   population   climate   scenery
music   entertainment   family life   travel and transport
food and eating habits: breakfast, lunch, dinner, snacks

2 Write a paragraph (about 60 words) summarising some of the differences.

17.3 A nice place   READING

A Read this newspaper article, then answer the questions below, choosing the best alternative according to the article.

Norwich is pleased to pull off a nice one

1 If you're reading this in Norwich, the chances are that you got out of bed on the right side this morning, that the newsagent smiled and said thank you as he took your money, that your bus queue is orderly and well-behaved, and that all is peace and harmony.

2 That's because the British Polite Society has just named the good people of Norwich as the 'courteous community of the year'.

3 The society's secretary, the Reverend Ian Gregory, said Norwich received the most recommendations from members this year, beating Swansea, Northampton and Portsmouth, and squeezing Alresford, Hampshire, into second place.

4 Polite Society agents tested the city's reputation, and returned with nothing but praise for the manners of its hoteliers, shopkeepers and publicans.

5 'We found Norwich to be a city with a smile,' says Mr Gregory, who will visit the town for the first time this week. 'Last year Shrewsbury won the award, and I hear they've just been placed top of a list for healthy living.'

6 Could he name the rudest place in Britain? 'No, we don't do that sort of thing,' recalling the commitment to good manners. What about a clue, then? 'Well, we did have a problem with doctors' receptionists about six months ago, and we get a lot of complaints about bar staff. But then, we also get complaints from bar staff about the customers.'

7 None of this, needless to say, concerns Norwich. Julian Roux, landlord of the Louis Marchesi pub, swears he knows not a single unpleasant person, and rates only Lowestoft, his birthplace, as a nicer place. 'The people here are very relaxed, which a Londoner would probably mistake for stupidity. If you played poker here, you'd discover we can be very cunning.'

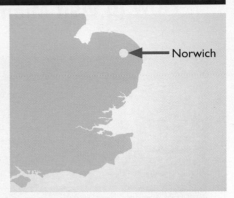
Norwich

8 Probably none of this will come as a surprise to the citizens because a year or two ago the European Union decided that Norwich possessed the most pleasant environment in Europe.

9 It fell to Norwich council's public relations officer, Mr Tim Anderson, to offer the only consolation non-Norwich residents can expect.

10 'We're reasonably nice to each other, but I'm sure that many other towns are equally as nice.' Now isn't that nice of him to say so?

1 The second politest place in the country is
a) Alresford   b) Northampton   c) Norwich   d) Swansea

2 The British Polite Society tested Norwich by
a) asking visitors to the city   c) sending people to find out about the city
b) asking the citizens of the city   d) counting its members' votes

3 The rudest people in Britain are
a) doctors' receptionists   b) bar staff   c) bar customers   d) not named

4 The secretary of the British Polite Society
a) visited Norwich last year   c) has no plans to visit Norwich
b) visited Norwich recently   d) is going to Norwich very soon

5 People from London might not realise that Norwich people are
a) lazy   b) friendly   c) stupid   d) cunning

6 A few years ago Norwich was named as the
a) healthiest place in Europe   c) most pleasant place in Europe
b) politest place in Europe   d) cleanest place in Europe

B Find the word or phrase in each paragraph of the passage that has a similar meaning to these words and phrases:

¶1 in a good mood *got out of bed on the right side*

¶2 polite   ¶5 prize   ¶8 people

¶3 pushing   ¶6 behaviour   ¶9 comfort or reassurance

¶4 representatives ¶7 of course   ¶10 fairly

C **Work in groups**   Discuss these questions:

• How polite are people in different parts of your own country?
• Which place would win the 'most courteous community' award in your country?
• Which country in the world would win the 'most courteous nation' award?
• Why are people sometimes rude or unpleasant to one another?
• What kind of behaviour would you describe as 'nice' and 'polite'?

17.4 Not such a nice place

READING

A Choose a suitable headline for this article:

Enjoying a holiday in Miami

How to visit Miami and survive

Miami for beginners

THINKING Miami? Blue skies, warm winds and drinks by the beach? Maybe not. When you think of Miami, you may not think fun in the sun, but crazy teenagers driving around, ramming and robbing and attacking people like you, the tourist.

1 [____]

Your chances of dying in Miami are remote. Of the 40 million tourists who visited Florida last year, only 0.1 percent were victims of crime. And of 1,191 people murdered in 1992, only 22 were non-residents.

To improve these already favorable odds of surviving, check out these suggestions.

Dress: Criminals like lost tourists, so it makes sense not to look like one from 200 yards away. **2** [____] Think rayon.

Got chest hair? Miami wants to see it. Trust me.

Look sinister. Visiting New Yorkers – pale, tetchy, chain-smoking, dressed entirely in black – do well here. Some criminals also shy away from people they consider 'visiting criminals.'

Think about this, ladies – women with heels and big hair most often possess permits for semi-automatic pistols, carried in their designer handbags. Criminals avoid them.

At the airport: Immediately on arrival, walk to one of Miami International Airport's coffee stands and order an espresso, here called a *café cubano*. After two or three thimbles of this incredibly powerful stimulant, you too will become highly agitated and more closely resemble a resident. You will also drive much faster, which will be helpful later on. Suitcases and bags are often stolen.

3 [____]

Taxis: Most cab drivers seem to be Cuban or Haitian. **4** [____] The Haitians are, shall we say, less linear in their world-view, but often sweeter. Almost all can find Miami Beach, Coconut Grove and Coral Gables. If you are staying somewhere else, you must be a risk-taking Scorpio. Cabs aren't cheap, but if you're going to be vacationing in South Beach, you do not need a rental car, or more accurately, a place to park the car.

Hire cars: This is the scary part. Hire-car lots are located in a dimly-lit, creepy corner of the airport. In the bad old days of 1993, roving criminals would prowl around waiting to see what tasty morsels emerged from the Hertz and Avis lots. Now, a crime task force also prowls the area, looking for criminals and assisting lost tourists. But don't be lulled. In Miami, I would advise hiring a car with a little power, the better to escape unpleasant scenes and keep up with the flow of traffic. **5** [____] Still, there is no getting around the fact that you will be immediately recognizable as a Person Driving a Hired Vehicle. But there is help. See *Driving*.

It is also a good idea to have the rental-car folks explain to you in painstaking detail how to drive the two miles from the airport to the major highways and then on to your hotel.

6 [____] Do not get lost.

Driving: To drive like a local – and avoid getting rammed – one should drive quickly. **7** [____] Whatever you do, never, ever use your turn indicator.

To get from the airport to the beaches a visitor literally drives over – via an elevated expressway – some of America's most impoverished neighbourhoods. If you get lost in a rough-looking spot, it is imperative that you keep moving. Do not pull over, turn on your interior lights and look at a map. If you need directions, get yourself to the most brightly-lit 24-hour gas station you can find.

Also, the police are very tolerant of tourists who treat stop lights as yield signs when they are lost in the inner city. Indeed, being pulled over by the police might be your ticket out of the area.

8 [____]

If you are approached at a stop light, and you think you are about to get robbed, look both ways – and floor it. The police will understand.

Being attacked: In the unlikely event that you are bumped from behind while driving or at rest: DO NOT STOP. Indeed, if it were me, I would accelerate, and drive off as fast as I could!

B Eight sentences have been removed from the article opposite. Choose from sentences A–I below the one which fits each gap 1–8. There's one extra sentence you don't need to use.

  A But mere speed is not enough to fool a resident.

  B You will have to pay them $50 but then they'll help you.

  C Generally the Cubans seem to know the city a bit better.

  D It is always better to carry them yourself.

  E Most tourists who get carjacked or robbed in Miami first get lost.

  F Save the green Bermuda shorts and yellow polo shirts for Orlando.

  G That is understandable but hysterical.

  H They will escort you back to the freeways.

  I Tinted windows would be nice. So would a car phone.

17.5 Stressing the right syllable   WORD STUDY

A 1 It's important to stress the right part of a word. Mark the stressed syllables in the words in green.

verbs and *-ing* forms	nouns and adjectives
They expórted the goods to the USA.	Tourism is an invisible éxport.
These bananas are impórted.	Ímports have risen this month.
He insúlted me.	That was a terrible ínsult.
They perfécted a new method.	Your work is not quite pérfect.
Smoking is not permítted.	You need a pérmit to fish in the river.
His work is progréssing well.	New Prógress to First Certificate
They protésted about the situation.	They held a prótest meeting.
Listen to the recórding.	Have you heard their new récord?
He is suspécted of the crime.	He is the main súspect.

2 📼 **Work in pairs** Listen to the recording. Take it in turns to read the sentences aloud.

B 1 When a word has two or more than two syllables, it's sometimes difficult to remember where the main stress is placed in the word – especially when there is a similar word in your language. Mark the main stressed syllable in each of these words.

emplóy emplóyer employée emplóyment applý applicátion advertising
advertisement attraction certificate comfortable communication deputy desert
dessert desirable details development experience girlfriend information
intelligence machine permanent photograph photography qualification
receptionist reservation secretarial secretary telephone telephonist temporary
themselves toothache vegetable yourself

2 📼 **Work in pairs** Listen to the recorded answers. Take it in turns to read the words aloud.

C 1 📼 Generally speaking, grammatical words (modal verbs, articles, prepositions, etc.) are *not* stressed in a sentence. Content words (nouns, adjectives, verbs and adverbs) *are* stressed. Listen to the recording and mark the stressed syllables in these sentences.

  1 Stréss is júst as impórtant in a conversátion as whén you're réading sómething alóud.

  2 It takes most people a long time to perfect their pronunciation in English.

  3 Norwich is pleased to pull off a nice one.

  4 We found Norwich to be a city with a smile.

  5 We're reasonably nice to each other, but I'm sure that many other towns are equally as nice.

  6 Save the green Bermuda shorts and yellow polo shirts for Orlando.

  7 How to visit Miami and survive.

  8 Tinted windows would be nice. So would a car phone.

2 **Work in pairs** Take it in turns to read the sentences aloud yourselves.

17.6 *Bring, call* and *cut*   VERBS AND IDIOMS

Fill the gaps in the sentences below with a suitable form of the phrasal verbs listed:

bring about   bring back   bring down   bring up   call back   call in   call for   call off
call off   cut down   cut off   cut out

bring

1 Can you explain what .... these problems?

2 They were .... by their grandmother after their mother died.

3 My glasses are upstairs, could you .... them .... for me please?

4 When you've finished with the books, please .... them ....

call

5 Not enough people booked for the excursion, so it has been ....

6 If you're ever in the area, do .... and see me.

7 They were engaged for six months but they decided to .... it ....

8 I'll .... you at 7.30 – will you be ready?

9 I'm very busy at the moment, could you .... me .... later, please?

cut

10 I can't give up smoking altogether but I'm trying to ....

11 Do you need a pair of scissors to .... the coupon?

12 During the strike all electricity supplies were ....

17.7 When in Rome . . .   LISTENING

 You'll hear five people describing their first visit to another country. Choose from the list A–F what each person says about the country. Use the letters only once. There's one extra letter you don't need to use.

A Behaving in the right way can bring you success.

B If you give someone a present, it has to be wrapped beautifully.

C You see two completely different types of people there.

D The people are very hospitable.

E You feel quite unsafe there.

F It's hard to believe that the country is really so beautiful.

Nick	1
Susanna	2
Neil	3
Gertrud	4
Nigel	5

17.8 Paper 2: Writing   EXAM TECHNIQUES

A 1 **Read this information about the Writing paper and highlight the important points which are new to you, or which you want to remember.**

Paper 2 is in two parts and lasts 1 hour 30 minutes. You have to write two compositions of 120–180 words. In each case you'll be told who the *reader* is and what the *purpose* of your writing is.

PART 1   Question 1 is compulsory. You have to write a letter after reading the information given in the texts and illustrations (you won't have to read more than 250 words). Follow the instructions carefully and include all the relevant information.

PART 2   Questions 2–4 are on a variety of topics. Question 5 contains two choices about the set books. You have to select one question, which could be a task in any one of these styles:

article   report   letter   story   description   account   composition

Marking Both compositions are marked on the same basis. The examiners do *not* count up the number of mistakes and deduct marks for each one! They read the whole composition and give an impression mark, looking at these aspects:

– range and variety of vocabulary and grammar
– accuracy, including spelling and punctuation
– organisation (planning) and the use of paragraphs and joining sentences
– style suitable for the task
– effect on the reader
– including all the relevant points (especially in Part 1)

You will pass if your composition is written in fairly good English, if it doesn't contain many errors, and if you have followed the instructions.

2 Work in pairs **Compare the points you've highlighted. Then look at the following tips and decide which of the advice is the most important for you:**

- How do you decide which of the questions to choose? If you like writing stories, you'll pick the story-writing task if there is one. But if you don't quite understand the instructions for any question, *don't* do that one.
- What about style? Our advice is to use a neutral, not-too-formal, not-too-informal style for both compositions, and don't try to write in a style you don't feel comfortable with.
- For the transactional letter in Part 1 make sure you cover all the points mentioned. And make sure that you do *exactly* what the instructions at the beginning tell you.
- Try to avoid the mistakes your teacher has corrected in the past. Check your work through at the end. Follow the instructions completely.

B 1 **Work in pairs** **Look at this Part 1 task. Highlight the important points in the instructions:**

- What are the points you have to cover?
- Do you need to make notes? Or can you plan this type of question by highlighting the points in the information given and in the instructions, without needing to write notes?

2 **Write the letter and time how long it takes you to complete.**

PART 1

Read this postcard from your penfriend in Japan and the notes you have made about it below. Write a **letter** (**120–180 words**) in an appropriate style replying to your friend and answering your friend's questions.

> Dear J—
>
> Hope you like this card: it's a temple in the city of Kyoto. I'm really looking forward to coming to see you in July. This will be my first visit to your country, but I have been to the USA – I spent two weeks in Florida last April, where I went to Disneyworld and to the Gulf Coast. I must say, I'm feeling quite excited, but also nervous.
>
> What kind of clothes do I need to pack? How much spending money do you think I'll need? I'd like to spend some time travelling round the country – where would be nice? I hope you can meet me at the airport – I've booked my flight and I'll arrive on Friday 13th at 16:45.
>
> Best wishes to you and your family,
> Yoshi.

> I'll be away when you arrive.
> Back on Monday 16th.
> Booked a room for you in hotel opposite main rail station (enclose brochure). How to get there.
>
> After that, stay with me.
> Possible to change flight date?

Four Golden Rules for Paper 2:

1 Read the instructions twice very carefully.
2 Make notes before you start writing. Re-read the instructions to make sure the points you've noted are relevant.
3 Make sure you include *all* the relevant details.
4 Check your finished work through for mistakes and slips of the pen.

18

Yes, but is it art?

18.1 The arts   VOCABULARY AND SPEAKING

(A) 1 Work in pairs   What's happening in each of the pictures above? Which place would you most like to be, and why? Write down three adjectives to describe the atmosphere or people in each scene.

2 Join another pair   Compare your lists of adjectives.

3 🔊 You'll hear ten different musical instruments being played. Identify each one and put them in order of preference.

4 Work in pairs   Compare your answers. Do you have similar tastes?

(B) 1 Write down your answers to these questions.

What do you call someone who:

1 performs on a stage?	6 plays a musical instrument alone?
2 plays a piano?	7 makes plates, bowls and cups?
3 plays a guitar?	8 makes statues?
4 plays a violin?	9 writes plays?
5 stands in front of an orchestra?	10 is absolutely brilliant?

2 Work in groups   Discuss these questions and note down your answers:

- Why do we need the arts? Think of several reasons.
- Which art form is most important for you, personally? Why?
- What would life be like without artists?

3 Join another group   Compare your answers.

C 1 Work in groups Carry out this survey among the members of your group. If their favourite in any category is missing, ask them to add it to the list.

Arts Survey

1 What kinds of music do you like? Put these in order of preference:

opera   pop   folk   jazz   chamber music   orchestral music
rock   other

2 Who is your favourite composer?

3 Who is your favourite singer?

4 Who is your favourite band or group?

5 What kinds of paintings do you like? Put these in order of preference:

abstract   great masters   French impressionists   20th century
landscapes   medieval   portraits   surrealist   other

6 Who is your favourite painter or sculptor?

7 Who is your favourite dramatist?

2 Compare your answers – do you have similar preferences? Were there any surprises?

18.2 Mozart   READING

A 1 **Work in pairs**   What do you know about Mozart? Note down three things you already know about him or his works.

2 Read the text and find the answers to these questions. Each answer is a number.

1 How many years did Mozart spend on tour?   11
2 How old was he when he first played the harpsichord?
3 How old was he when he composed his first work?
4 How old was he when he first performed in public?
5 How old was he when he first played the violin?
6 How many violin lessons had he had?
7 How many children did his mother give birth to?
8 How many of her children died in infancy?
9 How many years did Mozart's tour of France and England last?
10 What was the number of the symphony he composed in London?
11 How many times did he return to England?
12 How old was he when his first opera was performed?
13 When did he die?

The life and times of a young musical genius

Wolfgang Amadeus Mozart

MOZART, who was born on January 27 1756 in the Austrian city of Salzburg, was neither the first nor the last child prodigy, but he was certainly the greatest. From the age of six, when his father took him on his first foreign tour, Mozart toured the courts and musical centres of Austria, Germany, France, England, Holland, Switzerland and Italy. It has been calculated that Mozart spent almost a third of his short life – he died at the age of 35 – travelling.

He was born into a moderately prosperous family where his unmatched musical genius made itself known extremely early. Mozart began learning the harpsichord at three and his earliest known work was composed in 1761 when he was five, the age at which he also first appeared in public. At seven, never having had a violin lesson, he picked up the instrument and played it perfectly and at sight.

Mozart and his older sister Nannerl were the only survivors of seven children. Both were exceptional musicians and their father Leopold, who was himself a noted violin teacher, took them on several tours. At six, the children played before the Austrian empress Maria Theresa in Vienna where 'little Wolfgang sprang on to the lap of the Empress, threw his arms around her neck and kissed her properly'.

The following year they set out in their own carriage, with a servant, on a tour of France and England which took almost two and a half years. Mozart lived in England from April 1764 until August 1765, mainly in Chelsea, giving concerts and composing. It was here, probably, that he wrote the first of his symphonies. Mozart never revisited England, although he frequently planned to return.

As Mozart matured, he continued to tour and give concerts. From his early teens, however, composition became increasingly important, especially opera, and Mozart made three journeys to Italy to acquire mastery of such music. His first opera, Mitridate, Rè di Ponto, was performed in Milan when he was 14 and was the first of many triumphs in the theatre.

B **Work in groups**   What would you say to a foreign visitor who asked you these questions?

- Who is your country's most famous composer (or most famous musician or singer)?
- What do you know about his or her life?
- What kind of music did/does he or she compose (or perform)?

"Look on the bright side, dear – when Mozart was your age he'd been dead fifteen years . . ."

18.3 The future GRAMMAR REVIEW

See the Grammar Reference section on pages 173–174.

A **Work in pairs** **Fill the gaps in these sentences.**

1 She is very clever, so I expect that she .... her exams next summer.
2 Look at those black clouds – it .... soon.
3 The Joneses .... to dinner tomorrow.
4 Tomorrow, according to my diary, the sun .... at 5:09.
5 By the time our guests .... , the food .... eaten.
6 When my friends .... here, I .... them some coffee or tea.
7 Your room is in a terrible mess – when .... ?
8 I promise that I .... the money that you lent me as soon as I ....

B **Underline the errors in these sentences and correct them. If there are no errors, put a tick.**

1 *I tidy up my room when I get home this evening.* I'll tidy up
2 *If the telephone rings, I'll answer it.*
3 *After the floor will have been cleaned, I'll polish the furniture.*
4 *By the time you get home we will finish dinner.*
5 *We'll be waiting for you when your plane is going to land at the airport.*
6 *Liz has a baby next month.*
7 *The new bypass shall be finished in the spring.*
8 *You won't be able to unlock the door if you won't remember your key.*

C **Here are some *formal* announcements. Write down what you would say to your friends to give them the same information, using the word in red. (You may need more than five words in some sentences.)**

here
1 The 9:30 train has been delayed and will arrive in approximately 30 minutes.
The 9:30 train's late – it's not .....going to get/be/arrive here..... for another half an hour.

worse
2 The weather is expected to deteriorate at the weekend, and snow is forecast.
This weekend the weather .... snow.

why
3 Due to unforeseen circumstances, there will be no lessons next week.
Nobody seems to know .... any lessons next week.

exhibition
4 Students' work will be exhibited in the main hall next week.
They .... of students' work in the main hall next week.

find
5 The results of the examination will be published towards the end of September.
We .... exam results until the end of September.

start
6 This evening's performance in the Wessex Hall will commence in five minutes.
The performance .... five minutes' time.

D **1** **Work alone** **Note down your plans for each day next week: before lunch, after lunch and in the evening. If you have no plans, maybe invent some!**

2 **Work in groups** **Find out about each other's plans. Then find out how your partners' plans would change if unexpected things happened, by asking questions like these.**

> What if you're not feeling well?
> What if the weather's bad that afternoon?
> What if there's a public transport strike?
> What if you don't feel like going to school?

> If I'm not feeling well, I'll stay in bed.
> If the weather's bad, I'll . . .
> In that case, I'll . . .
> I always feel like going to school, so I will go anyway.

18.4 Art in New York   READING

A Find the following information in the text and write the number of the museum(s) beside each question. In some cases you have to write more than one number.

Which of the museums:

A is closed on Fridays?

B is open on Mondays?

C may only be partially open?

D spans the widest historical period?

E is like someone's house?

F has the two most important paintings in the city?

G exhibits photographs?

H is the most impressive architecturally?

I lets visitors decide how much to pay to get in?

J Where has this text come from?
a) a holiday brochure
b) an advertisement
c) an encyclopedia
d) a guide book

K What can you *not* find out from this text?
a) phone numbers
b) which is the best museum
c) admission charges
d) opening hours

Art Factory

The Guggenheim

Unmissable

1. THE FRICK COLLECTION
The private collection of Henry Clay Frick is arranged and furnished as if the man himself were still living there. European painting from the 14th–19th centuries, include Bellini's St Francis, Holbein the Younger's Thomas Cromwell, and Corot's Ville d'Array. There are also small collections of Hogarth and Gainsborough.
1 East 70th St at Fifth Ave (212-288 0700). Tue–Sat 10am–6pm, Sun 1pm–6pm, $3

2. GUGGENHEIM MUSEUM
A stunning building. Look also in the newly constructed towers, where there are intimations of the splendour of the permanent collection: Kandinsky's Landscape with Rolling Hills; Braque's Teapot on a Yellow Ground and Chagall's Green Violinist.
1071 Fifth Ave at 88th St (212-423 3500). Fri–Wed 10am–8pm, $7

The Metropolitan Museum of Art

3. ICP (INTERNATIONAL CENTER OF PHOTOGRAPHY)
A changing exhibition featuring collections of Capa, Cartier-Bresson, Strand, Edward Weston and more.
1130 Fifth Ave at 94th St (212-860 1777). Tue 11am–8pm, Wed–Sun 11am–6pm, $4

4. THE JEWISH MUSEUM
Seventeen galleries representing the history of Jewish culture, and a recreation of an ancient synagogue.
1109 Fifth Ave at 92nd St (212-423 3200). Mon–Thu and Sun 10am–5pm

5. METROPOLITAN MUSEUM OF ART
Thirty-six centuries are represented in the Egyptian collection alone and the gallery, if overwhelming, is unmissable. There are no less that 17 Rembrandts and a whole room devoted to Rodin. Special highlights include Rembrandt's Aristotle with a bust of Young Woman with a Water Jug; Monet's Ice Flows; Degas's A Woman Ironing (plus a superb collection of his sculpture); and Van Gogh's Wheat Field with Cypresses.

Fifth Ave at 82nd St (212-879 5500). Tue, Thu and Sun 9.30–5.15, Fri–Sat 9.30am–8.45pm. (Pay what you like but they suggest $7 on the door. Expect some galleries to be closed.)

6. MOMA (MUSEUM OF MODERN ART)
'Modern' as in Post Impressionism onwards. Extensive collections of painting, sculpture and design, plus a small display of photography. If you only get to see two paintings in New York, go for Picasso's Les Demoiselles d'Avignon and Matisse's Dancers.
11 West 53rd St, between Seventh and Sixth Aves (212-708 9480). Fri–Tue 11am–6pm, Thu 11am–9pm, $7

7. WHITNEY MUSEUM OF AMERICAN ART
The Whitney has five special exhibitions a year, and a permanent collection of 6000 American paintings and sculptures.
945 Madison Ave at 75th St (212-570 3676), Wed–Sun 11am–6pm, Thu 11am–8pm, $6

B 1 Work in pairs   Discuss these questions:

- What are the important museums or galleries in your city (or a city you know well)?
- What makes them attractive to tourists? Which would you recommend, and why?

2 ✍ Write a short description (about 120 words) of the two museums which might be included in a guide book or on a handout for visitors to your city.

18.5   Joining up words   SPEAKING

A **1** 🔊 Listen to these sentences:

It is very hard to understand someone if they pause between each of the words in a sentence.

It's much easier to understand someone if the words are joined up like this. When the last sound in a word is a consonant, and the first sound in the next word is a vowel, the words in a sentence are joined up.

2 Mark the places in this article where the words are joined up, when spoken.

SOUND OF MUZAK SOOTHES PATIENTS

IT'S heard in supermarkets, cinemas, lifts and on the telephone as callers wait to be connected. But – muzak in the doctor's consulting room?

A family doctor trainee has found that background music relaxed patients, allowing them to absorb more information during a consultation.

Dr Jonathan Kabler, of St Helier, Jersey, played continuous music during consultations with a hundred and two patients. He chose Mozart's piano concertos seven and twenty-one.

Sixteen patients reported not hearing the music. Of the rest, one felt the music interfered with the consultation, eighty-three per cent found it relaxing, and sixty-seven per cent said it helped the consultation.

'The result appears to be a more enjoyable surgery with lower levels of stress for patients,' Dr Kabler writes in a letter to the British Journal of General Practice.

3 🔊 Listen to the recording and compare your marks with the voices on the tape.

4 **Work in pairs**   Take it in turns to read each paragraph aloud.

B **1** Look again at the passage about Mozart in 18.2 and find two sentences containing the most surprising facts about his life and one sentence containing a fact about his life that you already knew. Mark where the words in the sentences you have chosen are joined up.

2 **Work in pairs**   Read the sentences to your partner.

18.6   *Fall* and *hold*   VERBS AND IDIOMS

Fill the gaps in the sentences below with suitable forms of the phrasal verbs listed:

fall for   fall in   fall out with   fall over   fall through   hold against   hold on   hold on
hold up   hold up

fall

1 In a romantic novel the heroine always .... the handsome hero.

2 She .... him because he was very rude to her.

3 As he wasn't looking where he was going, he tripped and ....

4 Unfortunately, our plans to spend the weekend away have ....

5 He was looking at his reflection in the lake but he lost his balance and ....

hold

6 The robbers .... the bank and got away with £200,000.

7 If you don't .... tightly, you may fall over if the bus brakes suddenly.

8 If you could just .... a minute, I'll try to find the information you require.

9 All the traffic was .... because a lorry had overturned on the motorway.

10 She made a fool of him but he didn't .... it .... her.

18.7 **Works of art?**   LISTENING AND SPEAKING

'Surrounded Islands, Biscayne Bay, Greater Miami, Florida, 1980–83.' Photo: Wolfgang Volz, Copyright Christo.

'The Pont Neuf Wrapped, Paris, 1975–85.' Photo: Wolfgang Volz, Copyright Christo.

A Look at the pictures and discuss these questions:
- Is it art?
- What makes something art?
- Why do museums pay millions for works of art?
- Should works of art taken from their country of origin be sent back home?

B 🔊 You'll hear part of a radio broadcast about Christo and Jeanne-Claude, the artists responsible for the works in the pictures. Complete the notes which summarise the information given in the broadcast.

1 Christo and Jeanne-Claude were both born in	_____ 1
2 Their most expensive project cost	_____ 2
3 They wrapped the Reichstag in Berlin in	_____ 3
4 While the Pont Neuf in Paris was wrapped everything around it looked	_____ 4
5 The number of islands in *Surrounded Islands* was	_____ 5
6 The length of the *Running Fence* was	_____ 6
7 All Christo and Jeanne-Claude's works of art are	_____ 7
8 While each project is being planned, people all over the world are	_____ 8
9 The money they make pays for their	_____ 9
10 The purpose of their works is to persuade people not to	_____ 10

C 👥 **Work in pairs** One of you should look at Activity *18*, the other at *21*. You'll each have a reproduction of another work of art to describe to your partner.

We all make mistakes

EXAM TECHNIQUES

How many mistakes can you find in this student's work? Underline them and then correct them.

```
I enjoy to visit galleries becaus I'm really interested for art. My
favourite paintings are modern paintings, painted by painters like Picasso
and Matisse. Whenever I visit another city I allways try to find time to
waste an afternoon looking for paintings in an art museum. Some quite small
cities have an art gallery, which may not contain any really famous or
valuble works of art. But every museum has it's surprises and there are
often facsinating things to see – especially works by local artists who are
unknown in another countries.
    But I must confess that sometimes it's the people, who are more
interesting as the paintings. As you wander round a museum it's wonderful
to watch different people looking at the exhibits and reacting in different
ways. It's a bit like sitting in a pavement café because you can watch
other people without feeling embarassed about stairing at them.
    So, I'd recommend a visit to a museum next time you're having noting
else to do on a raining day!
```

B 1 Read these notes:

Mistakes in grammar, vocabulary, spelling and punctuation fall into four categories:

1 Slips of the pen.

2 'Silly' or careless mistakes you make frequently – and which your teacher is always correcting.

3 Mistakes you make because you're experimenting with new words and structures – this is fine when you're learning and writing compositions that your teacher will mark. But it isn't advisable in the exam, where it's probably better to play safe and stick to vocabulary and grammar you know are right.

4 Mistakes due to lack of knowledge, where you don't know how a word is spelled, or you haven't learnt the grammatical rules involved. These are mistakes you can't help making.

2 Look at the last two compositions you wrote. How many of the mistakes your teacher has marked could you have corrected yourself? Which category do most of your mistakes fall into? Don't worry about the third kind: these are the kind of mistakes you *should* make if you want to go on learning.

3 **Work in pairs**   Plan two paragraphs of about 50 words each beginning with one of these phrases:

The last time I went to an art gallery . . .
The last time I went to a concert . . .
The last time I went to a museum . . .

4 **Work alone**   Write your two paragraphs. In the first, play safe and try to avoid all possible mistakes by using only words and structures you know are right. You may have to avoid expressing some of your ideas if you don't know the right words. In the second, experiment with your English and try to express all the ideas that occur to you.

5 **Work in pairs**   Look at each other's completed paragraphs, and discuss your reactions to this exercise. Which of your partner's paragraphs do you prefer? When you do the task in C below, which approach will you use?

If you don't know a particular word in English, try to think of other words to express the idea – maybe using a phrase. Alternatively, it may be safer in the exam to move on to your next point and forget about the one you can't express!

C Write an account of a visit to an exhibition, museum, concert or show (120–180 words). Explain what you enjoyed about it and why you would recommend it to other people. (Time yourself. Make notes before you start writing. Correct the mistakes of categories 1 and 2 that you spot.)

19 Other people

19.1 It takes all sorts . . .   VOCABULARY

(A) 1 Work in pairs   Discuss these questions:

- What is your birth sign? Do you think this affects your character?
- What kind of people do you get on with best?
- What kind of people do you find it hard to get on with?

2 Write down five adjectives that describe people you dislike, e.g. dishonest, bad-tempered, and five that describe people or behaviour you approve of, e.g. honest, kind.

(B)   Choose the best alternative to complete these sentences.

1 She's a very .... person – always smiling and in a good mood.
   cheerful   delighted   glad   pleased

2 He's a very .... person – I do wish he was more easy-going.
   bad-tempered   furious   mad   wild

3 Don't tell her off – she's very .... and she may start to cry.
   responsive   sensible   sensitive   responsible

4 People enjoy his company very much because he's very ....
   adorable   likeable   lovable   sympathetic

5 If you've got a problem, go and talk to her – I'm sure she'll be ....
   patient   sympathetic   tolerant   warm-hearted

6 When his wife started seeing more of the tennis coach, he became very ....
   arrogant   envious   jealous   selfish

7 The twins keep pretending to be each other – they're such .... children!
   evil   miserable   naughty   wicked

8 Thank you for my beautiful present. It was very .... of you to buy it for me.
   charitable   generous   loyal   reliable

9 You have to be quite .... to stand up in front of an audience.
   selfish   self-confident   self-conscious   self-satisfied

10 He's a very .... little boy – his parents give him everything he asks for.
   consented   discriminating   generous   spoilt

(C)   Work in groups   Describe the character and appearance of some of these people, but not in this order. *Don't* name them because your partners should try to *guess* the name of the person you describe, or their relationship to you.

- one of your relatives   – a close friend
- a well-known public figure   – someone your partners don't know
- a well-known film star, singer or musician

Work in groups Just suppose you wanted to find a partner by joining a dating agency. Look at the advertisement below and discuss these questions:

- Would you be totally honest about filling it in?
- Or would you make yourself out to be more attractive, interesting or intelligent?
- Is it possible to find a perfect partner for life through an agency like Dateline?

You too can find ...

... but if you can't
don't worry – just fill in the questionnaire below and we will send you
a *free* test to find your perfect partner

If you want to meet the partner of your dreams, why not take part in our new campaign? Whether you are young or old you could find the person you have been looking for amongst many thousands of our members throughout the country, all seeking their special partner.

A friend who is always there for you! Someone who understands you. A partner who loves you and accepts you as you are.

Please complete in block capitals
1. Mr ❐ Mrs ❐ Ms ❐
Surname: _____
First Name: _____
Address: _____
_____
_____ Post Code: _____
Tel No. _____

2. Personal information
Marital Status: Single ❐ Divorced ❐
Widowed ❐ Separated ❐
Religion: _____
Age: _____
Place of Birth: _____

PLEASE ENCLOSE 3
FIRST CLASS STAMPS

3. Your personal details
Height: _____
Build: Slight ❐ Medium ❐ Large ❐
Hair colour: _____

4. Your work
Present job: _____
Self-employed ❐ Employed ❐
Part-time ❐ Not working ❐
Unemployed ❐ In training ❐

5. Your personality
❐ Warm-hearted   ❐ Fashionable
❐ Serious   ❐ Practical
❐ Considerate   ❐ Conventional
❐ Shy   ❐ Reliable
❐ Romantic   ❐ Adventurous

To find the hidden word
Place the picture an inch in front of your eyes. Let your eyes get a little used to it. Then, without changing focus, slowly move the picture away. Stop when the picture is at arms length and gradually the image should become apparent.

Here's Your Chance!
Simply complete this questionnaire and send it to us today! You will receive in the **strictest confidence**, entirely **free of charge** and with no obligation:

1. The name and brief description of someone who could be your perfect partner.
2. Our colour brochure with lots of information about seeking a partner and meeting people.
3. A copy of our paperback '*All You Need is Love*' (R.R.P. £3.99).

6. Your interests
❐ Wining/Dining   ❐ Jazz/Folk music
❐ Pubs   ❐ Classical music
❐ Sports/Keep fit   ❐ Theatre/Arts
❐ Politics/History   ❐ Watching TV
❐ Reading   ❐ Smoking
❐ Travelling   ❐ Astrology
❐ Science/Tech   ❐ Children
❐ Cinema   ❐ Homemaking
❐ Pets/Animals   ❐ Gardening
❐ Pop music   ❐ Countryside

7. The partner you would like:
Minimum age: _____ Maximum age: _____
Height: min. _____ max. _____ Don't mind ❐
Marital status: Single ❐ Divorced ❐
Widowed ❐ Separated ❐ Don't mind ❐

19.2 **Adverbs and word order** GRAMMAR REVIEW

A Correct the mistakes in word order in these sentences. If a sentence is correct, put a tick ✓.

1 *I've met such a nice person before never.* I've never met such a nice person before.

2 *You never know how he's going to react.*

3 *I bumped into Bill the other day.*

4 *He ran very suddenly into the room.*

5 *I really badly had toothache yesterday.*

6 *She tripped over the cat and fell nearly over.*

7 *He completely had misunderstood what I told him to do.*

8 *Surprisingly enough, they rarely make mistakes with word order.*

See the Grammar
Reference section
on page 170.

B **1** **Work in pairs** Decide which are the most 'comfortable' positions (see page 170) that the adverbs below can be placed in for each sentence. In some cases there may be more than one comfortable place.

1 ....a.... She ....b.... was ....c.... able to finish her meal ....d.... .

2 ....a.... He ....b.... managed ....c.... to arrive on time ....d.... .

| almost 1c 2b | always .... | hardly ever .... | nearly .... |
| never .... | rarely .... | seldom .... | |

2 Now do the same with these adverbs and phrases:

as usual certainly definitely maybe normally obviously often on Friday
one day perhaps possibly probably really still surely usually yesterday

C Complete the second sentence so that it has a similar meaning to the first sentence, using the word given in **red**. Do not change the word given. You must use between two and five words, including the word given.

hard
1 She put in a lot of effort to finish the essay.
She ....worked hard to.... finish her essay.

hardly
2 It's unusual to meet people who are so charming.
You .... charming people.

unexpectedly
3 I'm surprised the task took me so long to finish.
The task .... time to finish.

annually
4 In a year the Italians eat 130 km of spaghetti each.
130 km of spaghetti .... the average Italian.

rarely
5 She's a very even-tempered person.
She .... temper.

probably
6 I expect you've already done some FCE practice tests.
By now you .... already done some FCE practice tests.

definitely
7 Don't forget to revise thoroughly before the exams.
You .... revision before the exams.

certainly
8 I'm sure you'll do well in your exams.
You .... do well in your exams.

If there are a few
difficult questions
you can't answer
in the exam, don't
panic – just leave
a blank, put a
pencil mark in the
margin to remind
you where they
are and come
back to them
later.

*"Is it something I've done? Is it something
I've not done? Is it something I've said?
Is it something I haven't said, or is it the
way I didn't say it?"*

This section covers some difficult points which might come up in the Use of English paper.

A Complete the second sentence so that it has a similar meaning to the first sentence, using the word given in red. Do not change the word given. You must use between two and five words, including the word given.

1 You should be very careful.

better   You .... more careful.

2 I'm not very happy.

wish   I .... so unhappy.

3 Please use a dictionary.

like   I .... use a dictionary.

4 Tony told me to do that.

who   It .... told me to do that.

5 It's advisable to arrive a few minutes early.

suggest   I .... arrive a few minutes early.

6 You should do the work soon.

time   It .... the work.

B Find the mistakes in six of these sentences and correct them.

1 *It's better to revise carefully than trust to luck.*

2 *You had better to do some revision.*

3 *It's best to make notes before you start writing.*

4 *I suggest you to read the questions very carefully.*

5 *We'd prefer you not to smoke, if you don't mind.*

6 *They wouldn't like you to use a dictionary.*

7 *Would you rather being healthy or rich?*

8 *I would rather to wear a sweater than a jacket.*

9 *I'd rather you didn't smoke in this room.*

10 *It will soon be time to stop.*

11 *It's time you went home.*

12 *I wish to make a complaint.*

13 *I wish they wouldn't smoke – it makes me cough.*

14 *He wishes he is more intelligent.*

15 *He wishes he had worked harder, but it's too late now.*

16 *If only I have worked harder.*

C Now try this exam-style exercise. Complete the second sentence so that it has a similar meaning to the first sentence, using the word given in red. Do not change the word given. You must use between two and five words, including the word given.

1 Please don't interrupt me when I'm speaking.

rather   I'd .... interrupt me when I'm speaking.

2 It would be a good idea to phone and ask for information.

suggest   I .... phone and ask for information.

3 Don't be so frank – be tactful.

better   It's .... frank.

4 It would be better for me to know your decision now.

prefer   I'd .... me your decision now.

5 Please fill in this questionnaire.

like   I .... fill in this questionnaire.

6 We ought to find out how much it's going to cost.

time   It .... how much it's going to cost.

7 I've got so much to do today.

wish   I .... so much to do today.

8 What a shame you didn't tell me earlier!

only   If .... me earlier.

If you try to remember the grammar points in this section, you should be able to cope with questions like these. But don't forget that losing a couple of marks on very difficult questions like these is not a great disaster – it's the questions that you *can* answer that will help you to succeed in the exam.

19.4 First impressions   READING

 A   🖉   **Highlight the words in the text that mean the same as these words and phrases:**

¶1 frightened   surprised and frightened   without intending   step

¶2 bumped into   remove his fears

¶4 communicated   nervousness

¶6 gently and carefully   revealed

¶13 mood   overemphasised   own individual   suspicious   anticipated   complete

1 My first impression was that the stranger's eyes were of an unusually light blue. They met mine for several blank seconds, vacant, unmistakably scared. Startled and innocently naughty, they half reminded me of an incident I couldn't quite place; something which had happened a long time ago, to do with the upper fourth form classroom. They were the eyes of a schoolboy surprised in the act of breaking one of the rules. Not that I had caught him, apparently, at anything except his own thoughts: perhaps he imagined I could read them. At any rate, he seemed not to have heard or seen me cross the compartment from my corner to his own, for he started violently at the sound of my voice; so violently, indeed, that his nervous recoil hit me like repercussion. Instinctively I took a pace backwards.

2 It was exactly as though we had collided with each other bodily in the street. We were both confused, both ready to be apologetic. Smiling, anxious to reassure him, I repeated my question:

3 'I wonder, sir, if you could let me have a match?'

4 Even now, he didn't answer at once. He appeared to be engaged in some sort of rapid mental calculation, while his fingers, nervously active, sketched a number of flurried gestures round his waistcoat. For all they conveyed, he might equally have been going to undress, to draw a revolver, or merely to make sure that I hadn't stolen his money. Then the moment of agitation passed from his gaze like a little cloud, leaving a clear blue sky. At last he had understood what it was that I wanted:

5 'Yes, yes. Er – certainly. Of course.'

6 As he spoke he touched his left temple delicately with his finger-tips, coughed and suddenly smiled. His smile had great charm. It disclosed the ugliest teeth I had ever seen. They were like broken rocks.

7 'Certainly,' he repeated. 'With pleasure.'

8 Delicately, with finger and thumb, he fished in the waistcoat-pocket of his expensive-looking soft grey suit, and extracted a gold spirit-lighter. His hands were white, small and beautifully manicured.

9 I offered him my cigarettes.

10 'Er – thank you. Thank you.'

11 'After you, sir.'

12 'No, no. Please.'

13 The tiny flame of the lighter flickered between us, and as perishable as the atmosphere which our exaggerated politeness had created. The merest breath would have extinguished the one, the least ludicrous gesture or word would have destroyed the other. The cigarettes were both lighted now. We sat back in our respective places. The stranger was still doubtful of me. He was wondering whether he hadn't gone too far, delivered himself to a bore or a crook. His timid soul was eager to retire. I, on my side, had nothing to read. I foresaw a journey of utter silence, lasting seven or eight hours. I was determined to talk.

14 'Do you know what time we arrive at the frontier?'

15 Looking back on the conversation, this question does not seem to me to have been particularly unusual. It is true that I had no interest in the answer; I wanted merely to ask something which might start us chatting, and which wasn't, at the same time either inquisitive or impertinent. Its effect on the man was remarkable. I had certainly succeeded in arousing his interest.

B   **Answer these multiple-choice questions on the text.**

1 The stranger at first looked

   a) frightened   b) harmless   c) childish   d) surprised

2 Hearing the narrator speaking for the first time made the stranger

   a) gasp   b) get up   c) jump   d) scream

3 The narrator had

   a) sat down beside the stranger   c) walked across to the stranger
   b) sat down opposite the stranger   d) walked up behind the stranger

4 The narrator asked the stranger for a light

   a) once   b) twice   c) three times   d) four times

5 Before replying, the stranger

a) adjusted his waistcoat   c) thought for a while
b) looked for his lighter   d) wondered if the narrator was a thief

6 The stranger gave the narrator a

a) delicate smile   b) nervous smile   c) pleasant smile   d) wicked smile

7 The narrator gave the stranger

a) a cigarette   b) a light   c) a reassuring smile   d) his hand

8 The stranger seemed to be afraid that the writer might be a

a) dull companion   b) murderer   c) foreigner   d) policeman

9 The narrator wanted to start a conversation because he

a) found the stranger fascinating   c) had nothing else to do
b) found the stranger interesting   d) respected the stranger

10 The meeting described in the passage took place

a) in a café   b) on a bus or coach   c) on a plane   d) on a train

C **Work in pairs**   **In your own words, describe the stranger. Then discuss these questions:**

- Why would you have chosen or not chosen to start a conversation with him?
- Have you ever had a conversation with a total stranger on a long journey or in a public place? How did the conversation start and what did you talk about?
- How usual is it to start speaking to strangers on trains or buses in your country?
- Think of your first meetings with two good friends of yours. What were your first impressions? Were they right or wrong?

D **Work in pairs**   One of you should look at Activity 37, the other at 62. You'll each have a picture of some people to describe to your partner.

19.5 **People talking . . .**   **LISTENING**

You'll hear people talking in eight different situations. Choose the best answer, a, b or c.

1 Listen to these two friends talking. What kind of document is the man filling in?
a) an application form   b) a computer dating questionnaire
c) a competition entry form

2 Listen to this woman talking about a man called Bill. Why can't she describe him?
a) They haven't met.   b) She has a bad memory.
c) She didn't think he was important.

3 Listen to the man talking about a friend called Jane. What is Jane's greatest fault?
a) She is too outspoken.   b) She sulks when she loses an argument.
c) She doesn't know when to stop.

4 Listen to this woman talking. When must the work be finished?
a) Friday   b) Tuesday   c) Wednesday

5 Listen to this man talking. Who is he speaking to?
a) a child   b) a good friend   c) a stranger

6 Listen to this man talking to a friend. Why is he late?
a) He has been running.   b) He had to make a telephone call.
c) Someone on the phone wouldn't stop talking.

7 You're staying at a friend's flat. What does she want you to do?
a) take a message if anyone phones   b) give someone a message
c) make breakfast for her

8 You're sitting in a restaurant when you overhear this conversation. How many pizzas are ordered?
a) one   b) two   c) three

19.6 Synonyms WORD STUDY

Some words which are perfectly all right in conversation are best avoided if you want to make your writing more interesting, and if you want to gain marks in the exam for using a wide vocabulary.

(A) 1 Work in pairs Look at these examples. What is the difference between them?

1 She's a very nice person. It was nice of her to help me and she was nice to you too, wasn't she?

2 She's a very likeable person. For example, it was kind of her to help me and she was friendly to you too, wasn't she?

2 Write down at least *two* synonyms that can be used in place of:

nice good bad thing like dislike

3 Write down at least *two* synonyms you can use instead of these adjectives (to avoid having to repeat the same word in a paragraph).

large small important intelligent interesting strange unpleasant beautiful

4 Write five sentences, using some of the words in 2 and 3 above. Pass them to another pair to rewrite more interestingly or more clearly.

(B) Sometimes you may not be able to think of exactly the right word you need:

The carpenter wanted to tighten the screws, so he used a...you know...a whatchmacallit.

But it's sometimes possible to use a less exact word which still shows what you mean:

*He used a special **tool** to tighten up the screws.*

Many synonyms either don't mean exactly the same as each other, or are used in different contexts. For example, *startled* and *terrified* don't have quite the same meanings. But *scared* and *frightened* do mean the same.

1 screwdriver hammer spanner *tools*	13 bread cake meat
2 brother cousin uncle *relatives*	14 dollar pound franc
3 grass cactus bush	15 racket bat stick
4 rabbit lion mouse	16 rugby tennis squash
5 lamb beef chicken	17 photography stamp-collecting reading
6 bus train lorry	18 medicine law accountancy
7 house flat room hotel	19 parrot goldfish cat
8 parrot sparrow pigeon	20 wheat rye oats
9 copper steel iron	21 rose carnation daisy ·
10 breakfast supper lunch	22 ant bee wasp
11 autumn spring winter	23 book newspaper brochure
12 suit socks sweater	24 violin guitar piano

19.7 Leave, let, pull and run VERBS AND IDIOMS

(A) Fill the gaps in these sentences with suitable forms of the verbs, *leave, let, pull* or *run*.

1 Could you .... him know the news?

2 I'm not serious, I'm just .... your leg.

3 Don't push the door, ... it to open it.

4 I asked him to .... me alone.

5 Let's .... the washing-up till tomorrow.

6 They .... the flat for £200 a month.

7 When does the London train .... ?

8 He .... five kilometres before breakfast.

9 She was .... £2,000 in her aunt's will.

10 I'm just going to .... the bath.

11 Hold tight and don't .... go.

12 My uncle .... a restaurant in the old city.

B Fill the gaps in the sentences below with suitable forms of the phrasal verbs listed:

leave behind   leave out   leave over   let down   let in   let off   pull down   pull out
pull up   run after   run into   run into   run off with   run out of   run over

leave

1 If you can't answer a question, don't .... it .... – guess the answer.

2 There was a lot of food .... after the party.

3 I .... my coat .... in the classroom last week.

let

4 I'm sorry that I .... you .... by arriving so late.

5 It's a very exclusive restaurant – they won't .... anyone .... wearing jeans.

6 It's very dangerous to .... fireworks .... indoors.

pull

7 You can't get on or off a bus when it .... at the traffic lights.

8 If you've got toothache, you may have to have that tooth ....

9 It's a shame that all the old buildings have been ....

run

10 He braked suddenly to avoid .... a dog but he lost control and .... a tree.

11 You won't believe this: the pub has .... beer.

12 We were walking past the farm when a large black dog started to .... us.

13 I .... an old school-friend of mine the other day.

14 Mrs Brown has .... her best friend's husband.

19.8 Describing people   WRITING

A 1 Write four paragraphs (about 40 words), incorporating all the points listed.

1 Andrew: overweight   mid-30s   selfish   dishonest   loses his temper
people disagree with him

2 Becky: slim   late 50s   absent-minded   delightful sense of humour
helps other people with problems

3 Carl: 18   athletic   loves sport   favourite game: football
spare time: likes going out with friends and cinema

4 Debbie: 16   studious   enjoys reading   four brothers and two sisters
hopes to go to university   wants to study engineering

2 Work in pairs   Compare your paragraphs and suggest improvements.

B Write 120–180 words on one of these topics.

1 Write an **article** for a magazine describing two people you admire or like OR two people you dislike very much. Explain why you feel this way about these people.

2 Write a **story** for a school magazine describing your first meeting with someone who became a close friend OR someone who later became an enemy.

3 Write a **letter** to a new pen-friend. Imagine that this is your first letter and give your pen-friend a good idea of your appearance, interests and personality.

4 If you have read one of the prescribed books, write an **article** for a student newspaper explaining which of the characters you liked best OR which of the characters you found least attractive.

• Complete the task in 45 minutes. Don't use a dictionary.
• Make notes before you start. Decide how you will begin and end your composition.
• Check your work through afterwards.

In questions like 1–3, the examiners are interested in how well you can express yourself, not in how truthful you are. Imaginary ideas may be more interesting – or easier to describe. Your imagination can steer your composition towards using the words you know.

For example, you could describe a wonderful imaginary aunt and uncle in 1 or write about an exciting imaginary meeting in 2 – and you don't have to tell the truth about yourself in 3!

20 Memories

20.1 Paper 1: Reading   EXAM TECHNIQUES

 Work in pairs   What do you know about the Reading paper?

- How many parts are there in this paper?
- How long do you have?
- What do you have to do in each part?
- What do you think is the most important piece of advice about this paper which you really must remember?

B Complete the exam-style reading task below from Part 3 of Paper 1.

C **1** Do a complete run-through of the Reading paper using a practice test. Time how long it takes you to do all four texts and all the questions.

It may be best to read the questions quickly through before you read each passage, so that you know what you have to find out. Alternatively, you may prefer to read the text quickly through (to get an idea of what it's about) before you read the questions and then read more carefully, looking for the answers in the text.

If you spend too long trying to find a particular answer, you may run out of time. It may be best to make a pencil mark beside a tricky question and come back to it at the end.

Use a highlighter to mark the places in each text where the important information is to be found.

2 **Work in pairs   Afterwards, discuss these questions:**

- If you ran out of time before the 1 hour 15 minutes was up, how can you get faster next time?
- Did you spend too long on one of the texts? Which one?
- If you had more than ten minutes to spare at the end, what did you do during this time?

You can prepare for the Reading paper by doing more practice tests and also by spending some of your free time reading newspapers, magazines or stories in English.

PART 3

You are going to read a brochure for tourists. Six sentences have been removed from the brochure. Choose from the sentences **A–G** the one which fits in each gap **1–6**. There is one extra sentence you do not need to use.

A For a while, modern time-travellers explore Coppergate and a little alley, Lundgate, which runs off it.

B Four rows of buildings were found, running back from Coppergate itself, almost exactly in the same positions as their modern successors.

C Jorvik has become York's favourite tourist attraction.

D Most of the city's buildings were made of wood, and have long since been demolished, or have burnt down or rotted away.

E People in the 10th century called it Jorvik, and knew it as the capital of the North of England, and one of Europe's greatest trading ports.

F Two of the rows of buildings were reconstructed as we think they were.

G Whole streets of houses, shops, workshops and warehouses are to be found, often still standing shoulder high.

JORVIK –
LOST VIKING CAPITAL

A thousand years ago York was one of the largest, richest and most famous cities in the whole of Britain. A monk at that time described it as packed with a huge population, rich merchandise, and traders 'from all parts, especially Danes.' **1** [ ] It owed its prosperity to the hard work and commercial enterprise of Viking settlers from Scandinavia who had captured it in AD 866 and almost totally rebuilt it.

Viking Jorvik has now completely disappeared. **2** [ ] In some parts of modern York, however, near the rivers Ouse and Foss, which run through the centre of the city, archaeologists have found that remains of Jorvik do still survive. They are buried deep below the streets and buildings of the 20th century city. Here the damp soils have preserved the timber buildings. **3** [ ] All the debris and rubbish left by the people of Jorvik in and around their homes is still there, awaiting discovery.

Between 1976 and 1981 archaeologists from the York Archaeological Trust excavated a part of this lost and all-but-forgotten city. The dig took place in Coppergate, before the city's new Coppergate Centre was built. **4** [ ] The remains were so well preserved – even

down to boots and shoes, pins and needles, plants and insects – that every aspect of life at the time could be reconstructed.

York Archaeological Trust decided to try to tell the story of Jorvik as it was a thousand years ago. To do so it built the Jorvik Viking Centre in the huge hole created by the dig. **5** [ ] A further two were preserved just as the archaeological team discovered them, the ancient timbers set out as they were found in the late 1970s, deep below the new shopping centre, where they have lain for centuries.

In the Jorvik Viking Centre people from the 20th century journey back in time to the 10th century. The journey is done in time-cars, which silently glide back through the years, past some of the thirty or so generations of York's people who have walked the pavements of Coppergate, until time stops, on a late October day in 948. **6** [ ] The neighbourhood is full of the sights and sounds and smells of 10th century Jorvik. Townspeople are there, buying and selling, working and playing.

20.2 Paper 2: Writing EXAM TECHNIQUES

When you check your compositions through for mistakes, you need to notice and correct spelling errors and grammatical mistakes. Some of these may just be careless mistakes or slips of the pen – others may be harder to recognise.

A **1** **Work in pairs** Find the mistakes in these sentences and correct them – in some cases there are two or more mistakes.

Careless mistakes and slips of the pen:

1 *The castle contain many treasure and painting.*
2 *Spelling mistakes are not serious but they do lost you marks.*
3 *My brother has brown eyes and so do my sister.*
4 *Could you tell me what time does the museum opens?*
5 *Which one of you payed for the tickets?*

Mistakes that may be harder to notice:

6 *After visiting the museum he had not very much time left.*
7 *His hair is very long, it's time for him to have cut it.*
8 *I am waiting for you since four hours.*
9 *They never visited Rome before their first visit in 1987.*
10 *She never wrote a letter by hand since she has bought a computer.*
11 *I am learning English during five years.*
12 *A suspicious is questioning by the police.*
13 *Before they had gone out they had been watched the news on TV.*

2 Look at your four most recent compositions and read all of your teacher's corrections and comments. Would you make the same mistakes again?

B **Work in pairs** What do you know about the Writing paper?

- How many parts are there in this paper? How long do you have?
- What do you have to do in each part?
- What do you think is the most important piece of advice about this paper which you really must remember?

In the exam, before you start writing:

1 Make sure you fully understand the instructions for each question. If you don't quite understand a particular question, it's best not to answer it.

2 For Question 1 (which is compulsory) make sure you include every point you're supposed to.

3 Decide which of the questions in Part 2 is the easiest for you to answer.

4 Make notes on both questions. If you find you haven't got enough ideas for the one you've chosen in Part 2, there may still be time to choose a different one.

5 If you've read one of the set books, you have an extra topic to choose from. But you don't have to do that question unless you want to: you may prefer to write a story, for example.

C Write your answers to the exam-style tasks on pages 163–164 under exam conditions in 1 hour 30 minutes.

PART 1

You **must** answer this question.

1 Read this information about the cities of York and Cambridge and the extract from a letter from your friends Bob and Mary Green and their children, Helen (14) and Richard (16).

Write a **letter** to them of between **120–180** words in an appropriate style, advising them which city they should go to and what you think they should do together (or separately) once they get there. Do not write any addresses.

York
Historic city with many ancient buildings

- Roman city walls – walk around the city
- York Minster: one of largest churches in Europe, stained glass windows
- Jorvik Viking Centre: experience the sights, sounds and smells of daily life in Viking times
- The Shambles: old street lined with fascinating shops
- Castle Museum: contains a reconstructed street with shops of various periods
- National Railway Museum: historic engines, carriages and history of railways in Britain

Journey time from London 2 hours – day return £48

CAMBRIDGE
Historic university city with old colleges

■ King's College Chapel: tall windows and superb ceiling

■ Colleges – many are open for the public to walk through: peaceful courtyards

■ Fitzwilliam Museum: paintings and antiquities

■ Kettle's Yard: delightful artist's house full of paintings and beautiful furniture

■ River Cam: walk beside river or hire a boat

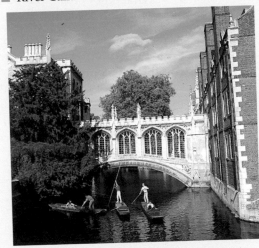

Journey time from London 1 hour – day return £25

... Mary will be attending a conference in London next month and I've decided to join her at the weekend with the children. It's Mary's birthday on Sunday, so we'd like to do something special. We're thinking of taking the train to either York or Cambridge. The problem is that, although we're all interested in history, Helen prefers looking at paintings, Mary doesn't like walking, I don't like museums and Richard is still crazy about railways!

You know both cities: which do you recommend? What can we do together when we arrive there? Or should we split up and meet later in the day for lunch or tea?

PART 2

Write an answer to **one** of the questions **2–5** in this part. Write your answer in **120–180** words in an appropriate style.

2   What was life like in your country 20 years ago? Write an **account** of the changes that have taken place and explain how the quality of life has improved or got worse.

3   Write a short **story** that includes this phrase:
'... everything seemed to be going well until ...'

4   You have been chosen by the other members of your class to present a gift to your teacher. Write a **letter** to accompany the gift, explaining why you have chosen this particular gift and thanking your teacher for everything he or she has done for you.

5   **Background reading texts**

Answer **one** of the following two questions based on your reading of **one** of the set books.

(a) Write an **article** telling the story of the book from the point of view of one of the characters (but not the storyteller).

(b) An English-speaking friend has asked about the book. Write a **letter** recommending it.

Your teacher will give you a mark for the two compositions and also tell you what particular points you should be careful about in the exam.

D   **Work in pairs**   **Discuss these questions:**

- What are your typical 'careless mistakes' of spelling and grammar that you should notice when checking your work?
- What types of composition do you feel more confident about (e.g. writing a story) and which do you dislike (e.g. writing an essay)?

In the exam it's a good idea to leave fairly wide margins and to leave a line or two between each paragraph. Then, if you want to add anything or cross a sentence out and rewrite it, you'll have plenty of space.

Don't forget to put the number of the question you've chosen in Part 2 in the box at the top of the page in the answer booklet.

The type of writing required is shown in bold letters on the exam paper: **report**, **letter**, **story**, etc. Make sure you notice this – but remember that different types of writing can overlap. A story could be written in letter form, for example.

20.3   Paper 3: Use of English   EXAM TECHNIQUES

Do the revision exercises on the next pages 'against the clock' in 1 hour 15 minutes. Or do each part separately and discuss the answers as you go along.

The texts in parts 1, 2, 4 and 5 are adapted from *Dreams for Sale*, a history of popular culture in the 20th century. (In the exam the texts will all come from different sources and be about *different* topics.)

PART 1

For Questions **1–15**, read the text below and decide which answer **A**, **B**, **C** or **D** best fits each space.

Note: *ephemeral = lasting for only a short time

When we **(1)** .... nostalgically at the recent past, we often recognise it by the things we **(2)** .... to buy, or else by such modern 'heroes' **(3)** .... movie stars and sports celebrities. The movies, music, fashions, sport and designs **(4)** .... a vivid map of our past, because they all share ephemerality*. They are all things of the **(5)** .... , designed to have a brief life, to burn brightly for the **(6)** .... and disappear, but are always replaced by other **(7)** .... more brightly coloured things of the hour.

An athletic record or popular song is **(8)** .... by another which is little different from it. These **(9)** .... us in an endless parade with **(10)** .... functions but different details. In the details of **(11)** .... parade is contained a history of our century. At **(12)** .... level it is a history of skirt lengths and Top Ten hits, a history of the ephemeral* things in **(13)** .... we wrap our sentimental memories of lost loves and long-ago summers. But it is also a history of **(14)** .... modern society has created images of **(15)** .... and expressed its fantasies, its fears, its ambitions.

1 A look	**B** regard	**C** see	**D** watch
2 A wanted	**B** like	**C** have	**D** used
3 A like	**B** than	**C** as	**D** and
4 A give	**B** provide	**C** are	**D** appear
5 A moment	**B** present	**C** history	**D** fashion
6 A while	**B** instant	**C** time	**D** day
7 A even	**B** sudden	**C** indeed	**D** very
8 A taken	**B** broken	**C** replaced	**D** released
9 A show	**B** pass	**C** reveal	**D** bring
10 A same	**B** similar	**C** different	**D** various
11 A any	**B** some	**C** a	**D** this
12 A a	**B** one	**C** every	**D** each
13 A that	**B** which	**C** this	**D** where
14 A how	**B** where	**C** when	**D** which
15 A it	**B** itself	**C** them	**D** this

PART 2

For Questions **16–30**, read the text below and think of the word which best fits each space. Use only **one** word in each space.

For 70 years, Hollywood, 'The Dream Factory', 'the entertainment capital of the world', has manufactured and marketed a consumer product: the **(16)** .... of 'going to the movies' rather **(17)** .... any particular film. In going to the movies, people consume *time* by renting **(18)** .... in the cinema for an **(19)** .... or two. What we are really buying is perhaps something different, something already our own. They steal our dreams, and then **(20)** .... them back to us for entertainment.

The buying and selling of time is the central activity of the leisure industry. This is what differentiates modern popular culture **(21)** .... the folk culture which preceded it, and from which it borrowed **(22)** .... of its forms. Football, for **(23)** .... , developed in the 19th **(24)** .... into its various modern forms out of local traditional games, but by 1900 it had become a professional **(25)** .... . The players earned their **(26)** .... by the game, and their spectators **(27)** .... for the pleasure of watching. Throughout the present century, adults have criticised their **(28)** .... for preferring to buy the products of popular culture **(29)** .... than 'make their own entertainment'. This offers a clear distinction **(30)** .... folk culture and popular culture: folk culture is something you make; popular culture is something you buy.

PART 3

For Questions **31–40**, complete the second sentence so that it has a similar meaning to the first sentence, using the word given. **Do not change the word given.** You must use between two and five words, including the word given.

31 I haven't seen my old school friend for ages.
   ages   It's .... my old school friend.

32 I found the questions difficult to answer.
   hard   The questions .... answer.

33 It was my first visit to North America.
   never   I .... North America before.

34 The ancient Egyptians built the Pyramids.
   built   The .... the ancient Egyptians.

35 It'll be necessary for her to give up her job soon.
   soon   She .... give up her job.

36 'Closed due to illness' said the notice on the door of the shop.
   found   We .... was closed due to illness.

37 In spite of the heat we had no difficulty climbing the hill.
   easy   The hill .... despite the heat.

38 It wasn't a good idea for you to put such a lot of salt in the soup.
   so   You .... much salt in the soup.

39 It's so salty that I can't eat it.
   too   It .... eat.

40 We couldn't finish the exercise because there was no time left.
   ran   We .... we didn't finish the exercise.

PART 4

For Questions **41–55**, read the text below and look carefully at each line. Some of the lines are correct, and some have a word which should **not** be there. If a line is correct, put a tick (✓) by the number. If a line has a word which should **not** be there, write the word. There are two examples at the beginning (**0** and **00**).

0	Among of the many fundamental social changes of the 19th century	*of*
00	was the way in which leisure was systematised. The factory system	✓
41	regulated time in a new way, making work time different from time spent not working.
42	In a sense that had not been true in pre-industrial culture, so time not working became
43	an empty period that needed to be occupied. For as much of the 19th century, leisure,
44	which can be defined as if the non-productive use of time, was only for rich people and
45	the upper classes. But by the early 20th century the idea of leisure it had spread down
46	through the social system in Europe and North America and new activities came into
47	an existence to occupy leisure time.
48	The city amusements of the late end 19th century included such things as bars,
49	dance halls, games rooms and roller-skating rinks; cheap novels and illustrated
50	papers, circuses, amusement parks, and with professional sports. There were
51	also cheap seats in theatres and concert halls. Most spectacular of all were
52	the so great exhibitions of the second half of the 19th century, beginning at London's
53	Crystal Palace in 1851 and culminating in the Paris Exhibition of 1900. These
54	architectural extravagances, which displayed so many of the new wonders of
55	about the worlds of industry and commerce, were available to anyone who could pay.

PART 5

For Questions **56–65**, read the text below. Use the word given in capitals at the end of each line to form a word that fits in the space in the same line.

By 1900 (**56**) .... output had developed so much that consumption as well as | **INDUSTRY**
(**57**) .... had to be managed and controlled. In the 19th century, industrialists had | **PRODUCE**
treated their (**58**) .... simply as workers who would produce their goods, but in | **EMPLOY**
the early 20th century, these workers became (**59**) .... as well. | **PURCHASE**

Advertising and **(60)** .... soon became industries themselves, developed out of a need to persuade people to buy. In the 19th century **(61)** .... merely made and sold products, but in the 20th century **(62)** .... were needed to create and sustain a demand for each new product. Consumers were not just given **(63)** .... of the new products but they were shown the emotional **(64)** .... that they could gain by buying products for **(65)** .... and pleasure.

MARKET
MANUFACTURE
ADVERTISE
DESCRIBE
SATISFY
ENJOY

20.4 Paper 4: Listening   EXAM TECHNIQUES

A **Work in pairs**   What do you know about the Listening paper?

- How long does it last? How many times do you hear each part?
- How many parts are there?
- What do you have to do in each part?

B Complete these exam-style listening tasks from two parts of Paper 4.

You'll hear Liz talking about a childhood experience. Complete the notes which summarise what she says. You will need to write a word or a short phrase in each box.

1	The incident happened to Liz when she was	**1**
2	Liz and her brother used to go together to the	**2**
3	While she was on one of the swings, she realised she was	**3**
4	She was sitting on the swing with	**4**
5	The dog tried to	**5**
6	In the end, the dog	**6**
7	After that she didn't go to the playground if it was	**7**
8	She didn't realise it then, but her brother had gone home to	**8**
9	Her brother came back with	**9**
10	Since then she has never	**10**

You'll hear five people talking about events they remember. Choose from the list **A–F** what happened to each one. Use the letters only once. There is one extra letter which you do not need to use.

A	This person had a lucky escape.	Speaker 1	**11**
B	A child was badly hurt.	Speaker 2	**12**
C	The experience made this person cry.	Speaker 3	**13**
D	A mother was very worried about her child.	Speaker 4	**14**
E	This person couldn't believe their eyes.	Speaker 5	**15**
F	This person was afraid burglars were inside.		

C **Work in pairs**   **Discuss these questions.**

- Which parts of this paper have *not* been practised in this section?
- What do you find hardest about the Listening paper?

Make sure you read the questions through carefully while you're waiting for the recording to be played to you.

If you are slightly unsure about any answers, lightly pencil in the answer you think might be best, then listen carefully for the answer to that question on the second listening.

If you have no idea about an answer, don't leave a blank – guess!

You can prepare for this paper by spending some of your free time listening to English-language radio programmes, or by watching videos in English.

20.5 Paper 5: Speaking   EXAM TECHNIQUES

A **Work in pairs**   **What do you know about the Speaking paper?**

- How long does it last? How many people are in the room with you?
- How many parts are there?
- What do you have to do in each part?

B 1 **Work in pairs**   **Let's suppose the topic of the paper is the past and history. Rather than pretending to do a complete exam with 'examiners', like we did in 14.2, let's just try some discussion tasks which involve everyone.**

👥 **One of you should look at Activity 2, the other at 30. You'll each have two pictures from the past to discuss.**

2 **Look at the brochure below and discuss these questions:**

- Would you like to visit this place? Why/Why not?
- What would you enjoy most about it?
- What historical buildings or monuments have you visited? What did you find interesting about them?
- What buildings or monuments should a visitor to your city or area go and see? Why?

"The loveliest castle in the world."

LORD CONWAY

Leeds Castle, Kent. Named after Led, Chief Minister of Ethelbert IV, King of Kent, in AD 857.

It is situated about 4 miles to the East of Maidstone on the A20 London–Folkestone Road, in some of England's loveliest countryside.

Built on two islands in the middle of a lake, the Castle was originally a stronghold until it was converted into a Royal Palace by Henry VIII.

Beautifully furnished and lovingly restored, its truly historic atmosphere gently reminds one that it was a Royal Residence for over 300 years.

The surrounding parklands offer many magnificent views and walks as well as a charming woodland garden.

Lunch, tea and light refreshments are available and picnics are welcome in the grounds surrounding the car park area.

Leeds Castle, Maidstone, Kent.

In the exam, the examiner will give you marks for the following aspects of your spoken English:

Fluency – Do you speak without too much hesitation?
Grammatical accuracy – Do you speak without making too many mistakes?
Pronunciation – Can people understand you easily?
Communication – Do you communicate your ideas effectively in a conversation?
Vocabulary – Do you know enough words to be able to express your ideas?

There's not a great deal you can do to avoid making mistakes when you speak. It's probably best just to concentrate on the ideas you want to communicate. If you're naturally a shy person, perhaps pretend to be someone more confident when you're talking. The examiner wants to hear you talking: it's better to keep on talking than to give very short answers to the examiner's questions.

3 Discuss these questions:

- Why do people study history?
- In what ways is studying history relevant to our present-day lives?
- What important historical events have happened in the history of your country? (In Britain everyone learns what happened in 1066 and 1588, for example. What equivalent 'memorable dates' are there in your country's history?)
- What would have happened if those events had turned out differently?
- If someone who had emigrated from your country or city 20 years ago returned now, what changes would they notice?

You can prepare for this paper by teaming up with another student in your free time and talking English together, instead of your own language.

Remember that in the interview you should try to be as relaxed as possible – and as talkative as you normally are in class. The best way to do this is to talk nothing but English (or as much English as you can) for 24 hours before the exam.

20.6 Good luck!

Don't forget:

– keep cool and don't panic if there are some questions you can't answer

– use your time sensibly

– read all the instructions and examples very carefully

– check all your written work and correct any careless mistakes you've made

– show the examiners how much you know!

Best of luck and good wishes from

Leo Jones

P.S. Take two of everything with you to the exam, just in case:

two pens (and cartridges or refills)

two highlighters

two pencils (and a pencil sharpener)

two rubbers

Grammar reference

CONTENTS

In the examples in these sections ✓ indicates a correct sentence and ✗ indicates an incorrect sentence.

Adverbs and word order

SEE 19.2 FOR EXERCISES AND MORE EXAMPLES

1 Different adverbs and adverb phrases may fit 'comfortably' in different places in a sentence: at the beginning, in the middle or at the end.

Some can go in **all three** positions:

> Recently, he was arrested.
> He was recently arrested.
> He was arrested recently.
> Unexpectedly, he was arrested.
> He was unexpectedly arrested.
> He was arrested unexpectedly.

2 Some feel most comfortable **at the end**:

> He was arrested by the police.
> He was arrested yesterday.
> I'll phone you tomorrow.
> Can you phone me in the afternoon?

3 These adverbs usually feel most comfortable in the **middle** position:

almost   always   certainly   completely   ever   frequently   hardly   hardly ever
nearly   never   obviously   often   probably   rarely   seldom

> He was certainly arrested.
> He has never been arrested.

Notice where middle position adverbs are placed when there is a modal verb in the sentence:

> He will certainly be arrested. ✓   He will be certainly arrested. ✗
> He will never be arrested. ✓

4 An adverb is not normally placed between a verb and a direct object:

> I like tennis very much ✓   I like very much tennis. ✗
> He drove the car very fast. ✓   He drove very fast the car. ✗

Articles and quantifiers

SEE 5.5 AND 6.4 FOR EXERCISES AND MORE EXAMPLES

1 Most nouns are **countable**, for example:

car   bus   train   tram

We can talk about a car, cars and some cars.

But some nouns are **uncountable**, for example:

petrol   wine   freedom   safety   water   rain

We can't say: a petrol ✗ or petrols ✗
But we can say: some petrol

Remember that these common English nouns are **uncountable**:

furniture   information   weather   advice   hair   progress   news

We can't say: a good news ✗ or a furniture ✗
But we can say: some good news or some furniture

Or we can refer to a singular item by using words such as *piece*, *slice*, *cup*, etc.:

a piece of good news   three cups of water

Remember that uncountable nouns take a singular verb:

The news is good.   The weather was awful.

2 **Quantifiers** are words like *few, less, some, any, much* and *many*:

There's some tea left in the pot, and there are some biscuits in the packet.
There isn't any tea left in the pot, and there aren't any biscuits either.
Is there any tea left in the pot? Are there any biscuits left in the packet?
Is there some tea left? (hopefully expecting the answer *yes*)

Less, the least, little and *much* are only used with uncountable nouns:

There isn't much tea left.   Beth's got less money than Jane.
There's very little tea left.   But Dave's got the least money of all.

Few, fewer, the fewest and *many* are only used with plural countable nouns:

There aren't many biscuits left.   Alan's got fewer friends than Sue.
There are only a few biscuits.   But Dave's got the fewest friends of all.

3 *The* is used in these cases:

a) Referring to things that are **unique** (in other words, only **one** of them exists):

Cricket is the most popular summer sport in Britain.
the Queen of England
The sea is too rough to swim in.
Is Manchester United the best football team in the UK?
I'm worried about the future.
What time does the sun rise?

(BUT: see the notes on planets, mountains, parks, etc. which follow)

b) When it's **obvious** which one you mean:

We're going to the pub; you can join us there later.
I'm taking the dog for a walk.
How many students are there in the class?
We are taking the exam in the summer.

c) When we mean a **particular** person or thing:

the actor who played the villain
The big question fitness experts are asking is . . .
The director of the film *Psycho* was Alfred Hitchcock.

d) Oceans, seas and rivers:

the Atlantic   the Aegean   the Mediterranean   the Thames   the Rhine

e) **Plural** mountain groups, island groups and countries:

the Andes   the Canary Islands   the Netherlands   the Philippines

f) Hotels, cinemas, theatres, museums:

the Ritz   the Gaumont   the Playhouse   the National Gallery   the Tate Gallery

4 *A* or *an* is used in these cases:

a) Referring to a **single** thing or person:

There's a bank opposite the cinema. (one of several banks in the town)
It's a difficult exercise.
a friend of mine
She's a friend of Peter's.
It was quite an interesting story.
She's such an active person.

b) **Professions** or **jobs**:

He's an actor.   She's an engineer.
My father's a taxi-driver.   My mother's a teacher.

c) **Generalisations**:

An actor performs in front of an audience.
A leisure pool usually has a water slide.
A manager has to be a good leader.

5 Ø – the '**zero article**' is used in these cases:

a) **Generalisations** about plural ideas, people or things:

Actors perform in front of audiences.   Managers have to be good leaders.
New cars are expensive.   Bicycles are pollution-free.
Dictionaries are useful.   Babies are noisy.

b) Referring to concepts and ideas that are **uncountable**:

shopping   freedom   knowledge   pollution   liberty   democracy   history   music
tennis   stamp-collecting   watching television   swimming

Are you keen on shopping?
Freedom is more important than wealth.
. . . certain inalienable Rights . . . Life, Liberty and the pursuit of Happiness.
Freedom from want, freedom from hunger.

c) With these places, but only when they're used for their **main** purpose, rather than just for a visit or when they are considered as buildings:

He went to school in England.   = he was educated
You mustn't smoke in class.   = during lessons
We go to church every Sunday.   = to worship
She's in hospital.   = for treatment
He's going to university.   = to study

BUT: She drove to the school to pick up her son, then to the university to pick up her daughter.

d) Planets, continents, countries, states:

Jupiter   Europe   Britain   Holland   France   California   Texas

BUT: the Earth   the Sun   the Moon   the United Kingdom   the Netherlands

e) Languages:

English   Dutch   Swahili   Greek

f) Mountains and lakes:

Mount Fuji   Lake Geneva   Ben Nevis   Lake Superior

g) Streets, roads and squares:

Oxford Street   Fifth Avenue   Trafalgar Square   Regent Street

h) Parks, stations and public buildings:

Central Park   Victoria Station   Gatwick Airport   Buckingham Palace   Windsor Castle

BUT: the Acropolis   the Statue of Liberty   the Eiffel Tower   the Empire State Building

Comparing and contrasting

SEE 17.2 FOR EXERCISES AND MORE EXAMPLES

Retired people aged over 60 per 1,000 workers

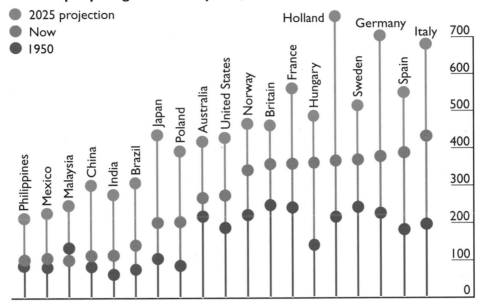

These examples show the principal uses of comparatives and superlatives. Pay particular attention to the way in which **similar** ideas can be expressed in **different** ways.

According to the chart:

> People in Italy live longer than anywhere else in the world.
> > = There are more retired people in Italy than anywhere else in the world.
> > = Italy has the oldest population in the world.

> Far more people live to retirement age in Britain than in the Philippines.
> > = Not as many people live to retirement age in the Philippines as in Britain.

> There are about the same number of old people in Australia as in the USA.
> > = The number of old people in Australia is similar to the number in the USA.

> There are not as many old people in Mexico as in Japan.
> > = There are fewer old people in Mexico than in Japan.

> The population of France is less youthful than the population of Brazil.
> > = The population of France is not as young as the population of Brazil.

> There are about twice as many retired people in the USA as in Brazil.
> > = There are about half as many retired people in Brazil as in the USA.

> Spain has the second oldest population in the world now.
> Throughout the world, people live much longer nowadays than they used to.
> The number of old people in China is nothing like as high as in Sweden.

The future

SEE 18.3 FOR EXERCISES AND MORE EXAMPLES

1 For **predictions** and **general** statements about the future *will* or *will be doing* or *will have done* are used:

> In the future the Earth will be hotter.
> I expect it will rain tomorrow.
> By the end of this year I'll have taken my exam.
> While I'm studying, my younger brother will be enjoying himself.
> I'm sure the weather will have improved by the end of the week.
> If you don't hurry up, the bus will have left before we get to the bus stop!
> This time next year we'll be in our new flat – if everything goes according to plan.

Remember that *will* and *'ll* are not normally used in a clause following a **time conjunction**:

when   if   until   before   after   while   by the time

> If you do your work tonight, you'll be able to go out tomorrow.
> We'll tidy up our rooms before she arrives.
> After he has done the housework, he'll have to start cooking the dinner.
> If you use a highlighter, you'll find it easier to remember the new words.

The short form *'ll* is normally only used after pronouns:

> I'll do it.   It'll rain tomorrow.

but in writing, or for emphasis, the full form *will* is often used:

> I will do it.   It will rain tomorrow.

2 For **inevitable** future events that we can 'see coming' *going to* is used:

> One day there's going to be a terrible accident on that road.
> My wife's going to have a baby.
> Look out! That dog is going to bite you!

3 For **intentions** *going to* is used:

> I'm going to leave now.
> We're going to visit Spain next year.
> I'm going to do the work later when I've got more time.

4 For **arrangements** the **present continuous** is used:

> I'm seeing the dentist at 2.30.
> We're visiting Spain next year.
> She's meeting her friend this afternoon.
> I can't meet you this evening because I'm washing my hair.

5 For **fixed events** on a timetable or calendar the **present simple** is used:

> The exam takes place on June 13th and 14th.   (= it's in the calendar)
> The plane from London lands at 09.30.

6 For **promises**, **suggestions** and **offers** *will* is used:

> I'll pay for lunch if you help me with my work.
> I'll help you tomorrow.
> Give me your suitcase and I'll put it in the boot of the car for you.

Normally, *shall* is only used when making an offer or a suggestion:

> Shall I help you? ✓   Will I help you? ✗
> Shall we take a break now? ✓   Will we take a break now? ✗

and not in these cases:

> He shan't arrive on time. ✗   He won't arrive on time. ✓
> They shall be late. ✗   They'll (will) be late. ✓

7 In most of the examples in 1–5 *going to* could be used instead of *will* or a **present tense**. In informal conversations, *going to* is more common than *will*. In formal writing, *will* is more often used.

A rule of thumb for conversation is: if in doubt, use *going to*, except if you're making a promise, offer or suggestion (when *going to* may sound like a threat).

If . . . sentences (Conditionals)

SEE 9.5 AND 11.2 FOR EXERCISES AND MORE EXAMPLES

If . . . sentences are used to describe or imagine the consequences of events. There are three basic types of conditional sentences:

1 **First conditional**
If + **present** followed by *will* is used to imagine the **consequences** of events that are **likely to happen** or to describe the consequences of events that **always happen**:

> If our flight lands on time, we'll arrive in time for lunch.

If you book your summer holiday in December, you'll get a discount.
If you intend to go to the USA, you'll have to get a visa.
If you've seen *Rambo*, you'll love *Rambo II*.
If water is heated to 100°, it will boil.   (OR: If water is heated to 100°, it boils.)

The example in brackets is sometimes called a 'Zero Conditional'. It is only used to talk about events and consequences that **always** happen:

If the sun shines, the temperature rises.
Water freezes if the temperature falls below 0°.

Unless (= '*except if* ') and *in case* can also be used in the first type of conditional sentences:

I won't give you a present unless it's your birthday.
You won't be able to get into the concert unless you've got a ticket.
I'll bring a jumper in case it gets colder in the evening.
I'll take a map with me in case I get lost.

2 Second conditional
If + **past** followed by *would* is used when we want to imagine the **consequences** of events that are **unlikely to happen** or events that **can't possibly happen**:

Which country would you visit if you could go anywhere in the world?
– If I had enough money, I'd go to Brazil.
If you had £1,000 to spend, where would you spend your holiday?
If I was (or were) English, I wouldn't need to take this exam.

In some situations, we can use either type, depending on what we mean exactly:

I would go to the USA if I had enough money.   (but I haven't got enough)
I'll go to the USA if I manage to save up enough money.   (more optimistic)
If I pass my driving test first time, I'll think about buying a car.   (more confident)
If I passed my driving test first time, I'd think about buying a car.   (less confident)

If I were you is often used for giving advice:

What would you do in this situation?
– If I were you, I'd stay at home.

3 Third conditional
If + **past perfect** followed by *would have* is used when we want to imagine the **consequences** of events that **happened**, or **didn't happen**, or **began to happen** in the **past**:

If I had known about the delay, I wouldn't have got to the airport so early.
If there hadn't been a mix-up with our booking, we'd have had a room with a view.
If you had reminded me to confirm the booking, I'd have written a letter.

Remember that *'d* is the short form of both *had* and *would*:

If he'd (he had) reminded me, I'd have (I would have) arrived on time.
If I'd had (I had had) more time, I'd have (would have) finished my work.

4 Second and Third conditionals (mixed)
We can also 'mix' types 2 and 3 in the same sentence if the meaning requires. These 'mixed' conditionals are often used to imagine the **present** or **future consequences** of events that **happened** or **didn't happen** in the **past**:

If you'd done more work (in the past), you'd get higher marks (today or in the future).
If the sun had shone more while I was on holiday, I'd have a suntan now.
If I'd been born in 1975, how old would I be now?

-ing and to . . .

SEE 10.3 AND 12.3 FOR EXERCISES AND MORE EXAMPLES

The *-ing* form can be a present participle (as part of a verb or as an adjective) or it can be the noun form of a verb ('a gerund'):

VERB	ADJECTIVE	NOUN
I'm eating my dinner.	a running man	Baking cakes is fun.
Are you feeling OK?	a mixing bowl	brown sugar for sprinkling

1 *-ing* is used as the **subject** of a sentence:

Preparing a meal every day is hard work.   Eating out every day is expensive.
Living abroad is interesting.   Washing-up after a meal isn't much fun.

2 *-ing* is used after **prepositions**:

Is anyone interested in joining me for a drink after work?
I'm looking forward to going away on holiday.
I can't get used to drinking tea without sugar.
I had an upset stomach after eating oysters.

3 Most **adjectives** are followed by *to . . .* (the infinitive). For example:

pleased   glad   surprised   disappointed   relieved   shocked   interesting   kind   hard
essential   difficult   easy

I was pleased to receive your invitation.   It was kind of you to invite me.
I was glad to meet my old friends again.   It was easier to do than I had expected.
We were surprised to get a bill for £45.   He was afraid to open the door.
We were sorry to hear your bad news.   The exercise was hard to do.

BUT: many common adjectives are followed by a **preposition + *-ing*** (see 2 above).
For example:

afraid of   interested in   sorry about   good at   capable of   famous for   fond of

She's afraid of flying.   He's fond of collecting butterflies.
We're sorry about interrupting.   They're very good at skiing.

4 *To . . .* is also used in the structures: *too . . . to . . .* and *. . . enough to . . .*

We arrived early enough to get a seat.   This coffee is too hot to drink.
The tray was too heavy for me to carry.   Boiled eggs are easy enough to cook.

5 There are some **verbs** which are usually only followed by *-ing*:

avoid   can't help   delay   dislike   don't mind   enjoy   finish   give up   go on   practise

I've finished preparing the salad.   I'm trying to give up smoking.
I avoid staying in expensive hotels.   I dislike doing the washing-up after a meal.
I couldn't help laughing when he fell over.   I always enjoy trying new dishes.

6 There are some **verbs** which are usually only followed by *to . . .* :

afford   agree   allow   choose   decide   encourage   expect   forget   help someone
hope   learn   manage   mean   need   offer   persuade   pretend   promise
recommend   refuse   teach   train   try   want   would like

I'd like you to help me with the washing-up.   He didn't mean to spill the soup.
They promised to invite me to lunch.   We decided to have a drink in the pub.
I can't afford to stay at the Ritz.   He tried to open the lid of the jar.
We managed to get a table by the window.   She offered to help him.

7 Some verbs are followed by *-ing* or by *to . . .* with **no** difference in meaning:

begin   continue   intend   hate   like   love   prefer   start

She began to eat/eating her meal.
I love to eat/eating Chinese food.
I don't like eating/to eat alone in restaurants.
Which dessert do you intend to order/ordering?
After the meal we continued chatting/to chat for a long time.

But when *stop* is followed by *-ing* or by *to . . .* there is a **difference** in meaning:

Please stop making that noise, it's driving me mad!   (= don't continue)
Their mother told them to stop quarrelling.
We stopped to get some petrol and have some lunch.   (= stop in order to)
I was half-way through my meal but I had to stop to answer the phone.

And when *remember* is followed by *-ing* or by *to . . .* there's also a **difference** in meaning:

Did you remember to buy the lettuce for dinner?   (= did not forget)
I don't remember you asking me to buy a lettuce.   (= I have a clear memory of it.)
You must remember to send Jill an invitation to the party.
I remember posting the letter yesterday evening after work.

Joining sentences and relative clauses

SEE 13.4 AND 14.3 FOR EXERCISES AND MORE EXAMPLES

1 **Identifying relative clauses** identify which person or thing is meant. Notice that commas are **not** used:

> Jay Gatsby is the man who is the main character in the book.
> ABC Enterprises is the only company that makes this product.
> The ghost which he had seen that night was his dead father.
> One writer whose books I always enjoy is Graham Greene.
> I liked the part of the story where the car broke down.

When *who*, *that* or *which* is the **object** of the relative clause it can be omitted:

> It was a skill (that) he had learned years before.
> The person (who) I liked best in the story was the father.
> *The Great Gatsby* is a book (which) I'm sure you'll enjoy.

Notice that *whom* is uncommon in informal writing and in conversation.

Instead of:	we'd normally say:
The person to whom you spoke was . . .	The person you spoke to was . . .
The people with whom I am working . . .	The people I'm working with . . .
The man from whom I received the letter . . .	The man I received the letter from . . .

2 **Non-identifying relative clauses** give extra information. They are often used to join sentences and are more common in writing than in speech. Notice that commas **are** used in these clauses. *That* is not used.

> Jay Gatsby, who is the main character in the book, is a millionaire.
> *Hamlet*, which is a famous play by Shakespeare, is a tragedy.
> Hamlet's father, who has died before the play begins, appears to Hamlet as a ghost.
> Hamlet's mother, whose husband has died, marries her husband's brother.
> Shakespeare, most of whose plays were written in the 16th century, died in 1616.

3 Sentences can be joined by using these conjunctions:

Time conjunctions and before after while as

Reason, cause or consequence conjunctions
and because as so that so . . . that such a . . . that

Contrast conjunctions but although even though

> I took some books with me so that I would have something to do on my holiday.
> I read the book while I was on holiday.
> The book was so exciting that I couldn't put it down.
> It was such a good book that I stayed up all night reading it.
> Even though I tried very hard, I didn't manage to finish the book.

4 Sentences can also be joined by using these prepositions:

Time prepositions before after during

Reason, cause or consequence prepositions because of due to

Contrast prepositions in spite of despite

> It was impossible to concentrate because of the noise of the traffic outside.
> I read the book during my holiday.
> In spite of spending all night reading, I wasn't able to finish the book.

To show **purpose**, a clause with *to* . . . can be used:

> I used a dictionary to/in order to/so as to look up any unfamiliar words.

5 Two sentences can also be connected by using these conjunctions, without actually making a single sentence from the two:

Time then afterwards beforehand meanwhile

Reason, cause or consequence
consequently therefore that's why that was the reason why

Contrast however nevertheless

> I tried to finish the book. However, I didn't manage to.
> We all read the book. Afterwards, we discussed it.
> It's a wonderful book. That's why I recommend it to you.

Modal verbs

SEE 7.6 AND 8.3 FOR EXERCISES AND MORE EXAMPLES

1   **Modal verbs** are used to express ideas like ability, possibility, certainty, etc.:

can   could   have to   may   might   must   need   ought to   should   will*

The same ideas can also be expressed in other words such as:

be able to   be obliged to   it's possible that   it's unnecessary to

*See The future on pages 173–174 for more about *will*.

2   Modal verbs can refer to **ability**:

PRESENT OR FUTURE	PAST
Ability	
can/be able to	was able to/managed to
Inability	
can't/be unable to/not be able to	couldn't/was unable to/wasn't able to
Questions about ability	
Can he?/Is he able to?	Was he able to?

Tony can speak Spanish very well.
I can't find my pen anywhere.
Can you drive a car?
Alex can't swim.
I know you're a good swimmer, but how well can you swim on your back?
Ann was able to do the research, but she couldn't write the report.
I was unable to finish all my work yesterday, but I hope to be able to do it tomorrow.
I couldn't finish all my work yesterday, but I hope I can tomorrow.

3   Modal verbs can refer to **possibility** and **certainty**:

PRESENT OR FUTURE	PAST
Possibility	
may/might/could	may have/might have/could have
Certainty or near certainty	
must	must have
Impossibility	
can't/couldn't	can't have/couldn't have
Questions about possibility	
Could/Might it?	Could/Might it have?

It could/may/might rain later.
We may not be able to get on the bus. It may be full up.
If his name's Spiros, he can't be Italian. He must be Greek.
It might be difficult to get a seat at such short notice.
Jane is always so punctual. She must have missed her train.
Her train might have been delayed. Or the train might have been cancelled.

4   Modal verbs can be used when giving or refusing **permission**:

PRESENT OR FUTURE	PAST
Giving permission	
can/may	was allowed to
Refusing permission	
can't/mustn't	couldn't/weren't allowed to
Questions about permission	
Can/Could/May we?	Was he allowed to?

You can/may make notes during the talk if you like.
Can/Could/May I finish off this work tomorrow?
We were allowed to look round the church after the service was over.
You can't/mustn't smoke when you're in a non-smoking seat.
We couldn't/weren't allowed to use our calculators in the maths test because it was
   against the rules.

5 Modal verbs can refer to **obligation** and **responsibility**:

PRESENT OR FUTURE	PAST
Obligation or responsibility	
must/have to/have got to/should/ought to	had to/should have
Lack of obligation or responsibility	
don't have to/needn't	needn't have
Obligation or responsibility NOT to do something	
can't/mustn't/shouldn't/oughtn't to	wasn't allowed to/shouldn't have
Questions about obligation or responsibility	
Must we/Have we got to/Do we have to?/	Did he have to?
Should we/Ought we to/Do we need to?	

Do I have to hand the work in tomorrow?
You don't have to/needn't book in advance if you're going by rail.
You must/should arrive at 4.30 if you want to get a good seat on the train.
You don't have to/needn't stand up on the bus unless all the seats are occupied.
In the exam do we have to write in pen or are we allowed to use pencils?
You shouldn't spend so much time watching TV when you should be studying.

The passive

SEE 15.2 FOR EXERCISES AND MORE EXAMPLES

1 The passive is used when the person responsible for an action is **not known** or **not important**:

Beer is made from water, hops and malted barley.
I was given a watch for my birthday.
These problems will have to be solved before we can go ahead.
The results are being published on Monday.

Or when we want to **avoid** mentioning the person responsible for an action:

You were asked to arrive at 8 am.   (less 'personal' than: I asked you to arrive)
This composition must be handed in by next Monday.

2 *By* is often used with the passive to emphasise **who** was responsible for an action:

Penicillin was discovered by Alexander Fleming.
The first CDs were marketed in 1982 by Philips and Sony.
The research is being done by a team of European scientists.

3 Often there's no great difference in meaning between a passive and an active sentence.
The passive can be used to give variety to the **style** of a passage, as in these examples:

Only 17 muscles are used when you smile but 43 are used when you frown.
You only use 17 muscles when you smile but you use 43 when you frown. (more personal)
Light bulbs were invented in 1878 (by Joseph Swan).
Joseph Swan invented the light bulb in 1879.
The committee will announce the names of the Nobel Prize winners in May.
The names of the Nobel Prize winners will be announced (by the committee) in May.

Using the passive tends to make a sentence sound **more formal** and **less personal** than
an active sentence, as in these examples:

It can be legally ridden by anyone over the age of 14.
Anyone over the age of 14 can legally ride it.
The battery pack and charger are included in the price.
We include the battery pack and charger in the price.
Your money will be refunded in full if you are not totally satisfied.
We will refund your money in full if you are not totally satisfied.

Past tenses

SEE 3.2 AND 4.6 FOR EXERCISES AND MORE EXAMPLES

Past **time** and past **tenses** are not always the same. We can use a past tense to refer to an imaginary event or situation:

> I wish my friends were here.

or a **present** tense to refer to past events (when telling a story, for example):

> So I get out my keys and unlock the door. You can imagine how I feel when I see that . . .

1 The **simple past** is the tense most commonly used to refer to events that happened at a particular time in the past:

> The Second World War started in 1939.
> My sister got married last year.
> I saw a film about animals on TV last Wednesday evening.
> In 1995 I spent my summer holidays in Wales.

2 The **past continuous** is used to refer to activities that were interrupted or hadn't finished at the time mentioned:

> At 7.45 last night it was still raining.
> It was raining when we arrived but now it has stopped.

or to refer to simultaneous events or activities:

> We were lying in the sun while she was revising for her exam.

3 *Used to* emphasises that the activity happened frequently in the past – but that it probably no longer takes place:

> He used to smoke 20 cigarettes a day. (but not now)
> Before the war, more people used to work on the land.
> When I was a child, we used to have a dog.
> Before he got married he didn't ever use to cook a meal or wash up.

4 The **present perfect simple** is used to refer to the past in these cases:

When no definite time in the past is given or known:

> I have been to Italy several times.
> He has seen that film three times.

When the activity began in the past and has not yet finished:

> I have (already) read 100 pages of the book.

When the activity finished recently:

> I have (just) been to the dentist's.

The **present perfect simple** is often used with these adverbs:

just   already   never   yet   so far

> Have you done your homework yet?
> I have never seen a lion in the wild.

Remember that the **present perfect** is **not** used to refer to a **definite time** in the past and is **not** normally used in questions that begin: *When*?

We always use the **past** with phrases like these:

last month   in July   on Wednesday   yesterday   a few minutes ago

> I saw that film last week. ✓   I have seen that film last week.   ✗
> We did this exercise on Monday. ✓   We have done this exercise on Monday.   ✗
> When did you go there? ✓   When have you gone there?   ✗

5 The **present perfect continuous** is used to emphasise that an activity started in the past and is still going on. It's commonly used after *for* or *since*:

> I have been playing football since I was seven.
> She has been feeling unwell for two days.

6 The **past perfect** is normally used to **emphasise** that one past event happened before another:

> I had been feeling quite depressed until my friend called round to cheer me up.
> I hadn't realised he was married until I noticed his wedding ring.
> Before we got our cat, we had never had a pet in our family.

It is very common in **reported speech**:

> 'I went there last year.' → He said that he had been there the previous year.
> 'I've been there once.' → She said that she had been there once.
> 'I paid you yesterday.' → I told you that I'd paid you the day before.
> 'I was feeling all right till you turned up.' →
> She said that she had been feeling all right until I turned up.

For more on **reported speech** see pages 184–185.
For more on the **present perfect** see pages 182–183.

Phrasal verbs and verbs + prepositions

SEE 3.6, 4.5, 6.3, 7.4, 15.7, 16.7, 17.6, 18.6 and 19.7 FOR EXERCISES AND MORE EXAMPLES

1 A **verb + preposition** is followed by a noun or pronoun that **cannot** be moved. You can sometimes guess the meaning of a verb + preposition from its parts:

look for (= try to find)
> I'm looking for my keys, but I can't find them. ✓

> BUT NOT:
> I'm looking my keys for, but I can't find them. ✗

look at (= observe)
> I looked at the instructions for a long time, but I couldn't understand them. ✓

> BUT NOT:
> I looked the instructions at for a long time, but I couldn't understand them. ✗

Some verbs + prepositions have an **idiomatic** meaning and it's hard to guess their meanings from their parts:

look after (= care for)
> I looked after the children. ✓   I looked after them. ✓   They were looked after by me. ✓

> BUT NOT:
> I looked the children after ✗   I looked them after ✗

Other examples: see to   see through   do without   make for   get over

2 A **transitive phrasal verb** (verb + adverb) is followed by a noun that **can** be moved. When a pronoun is used it must come between the verb and the adverb and **cannot** be moved. Notice how the word order is different from the examples above:

look up (= find information)
> I looked up a word. ✓   I looked a word up. ✓   I looked it up. ✓
> The word was looked up. ✓

> BUT NOT:
> I looked up it. ✗

Other examples: see off   do up   make up   find out   give away   give back

3 A **phrasal verb + preposition** (verb + adverb + preposition) is followed by a noun or pronoun that **cannot** be moved:

look up to (= respect)
> I look up to my aunt. ✓   I look up to her. ✓   She was looked up to by everyone. ✓

> BUT NOT:
> I look my aunt up to. ✗   I look her up to. ✗

Other examples: look forward to   look out for   make off with   make up for
run away with   run out of

4 An **intransitive phrasal verb** (verb + adverb) is **not** followed by a noun or pronoun:

look out (= be careful)

You must look out! ✓

BUT NOT:

You were looked out. ✗

Other examples: run away   read on   get out   get up   give up

---

Present tenses

SEE 1.4 FOR EXERCISES AND MORE EXAMPLES

There are four present tenses:

Present simple	She lives in London.
Present continuous	She's living in London.
Present perfect simple	She has lived in London all her life.
Present perfect continuous	She has been living in London for a few years.

1 The **present simple** describes general truths, complete events and unchanging or regular events or actions:

Water freezes at 0° Celsius.
I always have two cups of coffee for breakfast.
Where do you live?   (= What is your permanent address?)
After lunch I sometimes have a cup of black coffee.

Some common **adverbs** that are often used with the **present simple** are:

usually   often   generally   normally   frequently   never   hardly ever   sometimes
occasionally

2 The **present continuous** describes events happening at this moment or which haven't finished happening:

I'm trying to concentrate, so please don't interrupt.
Where are you living?   (= What is your temporary address?)
This year I'm doing a First Certificate course.

Some common **adverbs** that are often used with the **present continuous** are:

at the moment   today   this morning   this week   this month   this year   now

The **present continuous** with *always* describes habitual or annoying events that happen all the time or often:

She's always shouting
He's always arriving late.
They're always talking when they should be studying.

3 Some verbs (**stative verbs**) are not normally used in the continuous form, because they usually refer to permanent states or situations:

How much does this cost? ✓   How much is this costing? ✗
He has owned a car for two years. ✓   He has been owning a car for two years. ✗

Here are some common **stative verbs**:

believe   contain   cost   deserve   fit   know   like   look like   love   matter   owe
realise   remember   seem   smell   suit   understand

She doesn't look like her sister.
He deserves to do well in the interview.
Do you believe me?

4 The **present perfect simple** refers to actions or situations that began in the past and which are still true or relevant now, or are now finished:

> I've never smoked a cigar in my life.
> Someone has eaten all the cakes.
> We haven't spent very long on this unit so far.
> Have you finished your meal?

The **present perfect continuous** refers to actions or events which started in the past and haven't finished happening, or repeated actions:

> We've been waiting for twenty minutes.
> What have you been doing since we last met?
> I have been learning English for five years.
> I've been knocking for five minutes but nobody has answered the door.

The **present perfect** is often used with these **adverbs**:

ever   so far   never   this year   this week   all my life   recently
for a long time   since 1995

for is used with a period of time and *since* is used with a point in time:

for two years   for a long time   for a few minutes   for the last three days
since 1988   since yesterday   since 5 o'clock   since lunchtime   since April

We can't say: since two years ✗

5 Although present tenses often refer to **present time**, they can also refer to **future time**:

> When does this lesson end?
> I'll phone you when I arrive.
> When is your sister getting married?

and **past time**:

> I've been to the USA several times.
> Teacher wins jackpot in lottery. (Newspaper headline)

For more on the **present perfect** see page 180.
For more on the use of present tenses to refer to **the future** see pages 173–174.
For more on the use of present tenses in *If . . .* **sentences** see pages 174–175.

Questions and question tags

SEE 2.4 FOR EXERCISES AND MORE EXAMPLES

1 *Yes/No* **questions** expect the answer *Yes*, *No* or *I don't know*. *Yes/No* questions usually end with a rising tone (↗). Pay particular attention to the word order and the use of *do* and *did* in these examples:

> Do you like sports?
> Are you feeling all right?
> Have you ever been to Spain?
> Did you see the news on TV last night?
> Is New York the capital of the USA?

A **negative** *Yes/No* **question** may be a surprised reaction to what someone has said or done, or a question which expects the answer *Yes*:

> This football match is boring.
> – Don't you like sports? I thought you did.
> I like some sports but not football.
>
> Aren't you Thomas's sister?
> – That's right, yes.
> I thought so, you have the same eyes.

2 **Wh- questions** ask for specific information, and can't be answered with **Yes** or **No**. **Wh-** questions usually end with a falling tone (↘). Pay particular attention to the word order and use of **do** and **did** in these examples:

Who did you write to?
What does she do for a living?
Where have you put my keys?
When did you see them last?

Who, **What** or **Which** can also be the subject of the sentence. Pay particular attention to the word order (**do** or **did** are not used in these cases):

Who wrote to you?
What surprised you most about her behaviour?
Which of the letters seems more important?

3 It is sometimes more polite to use an **indirect question** rather than a direct question. Pay particular attention to the word order in these examples:

How old are you?	May I ask how old you are?
Where do you live?	Could you tell me where you live?
Are you feeling all right?	I'd like to know if you're feeling all right.
Where is the toilet?	Do you know where the toilet is?

4 **Question tags** are used to check up if we are correct, by asking another person to confirm if we are right or not. There are two **intonations**:

Your name's Leo, isn't it?	falling intonation = I'm fairly sure. (The listener will probably agree.)
Your surname's Jones, isn't it?	rising intonation = I'm not sure. (The listener will confirm whether or not you're right.)

A positive verb is usually followed by a negative question tag, and a negative verb is usually followed by a positive question tag, as in these examples:

The shops will be closed by now, won't they?
They won't open again till 9 o'clock, will they?

They always close at 6 pm, don't they?
Most shops don't open on Sundays, do they?

She must be more careful, mustn't she?
He mustn't be so careless, must he?

He really ought to write some thank-you letters, oughtn't he?
We have to write 120–180 words in the exam, don't we?
You haven't finished yet, have you?

A positive verb is sometimes followed by a positive question tag to express interest, surprise or some other reaction:

Bananas are more tasty than apples.
Oh, you prefer bananas, do you?

Reported speech

SEE 16.5 FOR EXERCISES AND MORE EXAMPLES

1 In reported speech the tense usually changes back into the past or past perfect:

'I haven't watched the news on TV for ages.' →
He said that he hadn't watched the news on TV for ages.

'I don't often read the newspaper.' →
She said that she didn't often read the newspaper.

'I'll phone you when I get home.' →
He said that he would phone me when he got home.

'Why are you looking so surprised?' →
She asked me why I was looking so surprised.

But if the information is still relevant or true, the tense needn't be changed:

> My boss refused to let me know whether I'm going to get a pay rise next year.
> We were told that Jupiter is the largest planet.

2 Reported **statements** are introduced by verbs like these, followed by *that*:

add   admit   announce   answer   complain   explain   find out   inform someone
let someone know   reply   report   say   shout   suggest   tell someone   whisper

> 'I'm afraid I made a mistake.' →
> She admitted that she had made a mistake.
>
> 'Oh, and I'm sorry.' →
> She added that she was sorry.
>
> 'Listen everyone: we're getting married!' →
> They announced that they were getting married.

Reported **orders**, **promises**, **offers**, **requests** and **advice** are introduced by verbs like these, followed by *to . . .* :

advise   ask   encourage   invite   offer   order   persuade   promise   recommend
remind   tell   threaten   want   warn

> 'You'd better be careful.' → She advised me to be careful.
> 'Will you help me, please?' → He asked me to help him.
> 'Don't drop it.' → She warned me not to drop it.
> 'Go on, have another try.' → She encouraged me to try again.

Reported **questions** are introduced by verbs like these, followed by a *Wh-* question word:

ask   inquire   try to find out   wonder   want to know

> 'What are you doing?' → He asked me what I was doing.

Yes/No questions are reported with *if* or *whether*:

> 'Are you feeling all right?' → She asked me if/whether I was feeling all right.

3 When you're reporting **times** and **places**, words like these may have to be changed, depending when the original conversation took place:

here → there   now → then   this → that
tomorrow → the next day   yesterday → the day before   this week → that week
last week → the week before   next week → the week after

> *Reporting the next day:*
>
> Some days ago she said, 'Phone them tomorrow.' →
> She told me to phone them the next day.
>
> Yesterday she said, 'Send them a fax tomorrow.' →
> She told me to send them a fax today.
>
> 'Don't forget to include this information.' →
> She reminded me to include that information.

But if the time and place haven't changed since the conversation you're reporting, these words don't change:

> *Reporting the same day:*
>
> Earlier today she said, 'Go and see them tomorrow.' →
> She told me to go and see them tomorrow.
>
> Five minutes ago she said, 'I will meet you here at lunchtime today' →
> She told me that she'd meet me here at lunchtime today.'

4 The exact words used in the original conversation are usually **summarised** in reported speech:

> 'I wonder if you'd mind helping me?' → She asked me to help her.
> 'Why don't we have lunch together?' → He invited me to have lunch with him.

Communication activities

1 Imagine that you're talking on the phone. Your partner is spending a few days in London while you are in New York for a few days. You want your partner to contact four people you know in London. Dictate their names, addresses and phone numbers to your partner. Spell out the difficult names if necessary.

✉ Ms Fiona Farquharson 13 Gloucester Rd, Kensington, London SW1 4PQ	☎ 0171 819 3232
✉ Mr Thomas Twining 70 St Andrews St, St John's Wood, London NW3 6OR	☎ 0181 678 9995
✉ Mrs Anne Greene 16 Acacia Ave, Streatham, London SW19 4KE	☎ 0181 331 4499
✉ Mr & Mrs Tony Brown 14 Grosvenor Square, London SW1 9US	☎ 0171 555 2347

2 Find out about your partner's pictures and answer your partner's questions about your photos. Take it in turns to ask and answer questions. Then compare all four photos.

3 This is the story that followed one of the headlines. Read it through and then tell your partners about it *in your own words* without reading it out to them.

A WOMAN trying to sell her Ford Fiesta for £500 was left with a rusty Skoda and an old lady yesterday, when a prospective buyer went on a test drive leaving them both as 'collateral'.

After Patricia Wakelin, of Westbury, Wiltshire, advertised her car, a man arrived to see it, apologising for bringing his granny along. When he went on a test drive, he left his Skoda and 'granny' as collateral. But the man – and Ms Wakelin's Fiesta – never came back.

Police have found the Skoda was stolen – and the confused old lady was from a home and thought she was being taken out for a drive.

4 First describe this poster to your partner. Then find out about your partner's poster.

See the new you after just two weeks.

You need to choose... **?**

5 These are the correct spellings of the words on the tape:

slipping sleeping   trouble robber   total putting   address doubled   request Christian
angle ignorant   engine average   adventure butcher   careful million   often sudden
immense coming   worry railway   assistant   please   insurance   pleasure   laughing rough
convince live   theory themselves   twelve while   university yawning

6 Read this information about global warming and then, *in your own words*, tell your partner what you have found out.

WORLDWIDE EFFECTS OF GLOBAL WARMING

The most dramatic result of higher temperatures would be the rise in sea level. Climate change would also have far-reaching consequences. Some parts of the world would receive more rain than before: others, including the productive croplands of the Northern Hemisphere, very much less.

USA
A farmer in South Carolina shows the effect of the 1986 drought on his soybean crop, five times smaller than in a normal year. Agricultural land in the USA could suffer from greatly reduced rainfall.

SUDAN
In the Sahara and sub-Saharan regions of Africa, scenes of drought and famine like this would become even more common than they are today.

JAPAN
Some parts of the world would benefit as a result of global warming. With changing patterns of rainfall, the area of land in Japan that could be used for rice-growing would double.

The poles are melting

CROPS ARE DYING

People will starve

HURRICANES ARE GETTING WORSE

Droughts are spreading

Governments don't care

Seas are rising

USE THE POWER OF THE WIND

Build railways not roads

7 Instruct your partner how to draw this picture on the grid on page 21. Just describe the direction the pencil should take to draw a continuous line. *Don't* tell your partner what animal it represents.

8 This is the story that followed one of the headlines. Read it through and then tell your partners about it *in your own words* without reading it out to them.

A PREGNANT teenage student was left with the clothes she was standing in after council workmen dumped everything she owned on a tip.

Jill Naylor, aged 17, had asked the local authority to *clean* a room at her new council flat in Bradford, West Yorkshire – but instead her message was misinterpreted as wanting her home *cleared*.

The teenager, who is four-and-a-half months pregnant, said: 'The flat had been completely stripped. Everything has gone into the crusher.' She had moved in two weeks earlier. Her parents, Margaret and Graham Naylor, bought furnishings and were set to help decorate. But when the student returned home from college she found her flat was totally bare – everything from the underlay on the floors to the television, and even exam notes, had gone.

She declared yesterday: 'My whole past life has been wiped out. I am in a state of shock.' Her father added: 'One of the rooms needed disinfecting and we wanted the council to clean it.

'Somewhere along the line the message has been misinterpreted and they have just cleaned it all out.'

The council admits its mistake and will compensate Ms Naylor. It has given her £100 to buy clothes, and is trying to find her somewhere to stay.

9 **1** These places are *not* on the map. Find them and mark them on.

The Free Press pub is in Prospect Row, just off Adam and Eve Street (parallel to East Road).
McDonald's is down Rose Crescent, just off Market Street.
The Cambridge University Press shop is opposite the Senate House.
Waterstone's bookshop is in Bridge Street before The Round Church.

2 Imagine that you are a visitor to Cambridge staying at the Regent Hotel. Find out from your partner (a resident) how to get to these places:

from the Regent Hotel to the Tram Depot pub
from there to Robert Sayle department store
from there to Brown's bistro
from there to Marks & Spencer's
from there back to the hotel

3 Now imagine that you are the resident and your partner is the stranger, staying at the same hotel. Explain how to get to the places you are asked about.

10   Talk for a minute about these pictures. Compare them and say what you think about them.

11   Here are explanations of some of the items on the menu on page 84, so that you can help your partners to understand them. *Don't* just read these descriptions out loud – try to remember them, so that you can answer your partners' questions.

Lancashire hotpot	Lamb and vegetables cooked in the oven with a layer of potatoes on top – very tasty!
Nut and mushroom roast	Nuts, mushrooms and rice made into a kind of loaf and cooked in the oven – tasty and suitable for vegetarians!

When you're all clear what each dish is, decide what you'll order for each course.

12   This is the story that followed one of the headlines. Read it through and then tell your partners about it *in your own words* without reading it out to them.

A SEVEN-month-old cat was last night looking forward to its remaining eight lives after being rescued from an automatic washing machine by the fire brigade.

Oscar, filthy after playing in the garden, was sprinkled with washing powder and placed in the wash by four-year-old Stephanie Lefevre of Widnes, Cheshire.

'It was set on a 40 degree wash, and the poor cat went round a few times before Stephanie's brother John switched the machine off,' said her mother, Pamela Lefevre. 'I tried to open the door but it was locked shut.'

She called the brigade. Sub-officer Graham Kirby, of Widnes fire station, said: 'We opened the top of the machine, unscrewed a couple of bolts and opened the door. He looked up at us as though he was quite grateful to be out.'

The cat came out clean.

13 Find out as much as possible about your partner's pictures by asking Yes/No questions or indirect questions. Take it in turns to ask and answer questions.

14 Dictate these words to your partner:

abbreviation   alive   butter   chalk   charming   correct   debt   half   hopeless   island
juice   knot   lucky   ready   scared   social   soften   surprise   telephone   thorough
vehicle

15 Look at this explanation of how a microwave works. If you would like more detailed information, look at Activity *23*. *In your own words*, without reading the text out, explain how it works to the other students. They will tell you how a computer mouse works.

MICROWAVE OVEN

A MICROWAVE OVEN cooks food in a fraction of the time it would take in a conventional oven. Microwaves, produced by a magnetron, penetrate the food, transferring **heat** to the water **molecules** in it by radiation. Heat then passes to the rest of the food by conduction.

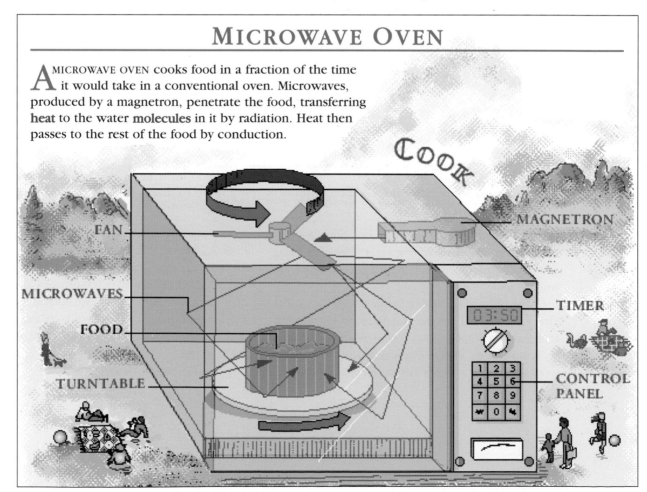

16　Here is some more information about five of the activities you discussed in B1 of Unit 8.8.
Tell your partner any extra information you didn't mention earlier.

Walking

The most natural exercise.
Brisk walking improves
stamina, but for strength and
suppleness it is best to turn
to other activities.
Walking is
excellent for
relieving
tension and
stress.

Swimming

The best all-round activity for fitness.
Extremely good for strength and
stamina and good for suppleness,
especially if you use different strokes.

Cycling

Good for stamina and improving
leg strength. It is also good for
suppleness in older people.
The negative factors are
pollution and traffic accidents.

Bowling

Good for improving flexibility
in arms and shoulders and for
building up strength. Not much
stamina is needed. Mainly an
activity for older people, but
many young people are now
taking up the game.

Jogging and running

Good for stamina, but not for
suppleness or upper body strength.
There is also risk of damage to feet,
knees, ankles and hips. If possible it
is best to run on grass.

17　Here are three more news items for you to read to your partner, who will listen and suggest
how you can improve your pronunciation. Before you read them, mark the places where
you're going to pause and the stressed syllables.

1

Mr Oliver Huskinson of
Middlesborough has been
advised by his doctor to
give up weight-lifting. He
is ninety-nine years old.

2

The Tea Council's
annual award for the
best in-flight cup of
tea has gone to
Iberia, the Spanish
airline.

3

STONEMASONS have
adjusted the inscription,
'To the glory of God',
on Porthleven's war
memorial after residents
of the Cornish fishing
port complained that
the letter G might be
mistaken for a C.

18　Describe this picture to your partner. Explain what you like (or don't like) about it.

19

If you're reading a set book, you'll need to discuss it in class regularly. And you'll need to do some preparation if you'd like to write about it in the exam. The following steps will take quite a long time to do, and can't all be covered in a single lesson!

1 Here are some typical questions that might be asked about a set book in the Writing paper. Which of them would be most relevant for your set book?

1 What lesson or message does the story have for the reader?

2 Who is the most interesting or attractive character in the story? Why do you find him/her interesting or attractive?

3 Who is the most unpleasant character in the story? Why do you find him/her unpleasant?

4 Describe the main character in the story.

5 Describe one of the minor characters and what happens to him/her in the story.

6 Tell the story of the book from the point of view of one of the minor characters.

7 Describe the setting or background of the story.

8 What have you found especially interesting about the book?

9 What makes the book 'different' from other books you have read?

10 Which parts of the book did you enjoy most? Why?

11 Why would you (or would you not) recommend the book to a friend?

2 Note down *two* more questions that might be asked about your set book.

3 Make notes on all the above questions that are relevant to your set book. When you've finished compare your notes with a partner.

4 Write at least *three* compositions, using the notes you've made.

Part of your revision programme before the exam should be to re-read the whole set book, so that the story and characters are still fresh in your mind.

In the exam, your answer should refer to events in the story to support your views. It doesn't matter if you haven't really enjoyed the book, but you must know the story well and be able to describe the characters and the relevance of the story to your own life. Don't attempt to answer the question if you're asked about an aspect of the book you haven't considered before. Or if you haven't read the whole of the book.

In the exam, even if you have read a set book, you can of course decide *not* to answer that question. This will depend on whether you think that the prescribed book question you actually get in the exam is easy or not.

20

Here are three more items for you to read to your partner, who will listen and suggest how you can improve your pronunciation. Before you read them, mark the places where you're going to pause and the stressed syllables.

1

Plastic ducks and other bath toys, washed overboard in the north Pacific two years ago, are now drifting through the Arctic. They are expected to reach Britain in nineteen ninety-nine.

2

In Taunton, two men signed a petition calling for better policing, then robbed a sweetshop. Detectives are studying their handwriting for clues.

3

WESSEX WATER COMPANY, which sent three thousand letters to householders in Lyme Regis, Dorset, telling them to stop wasting water, has found it does not supply the town with water.

21 Describe this picture to your partner. Explain what you like (or don't like) about it.

22 Dictate these words to your partner:

approximately   arrive   beauty   calm   cheerful   collect   cough   doubt   edge
exhibition   halve   heart   height   information   knowledge   lazy   matter   quickly
whistle   wreck

23 Here's some more information about microwaves.

HOW IT WORKS

MICROWAVES

HEAT

WATER
MOLECULES

Microwaves consist of intense electric and magnetic fields, which change direction many billions of times each second. Water molecules in the food twist in tune with the changes in these fields. This twisting gives the molecules extra kinetic energy, heating them and the surrounding food.

24

1 Imagine that a friend of yours was the man in this story. The pictures are in the wrong order. Work out what happened.

2 Now join another student and tell your story, beginning: 'This is what happened to a friend of mine . . .' Then listen to your new partner's story.

25

One of you will be asking the questions and telling the Candidates what to do. The other will be listening and making notes so that you can give the Candidates feedback later and advise them how to perform better.

> **FEEDBACK CHECKLIST:**
>
> | | | |
> |---|---|---|
> | Grammar | Pronunciation | Interactive Communication |
> | Vocabulary | Fluency | Task Achievement |

Part 1

1 Greet both Candidates.

2 Ask each Candidate these questions:

- What's your name?
- Where are you from?
- How long have you lived there?

- What's your home like?
- How do you usually spend your free time?
- What are your plans for the future?

Part 2

1 Ask the first Candidate to look at the photos in Activity *26* and to talk about them for one minute, comparing and contrasting the two jobs shown there. After one minute ask the second Candidate to comment briefly on the same pictures.

2 Ask the second Candidate to look at the photos in Activity *27* and to talk about them for one minute, comparing and contrasting the two jobs shown there. After one minute ask the other Candidate to comment briefly on the pictures.

Part 3

Ask both Candidates to look at the pictures in Activity *28*. Ask them to talk to each other about the kind of work that's being done in the pictures. Which of the jobs would they prefer to do themselves? Why?
After three minutes, go on to Part 4.

Part 4

Ask the Candidates to discuss these questions together for about four minutes:

- If you could have any job at all, what would it be? Why?
- What are the worst things about having a job?
- What jobs can you think of that are over-paid? Why do you think this?
- What work do you want to do when you finish your studies? Why?

That's the end of the first mock exam.

26

27

28

29 Imagine that you're talking on the phone. Your partner is spending a few days in New York while you are in London for a few days. You want your partner to contact four people you know in New York. Dictate their names, addresses and phone numbers to your partner. Spell out the difficult names if necessary.

✉ Ms Mary Fitzgerald 44 W 72nd St, Manhattan, New York	☎ 212 555-1265
✉ Andy Sipowicz 12 E 14th St, Manhattan, New York	☎ 212 555-7070
✉ Mr John Kelly 1222 46th Avenue, Queens, New York	☎ 718 699-0005
✉ Ms Rose Weinbaum 210 Lafayette Avenue, Brooklyn, New York	☎ 718 636-4100

30 Find out about your partner's pictures and answer your partner's questions about your photos. Take it in turns to ask and answer questions. Then compare all four photos.

31 **1** Imagine that a friend of yours was one of the people in this story. The pictures are in the wrong order. Work out what happened.

2 Now join another student and listen to your new partner's story. Then tell your story, beginning: 'This is what happened to a friend of mine . . .'

32 Find out about your partner's poster first. Then describe this poster to your partner.

See the new you after just two weeks.

First Choice Holidays

33 If any of these phrasal verbs are new to you, can you *guess* their meanings now?

1 looked up to   2 look out for   3 looked through   4 looking forward to
5 look after

34 Read this information about global warming and then, *in your own words*, tell your partner what you have found out.

WORLDWIDE EFFECTS OF GLOBAL WARMING

The most dramatic result of higher temperatures would be the rise in sea level. Climate change would also have far-reaching consequences. Some parts of the world would receive more rain than before: others, including the productive croplands of the Northern Hemisphere, very much less.

BRAZIL

Coastal cities like Rio de Janeiro would experience severe flooding. The floods that swept through the slum district of Santa Teresa in 1988 were perhaps a foretaste of even greater destruction to come.

MALDIVE ISLANDS

Rising sea levels would have catastrophic consequences for low-lying islands. If the sea level rises by 3 metres (10 feet), coral atolls like the Maldives will disappear completely beneath the waves.

CARIBBEAN

Tropical storms would become far more frequent, inflicting greater damage than ever on the islands' houses and vegetation.

Governments don't care

Use the sun's energy

TEMPERATURES ARE RISING

Use less energy

PEOPLE ARE DROWNING

Lands are flooding

Crops are dying

Forests are burning

DISEASES WILL SPREAD

COMMUNICATION ACTIVITIES

35 Instruct your partner how to draw this picture on the grid on page 21. Just describe the direction the pencil should take to draw a continuous line. *Don't* tell your partner what animal it represents.

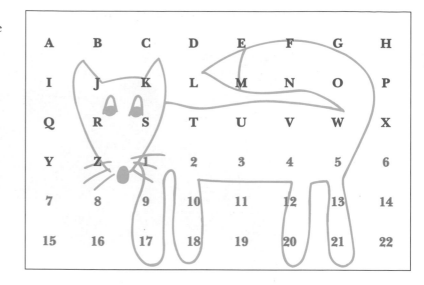

36

1 These places are *not* on the map. Find them and mark them on.

Brown's bistro is in Trumpington Street opposite the Fitzwilliam Museum.
Marks & Spencer's is in Sydney Street just past Hobson Street.
Robert Sayle department store is in St Andrews Street before Lion Yard.
The Tram Depot pub is in Dover Street, off East Road.

2 Imagine that your partner is a visitor to Cambridge staying at the Regent Hotel. Explain how to get to the places you're asked about.

3 Now imagine that you are the stranger in town, staying at the same hotel. Find out from your partner (a resident) how to get to these places:

from the Regent Hotel to McDonald's
from there to the Cambridge University Press shop
from there to the Free Press pub
from there to Waterstone's bookshop
from there back to the hotel

37

1 Describe each person in this picture to your partner, mentioning their appearance, clothes and personalities. Take turns to describe the people one-by-one, from left to right.

2 Which of the people your partner has just described would you choose to start a conversation with if you were on a train with them?

38   Talk for a minute about these pictures. Compare them and say what you think about them.

39   Look at this explanation of how a computer mouse works. If you would like more detailed information, look at Activity **45**. *In your own words*, without reading the text out, explain how a mouse works to the other students. They will tell you how a microwave oven cooks food.

MOUSE

WITH A MOUSE connected to the computer, it is easy to point at anything on the screen. As you move the mouse, a ball rolls inside, turning a pair of wheels. These translate the movement into separate left-right and up-down instructions. Pulses are then sent to the computer, telling it where to move the pointer.

BUTTON

VERTICAL WHEEL

CABLE

GUIDE ROLLER

ROLLER BALL

HORIZONTAL WHEEL

PHOTODIODE

MICROPROCESSOR

40

Find out as much as possible about your partner's pictures by asking indirect questions or Yes/No questions. Take it in turns to ask and answer questions.

41

1 The original version of the story uses the past tense, which makes it sound like a true story. But of course it's the plot of a film. The lack of detail also makes it very dull.

2 What makes the following version of the story better than the one on page 31? Highlight the *extra information* that helps to improve the story.

CASABLANCA

'Casablanca' is set in Morocco during the war. Rick, played by Humphrey Bogart, is an American who owns a night club in Casablanca. Before he came to Morocco, he has had an affair with Ilsa (Ingrid Bergman) in Paris before the German occupation of the city. Unexpectedly, Ilsa arrives at Rick's with her new husband, Victor Laszlo (Paul Henreid). Victor is a resistance leader and is in danger in Casablanca, but if he can escape to Lisbon, he can then get to the United States, where he can continue his resistance work. But without a visa he cannot leave Morocco, and he is unable to get visas from the authorities. Ilsa still loves Rick but she asks him to help Victor. Rick has two visas but he tells Ilsa that he intends to use them to fly with her to Lisbon, leaving Victor to his fate. At the last minute, he gives the visas to Victor, who flies off with Ilsa. Rick and the Chief of Police, Renault (Claude Rains) are left together at the airport watching the plane carry Ilsa and Victor to freedom.

42

Here is some more information about four of the activities you discussed in B1 of Unit 8.8. Tell your partner any extra information you didn't mention earlier.

Exercise classes/ dance/yoga

Aerobics and dance are a good all-round exercise, even for beginners. yoga is very good for suppleness and can also help you relax.

Racket sports

Badminton, tennis and squash are all good for all-round fitness, especially leg strength and suppleness. The better you get the more stamina is needed.

Weight-training

Becoming increasingly popular, especially among women. All weight-training improves strength and suppleness and repeating exercises improves stamina. It is important to have the proper training for more strenuous exercises.

Team games

Very good for stamina and strength and, depending on the sport, can be good for suppleness too. At a competitive level there is some risk of injury, and training is important.

43 This is the leaflet one of the slogans came from. Tell your partner about it in your own words, beginning, 'Did you know . . . ?'

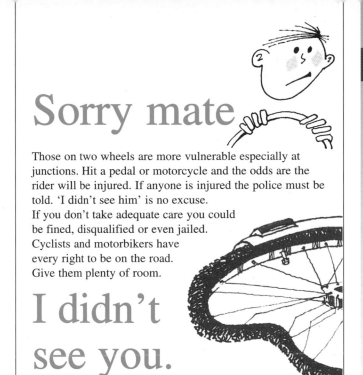

Sorry mate

Those on two wheels are more vulnerable especially at junctions. Hit a pedal or motorcycle and the odds are the rider will be injured. If anyone is injured the police must be told. 'I didn't see him' is no excuse.
If you don't take adequate care you could be fined, disqualified or even jailed.
Cyclists and motorbikers have every right to be on the road.
Give them plenty of room.

I didn't see you.

44 Here are explanations of some of the items on the menu on page 84, so that you can help your partners to understand them. *Don't* just read these descriptions out loud – try to remember them, so that you can answer your partners' questions.

Cottage pie	Minced beef in gravy topped with mashed potato – a favourite home-made dish!
Chicken Madras	Chicken pieces in an Indian curry sauce – very hot!

When you're all clear what each dish is, decide what you'll order for each course.

45 Here's some more information about the computer mouse.

PHOTODIODE

SLOTS

LIGHT-EMITTING DIODE (LED)

PHOTODIODE

Slots in the wheel allow light from a light-emitting diode to shine on a photodiode. When light hits the photodiode, current flows to the microprocessor; when the wheel blocks the beam, the current stops. As the wheel turns, the number of pulses tells the microprocessor how far the mouse has moved.

46 These marked up versions of the three articles show pauses and stress.

A woman in Ashford, Kent,| persuaded her husband to drive fifteen miles to return a live crab to the sea|after fighting gulls had dropped it in her back garden.|

A robber armed with a knife|stole a half-smoked cigarette from a man's mouth| in Commercial Road,|East London. |

The British lost forty million pounds|through holes in their pockets,|down the backs of sofas|and in other odd places last year.|The Royal Mint said four hundred and fifty million coins disappeared from circulation,|including twenty-five million one pound coins.|

47 One of you will be asking the questions and telling the Candidates what to do. The other will be listening and making notes so that you can give the Candidates feedback later and advise them how to perform better.

> **FEEDBACK CHECKLIST:**
>
> | Grammar | Pronunciation | Interactive Communication |
> |---|---|---|
> | Vocabulary | Fluency | Task Achievement |

Part 1

1 Greet both candidates.

2 Ask each candidate these questions:
- What's your name?
- Where are you from?
- How long have you lived there?
- What's your home like?
- How do you usually spend your free time?
- What are your plans for the future?

Part 2

1 Ask the first Candidate to look at the photos in Activity *48* and to talk about them for one minute, comparing and contrasting the two jobs shown there. After one minute ask the second Candidate to comment briefly on the same pictures.

2 Ask the second Candidate to look at the photos in Activity *49* and to talk about them for one minute, comparing and contrasting the two jobs shown there. After one minute ask the other Candidate to comment briefly on the pictures.

Part 3

Ask both Candidates to look at the pictures in Activity *50*. Ask them to talk to each other about the kind of work that's being done in the pictures. Which of the jobs would they prefer to do themselves? Why?
After three minutes, go on to Part 4.

Part 4

Ask the Candidates to discuss these questions together for about four minutes:

- What would be your ideal job? Why?
- What kind of work do you think you'll be doing in five years' time?
- What kind of job would you least like to have? Why?
- What jobs can you think of that are very badly paid? Why are they badly paid?

That's the end of the first mock exam.

48

49

50

51

This is the leaflet one of the slogans came from. Tell your partner about it in your own words, beginning, 'Did you know . . . ?'

(20 mph = 30 kph)

Kill your speed

If you are driving at 20 mph and a child runs out into the road 12 metres in front of you, in most cases you should be able to stop without injuring the child.

If you are driving at 40 mph you will not even have time to reach the brake pedal before you hit the child.

The child will probably be killed.

not a child

52

Here are explanations of some of the items on the menu on page 84, so that you can help your partners to understand them. *Don't* just read these descriptions out loud – try to remember them, so that you can answer your partners' questions.

Steak and kidney pie	A traditional English pie containing beef and kidneys in a rich sauce – delicious!
Blackberry fool	Cooked blackberries and sugar whipped up with fresh cream and served cold.

When you're all clear what each dish is, decide what you'll order for each course.

53

1 The original version of the story contains so little detail that it's impossible to get interested. It's supposed to be a personal story, so there should be personal details to explain why the night was unforgettable. The exact times and distances are irrelevant and distracting.

2 What makes the following version of the story better than the one on page 31? Highlight the main changes that have been made.

I'll never forget the night our car broke down. We were on our way home from a marvellous evening out with friends. It was well after midnight and we were still miles from home. We tried to get the engine started again, but in vain. There was no traffic on the road at all, so we couldn't get a lift and had to walk all the way home. To make matters worse it started to rain and by the time we arrived we were wet through. But worse was yet to come! It was then that we discovered that we'd left our front door key in the car.

We had no choice but to break a window and climb in. Unfortunately, just as we were doing this, a police car stopped in the road. At first, of course, the policeman didn't believe our story and wanted to take us to the police station, but in the end we convinced him that we were telling the truth. By the time we got to bed it was past three o'clock and we were cold, wet, miserable and absolutely exhausted.

54 Here is version of a punctuated version of the paragraph in B3 of Unit 2.3. As there are no firm rules for punctuation in English, there are a number of possible variations to this version.

Every Tuesday, Friday and Saturday in our part of the city, there's an open-air market in the main square which everyone goes to. Farmers come in from the countryside to sell their fresh vegetables and fruit. Other stalls sell all kinds of things: cheese, jeans, fish and even second-hand furniture. It's almost impossible to carry on a conversation above the noise and shouting as customers push their way to the front, trying to attract the stall-holders' attention and demanding the ripest, freshest fruit or the lowest prices.

55 **1** Study this recipe with your partner. Is this drink something you'd like to try?

LASSI
a refreshing Eastern yogurt drink

¼ litre yogurt   ¼ litre milk (or water)   juice of 1 lemon

ice cubes   sugar to taste

1 Crush the ice cubes or put them in a food processor.

2 Put all the ingredients, except the sugar, into the food processor or liquidiser and blend well.

3 Add the sugar little by little until the liquid is sweet enough. It should NOT be too sweet!

4 Serve immediately in tall glasses with drinking straws.

2 Join another pair and explain this recipe to them *in your own words*. They'll tell you how to make old-fashioned lemonade.

56 Here are the correct figures:

Shoplifting, as percent of US sales

Ladies clothes 2.44   Men's clothes 1.84   Children's clothes 2.65   Health and beauty 3.51
Jewellery 4.71   Shoes 1.54   Fashion accessories 7.57   Toys, hobbies 2.10
CDs, cassettes 4.13   Radios, stereos 3.37   Sporting goods 3.44

57

12 April

Dear Mr Brown,
    I am interested in renting your flat at 44C Sandringham Gardens, which was advertised in the Evening Echo this week.
    As I am unable to view the flat myself, could you please give me some more information about it?
    First of all, could you tell me if the building has a garage or if there is a safe place where I could park my car off the road? Could you also tell me what equipment there is in the kitchen: does it have a dishwater or a microwave? Is there a security deposit which I would have to pay to cover possible breakages and if so, how much would this be?
    Finally, could you please tell me whether the flat is still available from July 7th to August 14th inclusive, and what the rent is per week?
    I look forward to hearing from you.

    Yours sincerely,

58   Here are some guidelines on writing a report:

1 Collect all the relevant information – in this case the notes you made on the survey.
2 Consider the purpose of your report: Who is it for? Why does he/she want it? How will he/she use it?
3 Which of the information is important? Which parts are irrelevant?
4 Arrange the points of information in a logical sequence and in order of importance.
5 What are your recommendations? Or what is your conclusion?
6 Make notes. Decide on your opening and closing sentences.
7 Write the report.
8 Check it through to make sure you have made all your points clearly.
9 Check it through for mistakes in grammar, spelling and punctuation.

59   This is an extract from the leaflet about one of the *Discover Scotland* excursions.

GLENCOE AND FORT WILLIAM

TUESDAY

We board the coach at 8:30 and head north over the Forth Road Bridge, where we enjoy a wonderful view of the river and the famous 19th century railway bridge. We continue across the beautiful Ochill Hills, stopping for coffee in the ancient town of Crieff.

We pass Loch Earn and then drive up into the Grampian Mountains, across the lonely Rannoch Moor and then down into Glencoe, an impressive valley surrounded by steep mountains. This is where the Macdonalds were massacred by the Campbells and the English in 1602. After that we join the coast road with magnificent views across Loch Linnhe. We stop for lunch at Fort William, which lies at the foot of Ben Nevis (Britain's highest mountain at 1,392 metres).

We now start our journey home, returning by a different route across the moors, where we may catch sight of red deer and other wildlife. We make a short detour to Loch Tummel, stopping at Queen's View to admire the famous view. We then continue south to Perth, where we will stop for tea if time permits, before joining the motorway to Edinburgh, where we arrive at around 17:30 in good time for dinner – and perhaps an evening out in the city.

60   **1** Study this recipe with your partner. Is this drink something you'd like to try?

OLD-FASHIONED LEMONADE
a refreshing drink, rich in vitamin C

4 large juicy lemons   500 g sugar (brown or white)   1 litre water

1 Peel the lemons thinly, removing only the rind, and squeeze the juice into a large bowl. Add the sugar.
2 Boil the lemon rind in the water for a few minutes.
3 Remove the rind and pour the water over the juice and sugar. Mix well to dissolve the sugar.
4 Pour the liquid into clean bottles and put them in the refrigerator to cool.
5 Shake well before serving. Dilute with cold water to taste – or use sparkling mineral water for a fizzy drink.

2 Join another pair and explain this recipe to them *in your own words*. They'll tell you how to make a refreshing Eastern yogurt drink.

61 If you're looking at another student's work, or looking critically at your own work, here are some questions to bear in mind when giving feedback. Some of these points are more important than others – and you may find it difficult to judge some points.

INTEREST	Is the composition interesting? Does the first sentence make you want to go on reading to find out more? Has the writer considered the reader's reactions?
COMMUNICATION	Is it clear what the writer means? Are there any points you don't follow because they aren't expressed clearly?
ORGANISATION	Does the composition look well organised? Does the writer seem to have made notes or just jotted down a series of random thoughts?
ACCURACY	This is difficult to assess, and perhaps should be left to your teacher. But have you spotted any obvious mistakes in grammar or spelling?
VOCABULARY	Is the vocabulary too simple? Has the writer used words which have come up in this unit – in the vocabulary section or in the other sections of the unit?
PARAGRAPHS	Is the composition divided into a good number of easy-to-read paragraphs? Are there too few (or too many) paragraphs?
STYLE	Is the style of the composition appropriate for the imagined reader and the type of text required (informal letter, formal letter, magazine article, story, etc.)? If not, what should be changed?
ACHIEVEMENT OF TASK	Has the writer answered the question adequately? Has the writer misunderstood the question in any way? Has the writer ignored part of it?
RELEVANCE	Is all the information given in the composition relevant to the question? (In Part 1 of the Writing paper in the exam it's important to include all the relevant information that's asked for – you lose marks for missing out the required information.)
ENDING	Does the composition end well? Does the last sentence leave you feeling that you've read something interesting or entertaining?
OVERALL	What did you think of the composition overall? How much did you enjoy reading it? How much did you learn from it? What is the *one* thing that most needs improving to make it better?

You might like to try giving a grade for each aspect, using this scale:

A excellent B good C OK D not so good E not good at all

62 **1** Describe each person in this picture to your partner, mentioning their appearance, clothes and personalities. Take turns to describe the people one-by-one, from left to right.

2 Which of the people your partner has just described would you choose to start a conversation with if you were on a train with them?

To the self-study student

Using the self-study notes

This part of the book contains:
- self-study instructions on how to use the main part of the book on your own (where necessary)
- answers and model compositions or paragraphs
- tapescripts for the listening exercises.

Follow this procedure when working on your own:

1 Read the self-study instructions for part A of the section
2 Do the exercise or activity in A in the main part of the book
3 Check your answers with the model answers (if these are given)
4 Follow the self-study instructions for part B of the section
5 Do part B in the main part of the book
6 Check your answers
. . . and so on.

Answers and models

The answers, model compositions and model paragraphs in this part of the book will help you to check your answers and learn more. In some cases, where the questions are open-ended, suggested answers are given and variations may be possible. When a model is given, you should compare your work with this – but you should ask a teacher or an English-speaking person to correct your work from time to time, so that you can find out what kind of mistakes you are making.

When you make mistakes or can't answer questions, make sure that you learn from your mistakes. In fact, it's impossible to learn if you don't make mistakes – if you get everything right it would mean you knew everything already!

Working without a teacher

Working alone using the self-study notes will help you to improve your reading, writing and listening skills, but you should try to get someone to read your written work and correct it. If you are using this book entirely on your own without a teacher or other students in a class, the self-study notes tell you how you can do the speaking activities using a cassette recorder with a microphone – but if possible, you should do some of these with another person.

Working regularly with a partner will give you a chance to discuss what you have been doing and read each other's work. You will find that you will learn a lot from each other and it will help you to feel that you are making progress. Perhaps arrange a regular session each week when you can work together.

Whenever you are doing an exercise in co-operation with another student, follow the instructions in the main part of the book.

The self-study notes at the back of the book tell you how to use each exercise in the main part of the book when you are working alone.

Working partly on your own

Parts of this book can be used in class and other parts can be done by you working alone. Your teacher will advise you which parts you should do on your own, depending on how much time is available for work in class – in this case you may be expected to check some of the answers yourself. You should try to work through any exercises for which there is no time in class on your own.

Students who are unable to follow a complete classroom course, through illness or other commitments, will find this book especially valuable. You will be able to catch up on work you miss and perhaps rejoin the class later – or go on working on your own if you are unable to continue attending classes.

What you need

- A piece of card, about the same size as this book, to cover up the model answers in this part of the book while you read the self-study notes. This will stop you seeing the answers by mistake.
- An exercise book in which to write your answers to the exercises and your compositions.
- A smaller pocket-sized notebook for your vocabulary notes.
- A yellow highlighter, for highlighting the useful vocabulary and expressions in the reading passages and in the tapescripts.
- 🔲 The set of two cassettes.
- A cassette recorder for listening to the cassettes and a microphone for recording your own voice.
- A good English-to-English dictionary, such as one of the following:
  BBC English Dictionary
  Cambridge International Dictionary of English
  Collins COBUILD Essential English Dictionary
  Longman Active Study Dictionary of English
  Longman Dictionary of Contemporary English
  Longman Dictionary of English Language and Culture
  Oxford Advanced Learner's Dictionary
  Oxford Advanced Learner's Encyclopedic Dictionary
  Oxford Wordpower Dictionary
- A good bilingual dictionary – but a tiny pocket-sized one is not good enough. Ask for advice on which one to choose if you don't already possess one.

- A good grammar reference book to answer your questions on English grammar: *English Grammar in Use* WITH ANSWERS by Raymond Murphy (Cambridge University Press) or *Basic English Usage* by Michael Swan (Oxford University Press) are recommended.

Shortly before the exam, you should work through the test papers in *Cambridge Practice Tests for First Certificate 1 and 2* (Cambridge University Press) and you'll need the accompanying Teacher's Book, which contains the correct answers.

Exam enrolment

If you are entering for the FCE exam (which is held in June and December), remember that you will need to enrol for it at least three months in advance. In some centres the latest date for enrolment is even earlier. If you are studying in your own country, the local British Council office can give you the address of your nearest centre.

Unit-by-unit guide

1 Learning languages   Gestures and body language
Dictionary skills

Communication

The notes for this unit are longer than later units – they explain how the different types of exercises work and suggest how you should use them. You should do all the exercises in this unit, but in later units you may decide to leave some exercises out.

1.1 Ways of communicating
VOCABULARY AND SPEAKING

A Imagine that someone is asking you these questions: say your answers aloud softly to yourself. Use a dictionary to look up any words you need. You may prefer to write down your answers to some of the questions.

B Do the whole exercise in the main part of the book in pencil or in your exercise book, using a dictionary to look up any words you are unsure of. There will probably be several gaps that you can't fill. When you have finished, check your answers below and correct any mistakes you have made.

If you have written the answers in pencil, you can rub them out and do the exercise again during another session – this will help you to remember the new words you are learning. If you have written them in your exercise book, use a fresh page when you do the exercise again.

ANSWERS

2 abstract   **3** adjectives   adverbs
4 pronouns   **5** prepositions
6 conjunctions   **7** parts   **8** phrasal
9 capital letter   **10** italics   **11** syllables
12 prefixes   suffixes   **13** phonetic
14 accents

C **1** There are no 'correct answers' for this task, but most of us notice other people's appearance long before we notice their voice or accent. And what they say is often the last thing we notice.

2

SUGGESTED ANSWERS

✓ sincere   attractive   intelligent   sensible
   artistic   pleasant
✗ arrogant   unfriendly   rude
   self-satisfied   bad-tempered   timid
   sensitive

D Remembering vocabulary is one of the most important things you will have to do during this course. There is no best way of doing this – different methods work well for different people.

Here is just one way a page in a Filofax might be organised:

> PEOPLE
>
> bad-tempered / bæd tempəd /
> – A bad tempered person easily gets angry, or loses his temper.
> sensible / sensɪbl /
> – A sensible person isn't silly – she has a lot of sense.
> sensitive / sensɪtɪv /
> – A sensitive person can get upset easily.

1.2 Signs
LISTENING

Before you listen to the recording, read these notes through carefully and look at the questions in the main part of the book. Then, if necessary, listen to each conversation two or three times.

The recordings on the cassettes are all unsimplified, natural conversations or interviews or radio programmes. The speakers talk at their normal speed. Each recording lasts only a few minutes, so it's quick and easy to listen to them several times if you need to. In the exam itself, you'll hear each listening passage through twice.

The questions you have to answer in the exercises or the gaps you have to fill in are the only things you need to worry about. Don't worry if you can't understand every word that's spoken or if parts of a conversation seem very fast to you. No one, not even a native speaker of English, can catch every single word that's spoken in a conversation. So, all you have to do is to concentrate on understanding the information given by the speakers. If you can answer the questions, then you have understood all the important information.

In other words, don't panic if the voices seem very fast or if the speakers use some words you don't know. Just listen to the recording again a couple of times, looking at the questions in the main part of the book, and you'll soon find that you do understand all that you need to in each conversation. If necessary, pause the recording while you note down the answers.

There is a tapescript for each listening exercise. Don't look at this until you have heard the recording at least twice through.

A

ANSWERS

1 Give priority to vehicles from the opposite direction   2 No bicycles allowed
3 No motor vehicles allowed
4 This way to the zoo   5 Mini-roundabout: give way to traffic from the immediate right
6 Road gets narrower on both sides
7 Elderly people   8 Traffic merging with equal priority from the right
9 Quayside or river bank

B Follow this procedure, and do the same with the other listening exercises.

1 Look at the task first and try to anticipate (or guess) what the answers might be.

2 Listen to the first 20 to 30 seconds of the recording so that you can get used to the unfamiliar voice. Don't try to answer the questions and don't look at the tapescript. (You may find it easier to concentrate if you close your eyes while you're doing this.)

3 Listen to the recording all the way through and do the task. If necessary, pause the tape during the conversation – this will give you time to think about the task.

4 If you have only been able to do part of the task, listen to the whole conversation again and concentrate on finding the answers you missed or were unsure about. Again, pause the tape where necessary.

5 Check your answers. If you have made any mistakes, it means you have misunderstood the speaker or the question.

6 Listen to the recording again, but this time follow it in the tapescript, checking any wrong answers as you go. Again, pause the tape where necessary. Use a yellow highlighter to mark any useful new words or expressions.

7 Listen to the whole recording all the way through. Sit back, close your eyes and listen – this will help you to appreciate and learn the sounds of English conversation, pronunciation and vocabulary.

Looking at the tapescript earlier would make the task much easier – but this will not help you to improve your listening skills.

A low-pitched tone is recorded between each section on the cassette. When the tape is played forwards or backwards fast on CUE or REVIEW you will hear this as a high-pitched beep which makes it easy to find where each new section begins on the cassette.

ANSWERS

3 Friendly people ○
4 Friendly, generous people ⊙
5 Very friendly, generous people ⊙̲

6 Work to be had here ⊖
7 Gypsies not liked ╪
8 Nothing to be had ╋
9 Work available with good pay ⊜
10 These people will buy from you ═
11 This place has been robbed ///

TRANSCRIPT   *3 minutes 40 seconds*

GUIDE: . . . and the gypsies also had a whole system of communications of...of...way of communicating with each other as well. When they went from house to house around the country they left behind chalk marks on the wall...um...and these were messages for any other gypsies who came along later. Now, these signs were useful because, for one thing, many gypsies were illiterate in those days but also the signs couldn't be understood by the country people, they were only intelligible to the gypsies themselves.

Now, I'll show you some of the signs, I'll draw them on this board. Now, if there was a dog at the house, then they used this sign, see: a triangle. If it was a fierce dog, then they put a horizontal line through the triangle like this. If the people in the house were friendly, then they'd draw a circle like so.

Now, what do you think this meant? This is a circle with a dot in the middle. Now, I wonder what that meant?

MAN: Angry? Angry neighbours?

GUIDE: No, no, no. It meant 'friendly and generous people'. Now what about this? This is a circle with a dot in the middle and a line underneath and this means very friendly and very generous people. Now, this one, this is a circle with a horizontal line through it and this meant 'work to be had here'.

Now if a house was known to be unfriendly, they would leave a sign like this, this is a vertical line with two horizontal lines and that meant 'gypsies not liked', so they could steer clear of that one.

Now, I wonder what you think about this one? This is a very common one: it's a cross made with one vertical line and one horizontal line. What...what do you think that might have meant?

WOMAN: No idea.

GUIDE: Any ideas? It meant 'nothing to be had' at this house, so again they could...er...they could go on by and not waste their time knocking on the door. Um...here's another one. This is a circle with two horizontal lines and...er...probably fairly uncommon in those days, this one meant 'work available and good pay'. So they'd obviously stop there. Er...now, three horizontal lines – any ideas what that might be? No? Now, this was a very hopeful sign for a gypsy because this meant 'these people will buy from you' so it would be well worth your time stopping by here. Now, here's the last one: three slanting lines, like this. Anyone care to guess? This was a very important one for the gypsies. Three slanting lines means 'don't stop here because this place has been robbed'.

C

SUGGESTED ANSWERS

✓ good   ✓✓ very good   ✗ one mistake
✗✗ two mistakes   P Punctuation mistake
Sp Spelling mistake   WO mistake in Word Order
G Grammatical mistake
V Vocabulary mistake   ! I'm surprised!
? What do you mean?

And to avoid repeating spelling mistakes:
write out the word again correctly, twice
and/or
have a special section in your vocabulary notebook for
'Words I often spell wrong' – when you've stopped
spelling them wrong, they can be crossed out or ticked
off (✓).

1.3 Using a dictionary
WORD STUDY

A Here are some suggested answers:

- more examples to see, definitions in other words, different dictionaries have different strengths and weaknesses in their coverage, not every dictionary is equally up to date or includes every specialised word
- quick to use, translations of every word
- more examples of words in sentences, usually more up to date

B All the answers can be found on the same or adjacent pages in any good English-to-English dictionary.

C **1** Not many people read a foreword or introduction, least of all in a dictionary. But the foreword gives essential information about the way a book is organised and the rationale behind it.

2 Highlighting words is a technique that will be used over and over in this book. As time goes by, you need to decide which words to highlight – not every word you don't know, but the ones you want to remember.

3 There is no 'correct' arrangement of the features.

1.4 Present tenses
GRAMMAR REVIEW

The GRAMMAR REVIEW exercises are **revision** exercises. Always consult the GRAMMAR REFERENCE section if you have any difficulties with the exercises.

A Study the GRAMMAR REFERENCE section on pages 182–183.

B

> **SUGGESTED ANSWERS**
>
> 2 What does she do?
> She's a student.
>
> 3 How long has she been writing?
> For about an hour.
>
> 4 How much has she written?
> About 200 words.
>
> 5 When are you having lunch?
> Later than usual today.'
>
> 6 When do you have lunch?
> Usually at one thirty.
>
> 7 Where are you going for lunch?
> Probably the cafeteria today.
>
> 8 Where do you go for lunch?
> To the cafeteria most days.
>
> 9 Does he speak Japanese or Chinese?
> Both, I think.
>
> 10 Is he speaking Japanese or Chinese?
> It sounds like Chinese to me.

C The error-correction exercises in the grammar sections will help you to recognise mistakes when you're checking your own written work.

> **ANSWERS** (Some variations are possible.)
>
> 2 *A dictionary isn't costing very much to buy.*
> doesn't cost
>
> 3 *She is living in London since she has been a child.*
> has been   was
>
> 4 *What time are you expecting her to arrive?* ✓
> (*or* do you expect)
>
> 5 *I am still waiting for her to answer my letter.* ✓
>
> 6 *Are you understanding me if I am speaking very fast like this?*
> Do/Can you understand   speak
>
> 7 *My sister's always annoying me.* ✓
>
> 8 *I am remembering his face but I'm forgetting his name.*
> remember   forget/have forgotten

D

> **ANSWERS** (Some variations are possible.)
>
> 2 I *(can) never remember* how to spell the word 'pronunciation'.
>
> 3 It *doesn't matter* if you don't understand every word.
>
> 4 I *have/'ve been learning English since* I was ten years old.
>
> 5 How *long has it been* raining?
>
> 6 He *is/'s always interrupting* and it's very annoying!
>
> 7 She *teaches people (how)* to drive.
>
> 8 Oh dear, *it's still raining*!

E Write a paragraph about what you do every morning.

1.5 Good manners
READING

The Reading sections in this book usually contain:

A A 'first reading' task which helps you to understand the main points of the passage, often by reading the passage through fairly quickly. In some cases there are questions about your previous knowledge of the subject.

B A 'second reading' task: reading comprehension questions which help you to develop your reading skills and understand the details of the text, by reading the passage again more slowly and carefully.

C A discussion activity in which you discuss the ideas given in the passage – this can be recorded on a blank cassette or done with a partner.

Some reading sections also contain vocabulary exercises, which will help you to understand difficult passages without using a dictionary to look up the unfamiliar words. Whenever you read a passage for the first time, it's best not to use a dictionary – you'll find that you can often guess the meaning of unfamiliar words from their context.

The passages in this book come from a wide variety of sources: magazines, newspapers, books, advertisements, etc. However, you should also read more English in books, newspapers or magazines for your own pleasure and to improve your vocabulary and reading skills.

A This is an exam-style reading task and it is quite difficult! It's necessary to read the passage quite carefully, looking for clues, but it is **not** necessary to understand every word (or even every sentence).

> **ANSWERS**
> **2** E   **3** G   **4** F   **5** C   **6** B   **7** D

B Decide which words to highlight, according to whether they are worth remembering or not. For example, words like *appendage* and *clammy* may not be worth remembering, whilst *appreciated* and *compels* may be.

C Decide how you would answer the questions and say your answers aloud softly to yourself (or under your breath). Perhaps record yourself on a blank cassette.

The author is American (he refers to *highways* and a *thousand-dollar bill*). *Exchanging cordialities* means saying a few friendly things to people you meet, such as commenting on the weather.

1.6 Remembering prepositions
PREPOSITIONS

The problem with prepositions is remembering them – especially when there seems to be no logical reason why one is used rather than another.

A

> **ANSWERS**
> **3** of/for   **4** for   **5** for (*or no preposition*)
> **6** on/about   **7** by   **8** of   **9** in
> **10** for/to   **11** by   **12** in   **13** on
> **14** by/on   **15** with   **16** with   **17** at/for
> **18** by   to   **19** in   **20** from/of   **21** of
> **22** at   **23** about (*or no preposition*)   **24** for

B There are 46 in the main text (*than* and *like* are also prepositions) and two in the sentences to be added.

1.7 Giving your opinions
LISTENING

A **1**   This exercise is similar to an exam-style listening task. It is definitely **not** necessary to catch every word to be able to answer the questions.

> **ANSWERS**
> **1** Julie   **2** no one   **3** Sally   **4** Tom
> **5** Anthony   **6** Bill

2 Tom sounded quite unpleasant. His tone of voice made him sound arrogant – and not using any of the phrases underlined in the tapescript to introduce his opinions contributed to this impression.

B **TRANSCRIPT AND ANSWERS**
2 minutes 40 seconds
(The phrases used to introduce opinions are underlined.)

ANTHONY: Well, <u>it seems to me</u> that some languages are easier to learn than others. I mean, what about if you had to learn Japanese? <u>I don't really think that</u> as an English speaker I could learn to speak Japanese as easily as I could learn...er...say Italian. I mean for a start I'd have to learn a completely new writing system, and there'd be hardly any words which are the same in English and Japanese. Do you see what I mean, Sally?

SALLY: Yes, but at least Japanese is a living language – ha...I mean millions of people speak it in Japan. So <u>I think it's true to say that</u> learning it would be useful and relevant. But Latin or Ancient Greek are languages that nobody speaks. <u>I mean, don't you agree that</u> learning a dead language is a bit of a waste of time? Some students find them interesting, but <u>I don't really believe that</u> there's any practical value at all in learning classical languages, do you, Bill?

BILL: Not really. But <u>you know what I think? I think that</u> if you learn a foreign language in your own country, it's quite difficult to appreciate the relevance of *any* language. I think this is particularly true if you're learning a language at school, where...er...studying languages sometimes doesn't seem relevant – any more than history or literature seem relevant. And don't you agree that...if your only contact with the language is in the classroom and you only speak and hear it there, you may forget all about it between lessons? So each new lesson begins...um...with time spent trying to remember what you did in the last lesson, doesn't it, Julie?

JULIE: Yes, but I think it's true to say that the reality for most people is that they have to learn foreign languages in classes in their own country. It takes a very long time to learn a language. I...I don't really think that many people can just travel to the country where the language is spoken and live there. The point is that most people have to continue their studies, or earn a living, they...they can't afford to take time off living in another country for as long as it takes for them to learn the language, can they, Tom?

TOM: No, but with a foreign language you never stop learning. You never reach a point where you can say: 'At the end of this course I'll know English and I can stop learning it.' It's a process that goes on and on – you can reach a certain level, or you can pass an exam or even get a university degree. But you still remain a learner all your life.

C Record yourself talking about some of the topics.

1.8 What are your strengths and weaknesses?

WRITING

If possible, ask another person (perhaps an English-speaking person or a friend whose English is reasonably good) to read and mark your work.

If this is not possible, check your own composition through a week or two later. By then you will probably be able to find mistakes of spelling and grammar in your work that you can correct yourself.

Shops and stores Using services: banks, post offices
Clothes and fashion

2 At your service!

2.1 Can I help you?

VOCABULARY AND LISTENING

A If you don't have a partner to do this with, record yourself on a blank cassette or make notes of your answers to the questions.

B

	Where are they?	**What does the customer want?**	**What will the customer say next?**
1	in a bank	to change $120 into pounds	'£90 in ten-pound notes and the rest in coins, please.'
2	in a pharmacy/ chemist's	something for her daughter's illness (sore throat or lost voice, perhaps)	'I'll take the tablets/ lozenges, I think.'
3	in a bookshop or newsagent's	a street map	'I'll have the ABC, I think.'
4	in a post office	to send a small packet abroad	'Oh, well I suppose I'll have to send it letter rate then, even though it does cost more.'

SUGGESTED ANSWERS (table title)

TRANSCRIPTS *2 minutes 50 seconds*

1 CUSTOMER: . . . OK, I've got two at fifty dollars and one at twenty dollars.
CASHIER: So that's 150 dollars altogether.
CUSTOMER: Er...no, that's 120.
CASHIER: Oh...right...um...could you sign them there please?
CUSTOMER: Here? Yep, OK, there you are.
CASHIER: Thank you. Can I see your passport please?
CUSTOMER: Ah...yeah, sure here it is.
CASHIER: OK...Right, so that's 94 pounds 45. How do you want the money?

2 CUSTOMER: . . . um...have you got anything suitable?
CHEMIST: Yeah, sure. But you don't sound as if you need anything.
CUSTOMER: Oh no, they're not for me. They're for my daughter.
CHEMIST: Oh I see. Well...um...these are pretty good. Or you could give her some of this. She should take one spoonful three times a day.
CUSTOMER: Mhm. Is there any limit to how many of those she can take?
CHEMIST: Er...yes, she should only take eight of them in one day.
CUSTOMER: Which do you recommend?
CHEMIST: Well, they're both pretty effective. It depends which is more convenient really. Which would you like?

3 CUSTOMER: . . . so what's the difference between them?
ASSISTANT: Well, the ABC covers a larger area a...and it's got the main tourist attractions marked.
CUSTOMER: Mm. And the A to Z?
ASSISTANT: Well, it does cover the whole town, um...but not the surrounding area. Er...what it does have is all the bus routes marked on it, see, there?

CUSTOMER: Ah yes...but it hasn't got an index of street names, has it?

ASSISTANT: Ah, w...i...it has, it has, look look, it's printed on the back.

CUSTOMER: And are they s...exactly the same price?

ASSISTANT: Aha, almost: the ABC is three ninety-five and the A to Z is three ninety-nine.

CUSTOMER: Ah.

ASSISTANT: Which one would you like?

4 CUSTOMER: . . . Mm, yes, I think so, would that be the cheapest?

COUNTER CLERK: Yes. Um...can you put it on the scales please?

CUSTOMER: OK.

COUNTER CLERK: That'll be four pounds twenty...Oh dear.

CUSTOMER: What's the matter?

COUNTER CLERK: Well, did you wrap this yourself?

CUSTOMER: Yes.

COUNTER CLERK: Well, I can't accept it as a 'small packet'.

CUSTOMER: Why not?

COUNTER CLERK: Well, to go as a 'small packet' it has to be easily openable. You've put sticky tape all over it. Look, do you want to take it away and repack it or do you want to send it at letter rate? If you do that, letter rate would be...six pounds sixty-five.

CUSTOMER: Mhm.

 C

ANSWERS

1 cash   cheque/check (*US spelling*)
2 assistant   counter/cash desk
3 help   looking   **4** receipt   **5** guarantee
6 trying   size   fit   **7** match   suit   **8** label
9 queue   **10** bargain   sale/sales

 D

SUGGESTED ANSWERS

2 butcher's – hardware store or ironmonger's or kitchen shop
3 electrical store – music shop or record shop
4 baker's – grocer's
5 *for both*: stationery shop or stationer's or newsagent's or newspaper shop or kiosk
6 *for both*: chemist's or pharmacy
7 souvenir shop or newspaper shop or kiosk – post office or the same shop you bought the card in!

2.2	**Abbreviations and numbers**
	WORD STUDY

 A

ANSWERS

c/o	care of
e.g.	for example
etc.	and so on/*et cetera*
FCE	First Certificate in English
GMT	Greenwich Mean Time
incl.	including/inclusive
info.	information
intro.	introduction

max.	maximum
min.	minimum
misc.	miscellaneous
No.	Number
N, S, E & W	North, South, East and West
PTO	Please turn over
Rd.	Road
RSVP	Please reply (to this invitation)
St.	Street
VAT	Value Added Tax
VIP	Very important person
vocab.	vocabulary
Xmas	Christmas
1st, 2nd & 3rd	first, second and third

 B

ANSWERS (Spelling is important!)

a hundred and forty-four
a hundred and thirteen
two hundred and twenty-seven
eight hundred and fifty thousand
five point seven five
one thousand nine hundred and ninety-two
seven-eighths
one and a quarter plus two and two-thirds equals three point nine one six seven
four and three-quarters minus two and a half equals two point two five

C   Play the recording and pause it after each sentence while you write down the numbers you hear. Then listen to the whole recording again to check what you wrote.

TRANSCRIPT AND ANSWERS   *3 minutes*

My phone number is 5180477.
The number is 617930.
Call me on 0171 2258915.
The fax number is 044 1202 892671.
You can contact me on this number: 01473 993313.
Leave a message at this number: 879615.

The total population of the city is 5,180,477.
Twenty years ago there were only 617,930.
The number of inhabitants of the town is 40,515.
Ten years ago there were only 14,550.
Can you make a note of this number: 17,170,660.
The value of pi is three point one four two – 3.142.

The time's three forty-five pm – 3.45 pm.
It's ten to eleven – 10.50.
It's twenty-five to eight – 7.35.
It's just after a quarter past seven – 7.15.

The total price is forty-five pounds ninety-nine – £45.99.
You'll have to pay twelve dollars and fifteen cents – $12.15.
The cost is £140 plus VAT – £140 + VAT.
You still owe me ninety p – 90p (pence).

D Use your cassette recorder with a microphone and a blank cassette:

1 Record all the information that is given in Activity *1* (page 186) on the cassette.

2 A little later, play it back to yourself and write down the information, pausing the tape frequently.

3 Look again at Activity *1* and check whether you got all the information correct – were any mistakes your fault as a reader or your fault as a listener?

4 Do the same with the information in Activity *29*.

2.3 **Spelling and punctuation**
WRITING

A The words containing a spelling mistake are underlined.

ANSWERS

2 *My brother is <u>ninteen</u> years old.*	nineteen
3 *One day he's <u>hopping</u> to go*	hoping
to <u>Amerika</u>.	America
4 *It was a <u>realy wonderfull</u> meal!*	really wonderful
5 *I <u>recieved you</u> letter this morning.*	received your
6 *He <u>want</u> to improve his*	wants
<u>knoledge of english</u>.	knowledge English
7 *Concorde <u>flys</u> across the Atlantic*	flies
in four <u>ours</u>.	hours
8 *Some people find <u>speling</u>*	spelling
<u>especialy dificult</u>.	especially difficult

B **1**

ANSWERS

exclamation mark   question mark
full stop / period   comma   semi-colon
colon   apostrophe   single quotes /
single quotation marks   double quotes /
double quotation marks   hyphen   dash
brackets / parentheses

2

CORRECTED VERSION
(Some variations are possible.)

Harrods (or Harrod's) is London's most famous department store. You can buy almost anything there and it's one of the landmarks of London. People come to eat at its restaurants and look round its 214 departments, but not everyone comes to buy. Many of the people who go there just enjoy looking at the enormous range of goods on display – and at the other customers.

3 & 4 Add your own punctuation before you look at the corrected version of the paragraph in Activity *54*.

2.4 **Questions and question tags**
GRAMMAR REVIEW

A Compare your questions with the examples in the GRAMMAR REFERENCE section.

B **1**

ANSWERS (Some variations are possible.)

2 When *were you born*?
   Could you tell me *when you were born*?
3 Where *were you born*?
   Can you also tell me *where you were born*?
4 Where *do you live*?
   I'd like to know *where you live.*
5 What *is your phone number*?
   Would you mind telling me *your phone number*?
6 Who *is the British prime minister*?
   Do you know *who the British prime minister is*?
7 How many *people live in the UK*?
   Do you happen to know *how many people live in the UK*?

2 Write down five questions you could ask about the pictures in Activity *13* and *40*. Then write down your answers to the questions.

C **1** 🔲 Pause the recording between each example, while you make up your mind.

ANSWERS
3 ✔   4 ?   5 ?   6 ✔   7 ?   8 ✔
9 ✔   10 ?

TRANSCRIPTS *2 minutes*

1 WOMAN: Today's the fourteenth, isn't it?
  •NARRATOR: She's unsure so put a question mark.
  MAN: No, it's the fifteenth.

2 WOMAN: Today's Monday, isn't it?
  NARRATOR: She's fairly sure so put a tick.
  MAN: Yes, Monday the fifteenth.

3 WOMAN: The capital of the USA is Washington, isn't it? *sounds sure*
  MAN: Yes, that's right.

4 WOMAN: And the capital of Canada is Toronto, isn't it? *sounds unsure*
  MAN: No, it's Ottawa.

5 WOMAN: There are five oceans, aren't there? *sounds unsure*
  MAN: Five? Yes, I think so.

6 WOMAN: And the biggest are the Pacific and the Atlantic, aren't they? *sounds sure*
  MAN: Yes, and of the two the Pacific is bigger.

7 WOMAN: Most people in Canada speak English, don't they? *sounds unsure*
  MAN: Yes, but there are lots who speak French.

8 WOMAN: Most people in Australia speak English, don't they? *sounds sure*
  MAN: Yes, I think so. It's the official language, anyway.

9 WOMAN: Marilyn Monroe was in *Some Like It Hot*, wasn't she? *sounds sure*
  MAN: Yes – great film!

10 WOMAN: And it was directed by Michael Curtiz, wasn't it? *sounds unsure*
   MAN: No, no, you're thinking of *Casablanca*. *Some Like It Hot* was directed by Billy Wilder.
   WOMAN: Oh, yes, that's right.

2

ANSWERS

3 can't it?   4 should they?   5 is there?
6 wasn't it?   7 mustn't they?   8 didn't they?
9 haven't we?   10 shall we?

3 & 4   Record the questions on a blank cassette. Then play the recording back and answer the questions.

2.5   ## Advertisements and commercials
SPEAKING AND LISTENING

A   Record your description on a blank cassette. Then listen to it and decide how you could improve it.

B   Record your descriptions of the posters in Activity *4* and *32*.

C   Listen to each commercial separately – it is not necessary to understand every word. These commercials are all authentic and may contain unfamiliar vocabulary.

Pause between each commercial to check your answers. Look at the next set of questions before you listen to the next commercial.

When you've checked all your answers, listen to all four commercials while looking at the tapescript.

Finally, listen to them again with your eyes closed – and **enjoy** them.

ANSWERS

1 video recorder   stupid/ignorant   Japan washing machine   2022   understand
2 beer   beautiful girl   slips away
3 film/movie   mother   elderly people   102
4 colour film   hear   symphony

TRANSCRIPTS
4 minutes 30 seconds

1 CUSTOMER   Morning, squire.
SALES ASSISTANT   Morning, sir.
CUSTOMER: I'd like a videocaster please.
SALES ASSISTANT: A video recorder, any one in particular?
CUSTOMER: Well, I'd like it to have some specifications, and functions, I must have some functions.
SALES ASSISTANT: I see. Did you have any model in mind?
CUSTOMER: Well a friend mentioned the Harikirikabukikasoonikawhatchamacallit. You know, the Japanese one, the 2000. Because I'm very technically-minded, you see.
SALES ASSISTANT: I can see that, sir.
CUSTOMER: So I want one with all the bits on it. All the Japanese bits. You know, the 2000.
SALES ASSISTANT: What system?
CUSTOMER: Er...w...well, electrical, I think. Because I'd like to be able to plug it into the television, you see. I...I've got a Japanese television.

SALES ASSISTANT: Have you?
CUSTOMER: Yeah, I thought you'd be impressed, the 2000, the Hokikoki 2000.
SALES ASSISTANT: Well sir, there is this model.
CUSTOMER: That looks smart, yeah.
SALES ASSISTANT: Eight hours per cassette, all the functions that the others have, and I know this will be of interest: a lot of scientific research has gone into making it easy to operate, even by a complete idiot like you.
CUSTOMER: Pardon?
SALES ASSISTANT: It's a Philips.
CUSTOMER: Doesn't sound very Japanese.
SALES ASSISTANT: No, Firrips, Firrips – it's a Firrips.
CUSTOMER: Oh it is a 2000 is it?
SALES ASSISTANT: No, in fact it's the 2022.
CUSTOMER: Mm...no no it hasn't got enough knobs on it...What's that one over there?
SALES ASSISTANT: That's a washing machine.
CUSTOMER: Yeah, what...sort of Japanese?
VOICEOVER: The VR 2022: video you can understand. From Firrips.

2 STORYTELLER: (*Irish music*) It was a Saturday and Joe was in the bar with Eddie. But Eddie wasn't necessarily with Joe. He was staring deeply into his glass of Beamish. He fancied he saw the girl with the dark ebony-coloured hair, and the moonlight skin, and the wild, wild eyes. But in no time at all, like his Beamish, she was gone. 'She was beautiful,' said Eddie quietly. 'Buy me a Beamish then,' said Joe, 'so I can have a look too.'
VOICEOVER: Beamish Stout – just slips away.

3 JOHN CLEESE'S MOTHER: Into this?...Hello, my name is Muriel Cleese and I live in a very nice elderly people's home in Weston-super-Mare. My son John is in a new Monty Python film *Life of Brian*. I do hope you'll go and see it because he's on a percentage and he said if it doesn't do well he won't be able to keep me on in the home any longer. So see *The Life of Brian* now because I'm 102 years old and if I have to leave here it'll kill me...Haha.
VOICEOVER: If you want to help Mrs Cleese, please go and see *Monty Python's Life of Brian*. Exclusive presentation at the Plaza from Thursday November 8. Certificate AA.
MRS CLEESE: Haha . . .

4 MAN FROM NEWCASTLE: To prove to you just how clear and vibrant Kodacolor Gold's colours are, I'm going to conduct a little exercise. Imagine for a moment that you can actually hear colour. Now you'll have to concentrate, mind.
   Right, this is the sound for blue: (*silence*). I said you'll have to concentrate: (*harps*). Right, thank you. And this is the sound for green: (*violins*). That's it and now let's hear it for yellow: (*flute*). And finally – (*trumpets*) er...wait for it lads, red: (*trumpets*).
   Right, I'm now showing you a photograph of a magnificent sunset over the Grand Canyon, as taken on Kodacolor Gold: (*full orchestra playing The Big Country*). And now I'm going to show you that very same sunset taken on ordinary film: (*kazoo*). Well, I suppose it had a certain raw charm.
VOICEOVER: Kodacolor Gold, for a symphony of colour we have the clicknology.

D **1** Saying to someone *You're wrong!* or *That isn't true!* can be very rude, and may upset someone or make them angry, and turn the discussion into an argument.

Here are some more ways of agreeing and disagreeing politely:

I quite agree.
I'm not sure that I entirely agree.
Absolutely!
I see. But don't you agree that . . .
I think you're absolutely right there.
Isn't it also true to say that . . .

2 Find some advertisements. Then record your answers to the questions on a blank cassette.

2.6 Position and direction
PREPOSITIONS

A **1 & 2** When you've done step 1, add letters G to L as follows:

G is inside the top left-hand corner of the box.
H is standing on top of the box, about a quarter of the way from the left.
I is right in the very centre of the box.
J is to the right of the bottom right-hand corner of the box.
K is below the bottom left-hand corner of the box.
L is just beside the 's' at the end of 'Prepositions' in the title of this section.

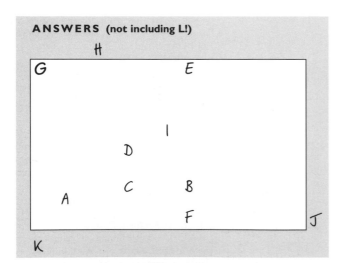

ANSWERS (not including L!)

3 Pencil in the letters. Then say to yourself where exactly each letter is positioned.

B Look at Activity **7** and, using a blank cassette, record yourself explaining the route that a pencil should take to draw the picture. Pause the tape when you need to stop and think. (This may be much harder than you expect – but quite enjoyable.) Then listen to what you said and try following your own instructions to draw the same picture on page 21.

Do the same with the picture in Activity **35**.

2.7 Department stores
READING

A Here are some possible questions:
Which is the cheapest store?
Which is the biggest store?
What is each big store most famous for?

B

ANSWERS

1 Macy's in New York
2 Harrod's, Harvey Nichols, Fortnum and Mason, and Marks and Spencer in London – and Bloomingdale's in New York
3 Bergdorf Goodman in New York
4 Saks Fifth Avenue, Bloomingdale's and Macy's in New York
5 Bloomingdale's in New York
6 Bloomingdale's in New York (and Harrod's in London?)
7 Most stores in New York
8 All the stores in New York
9 Marks and Spencer

C Record your answers to the questions.

2.8 Describing a place
WRITING

A & **B** If possible, ask another person (perhaps an English-speaking person or a friend whose English is reasonably good) to read and mark your work.

3 Friends and relations

Family life   Friendship   Relationships

3.1 Relationships
VOCABULARY AND SPEAKING

A Record your answers to the questions. Then look up any words you couldn't think of.

B

> **ANSWERS**
> 1 anxious   2 lonely   3 on   4 make
> 5 out   6 sight   7 engaged   8 wedding
> 9 got married   10 anniversary   11 best man
> 12 relations   13 guests   14 reception

C 1

> **ANSWERS**
> 2 nephew   3 grandson   4 second wife
> 5 ex-wife   6 brother-in-law
> 7 mother-in-law   8 aunt   9 (first) cousin
> 10 great-grandmother

2 & 3 Write similar sentences about the members of your own family.

D 1

> **ANSWERS**
> 1 Sarah   2 Charles   3 Sarah   4 Anna
> 5 Charles   6 Lenny   7 No one
> 8 No one   9 Lenny

TRANSCRIPTS   3 minutes 20 seconds

1 CHARLES: Um...my closest friend is...um...someone I've known since I was a baby. Um...our parents were friends and we've always lived in the same sort of neighbourhood. O...originally we lived...er...next door to each other, but now we live exactly three blocks apart. So...er...anyway, we see each other every day, usually in the evening. Um...we have the same interests.

   I...I mean, to be friends you have to share the...the same interests, don't you? And you have to be tolerant of each other's moods. I...I think being friends means making allowances for the other person's faults.

2 SARAH: Well, I've got...um...two close friends but they don't get on with each other, which means of course that I have to see them separately! Um...well, sometimes, as you can imagine, that...that's a problem. For example, if there's...um...a new film that I want to see, I have to decide which one I want to go with. And sometimes that means missing the film altogether so...um...neither of them gets upset. It sounds terrible, doesn't it? But, well actually, it's all right most of the time.

   I think a friend is someone you can have fun with, um...someone who finds the same things funny, and someone who doesn't take you too seriously a...and stops you taking yourself too seriously.

3 LENNY: Well, I don't have any really close friends, I suppose. I mean, I know a lot of people, you know: people I study with, people I play sports with, um...people I've known since I was a kid. But, you know, no one I could call my 'best friends'.
OTHERS: Oh, that's sad.
LENNY: I mean, well, it isn't really, you see. Friendship isn't really important for me.
   I think you have to get on well with everyone you come into contact with.
   I mean, being really close to someone can be...can be dangerous in a way...because, well, you come to rely on them too much and it excludes other people from your...from your social circle. You become sort of unfriendly.

4 ANNA: Well, believe it or not, my best friend is my sister. Um...she's two years older than me and she works in an insurance office. Um...we spend loads of time together. Er...the...it's funny actually because we used to really hate each other when we were younger. Yeah. And then...um...ooh, about three years ago she had a massive row with her...with her boyfriend at the time and...er...she came and actually she talked to me about how she felt for the first time really. And...um...since then, well, we've been really really close.

   Um...the most important thing about friends for me is being able to share secrets. Um...and, you know, and to be able to tell each other your problems and share your...your worries, and things like that. And...er...you know, to help each other out.

2 Record your answers to the questions.

3.2 The past – 1
GRAMMAR REVIEW

A

> **ANSWERS**
>
> 2 The weather <u>were</u> lovely yesterday and the sun <u>has been shining</u> all day.
>   was   shone
>
> 3 I <u>have gone</u> to the zoo last weekend.
>   went
>
> 4 Where <u>you went</u> on holiday last year?
>   did you go
>
> 5 They got married two years ago. ✔
>
> 6 She <u>has been</u> born in 1980.
>   was
>
> 7 Our family <u>was used to living</u> in a smaller flat when I <u>am</u> younger.
>   used to live   was
>
> 8 Our broken window still <u>wasn't</u> mended yet.
>   hasn't been
>
> 9 I've been here for two years but I've only made a few friends. ✔
>
> 10 The rain started <u>during</u> they <u>played</u> tennis.
>   while   were playing

219

B **1**

> **ANSWERS**
> 2 noticed   3 said   4 was looking   5 came
> 6 said   7 said   8 thought   9 offered
> 10 were   11 went   12 took   13 saw
> 14 looked   15 told   16 could
> 17 had grown   18 asked   19 was going

2 The actual ending was this:

'My husband and I have separated. He's been having an affair with his secretary. Before he went off on holiday with his new love, he asked me to sell all his belongings and give him whatever money I got for them. So that's just what I'm doing!'

C In the exam this kind of exercise requires two to five words, but some of the sentences in this exercise need more.

> **ANSWERS**
> 2 We *used to have* a dog.
> 3 *Have you been here* before?
> 4 We*'ve studied two* units in this book so far.
> 5 While you *were away we haven't done* much work.
> 6 What *were you doing when I phoned you* last night?
> 7 Although they *had a row yesterday they haven't* stopped being friends.

3.3 **Telling stories**
LISTENING AND SPEAKING

A **2**

> **ANSWERS**
> The correct sequence of pictures is:
> First story: f d b
> Second story: a e c

TRANSCRIPTS *4 minutes*

1 MAN: Well, this friend of my brother's called Alex...um...he was a medical student. He was getting married the next day and he was having a night out, you know, with his friends – his last night of freedom before the big day. Well, anyway, he got quite drunk and fell asleep before the end of the party. So his friends, supposed friends, took him back to the hospital and put both his legs in plaster, from hip to toe.
WOMAN: What? Goodness!
MAN: I know, so when he...when he woke up the next morning he was in bed at home, and his best man was there and so he says, 'Well, look, you're very lucky: you had a bad fall last night at the party and, you know, it was a good thing we were there because we were able to get you to the hospital.'
WOMAN: So what happened?
MAN: Well, so he went through the whole wedding ceremony at the church on crutches and then there was the reception, and he was still on the crutches. And it...it was awful for him –
WOMAN: What did his wife say?

MAN: I don't know, I guess she just accepted it like everybody else I suppose. So, I mean, everybody else thought it was hilarious. So, now his...his friends were then going to tell him the truth, but they decided that they were going to wait till he and his new wife got to the hotel in Spain where they were going to spend their honeymoon.
WOMAN: Oh, that's wicked.
MAN: Well, yeah, it gets worse actually. Now, Alex suspected that his friends would play some trick on him – so he gave them the phone number of a hotel in Spain, whereas in fact they were going to a hotel in Greece for their honeymoon. So his friends couldn't contact him till he got back from honeymoon two weeks later. So he spent the entire honeymoon –
WOMAN: Ohh! So he spent the whole honeymoon . . .

2 WOMAN: This friend of my brother called Andrew was going to spend Christmas with his girlfriend and her parents. Now, he hadn't met her parents before, so he was really nervous, like...you can imagine.
Anyway, he was going to drive down to their house from the north and the plan was that he was going to arrive very late on the Christmas Eve. So his girlfriend said that she'd leave the back door open so he wouldn't have to ring the bell and wake people up and all that sort of stuff.
Anyway, what happened was he arrived at the house at about two o'clock, two o'clock in the morning. The street lights were off but he worked out which house was number 31 Forest Avenue, because it was too dark to read the numbers on the front door but it was next to number 29 so he knew of course that it was going to be the right one. OK?
MAN: Right, right. So then what happened?
WOMAN: I'll tell you: what happened, he went round the back, but the door was locked. And because he didn't want to wake them up he saw there was a window open. Now he was just about to...he was just able, you know, to climb in and open the back door to get his things, so that's what he did. Well, after that drive he was quite hungry and everything, so he helped himself to some food from the fridge, like you would –
MAN: Yeah.
WOMAN: and he had a can of beer, a bit of drink, all the rest of it, and then of course he crept upstairs, not wanting to wake anyone up. And the first door he opened was the guest room, OK? So, naturally enough, he got undressed and went to sleep.
Well, the next morning, Christmas Day, he woke up quite late. He was late the night before –
MAN: Yeah.
WOMAN: so he woke up late Christmas morning, went downstairs in his dressing gown to say hello to his girlfriend, meet the parents, have breakfast and give them all their presents. OK? Now listen to this: he opens the kitchen door, he's got his arms full of wrapped presents, calls out: 'Merry Christmas, everyone!' But there was no one in that room that he knew. There was a man and a woman and two little kids sitting at the kitchen table staring at him with their mouths open wide in astonishment.
MAN: So what had happened?
WOMAN: Well, he was at number 27 Forest Avenue!
MAN: Oh no, haha, that's brilliant!

B Record your stories on a blank cassette. Listen to your recording and decide how your narrative could be improved.

C Make notes on the two stories before you record them on a blank cassette.

3.4 Special occasions
READING

 1

ANSWERS

1 special days like birthdays, anniversaries, Mother's Day
2 44%
3 10% of 7.3 billion (730 million)
4 It's a matter of opinion, but the one about the untidy room is certainly very strange!

2

ANSWERS
True: (1) 2 4 5 7
False: 3 6 8

The relevant phrases in the text are:
1 Halloween (October 31st) *in paragraph 1*
2 people send fewer cards than at any other time of the year *in paragraph 1*
3 (*they sell cards so obviously they don't want people to send letters*)
4 a market that threatens to stop growing for the first time since 1945 *in paragraph 2*
5 death-of-a-pet card *in paragraph 3*
6 (*not mentioned in the text*)
7 Others address almost every imaginable calamity *in paragraph 4*
8 (*it's ironic*)

3

ANSWERS
¶1 reviving
¶2 illiterate   scribes   sentiments
¶3 cope (with)
¶4 keep in touch   calamity
¶5 account for   saturation

C **1** Here are some questions that might be asked about the photos:
• How old do you think the boy is?
• What presents did he get for his birthday?
• Why do you think he's got his eyes closed?
• What do you think he's wishing for?

3.5 Using prefixes – 1
WORD STUDY

Here are some of the common prefixes with their meanings:
over = too much
under = not enough
re = again
post = after
pre = before

 A

ANSWERS

1 rearranged = to arrange something again, in a different way or in different places
2 overreact = to react in an excessive, unreasonable way
3 underestimate = to fail to guess the real amount, thinking it less than it really is
4 pre-holiday = before a holiday
post-holiday = after it

B

ANSWERS

re   reappear rebuild reconsider
          remarry reprint reread
pre-   pre-dinner pre-lunch pre-prepared
          pre-war
post-   post-dinner post-lunch post-war
over   overcharge overcrowded overexcited
          overprepared (overpay)
under   undercharge underprepared
          (underpay)

C

ANSWERS
2 rebuilt   3 pre-exam   over-confident
4 under-staffed   5 underpaid   undervalued
6 overeat   overweight   7 rewrote
8 overslept

3.6 Looking and seeing
VERBS AND IDIOMS

A

SUGGESTED ANSWERS
2 watched/saw/noticed
3 gazed/looked/stared
4 notice/recognise/see   5 recognise
6 stare   7 watch   8 see   9 see   10 looks
11 see   12 noticed/seen/recognised

B **1 & 2** The missing phrases are:
1 looked up to   2 look out for
3 looked through   4 looking forward to
5 look after

3 Many phrasal verbs can be replaced with equivalent 'normal verbs' – as this exercise shows. Quite often the phrasal verb is more **informal** than its 'normal' formal equivalent.

ANSWERS
3 Look out   4 look up to   5 see to (*or* look after)   6 looking into   7 saw through
8 look up   9 look in (*or* look it up)
10 looking forward to

3.7 Writing a story
WRITING

 An improved version is in Activity **53**.
The original version of the story contains so little detail that it's impossible to get interested. It's supposed to be a personal story, so there should be personal details to explain why the night was unforgettable. The exact times and distances are irrelevant and distracting.

 An improved version is in Activity **41**.
The plot of a film or book is generally told in the simple present tense, whereas a true story or a fictional short story would usually be told using past tenses.
The original version of the story uses the past tense, which makes it sound like a true story. But of course it's the plot of a film. And the lack of detail makes it very dull.

 If possible, ask another person (perhaps an English-speaking person or a friend whose English is reasonably good) to read and mark your work.

---

4 Time off
Hobbies and pastimes   Sports and games   Leisure

4.1 What do you enjoy?
VOCABULARY

A Some useful vocabulary:

*competitive   diving   energetic   fresh air   game
match   mountain bike   muddy   soccer/football
surf   swimming   underwater   windsurfing*

B

ANSWERS
1 collecting   taking   2 active   relax
3 professional   amateur   4 team   support
5 match   referee   whistle   cheer   crowd
draw   score   6 court   course   7 cup   prize
8 lottery   charity (*or* children!)

C **1 & 2** You'll need to do some 'research' for this using a dictionary. Then record a short talk about your favourite sport.

4.2 Leisure activities
READING

A

ANSWERS
1 walking   2 swimming
3 health and fitness clubs   4 1,500

B

ANSWERS

swimming	22 million
snooker and pool	12 million
cycling	9 million
keep fit, aerobics and yoga	10 million
darts	7 million
golf	4 million
bowling	6 million
running and jogging	4 million
football	4 million
weight training	5 million
badminton	5 million
squash	3 million
tennis	4 million
fishing	3 million

SUGGESTED PARAGRAPHS
(Some variations are possible.)

The fitness boom of the eighties led to a big rise in the numbers of people participating in sports. To cater for this boom and provide the up-to-date facilities people want, over 1,500 private health and fitness clubs and the same number of public leisure centres have been built during the past twenty years.

These modern centres, with their swimming pools (22 million people went swimming last year), squash courts, gyms and indoor courts for tennis and other sports, are competing with clubs, pubs and cinemas as places for people to go to spend their leisure time – and their money. Now practically every town has a leisure pool, often with a wave machine, water slides and tropical plants. Families can even spend their holidays at huge indoor water parks, where they can play or relax all day long in warmth and comfort without worrying about the weather outside.

But this may not be helping us to get fitter: we may be becoming a nation of splashers, but not a nation of swimmers. The big question fitness experts are asking is: should sport be taken seriously or should it just be fun?

4.3 ## Sorry to interrupt, but . . .
SPEAKING

ANSWERS

1 Amanda	2 Debbie	3 Tony	4 Tony
5 Debbie	6 No one	7 Amanda	
8 Tony	9 No one		

B The expressions that are used are <u>underlined</u> in the transcript below.

TRANSCRIPT AND ANSWERS
3 minutes 10 seconds

AMANDA: . . . It really really turns me on, I really, really enjoy it.

TONY: Amanda, really!

AMANDA: Well, I know in the long run I don't make a profit but it's great to have something to get really excited about! I enter all the competitions, and my favourite sport is horse racing. I just enjoy the betting and it's so exciting: you've got your own horse there and you're shouting for it – you just want to win.

TONY: <u>Just...just a minute</u>, Amanda.

AMANDA: Yeah.

TONY: I must say...I have to say I am shocked. Right, no, I think gambling is...I think gambling is terrible. No, it's a waste of money and what's worse it's...I mean, it's like a drug. The more you lose the more you want to play a...again and win. I mean, you know, and what about those fruit machines you find in the bars? They're terrible, they're the worst of all. You see people feeding money into them, all in the hope of winning the jackpot. I mean, it's pathetic. I mean, what about...and the people...and I must say –

DEBBIE: <u>Could I say something?</u>

TONY: Yes, Debbie.

DEBBIE: I think you're taking things far too seriously. It's only a bit of fun for most people. Nobody loses anything by it – if people want to spend their money, it's up to them. They may choose to spend their spare cash on drink, or food, or books, or whatever they want to –

TONY: <u>Yes, but</u> if they spend it on gambling it's just money down the drain. Look, the people who bet and, yeah, it's mostly men, right, who are gamblers, you know? Right, they're the ones who can least afford it. And...er...the ones who suffer are...are probably the wives and the children, not them –

AMANDA: Do you know, Tony, what you sound like? You sound like an ex-gambler who has seen the light. Like one of those ex-smokers who's given up smoking and they're passionate about anti-smoking.

TONY: Er... no no no no no no no. I just think it's wrong. It's this association of sport and gambling that I think is just so terrible –

AMANDA: You're a puritan!

TONY: No, sport should be something that you enjoy for its own sake, honestly, you...you –

DEBBIE: <u>I see, what you mean, but</u> I don't think you're being realistic. If Amanda wants to go to the races, that's her business. Personally, I'd never do...go to a betting shop or do the football pools.

TONY: Well, good for you!

DEBBIE: But going in for lotteries seems OK to me. I always buy a ticket for the National Lottery on a Saturday if I can afford it, and I don't see anything wrong with that.

AMANDA: I don't know, I think that *is* a waste of money. I mean, the chances of actually winning the jackpot are a million to one –

DEBBIE: So?

AMANDA: but with horses, right, you've got a question...it's like...you've got control, it's a skill. You know more about the horses, you know the jockeys, you've got more chance to win, you see?

DEBBIE: <u>I'm sorry, but</u> that's not fair. You say it's OK to bet on the horses, but a little flutter on the lottery is different according to you. There's nothing wrong with –

AMANDA: Look, did you know that since the National Lottery started people have stopped going to the cinema, they've stopped giving to charity? Attendances at cinemas are down by twenty per cent – and they say it's because people are spending their spare cash on the lottery. And I bet that if you did win, you wouldn't know what to do with a million pounds, you'd just squander it, you'd waste it . . .

DEBBIE: <u>Well, I'm sorry to interrupt you but</u> I did actually win last week.

AMANDA AND TONY: You won!?

DEBBIE: Yeah. Not the jackpot, just £100.

AMANDA: Well, that's not bad, is it?

TONY: OK, and how much have you paid for tickets over all those months?

DEBBIE: Well, I'd have to work that out –

TONY: Ahh!

C Record your views on the topics and try to experiment with the phrases in B.

4.4 ## Using prefixes – 2
WORD STUDY

A

ANSWERS

1 in the middle of a sentence
2 (approximately) half   3 partly retired works for himself not for an employer

B

ANSWERS

half- half-afraid   half-asleep   half-finished
semi- semi-automatic   semi-circle
mid- mid-air   mid-morning   mid-twenties
self- self-defence   self-pity   self-respect

C

ANSWERS

2 mid-fifties   3 half-price   4 mid-winter
5 self-service   6 semi-final   7 half-marathon
8 mid-afternoon

4.5 *Make* and *do*
VERBS AND IDIOMS

A

ANSWERS

Bill made . . .
Shirley laugh   a cake   a noise   a mistake
an arrangement   a comment   a decision
a good impression   me an offer   a promise
a statement

Shirley did . . .
Bill a favour   the washing-up   her duty
the shopping   an exercise   her homework
a good job   badly in the test   her best
very well   nothing at all

B

ANSWERS

1 (do with = need or want)
2 making up = inventing (a story)
3 doing up = redecorating – We can also do up a shoelace or coat.
4 make out = see with difficulty
5 make up for = repay or compensate for
6 making for = going in the direction of/heading for
7 made off with = stole
8 do without = manage without having something

4.6 The past – 2
GRAMMAR REVIEW

A 1

ANSWERS

Correct sentences: (1)   3   5   8
Incorrect sentences: (2)   4   6   7

2

CORRECTED PARAGRAPH
(Some variations are possible.)

It <u>was raining</u> when we <u>arrived</u> at the coast but by midday it had <u>stopped</u>. We thought the rain <u>would last</u> all day and we <u>were</u> very glad it <u>didn't</u> because we <u>wanted</u> to go swimming. We found a café where we could eat outside and <u>had</u> a nice meal. By the time we had finished lunch the sun <u>was shining</u> brightly and the temperature <u>had risen</u> to 30 degrees. We all <u>ran</u> down to the beach and, after we <u>had changed</u> into our swimming things, we dived in the sea.

B 1

SUGGESTED ANSWERS

2 had   3 seen   4 were   5 met   6 had
7 been   8 had   9 finished   10 was
11 were   12 told   13 had   14 was
15 had   16 used   17 went   18 was
19 did   20 have   21 agreed

2

SUGGESTED ANSWERS

2 were/was   3 had   4 was   5 came
6 continued   7 came   8 started   9 had
10 were   11 was   12 scored   13 was
14 was   15 have

4.7 Safety at sea
LISTENING

B

ANSWERS

1 a) 'I am OK.' – picture 3
   b) 'I need assistance.' – picture 1
   c) 'I have a diver down. Keep clear and proceed slowly.' – picture 2
   d) 'Faster!' – picture 7
   e) 'Slower!' – picture 6
   f) 'Speed OK.' – picture 8
   g) 'Back to jetty.' – picture 5
2 nod your head
3 shake your head
4 a) watch the skier   drive the boat
   b) above water
   c) start
   d) let go of the rope and sit down
   e) curl yourself into a ball
   f) they can help to keep you afloat

JENNY: After a series of accidents involving water-skiers, it's clear that there needs to be stricter rules and controls. Andy Brown is a lifeguard. Andy, what advice would you give to people taking part in water sports?

ANDY: Ah, well, Jenny, the first thing you have to know is the signals that you should use if you get into any kind of trouble...because it's difficult to hear, you know, somebody just shouting above the noise of waves and the wind and boat engines, and breathing apparatus or scuba gear if you happen to be wearing that, that kind of thing.

JENNY: Do you have any examples of that?

ANDY: Um...well, if...ah...if you're diving...um...you need to use these signals. You use: 'Now I'm OK' is holding the hand up with thumb and forefinger making an O, like that. You know, like the OK sign. And...um...'I need assistance', that signal is...you put the fist up and you move it from left to right a...above the water, if you can. And, if you're on a boat...um...you should always be flying the...er...correct international signal, which is a flag which is white on the side that's nearest the mast and blue on the other.

JENNY: Oh, what does that mean?

ANDY: Well, that means: 'I've got a diver down, so keep clear or drive slowly' for all the other boats around.

JENNY: I see, how about skiers, water-skiers?

ANDY: OK. Um...anybody who's going to be water-skiing should be taught a...several signs and signals. First of all the signal to go faster: you hold your palm up and you motion upwards or you can just nod your head.

JENNY: Right.

ANDY: And...and the signal for 'Slower' is you hold your palm down, and you motion downwards or you shake your head.

JENNY: Yes, of course.

ANDY: OK, now if you want to indicate that the speed is actually OK, you just give the OK signal with your thumb and forefinger making the O, just like I told you about. Um...and if you want to go back into the shore, you just point your arm downwards. Like that, just down toward your side.

JENNY: I see. Well...um, so much for signals. But water-skiing can actually be quite dangerous, can't it, even if you do know all the signals?

ANDY: Yeah, I guess, but not if you follow some basic safety procedures and you...you have to know what you're doing, like with any sport. There are three points really with water-skiing. There should always be two people in the boat. That's one person to drive the boat and one person to keep his eye on the skier. And before you start your...your ski-tips, if you're the skier, your ski-tips have to be above the water, so you don't get immediately dragged down to the bottom when the boat goes –

JENNY: And go under. Yes.

ANDY: Yes. And...um...if you're the skier, you have to give a clear signal to the helmsman, which is the guy who's driving the boat, when you're ready to start.

JENNY: And I suppose that...um...even the best water-skiers fall into the water sometimes. What do you do if you do fall?

ANDY: Well, no, *when* you fall!

JENNY: Oh, right.

ANDY: Um...well, if you...if you start to fall forwards, you should let go of the rope and try to sit down. If you're falling sideways, you've got to curl yourself up into a ball. And it's very important that if you do fall, you get a hold of your skis immediately because they can help you keep afloat.

JENNY: Yes, of course, right. Well, thank you very much, Andy.

ANDY: Hey, no problem, you're welcome.

4.8 Stimulating and satisfying
READING

B 1

ANSWERS
True: 1 6
False: 2 3 4 5

2

ANSWERS
gruelling   super-fit   modestly   agony
resentment   exhilaration   experience
the elements   stimulating

C This is how the article was originally split into paragraphs:

SUGGESTED PARAGRAPHS
(Some variations are possible.)

John Ridgway, the ex-Paratrooper famous for rowing the Atlantic, sailing twice around the world and canoeing down the Amazon, runs the most gruelling survival course in Britain. Perched halfway up a mountain in northern Scotland, overlooking a black lake, the Ardmore Adventure School is cold, bleak and forbidding.

In this week's *Cutting Edge* programme, *Exposure*, it serves as a temporary home for 24 business managers from a multinational company – all in search of their real selves.

The group are not super-fit athletes but very average 28–50-year-olds, ranging from the completely inactive to the modestly sporty. The film follows the men and women as they attempt abseiling, rock climbing, canoeing, orienteering, sea swimming and raft-building in the Scottish wilderness. It's only on the third day that they see their first glimpse of Ardmore House itself, with its relative comfort of bunk beds and cold showers.

Their agony and resentment is clear at the beginning of the course, but, as the days go by, the exhilaration starts to show through. As one participant says, 'It was hell, but it was worth it.'

It's a feeling Ridgway understands. 'I decided to create a small corner of the world where people could experience the confrontation with the elements that I find so stimulating and satisfying.'

4.9 Paragraphs
WRITING

Unfortunately, there are no fixed rules about when to start a new paragraph. Often paragraphs are used simply to split long stretches of text into shorter, more easily assimilated pieces.

Or they may be used to emphasise a sentence by giving it prominence. A new paragraph often signals a change of direction, or a digression.

The traditional reason for starting a new paragraph is when a new idea is begun. For example, if you're writing about the advantages and disadvantages of something, the introduction might be in the first paragraph.

And the advantages might be in the second paragraph.

Then the disadvantages would be in the third paragraph.

If there are lots of disadvantages, there might need to be a fourth paragraph to contain them all.

Finally, the conclusion would be in the final paragraph.

In a story, if there is a dialogue, each time a new speaker says something, the words in quotes should be on a new line.

'What are we going to do today?' I asked my friends.

'Let's go swimming!' they all shouted.

In the exam, paragraphs of 40 to 50 words are probably best. A single-paragraph 150-word composition is **not** recommended!

A There are no 'correct answers' to these questions, but any of the reasons outlined above may be relevant. You should try to develop a feeling for what seems right.

B Write your story. Then, if possible, show it to an English-speaking person or a friend, and ask for comments.

The environment   Nature   Animals and wild life
The weather

5 The world around us

5.1 Nature
VOCABULARY AND LISTENING

A Some useful vocabulary:

autumn/fall autumnal blanket blossom boiling cherry tree chilly forest freezing fresh frosty icy meadow mild picnic snowman spring-like summery wintry wood

B

SUGGESTED ANSWERS

Fruit:	apple, plum, pineapple, apricot, melon, raspberry, strawberry, blackcurrant, cherry, etc.
Vegetables:	cabbage, cauliflower, aubergine, onion, etc.
Trees:	fir, beech, palm, cypress, eucalyptus, etc.
Flowers:	buttercup, daffodil, crocus, dandelion, orchid, etc.
Wild mammals:	lion, wolf, fox, elephant, deer, monkey, whale, etc.
Birds:	blackbird, robin, stork, crow, swallow, kingfisher, budgerigar, parrot, etc.
Domestic animals:	cow, sheep, chicken, horse, donkey, cat, dog, canary, hamster, gerbil, etc.
Insects:	bee, mosquito, cockroach, beetle, locust, moth, butterfly, flea, etc.
Sea creatures:	sole, sardine, cod, anchovy, red mullet, lobster, mussel, squid, prawn, shrimp, jellyfish, etc.

C

ANSWERS

1 Steve	**2** Claire	**3** Steve	**4** Steve
5 Emma	**6** No one	**7** No one	**8** Claire
9 Emma			

TRANSCRIPTS *3 minutes*

1 CLAIRE: . . . Well, it seems to me that too many people own dogs in the city. I mean, they keep them in small apartments all day, take them out for short walks maybe twice a day. I mean, some of the dogs in our neighbourhood are huge. I think it's cruel to keep them inside an apartment all day.

STEVE: I think you're being sentimental. I mean, you know, dogs are really good companions, especially for people who live on their own. And they don't have feelings like people, I mean, they don't get lonely if they're alone all day, I mean, they just go to sleep. And then, you know, being alone makes them even happier to see their owners when they get back from work.

CLAIRE: Oh yeah, what do you think, Emma?

EMMA: Well . . .

2 STEVE: . . . I think all this stuff we hear about recycling is exaggerated. We have to put all our waste paper in one place, our bottles in another, and our cans in another, and our plastic in another one, I mean, on and on. I just don't believe that all these things really have to be recycled . . . Well, I'm sure it costs more to recycle them than to make new ones. I suspect some of these things are actually just buried so that everyone *thinks* they're helping the environment.

EMMA: That is a terrible attitude . . . Well, look, to make paper people have to cut down trees, to make bottles they have to use up huge amounts of energy, to make cans, well, they've got to find aluminium and melt it down, you know that. The point about recycling is that it saves energy and it stops us using up the resources that can't be renewed, well, like oil, metal . . . Well, it may not be much cheaper to recycle I agree, but it's much better for the future of the planet.

STEVE: Mm, well, let's find out what Claire thinks. Claire?

CLAIRE: Well, you know, I . . .

3 CLAIRE: . . . Anyway the reason I'm a vegetarian is, well, it's simple really: producing meat is a very wasteful way of producing food. I mean, if you think about it, farmers have to grow crops to feed the animals which people then eat. Now, that land could be used to grow crops to feed the people directly – simple! All the world's problems about lack of food, starvation, would be solved if everyone stopped eating meat and ate beans, nuts, vegetables, fruits instead.

EMMA: Mm, that's all very well but I, personally, don't want to do without meat. Well, you can't make people be vegetarians, can you? . . . I think you've got to be realistic . . .

CLAIRE: Or selfish . . .

EMMA: No, the...I mean...the people I know eat much less meat now than they used to – they eat a lot more pasta and...and more fish. Is it all right to eat more fish, I wonder? Aren't all the oceans being over-fished?

CLAIRE: Steve, what do you think?

STEVE: Well, I think people just . . .

5.2	**The weather**

READING AND LISTENING

(A) **2** The original headline for the article was 'Avoiding that unlucky strike'.

3 One or two of the answers given below are clearly implied rather than definitely stated.

ANSWERS
talking on the phone ✔
washing up ✔
watching television ✔
sitting near a closed window
looking out of an open door ✔
climbing stairs
working outdoors ✔
climbing a ladder
fishing ✔
playing golf ✔
sheltering under an isolated tree ✔
sheltering in a building
sailing ✔
cycling ✔
swimming ✔

4 One thing it doesn't tell you is where the **safest** place to be is. The safest place is probably inside a metal box (e.g. car or plane) – but don't touch the metal parts. If you're driving, it's safer to stay inside the car than to get out and become an exposed target.

(B)

ANSWERS

	Today	Tomorrow
heavy rain	(S + E)	(W)
dry and warm	W	
cloudy		S
hazy sunshine		W
temperatures above 25°		E
thunderstorms		E
scattered showers		W
gale-force winds		N
light breeze		S
temperatures below freezing and frost	N	

TRANSCRIPT *2 minutes*

PRESENTER: . . . denied that he has been having an affair with his secretary. And now for the weather. Over to Michelle Brown at the Weather Centre. Michelle, what have you got for us today?

FORECASTER: Thank you, Bob. Well it's not going to be very nice in the South today. There's going to be some very heavy rain in the South and also in the East.

In the West today it should be mainly dry and quite warm but overnight the rain will spread to the West and it's going to be very wet there during most of the morning tomorrow. After about lunchtime in the West there may still be a few showers but most of the region can expect some hazy sunshine.

Coming back to the South now, as I said, there will be a lot of rain today but as we move into the evening the clouds will clear and temperatures will fall to about 10 degrees during the night, so you'll need your blanket. Tomorrow a light breeze and cloudy with temperatures around the 20 mark.

In the East today's rain will die out overnight and tomorrow a complete change with temperatures rising to the mid-twenties or even higher, and with this rise in temperatures there may well be the odd thunderstorm during the afternoon and evening.

The North will be much colder today – sorry! – with temperatures falling below zero during the afternoon and a frosty evening and night can be expected. Tomorrow the temperature will be above freezing but it will feel very cold with winds picking up considerably, and some extremely strong winds on the coasts, making it a very rough, nasty day for sea crossings.

And the outlook for the day after tomorrow and the rest of the week: cool and dry in the South, warm and sunny in the West, hot with the chance of more thunderstorms in the East, and foggy in the North.

So that's it from me and back to Bob.

PRESENTER: Thanks, Michelle. And now sport, and good news for Manchester United fans . . .

5.3 Global warming
READING

 B This is a very tricky exam-style exercise. It may be best to do the easy parts first, leaving the harder parts till later.

ANSWERS
1 D   2 A   3 B   4 F   5 C   6 E
(Sentence G is not used.)

C Read the information in Activity **6** and **34**. Then record your views on a blank cassette.

5.4 Compound prepositions
PREPOSITIONS

A

ANSWERS
1 because of/owing to   2 because of/owing to
3 except for   4 in common with
As well as and *in place of* don't fit anywhere.

B

ANSWERS
1 (because of *or* owing to)   2 on behalf of
3 because of/owing to   4 instead of
5 as well as   6 apart from/except for
7 apart from/except for   8 according to

5.5 Articles and quantifiers – 1
GRAMMAR REVIEW

 1

ANSWERS
This is the only countable noun: disease
These are uncountable nouns: blood   salt
    money   mathematics   health
These could be either:
    glass – Windows are made of glass. /
    a glass of milk
    fire – Fire is a great danger. / What a nice fire!
These are usually uncountable, but they can be countable in these cases:
    food – Hamburgers and frankfurters are fast foods. (i.e. kinds of fast food)
    milk – Three coffees and two chocolate milks, please. (i.e. ordering in a café)

2

ANSWERS
bread – a slice (*or* a loaf)   education – a lesson
furniture – a sofa (*or* chair, table, etc.)
information – a fact   homework – an exercise
(*or* composition, assignment, etc.)

luggage – a suitcase   medicine – a tablet
(*or* drug, pill, etc.)   money – a dollar (*or* pound, coin, banknote, etc.)   news – a report
(*or* article, broadcast, etc.)   traffic – a car (*or* truck, bus, etc.)   vocabulary – a word (*or* phrase, expression, idiom, etc.)   water – a drop (*or* lake, river, bottle, etc.)   weather – a storm (*or* shower, gale, etc.)   wild life – an animal (*or* reptile, bird, mammal, etc.)

B

ANSWERS (Some variations are possible.)
2 More men are involved in politics than women in every country in the world.
3 If there were fewer cars in the city, there wouldn't be so many problems with pollution.
4 To get to the leisure centre, go along Coronation Avenue and take the first right.
5 Education is compulsory – all children have to go to school.
6 Anyone can have a look at the/a church even if they don't go to church on Sundays.
7 Pollution is a very great problem in the world today.
8 Few people realise that using the sun's energy is better than burning fossil fuels.

C

ANSWERS (Some variations are possible.)
2 My work took me all night *because there was so much information* to learn.
3 Do you know *how many plants and animals* become extinct every day? Fifty to one hundred!
4 There *are so many clouds* that there's sure to be some rain eventually.
5 Could *you give me some advice (about what to do)* please?
6 Vegetarians *never eat meat, but some (do) eat* fish.

 D Headlines and notes don't obey quite the same rules as normal prose in English. For example, articles are usually omitted ('Queen opens new hospital'), present tenses are used instead of past ('PM makes pro-Europe speech'), passives are just participles ('Princess given warm welcome'), and *to...* is used for the future ('President to visit language school').

SUGGESTED ANSWERS
(Many variations are possible.)
2 An escaped tiger has been found in a wood after a search lasting a week.
3 A family is angry because £60,000 has been left to a cat.
4 A man bit a dog.
5 A father lost a £200,000 lottery ticket.

6 A mother has been reunited with her daughter after not seeing her for 20 years.

7 A town is missing from the phone book (perhaps due to a computer error).

8 A golfer who was struck by lightning survived.

5.6 Talking for a minute
SPEAKING

(A) **2** Both speakers sound interesting, but the woman seemed to run out of things to say after her first comment.

They could also have mentioned:
- training animals to perform tricks
- keeping animals in captivity
- killing animals for sport versus killing them for food
- the intelligence and sociability of dolphins.

(B) Both speakers sound quite fluent because they have disguised their hesitation in various ways. The phrases used by the speakers are <u>underlined</u> in the transcript. The other technique they both used was **repetition** – also underlined in the transcript.

TRANSCRIPT *2 minutes 30 seconds*

EXAMINER: Now, I'd like you each to talk on your own for about a minute. I'm going to give each of you two different photographs and I'd like you to talk about them. Stephan, here are your two photographs. Please let Gertrude see them. They both show people and animals. Gertrude, I'll give you your pictures in a minute.

Stephan, I'd like you to compare and contrast your two pictures and tell me how you feel about them. Remember, you only have one minute for this so don't worry if I interrupt you. All right?

STEPHAN: <u>Well,</u> OK, <u>well,</u> the first picture is an aerial view of a woman...<u>um</u>...riding through the sea or riding through water on a dolphin. <u>Um</u>...and the second picture is...<u>um</u>...a picture of two men <u>in...in</u> khaki outfits in some sort of bamboo on a boat...<u>um</u>...with a dog and guns, and I would think they are probably hunting. <u>Er...well,</u> the pictures both seem to be about man and animal and their relationships. <u>Um</u>...the men are obviously hunting the animal, I would think for . . . using them to eat them, to eat birds I would think. <u>Um</u>...while the other picture is <u>of...of</u> the closeness of the woman with the dolphin <u>and...and</u> how they can relate to each other and be <u>kind of</u> friends with each other. <u>Um</u>...but I wouldn't want to...<u>um</u>...be very judgmental about this because the relationship you can have with a dolphin is very different <u>to...to</u> what you can have with birds, the relationship you could have with birds . . .

EXAMINER: Thank you. Gertrude, what are your feelings on the subject?

GERTRUDE: Well, yeah, <u>the...the</u> one with the dolphin and the woman <u>is...is</u> a picture of harmony, <u>um</u>...it's humankind and animals living together in harmony, and the other one is...<u>um</u>...the opposite. And so I definitely prefer the one with the dolphin.

EXAMINER: Thank you. Now Gertrude, here are your photographs, please let Stephan see them . . .

(C) Speak for one minute about the pictures in Activity **10**, recording your voice on a blank cassette. Then listen to the recording before you do the same with the pictures in Activity **38**.

5.7 Prefixes – 3
WORD STUDY

(A)

ANSWERS
1 a *or* an   the (!)
2 impossible to read   not tidy
3 connected with the topic   not connected
4 behave badly   not follow
5 peaceful   lack of approval
6 put paper round it   remove the paper from around it

(B)

SUGGESTED ANSWERS
un-	unable (*but* inability) uncomfortable unfair unfortunate unnecessary unpleasant unusual unwilling (unlike)
in-	inaccurate inactive inconvenient incredible indirect inexperienced informal intolerant
im-	impatient impossible
un-	unbutton unfold unpack
dis-	disagree dislike (disable)
mis-	mishear mispronounce misspell (misdirect)

(C)

ANSWERS
2 unlock   **3** impatient   **4** inconvenient
5 unreasonable   **6** inefficient
7 misunderstood   **8** misspelt/misspelled
9 disqualified   **10** disappear

5.8 Making notes
WRITING

(A) No particular style of notes is recommended here – experiment with various styles to find out which suits you best.

(B) Make notes on more than one topic, using a different note-making style for each.

(C) Show your article to an English-speaking person, or a friend, and ask for comments.

6 Public transport Cars and motoring
Giving directions

Going places

6.1 Mind how you go!
VOCABULARY AND SPEAKING

A The main message is 'Wear a seat belt' – 'Clunk' is the noise of the car door closing and 'Click' is the noise that fastening a seat belt makes.

Two other pieces of advice for pedestrians might be: 'Don't walk into the road suddenly' and 'If there isn't a pavement, walk on the side of the road facing oncoming traffic'. For cyclists: 'Always look behind before overtaking' and 'Assume every driver can't see you'. And for drivers: 'Always use your indicators' and 'Look behind before opening your door'.

The text here and in the Communication Activities comes from a British Department of Transport leaflet. (30 mph = about 50 kilometres per hour, 20 mph = about 35 kph and 40 mph = about 65 kph)

B

ANSWERS
1 seat belts **2** test licence **3** accident
mirror overtaking **4** roundabout
way right **5** lights lane **6** space park
meter **7** fine disqualified **8** pedestrians
pavement/path

C

ANSWERS
1 trip/journey/flight trip/journey/flight
2 flight/journey **3** crossing
4 excursions/trips/tours/outings **5** trip
6 cruise **7** excursion/tour **8** Travel
9 transport **10** trip/journey/flight
trip/journey/flight trip/journey/flight

D

ANSWERS
1 motorway (*but US* highway)
2 tube (*but US* subway *and other countries* metro)
3 coach **4** turning **5** brake **6** ticket

E Note down your questions. Then record yourself on a blank cassette.

6.2 Cars in cities
READING

A Record your answers to the questions.

B **1**

ANSWERS
1 D **2** A **3** E **4** F **5** C
(Sentence B is not used.)

2 The original headline was 'Running out of road'.

6.3 I don't get it!
VERBS AND IDIOMS

A

SUGGESTED ANSWERS
1 receive **2** became/grew have
3 arrived didn't have **4** buy/obtain catch

B

ANSWERS
2 get better **3** get started **4** get a headache
5 getting dark **6** get the joke **7** get ready
8 get into trouble **9** get to sleep
10 get an expert **11** got the sack/got into
trouble **12** get lost

C

ANSWERS
1 (get on with = continue)
2 get out of = avoid
3 getting at = suggesting/trying to communicate
4 got over = recovered from the disappointment or unhappiness
5 get (a)round = solve (a problem)
6 get off = alight from
7 getting on with = managing/progressing
8 get on with = have a good relationship with
9 get (a)round to = find the time
10 get through = get a connection (on the phone)
11 get together = meet
12 getting (me) down = making (me) feel depressed

6.4 Articles and quantifiers – 2
GRAMMAR REVIEW

A

SUGGESTED ANSWERS (Many more are possible.)
Countries in Europe:
Norway Belgium Switzerland
Countries in Asia:
India Thailand China

Countries in South America:
Peru   Brazil   Colombia
Oceans:
the Pacific   the Indian Ocean
Seas:
the Aegean   the Mediterranean
the Caribbean
Mountain ranges:
the Alps   the Andes   the Pyrenees
Mountains:
Mount Everest   Mount Olympus   Mount Fuji
Famous public buildings:
the British Museum   the Acropolis
the Statue of Liberty
Languages:
Welsh   Gaelic   Urdu
Cities in North America:
New Orleans   Chicago   Seattle
Rivers:
the Mississippi   the Rhine   the Nile
Groups of islands:
the Cyclades   the Balearics   the West Indies
Lakes:
Lake Titicaca   Lake Geneva   Lake Constance
Famous streets:
Bond Street   Fifth Avenue   Broadway
Planets:
Uranus   Jupiter   Venus

B 1

ANSWERS (In each case the first alternative is the one that appeared in the original article.)

4 Ø   5 Ø   6 Ø/the   7 Ø   8 a   9 a
10 Ø   11 the   12 the   13 Ø/the   14 Ø
15 the/a   16 the   17 the   18 the
19 Ø/the   20 the   21 Ø   22 an
23 the/a   24 a   25 a   26 the   27 Ø
28 the   29 Ø   30 the/a   31 the   32 Ø
33 the   34 the/a   35 Ø   36 a   37 the

2

ANSWERS (In each case the first alternative is the one that appeared in the original article.)

1 Ø   2 the   3 Ø   4 Ø   5 the   6 an
7 the   8 Ø   9 a   10 a   11 the   12 a
13 Ø/the   14 Ø/the   15 the   16 Ø/the
17 the/Ø   18 the   19 Ø   20 a   21 the
22 the/a   23 the

6.5 Boring in the Alps
LISTENING

B

ANSWERS

1 60 minutes   2 30 minutes   3 400 km/h
4 675 km   5 Zürich   6 4 billion
7 2000   8 25 billion   9 14 million
10 traffic off the motorways

TRANSCRIPT   *4 minutes 10 seconds*

HELEN: A few years ago the Channel Tunnel seemed like a fantasy. Even while it was being built it seemed hard to believe that it would ever really happen. Now, of course, we take it for granted. Just like the M25 motorway around London it seems as if it's always existed. But now there are plans in the Alps that would make the Channel Tunnel seem like a bypass. Martin Johnson reports.

MARTIN: Travelling in Switzerland seems to most people like an ideal world. The rail system is splendid – the trains are comfortable, they leave and depart on time and the views you get as you ride along are lovely. And the system is brilliantly integrated – bus timetables fit in with train connections, even the steamers on the lakes connect with trains, and little mountain railways and cable cars get you to the nearest mainline station in good time to make your connection to a train that will take you anywhere in the country.

A perfect world? Well, the Swiss themselves seem to think there's room for improvement. There are plans to build a new rail system underground – Swissmetro – which will link all the major cities of the country in at least a third of the time it now takes by normal train. I've been talking to Annemarie Studer, an engineer at the Federal Polytechnic in Lausanne. Annemarie, tell us about the project.

ANNEMARIE: Swissmetro is going to be environmentally friendly, it's technologically feasible and it's going to be profitable too. Let me explain:

The system will link all the major cities in the country: you'll be able to travel from Geneva to Berne in 30 minutes and then on to Zürich in another 30 minutes. That journey takes three hours now. And you'll be able to travel from Basle in the north down to Bellinzona in the south in half an hour too. To achieve this the trains will operate in tunnels which will be bored through the mountains or buried into the countryside.

The trains will fly along, floating on magnetic cushions, so there won't be any friction, and the tunnels will have linear electric motors all along them. Most of the air will be pumped out of the tunnels, so that there will be very little air resistance, just like with high-flying planes. This means that the trains will fly at up to 400 kilometres an hour. The trip will be comfortable and fairly quiet. We already have the technology to build these trains – and the Swiss have the longest experience of boring tunnels in the world. So technologically there would be no problems for us.

The whole scheme will take about 25 years to complete and will involve building 675 kilometres of tunnels. The first part of the scheme will be a line from Basle Airport to Zürich Airport and that will cost four billion Swiss francs. But once we have the go-ahead, this project will start in the year 2000. The whole project, linking all parts of the country, will cost around 25 billion Swiss francs.

MARTIN: Who's behind the scheme? Where's the money going to come from?

ANNEMARIE: A new company called Swissmetro has been set up. About 80 companies are putting up half of the 14 million Swiss francs needed for the feasibility study and the other half is coming from the Swiss government. And both the national airline, Swissair, and Swiss Railways have a five per cent share in the company. We're very confident that the scheme will pay for itself quite quickly because there will be a huge demand from passengers. But the main advantage is keeping traffic off the motorways – by the year 2000 the Swiss motorways are going to be absolutely full and the amount of pollution caused by traffic is getting worse and worse. Something has to be done about it, and Swissmetro is the best solution.

MARTIN: Thank you Annemarie. Well, that's how the future may look in the Alps – if the project goes ahead. Helen, back to you.

HELEN: Thank you, Martin. But are people really going to be in such a hurry to get across Switzerland? I wonder.

C Before you record your answers to the questions on a blank cassette, spend a few moments making notes.

6.6 Can you tell me the way to . . . ?
LISTENING AND SPEAKING

A

CORRECT ROUTE

TRANSCRIPT *2 minutes 20 seconds*

RECEPTIONIST: Regent Hotel, how can I help you?

GUEST: Er...hi. Look, this is going to sound really silly but I'm staying at your hotel...um...except I've forgotten the address.

RECEPTIONIST: Haha, oh I see, it's number 41 Regent Street.

GUEST: OK, I...I wonder, could you...could you give me directions how to get back to the hotel? I had this really nice little pop-up street map but I don't know, I seem to have lost it.

RECEPTIONIST: All right. Where are you now, sir?

GUEST: Um...I'm in Queen's Road. I've just crossed over Kitchen Bridge and I walked straight on till I came to Queen's Road.

RECEPTIONIST: OK, all right. Well, um...first of all you'll need to go back to Kitchen Bridge, you'll see the Bridge of Sighs on your left, cross the river and go straight on till you come to St John's Street – it's a pedestrian precinct.

GUEST: OK, St John's Street. Just a second, I'll write that down. OK.

RECEPTIONIST: OK?...Then you turn right and go down St John's Street and that leads you into Trinity Street. Carry on till you come to the Senate House – that's on the right. Then turn left into Market Street.

GUEST: OK, the Senate House, Market Street. OK.

RECEPTIONIST: Then at the end of Market Street you come to Sydney Street. Turn right and follow that street round a bend past Marks and Spencer's and Boots and eventually it leads into St Andrews Street. Go down there, leaving the pedestrian precinct...and keep walking and soon you'll see the University Arms Hotel on your left.

GUEST: OK, the University Arms Hotel.

RECEPTIONIST: And then just a little way further down you'll find the hotel on your left. It's more or less opposite Downing College.

GUEST: OK, thanks...thanks a lot. How...how long is this going to take me?

RECEPTIONIST: Oh not long. About 20 minutes.

GUEST: Fine. OK, well, thanks a lot for your...Oh, no! you're not going to believe this!

RECEPTIONIST: What's happened?

GUEST: I just found my map. It was inside my passport. I'm so sorry to have given you so much trouble.

RECEPTIONIST: That's quite all right, you're very welcome, sir.

B Practise explaining the routes in Activity **9** and **36** by recording your answers on a blank cassette.

6.7 Personal letters
WRITING

A

SUGGESTED ANSWERS

This is clearly a matter of opinion, but some of the more helpful bits of the first letter are perhaps:

There's a direct bus (number 108)
Ask the driver to tell you
I've drawn a little map (the map itself is also very useful)

And some of the less helpful bits are:

expensive – how expensive?
cheap, but slow – how slow?
you'd have to change twice – where?
Jan doesn't recommend a best option.

Some of the more helpful bits of the second letter are:

there is no easy way
I would suggest taking the underground
When you come out of the station . . . etc. – the clear directions
there is a stop opposite Greenwood Park Station
Ask the driver to tell you when to get off
If you get lost . . . phone me at work (the number)

Some of the less helpful bits are:

You'll have to change twice – where?
There's no map.

Three examples of informal style are:

Here's a quick note . . .
I've drawn a little map . . .
. . . which could be tricky . . .

Three examples of formal style are:

Therefore, if you do not have . . .
I would suggest taking the underground.
However, if you have time . . .

B Show your completed composition to an English-speaking person, or to a friend.

Homes and housing   Living conditions   Living in a city

7 There's no place like home

7.1 Make yourself at home!
VOCABULARY

 A Some useful vocabulary:

artistic   blanket   disorganised   duvet   furniture
mess   messy   methodical   musical   neat   organised
patterned   plain   radiator   reading lamp   sheet
sporty   studious   tidy   untidy   view   wastebasket

B

> **SUGGESTED ANSWERS**
> 2 floor   3 block   4 central heating
> 5 air conditioning   6 accommodation
> 7 outskirts   8 suburbs/surroundings
> 9 move   10 cottage   11 village
> 12 next-door neighbours   13 complaining
> 14 room   15 shelves   16 lounge/living room
> 17 wardrobes/cupboards/closets/
> chests of drawers   18 mortgage
> 19 rent   20 landlord/landlady
> 21 spacious/homely/convenient etc.

C

> **ANSWERS**
> 1 cellar   2 blinds   3 drive   4 shed
> 5 lawn

D Record yourself on a blank cassette.

7.2 Town or country?
LISTENING AND SPEAKING

A 2

> **ANSWERS**
> 1 John   2 Sarah   3 Sarah   4 no one
> 5 John   6 Terry   7 no one   8 Terry
> 9 Sarah   10 John

TRANSCRIPT   *3 minutes 40 seconds*

SARAH: Hello, Terry! Hi, John!
JOHN: Hello Sarah, how are you?
TERRY: Hi Sarah, haven't seen you for a while.
SARAH: Hello, no I've just got back from staying with my uncle in New York. Oh, what a wonderful city! I'd really love to live there. Have you ever been there John?
JOHN: No, I wouldn't want to. I can't think of anywhere I'd want to live less. I've heard all about it and it sounds absolutely terrible – so much crime and violence. Did you get robbed while you were there, Sarah?
SARAH: Of course not. As long as you take care and don't go anywhere you shouldn't go, like into Central Park after dark, or anywhere north of 110th Street, I mean you're perfectly safe. Why in any city you learn which districts to avoid and which are safe.

What I really love about cities is that there are so many different kinds of people to see, and w...so many different things to do. It's impossible to be bored. I mean, whatever your interests there's something to do: entertainments, artistic events, galleries, historic buildings, museums – I mean, you name it it's there.
JOHN: No, I...I'd rather live in the country because I like living in a...a little village where everyone knows everyone else, and people talk to each other, and they help each other out. In a city nobody knows who you are – everybody's in a hurry and nobody has the time to be friendly. I know Terry agrees with me, don't you, Terry?
TERRY: Err...well up to a point I do but, well, I think you're generalising a bit. Some villages are...are full of unfriendly people and...and some cities are full of friendly people . . . It all depends. Anyway, most cities are actually divided up into smaller neighbourhoods, which...which are sort of like villages within the city . . . Yeah, in a neighbourhood many people do know each other a...and they meet in the shops or the local market and they chat with each other . . . I mean, if you do want to be alone and you don't want to socialise then, well, you can do that, and you have that choice and...and nobody will mind if you keep yourself to yourself. But if you...you try doing that in a village and people will call you unfriendly and unsociable and, well, they'll make life quite difficult for you.
SARAH: Well, that's true. And anyway, what Terry said about neighbourhoods is certainly true of where my uncle lives in New York. I mean, where he lives everyone *does* know everyone else, I mean they're...they're really very sociable.
JOHN: Well, yeah, but I'm sure that's an exception. I mean most people in cities aren't friendly to each other. But y...I'll tell you what: the worst thing of all?
TERRY: What's that, John?
JOHN: The traffic and the public transport. Now, I'd hate to live in a place where the traffic never stops and where you just have to squeeze onto a bus or an underground train just to get anywhere.
TERRY: Oh, yeah yeah. Underground trains are terrible, aren't they? I...it's not so much the crowds as travelling in the dark, without being able to see where you're going, it's frightening.
SARAH: I do agree about the traffic, but the...the subway in New York – a...and the underground or metro in other cities – I mean it's really the best way to get around. I...it's so quick and...and convenient that it, well, it doesn't really matter if you're squashed together because you know you can get anywhere you want in just a few minutes.
TERRY: Yeah yeah, and I do have to agree that cities are exciting places to live in . . . Not like a village where nothing goes on from one week to the next.
JOHN: B...but that's the whole point, as far as I'm concerned, that's exactly what makes a village so great to live in, the peace and quiet!

B & C Record yourself talking about preferences and describing the photos.

7.3 Two cities
READING

A 2 The original headline was 'Not as different as they look'.

B

> **ANSWERS** (with comments in italics)
> 1 in government offices (*'in the afternoon' is also true, but the joke is about the behaviour of civil servants, not everyone in Madrid*)

2 a newcomer
3 took power away from Barcelona
4 old-fashioned
5 different
6 faster (*this is implied, though it could be argued that Madrid and Barcelona have a similarly fast pace of life*)
7 business centre (*it is also a banking centre, but the term 'business centre' covers this aspect*)
8 resentful of

C

ANSWERS

¶2 autonomous   have a dig
¶3 bossed about   squash
¶4 shuttling   plateau
¶5 caricatures   obsession
¶6 pace   cuisine   fanatical
¶8 chip on Barcelona's shoulder

7.4   *Have* and *give*
VERBS AND IDIOMS

A

SUGGESTED ANSWERS

Note that if more words are added, some different answers are also possible (e.g. Carol gave the information to her friend).

Alex had . . .
a quarrel with Carol   an order   no time to finish
permission to leave   a meal   a drink
a headache   his/her hair cut   a chance
a look   an interview   a good idea
the information   an accident   a rest   a swim
the details   no imagination   better be careful

Barry was having . . .
a quarrel with Carol   a meal   a drink
his hair cut   a look   an interview   a rest
a swim

Charlie gave us . . .
an order   no time to finish   permission to leave
a meal   a drink   his/her opinion   a headache
a chance   a look   an interview   a good idea
the information   a rest   the details

Carol gave . . .
an order   a sigh   a good performance
her opinion   an interview

B

ANSWERS

1 (give away = reveal)
2 gave back = returned
3 had given up = had quit/had stopped
4 giving out = distributing

5 gave up = surrendered
6 giving in = handing in
7 gave up = stopped trying (*or* gave in = admitted defeat)
8 had on = wore
9 have back = returned
10 having round = having a guest/visitor

7.5   A nice place to stay
LISTENING AND WRITING

A   2

MODEL NOTES

(The new information not given in the advertisements is <u>underlined</u>. It is a matter of opinion what each speaker's three main points are.)

BALMORAL WAY
seen by Bob:
    modern with <u>spacious</u> living room
    two <u>small</u> bedrooms
    <u>tiny</u> kitchen (<u>freezer and dishwasher</u>)
    <u>no TV</u>
    <u>5th floor: nice view</u>
    <u>may be expensive</u>

WINDSOR AVENUE
seen by Bob:
    ground floor of <u>old house</u>
    garden: <u>could eat outside</u>
    <u>comfortable furniture</u>
    one <u>big</u> bedroom: <u>two beds (could move one into living room)</u>
    big kitchen <u>with door to garden</u>

SANDRINGHAM GARDENS
seen by Louise:
    balcony
    <u>L-shaped bedroom (like two rooms)</u>
    light living room <u>(TV and video)</u>
    <u>2nd floor: view of railway line</u>
    <u>close to centre, station 20 mins</u>

WINDSOR AVENUE
seen by Louise:
    <u>full of dirty old furniture</u>
    nice garden
    one bedroom <u>with two uncomfortable beds</u>
    living room <u>with bed (black and white TV)</u>
    <u>close to centre, station 20 mins</u>

TRANSCRIPT   *3 minutes*

BOB: Hello...er...this is Bob. I've been to see two of the places you asked me to look at: er...13A Balmoral Way and 7B Windsor Avenue. Well, first of all the one in Balmoral Way: um...it's quite modern and the living room's very spacious. Both the bedrooms are small though and the kitchen's tiny but it does have everything you'd need, including a freezer and a dishwasher. Um...there's no TV, so you'd have to rent one. It's on the fifth floor and you can see the park and the fields beyond: that's quite nice, but I got the impression that it's quite expensive because it's modern and it's got two bedrooms.

Now, the other place is quite different. It's the ground floor of an old house and it's got its own garden, with trees and a nice lawn and a patio with a table and chairs so you could...er...eat outside in the evenings. Er...the furniture's comfortable and although it's only got one bedroom it's really big and it's got two single beds which are on separate sides of the room – or, well, you could move one bed into the living room. The kitchen's big and it's got a door onto the garden.

Ah...that's about it. They're both still free and they're both available from July. Er...well, let me know what you decide to do. Bye.

LOUISE: Louise here. Listen, I've been to see two flats: one was 44C Sandringham Gardens and the other one was 7B Windsor Avenue. I like them both actually.

Now, the one at Sandringham Gardens: it's got a balcony, which is nice. And the bedroom is quite unusual because it's a kind of an L shape; it's got one bed round the corner from the other. It's almost like two rooms in a way, it's really nice. Um...the living room has a TV and a video and it's very light and it's quite cheerful. It's on the second floor but the view of the railway line isn't what you'd call beautiful.

Now the one at Windsor Avenue: this is absolutely crammed full of dusty old-fashioned furniture and it's not very clean. The garden's nice, but it was raining when I was there, so I didn't actually go out. There's one bedroom and it's got a couple of beds in it – they didn't look very comfortable. And there's another bed in the living room. And there's an old black and white television.

They're both quite close to the centre, which is good. You could walk to the shops in a few minutes. The station's about 20 minutes away from both. Um...if you need to know any more just call me. I'll be in tomorrow. Bye then.

 Activity **57** in the Student's Book contains a model letter. Compare your letter with this.

7.6 Modal verbs – 1
GRAMMAR REVIEW

ANSWERS

1 I can't help you to find accommodation. = I'm unable to help you. (*But all three meanings could be implied in this sentence.*)
2 I don't have to help you to find accommodation. = It's not my responsibility to help you.
3 I won't help you to find accommodation. = I'm unwilling to help you.
4 She can't be joking. = I'm sure she isn't.
5 She can't tell jokes. = She's no good at it.
6 She must be joking. = I'm sure she is.
7 She mustn't tell jokes. = She isn't allowed to.
8 You can't leave now. = I won't let you go.
9 You could leave now. = It would be possible to go.
10 You don't have to leave now. = It's unnecessary to go.
11 You needn't leave now. = It's unnecessary to go.
12 You shouldn't leave now. = It's not a good idea to go.

ANSWERS

2 *I checked the timetable so I mustn't be wrong about the departure time!*
   can't

3 *You needn't to worry if I miss the last bus because I can get a taxi.*
   don't need to/needn't

4 *Do I ought to phone for a taxi, or may I pick one up in the street?*
   ought I to/should I   can

5 *I could get a taxi but I must waiting for five minutes for one to arrive.*
   would have to wait

6 *Don't be silly, you ought not to show your passport if you will buy a rail ticket.*
   don't need to/needn't   want to

7 *You mustn't write anything down unless you want to.*
   don't have to/needn't

8 *You need spend as much time as you can on your homework.*
   ought to/should/need to

SUGGESTED ANSWERS

- I still can't play the saxophone and I still can't speak Greek. When I was ten I couldn't do either of those things.
- I don't have to go to school and I don't have to do what my parents tell me to. When I was ten I had to do both those things.
- I still have to clean my teeth and I still have to wear glasses.
- One day soon I may visit the USA and I may buy a new car.
- I know I shouldn't laugh at people behind their backs and I shouldn't eat so much.

D Record yourself on a blank cassette.

7.7 Spelling and pronunciation – 1: Vowels **WORD STUDY**

A

ANSWERS

worn   meat   one   through

B 1 & 2

ANSWERS

/æ/	scandal	flat	marry
/e/	bury/berry		
	weather/whether		
	check/cheque		merry
/ɑː/	laugh	castle	half	guard

/ɔː/	wore/war source/sauce	
	raw/roar	walk
/ɜː/	turn firm	work
/iː/	weak/week seize/seas	
	wheel/we'll	receive
/ɪ/	guilty witch/which	
	mist/missed	business
/ɒ/	not/knot knowledge	
	quality	wander
/uː/	blue/blew root/route	
	new/knew	soup
/ʊ/	cushion butcher pull	push
/ʌ/	blood tongue country	
	thorough	wonder

3 The recorded answers include correct pronunciations of the examples on the left in the Student's Book, as well as the words listed in the answers above.

C

CORRECTED SENTENCES

1 *I am quite shore that this weak is going too be wonderful.*
   sure   week   to

2 *We are truely sorry that you had to weight so long four the delivery.*
   truly   wait   for

3 *He has dredful manners — he paws tomato source on all his food.*
   dreadful   pours   sauce

4 *They couldn't get thier new armchare threw the door.*
   their   armchair   through

5 *Witch of these too alternatives is the write one?*
   which   two   right

6 *He lent the ladder agenst the wall and climed onto the roof.*
   leant   against   climbed

7 *The cieling and walls of this room need peinting ergently.*
   ceiling   painting   urgently

7.8 **Starting and ending well**
WRITING

A The best opening sentence is probably number 5: 'G__ is a delightfully unspoilt village surrounded by fields and woods at the mouth of a river.'

B And the best closing sentence is probably number 4: 'Go there before everyone else discovers it!'

C This is a matter of taste.

D Show your letter to an English-speaking person, or to a friend.

---

8 Good health and illness   Keeping fit

Looking after yourself

8.1 **How are you feeling?**
VOCABULARY

A Some useful vocabulary:

cholesterol   drink less   get up late/early   give up smoking go to bed early/late   healthy diet   jog   keep fit medical examination/check-up   overeat   smoke stay up late   take exercise   walk

B

ANSWERS
2 prescription (*in some countries you can get antibiotics from a pharmacy without a prescription*)
3 injection   4 spots   5 headache
6 temperature   7 sneezing   8 diet

C

ANSWERS
1 off your food   out of sorts   under the weather
2 bruise   bump   cut
3 physically fit   living a healthy life   in good shape
4 affect   damage   ruin
5 dizzy   faint   funny

D 1

SUGGESTED ANSWERS
(Many variations are possible.)
2 leg/arm/collar bone   3 finger/leg/toe
4 elbow/knee/heel   5 shoulder/back/stomach
6 ankle/wrist/knee   7 head/tooth/back
8 bumped/hit

8.2 **Sleep and Dreams**
LISTENING AND WRITING

A 2

ANSWERS
1 Rapid Eye Movement
2 deep sleep
3 REM sleep
4 several minutes
5 hurt or caught
6 deal with problems
7 remember them
8 four or five hours/less
9 (ten-minute) nap/short sleep
10 waking up

TRANSCRIPT   *5 minutes 40 seconds*

INTERVIEWER: . . . Now, sleep...er...like the way our brains work, is still something of a mystery, but recent research into sleep has given us a few more answers. With me today is Dr William Johnson, who has just published a book called simply: 'Sleep'. Dr Johnson, hello.

DR JOHNSON: Hello.

INTERVIEWER: How many kinds of sleep are there?

DR JOHNSON: Er...well, there are three types of sleep: um...there's light sleep, deep sleep and REM sleep.

INTERVIEWER: REM sleep, what's that?

DR JOHNSON: REM...er...R E M, that stands for Rapid Eye Movement. Now our eyes move about very fast under our eyelids during...um...this particular type of sleep.

  Now...er...light sleep is 'optional' – we can actually do without it – and yet quite a lot of our sleeping time is actually spent sleeping lightly. But actually to restore our brains we require deep sleep.

INTERVIEWER: I see, and...er...is it true that dreams occur when you're just about to wake up?

DR JOHNSON: Well, haha, a lot of people actually think this but this is in fact wrong. Dreams take place during Rapid Eye Movement sleep...Yeah, now this type of sleep occurs every 90 minutes or so throughout the night. And...er...it usually goes on for several minutes.

INTERVIEWER: Oh, right...w...is there a...is there a particular reason why we dream?

DR JOHNSON: Um...well, that's a very good question...haha, well there's no...um...easy answer to it. Most of us can remember dreams where we are, I don't know, falling, flying, or being chased or something...Yeah and we wake up just before we hurt ourselves or just before we're caught. It seems that perhaps one purpose of dreams might be to help sleepers to deal with problems that they actually have in their waking lives, um...such as their fears or worries...Um...th...not exactly to solve those problems, but just to come to terms with them.

INTERVIEWER: But i...it's true, isn't it, that not everybody has dreams?

DR JOHNSON: Ah, well, ha, research has in fact shown that, yes, everyone *does* have dreams. The thing is that some people can't *remember* their dreams. Um...in fact, most people forget their dreams very quickly after waking up. For example, um...if I asked you now to tell me about your dreams last night, you...well, you probably couldn't remember, could you?

INTERVIEWER: Mm...well, no no, actually I can't, no.

DR JOHNSON: Haha, but if I asked you as soon as you'd woken up, you probably would have been able to tell me.

INTERVIEWER: Mm, yes, so...er...er...how much sleep do we really need? Um...you know, e...everyone says that eight hours is what...i...is...is the essential amount. Is that...is that right?

DR JOHNSON: Well, y...n...yes, in fact most people actually require *less* than eight hours' sleep a night – um...six or seven is enough for many people. And there are also many successful people who only need...er...a few hours sleep a night. I can think particularly of Napoleon, and...er...there's also Winston Churchill...um...also Margaret Thatcher...they all managed on four hours a night or...or even less – um...leaving them more time to keep one step ahead of their...their enemies, so to speak!

INTERVIEWER: Now then, what about...um...people who have...er...what...well, two sleeps? You know they...they sleep during the day and then they sleep at night as well? Um...now...er...presumably they get more sleep than people who only sleep at night?

DR JOHNSON: Well, if you split your sleep into two parts, you actually need *less* sleep. Um...for example, if someone takes a siesta and sleeps for say an hour, they only need to sleep for four or five hours at night. And presumably that's why people in the Mediterranean countries appear to be able to keep going until, you know, 2 am or...or even later than that.

  But...um...a sleep during the day has to be long enough to allow...er...plenty of time for deep sleep. So, for example, the benefit of a ten-minute nap is...is, well, it's only psychological really, it's not physical. It may make you *feel* better, but it doesn't really do you any good at all.

INTERVIEWER: Uhuh, right, so...er...what about things like...um...oh, I don't know, snoring, talking in your sleep, you know, er...are...is there...is there anything you can do about that, are there any cures?

DR JOHNSON: Haha, um...there's only one certain cure for snoring – and that is waking up! . . . Er...but some snorers...um...are cured by sleeping on their sides or by sleeping without a pillow.

  And...er...and talking in your sleep is something most people do, I think, at...at some point in their lives, it's, I don't know, it's not a problem exactly and surprisingly it occurs in all types of sleep, not...not just when you're dreaming.

INTERVIEWER: Mm. What about...er...insomnia, people who can't sleep, what...um...is there anything that you can do to help them?

DR JOHNSON: Err...well, there are many different causes for insomnia. Um...there really isn't time to deal with them all now. But if you do have trouble sleeping, the one thing you should *not* do is take sleeping pills.

INTERVIEWER: Oh really?

DR JOHNSON: Yeah, really. If you want to find out more you'll have to read my book.

INTERVIEWER: Haha, oh well, thank you, Dr Johnson, that's...er...that's marvellous, thank you very much.

DR JOHNSON: Thank you.

8.3 Modal verbs – 2
GRAMMAR REVIEW

ANSWERS

2 I had to give her my phone number. = I gave her the number.

3 I didn't have to give her my phone number. = I gave her the number.

4 She wouldn't let me give her my phone number. = I didn't give her the number.

5 He can't have gone to hospital. = I'm sure he didn't go.

6 He couldn't go to hospital. = He didn't go, because he wasn't able to.

7 He must have gone to hospital. = I'm convinced he has gone.

8 He needn't have gone to hospital. = He went, but it was unnecessary to.

9 He shouldn't have gone to hospital. = He went, but it was a mistake to do so.

B

ANSWERS

2 The doctor told me that *I had to take* the tablets three times a day.
3 She told me that *I could stop taking them when I felt* better.
4 She told me that *I might feel better* in a few days.
5 She told me that *I couldn't expect to get better if I didn't follow* her advice.
6 She told me that *I had to take* some exercise every day.
7 She told me that *I shouldn't/mustn't/hadn't to* sit around doing nothing.
8 She told me that *I ought to/should* eat less.

C

ANSWERS (Some of these require more than five words, so they aren't typical exam questions.)

2 He *can't possibly need an injection before* going to America.
3 You *shouldn't take aspirins if you're perfectly* all right.
4 Do *I really have to/need to* take more exercise?
5 I wonder how long I'll *have to wait?*
6 He *had to stay* in bed.
7 You *shouldn't have gone/needn't have gone/didn't need to go to the doctor/doctor's with* a cough.
8 The doctor *couldn't have/can't have cured* your cough.

8.4 What to do about flu
READING

A

ANSWERS

1 True
2 False (*They can't kill viruses.*)
3 False (*You shouldn't force yourself to eat.*)
4 False (*It can become serious for elderly or sick people.*)
5 True
6 False (*The text would say if this was advisable – but if it helps, why not?*)
7 False (*It only gives one year's protection.*)
8 False (*winter*)
9 True (*Dirty plates and cutlery can spread infection.*)
10 True

B **1** Here are some questions:

Have you got a headache?
Do you feel weak or shivery?
Are you sweating a lot?
Do you feel sick?
Have you lost your appetite?
Have you got a high temperature?

2 Some other ways of introducing advice:

I think you should . . .
You ought to . . .
It's best to . . .
My advice is to . . .

It's best to stay indoors.
You'd better keep away from other people.

3 & 4 Record your advice, as if you were talking to a friend on the phone.

8.5 Smoke-free zones
READING

A Laws on smoking in public places are moving closer to the ones explained in the article, and in some European countries, even exceeding them.

B

ANSWERS

2 c 3 b 4 c 5 c 6 a 7 a 8 c

C

ANSWERS

¶1 grimy consenting adults
¶2 harsher banned
¶3 polls hazard
¶4 hinted hefty kicking the habit

D The missing figures are:

Cigarettes – Czech Republic: 1,600; Greece: 2,900
Litres of beer – Brazil: 34; Germany: 140
Litres of wine – Italy: 70; Spain: 38

8.6 Spelling and pronunciation – 2: Diphthongs **WORD STUDY**

A

ANSWERS

aloud break hole write

B

ANSWERS

/aɪ/	climate	by/buy/bye	thigh	time
/aʊ/	proud	found		frown
/ɔɪ/	destroy	employer		point
/eə/	stares/stairs	fare/fair		
		pair/pear		share
/ɪə/	cleared	atmosphere		sincere
/eɪ/	wait/weight	male/mail		
		waste/waist		paint
/əʊ/	folk	nose/knows		soap

The answers to B1 and 2 are on the recording, which also includes the examples given on the left in the Student's Book.

C 1

ANSWERS AND TRANSCRIPT

1 The part of your leg above the knee is your *thigh*.
2 What is your *waist* measurement in centimetres?
3 What is your *weight* in kilos?
4 What is your *height* in metres?
5 If you jump out of this window, you'll *break* your leg.
6 The *mayor* of New York is against smoking.
7 Smoking isn't *allowed* in restaurants in Los Angeles.
8 *Walking* to *work* keeps me fit.

8.7 At . . .
PREPOSITIONS

A

ANSWERS

2 at last   3 At first sight   4 at a profit
at a loss   5 at war   at peace (*or vice versa*)
6 at a time   7 at least   8 at once
9 at the same time   10 at all

8.8 How to stay healthy
SPEAKING AND WRITING

A Record two one-minute talks on a blank cassette.

B The information here and in Activities *16* and *42* gives you ideas for the writing task in C.

C 2 Suggested opening and closing sentences:
I was really pleased to hear from you after all this time.

Let me know how you get on.

9 Tourism and travel Holidays and excursions

Having a great time!

9.1 Holidays
VOCABULARY AND SPEAKING

A

ANSWERS

The first speaker, Susanna, went to Paris (photo 2). Her holiday lasted ten days.

The second speaker, James, went to New York (photo 1). His holiday lasted a week.

The third speaker, Joan, went to Venice (photo 3). Her holiday lasted four days.

TRANSCRIPT   *2 minutes 40 seconds*

SUSANNA: . . . it was wonderful because it was the springtime and it's, you know, traditional sort of romantic place to be in the spring. Er...we went for about ten days, and it was glorious. All the blossom was on the trees and down by the river and...um...the people seem to rush around everywhere all the time and...er...we were just desperately trying to keep up, and didn't, and didn't. But...um...visited the churches and of course the Eiffel Tower – all the...all the old tourist spots, but it was really beautiful, had a lovely time.

JAMES: . . . it's...um...an extraordinary...er...jungle really...um...a fantastic mixture of different kinds of people...um...a...a mixture of different kinds of cultures...um...all sort of packed into a tiny area, considering how many people there are. Er...I was there for about a...a week...um...and it was March and it was beginning to hot up and...um...er...the street life is the thing that instantly hits you. And the number of cabs and the noise on the streets is incredible, there's almost a sort of sense of...a sort of...almost as if there's a permanent earthquake going on under...just under the surface, and you look up and there's just a thin blue strip and you realise that that's the sky and all around you are these incredible tall buildings . . .

JOAN: . . . it was absolutely beautiful. We booked last minute flights and...um...it was a long weekend, which was just perfect actually, we in fact had about four days. Um...and because it was springtime, the weather was ideal for walking, we travelled very lightly, and we just walked miles and miles, and it's just the perfect place to do that really. Um...we did, in fact, have one trip on a gondola, but it's quite a pricey way to...to experience, you know, the sights and sounds of the city. But...um...I loved it and I'd like to go back and spend more time and really explore the city because it's very old and crumbling and the...the artwork is just really quite exquisite, it really is splendid. I took rolls and rolls of film as well, wonderful!

B 1

ANSWERS

1 package   2 agency   3 arrangements
4 brochures   5 guide   6 resort
7 sunbathing   8 beach   9 excursions
10 self-catering   11 view   12 balcony
13 delightful

2 Presumably the reality didn't live up to expectations!

C

ANSWERS

1 day-trippers   holiday-makers   sightseers
2 bed and breakfast   full board   half board
3 active   busy   energetic
4 lazy   relaxing   restful
5 choice   range   variety
6 gift   present   souvenir

D   Here is some useful vocabulary:

*art gallery   castle   crowded   deserted   group   guide
hiking   historical monument   mountains   museum
package holiday   palm trees   path   pedalos
rucksack/backpack   sightseeing/seeing the sights
sunburn   suntan   track   work of art*

9.2   Brazilian Contrasts
READING

A

ANSWERS

2 Salvador   3 São Paulo   4 Rio   5 Rio
6 Rio   7 Brasilia   8 Rio   9 Iguaçu
10 Rio

B 1

ANSWERS

2 Early morning
3 Day 2: afternoon city tour and Days 11–13:
  Carioca night tour
4 Brasilia
5 No, winding (*streets wind up and down the hills*)
6 By a million new inhabitants every year
7 The noise (*the distant roar of the Falls increases
  to a deafening crescendo*)
8 Evening

2

ANSWERS

1 Luxor Continental
2 Yes (*290 rooms . . . high rise*)
3 No (*50 yards from . . . Copacabana Beach*)
4 Not necessarily (*rooms vary in size and location*)
5 No (*with shower only*)
6 No (*modern accommodation*)

C   Some of the other problems of holidays in exotic
places are malaria, yellow fever, snakes, sharks,
jellyfish, humidity, long-haul flights, crime, terrorism,
etc.

9.3   By . . .
PREPOSITIONS

1

ANSWERS

1 by name   2 by far   3 by heart
4 by accident/mistake   5 by train   by car
6 by day   by night   7 by surprise
8 by chance   9 by all means
10 by post   by hand   11 By the time
12 by yourself

The three superfluous phrases were:
by plane, *by ship* and either *by mistake* or *by accident*.

2 Example sentences:

You can cross the Atlantic quickly *by plane* or more
slowly *by ship*.

Oh dear, I've put down my old address on the form
by mistake.

9.4   Spelling and pronunciation – 3:
Consonants   WORD STUDY

A 1

TRANSCRIPT AND ANSWERS
3 minutes 30 seconds

slipping	He kept slipping on the ice.
sleeping	She was still sleeping at ten o'clock.
trouble	Don't worry, it's no trouble.
robber	The robber stole the money.
total	What's the total amount?
putting	You're putting on weight.
address	What's your name and address?
doubled	Their speed doubled.
request	I agreed to his request.
Christian	Is he a Christian or a Muslim?
angle	Ninety degrees is a right angle.
ignorant	They are very ignorant.
engine	This car has a petrol engine.
average	The average is 50 per cent.
adventure	We had an exciting adventure.
butcher	You get meat from the butcher.
careful	Please be very careful.
million	The population of Britain is 50 million.
often	How often have you seen her?
sudden	There was a sudden noise.
immense	The problems are immense.
coming	Are you coming to see us?
worry	It's all right, don't worry!
railway	I'll meet you at the railway station.
assistant	My assistant will help you.
please	Please don't smoke.
insurance	Don't drive without insurance.
pleasure	It was a pleasure to meet you.
laughing	He kept on laughing.
rough	The surface isn't smooth, it's rough.
convince	They tried to convince me.
live	Where do you live?
theory	In theory that sounds like a good idea.
themselves	They did all the work themselves.
twelve	Six plus six is twelve.
while	I'll wash up while you dry.
university	She's a student at the university.
yawning	I'm very tired, I can't help yawning.

B Some more examples of 'silent letters':

gh	through straight
b	crumb thumb
t	postman fasten
k	know knock knit
l	stalk talk would
r	far father farther confirm (only in RP)
h	honour dishonest exhausted
w	wrestle wrong wretched

C Look at Activity *14* which contains some words that may cause spelling difficulties. Read out the words and record yourself on a blank cassette. Then play back the cassette and write down the words, pausing the tape frequently. Check your spelling by looking at Activity *14* again.

Then do the same with the work in Activity *22*.

9.5 ***If . . .* sentences – 1**
GRAMMAR REVIEW

A

ANSWERS (The words that show the meaning differences are in bold italics.)

1 We can't go skiing *until* there's more snow on the mountains. = We're waiting for more snow – without more snow we can't go skiing.
2 *Unless* there's more snow on the mountains, we can't go skiing. = There's not enough snow now and there needs to be more snow for skiing (similar meaning to 1).
3 We can't go skiing *if* there's more snow on the mountains. = Too much snow will make skiing dangerous or impossible – there's already plenty of snow.
4 In April, *when* the weather *is* warmer, I*'ll take* a few days off. = I know the weather will be warmer then.
5 I*'ll take* a couple of days off *if* the weather *is* better in April. = I'm unsure whether the weather will be warmer then.
6 *If* the weather *were* nicer in April, I*'d take* a short break. = I know the weather won't be nicer then – I'm just imagining.
7 You'd better take an overnight bag *in case* you have to stay the night. = You may have to stay the night, so be prepared.
8 *If* you have to stay the night, you'd better take an overnight bag. = As you have to stay the night, be prepared.
9 I*'ll go* to Rio for the Carnival *if* I *can* afford it. = I may be able to afford it, and if I can I will go.
10 *If* I *could* afford it, I*'d go* to Rio for the Carnival. = I can't afford it and I can't go – I'm just day-dreaming.
11 I *might go* to Rio at Carnival time *if* I *had* enough money. = I can't afford it, but even if I could I wouldn't definitely go there.

B

ANSWERS

2 If *it's* my birthday tomorrow, I'd invite my friends out for a meal.	it was/were
3 If you *will need* any help, please let me know.	need
4 We'll enjoy our holiday unless it *will rain* all the time.	rains
5 If the sun's shining tomorrow, we'll go swimming.	✔
6 When I'm on holiday *I'd like* to relax rather than be active.	I like
7 Let's go to the mountains if the spring comes.	when
8 I'll be arriving on Sunday *until* there's a change of plan.	unless

C Most of these sentences require more than five words, so they are not the same as the equivalent part of the Use of English paper.

ANSWERS (Some variations are possible.)

2 If you go to Britain, *you'll be able to practise your English* all the time.
3 If you *stay in the sun all day long, you'll get* sunburnt.
4 If *I didn't have to work this summer, I'd go* on holiday.
5 Unless you book ahead *you won't find anywhere to* stay.
6 Pack a jumper to wear after dark *in case the evenings are* cool.
7 If we *go on holiday together, you'll certainly enjoy* yourself.
8 If *you could go anywhere in the world, which country would you* travel to?

D Write down six sentences using *If . . .*

9.6 **An excursion programme**
LISTENING AND WRITING

B

ANSWERS

Excursion programme

	Departure		Return
Sunday	14:00	Edinburgh city sightseeing *(no need to book)*	16:30
Monday	9:00	(Braemar Castle) and (Aberdeen)	17:30
Tuesday	~~7:45~~ 8:30	Glencoe and Fort William	17:30
Wednesday	8:00	Inverness and Loch Ness	~~18:30~~ 17:30
Thursday	14:00	Edinburgh City sightseeing tour	16:30
Friday *cancelled*	~~7:00~~ ~~9:15~~	*Glasgow and River Clyde steamer trip* ~~Galashiels and the Borders~~	~~17:45~~ ~~16:00~~

TRANSCRIPT *2 minutes 30 seconds*

TOUR LEADER: Good morning, everyone. Er...ha...sorry to...er...interrupt breakfast. I've got here a few changes to the excursion...er...programme, which I think you've all got. Um...I might as well go through them all and then you'll know where you are. In fact, they make absolutely no difference to the tours: in fact they...they improve them, which is basically why we've made the changes. Now, your Monday 9 o'clock...um...where you've got the Braemar Castle...er...Aberdeen: what we're going to do is we're going to swop round there and we're going to go to Aberdeen first and then on to Braemar, returning here at 17.30. Now we move to Tuesday. Ah...the only difference there...I'm going to make an earlier start for Glencoe and Fort William: ah...7.45 instead of 8.30. Ah...Wednesday: yes, the...the Inverness and Loch Ness – one of my personal favourites, I think...um...everyone – um...instead of returning at...er...17.30, we'll come back a...a...a little bit later there on that one...er...18.30... give us a bit more time actually at Loch Ness. Hope we spot the monster, eh? Ha! Well...er...Thursday...um...now this is...this is our...our big day in Edinburgh, where we're doing the city sightseeing. Um...also...er...we're going to do an Edinburgh this afternoon – that's today, Sunday, we're going to do an Edinburgh...um...because...er...we...we had nothing planned for today, but we're going to do an Edinburgh as well. Er...same time, no need to book. Er...now unfortunately on Friday we've had to cancel your Galashiels and your Borders. Er...but instead we're substituting Glasgow, leaving at seven for Glasgow and then I think a fitting end to your holiday, one I think you're going to go for: the River Clyde Steamer Trip. Yes, on an actual River Clyde steamer. Re...returning at...at 17...17.45. Er...I hope those are all satisfactory. Sorry we've had to make these changes, but I think you'll find that they'll improve the holiday and make it even better than it already is.

Oh, now I...can I remind you that the...the excursions are of course optional, you know, but I'm sure you'll all want to go on them. Er...and would you decide which ones you want to go on by lunchtime today. Thanks very much, everyone, enjoy the rest of your breakfasts.

C Activity **59** contains a description of one of the Scottish excursions as a model for your own writing.

9.7 Use of English: Fill the gaps

EXAM TECHNIQUES

A **1**

ANSWERS

2 noun   **3** verb
4 adverb   possessive pronoun
5 article   article
6 preposition   pronoun

2

SUGGESTED ANSWERS

1 bad   **2** night   **3** cross   **4** finally   our
5 A   the   **6** in   myself

B **1**

ANSWERS

1 usual   **2** himself   **3** minute   **4** airport
5 road   **6** time   **7** lounge   **8** flight
9 made   **10** desk

2

SUGGESTED ANSWERS

12 free   **13** technical   **14** take off
15 ages   **16** information   **17** night
18 expense   **19** happened   **20** asleep
21 behind   **22** passengers   **23** reason
24 imagine

10

Eating and drinking   Restaurants and cafés
Preparing food   Explaining recipes

Food for thought

 10.1

Mmm, this looks delicious!
READING

B

> **ANSWERS** (Some of these may have to be guessed by a process of elimination.)
>
> **Dorset Apple Cake:**
> ingredients C, instructions 3, photo a
>
> **Somerset Cider Cake:**
> ingredients D, instructions 1, photo c
>
> **Apple and Blackberry Pie:**
> ingredients A, instructions 2, photo b
>
> **Apple Crumble:**
> ingredients B, instructions 4, photo d

C

> **ANSWERS**
> A   filling   pastry
> B   ground   wholewheat flour
> C   peeled   chopped (into chunks)   zest
> D   cider   cored   self-raising flour

 10.2

Cooking and eating
VOCABULARY

A

> **SUGGESTED ANSWERS**
> Chicken can be fried, roasted, grilled or
>   barbecued.
> Potatoes can be steamed, boiled, fried, roasted
>   or baked.
> Rice can be steamed, boiled or fried (after it's
>   been steamed or boiled).
> Fish can be steamed, boiled (to make soup or
>   fish stew), fried, baked, grilled or barbecued.
> Bread can only be baked, or grilled (to make
>   toast).
> Steak can be fried, grilled or barbecued.
> Carrots can be steamed or boiled (and possibly
>   baked).

B   Some letters are harder than others (in italics below), but here are some suggestions.

> **SUGGESTED ANSWERS**
> aubergine   butter   chicken   duck   eggs
> French fries   garlic   hamburger   ice cream
> jam   kiwi   lettuce   marmalade   nuts   oranges
> peaches   *quince*   radish   spinach   tomato
> *unleavened bread*   vegetables   water melon
> *Xmas pudding*   yogurt   *zucchini* (= courgettes)

 C

> **ANSWERS**
> 1 hot   2 dishes   3 recipe   4 rare
> 5 additives   6 wine list   7 greedy
> 8 helping   9 avoid   10 off   11 still
> 12 bitter

 10.3

-ing and to – 1
GRAMMAR REVIEW

A

> **ANSWERS**
> 2 *I'm looking forward to go on
>   holiday.*   going
> 3 *To smoke is not allowed in
>   restaurants in New York.*   Smoking
> 4 *It was kind of you inviting me
>   joining you.*   to invite   to join
> 5 *At night it's too dark to see
>   without to use a flashlight.*   using
> 6 *Do you think that cooking for a
>   family is easier than running a
>   restaurant?*   ✔

B   Some of these sentences require more than five words, so it's not typical of the equivalent Use of English exercise in the exam.

> **SUGGESTED ANSWERS**
> 1 I'm looking *forward to having* something
>   to eat.
> 2 It is easier *to boil eggs than (to)* poach them.
> 3 It's *essential to phone the restaurant to* book a
>   table for twelve.
> 4 We got there *too late to have/for* lunch.
> 5 I'm always *interested in trying* new dishes from
>   abroad.
> 6 I was disappointed *to find that my favourite dish
>   wasn't* on the menu.
> 7 *Drinking* strong coffee *at night prevents me from
>   sleeping.*
> 8 Don't you realise *that eating sweets is bad for
>   your* teeth?

 C

> **SUGGESTED ANSWERS**
> 1 to visit   2 seeing   3 spending   4 using
> 5 to use   6 to go   7 sitting   8 eating/to eat
> 9 eating   10 eating   11 piling/filling
> 12 eating   13 sitting   14 talking/chatting
> 15 to stay/to sit

10.4 Eating out
LISTENING AND SPEAKING

ANSWERS

1 a gin and tonic   sparkling water
2 tomatoes   olives
3 chopped potatoes   onions
4 veal   breadcrumbs
5 wine   cream   starter   main course
6 grated   bacon   fried eggs
7 layers   pasta   meat   oven   cheese
8 *moules marinière*   Spanish omelette   green
9 Greek salad   lasagne
10 orange juice   a half bottle of the house
   red wine

TRANSCRIPT *3 minutes*

WAITRESS: Good evening. Would you like to see the menu?
AMANDA: Oh, yes please.
WAITRESS: Would you like a drink before you start?
PAUL: Oh, I think so, yes. Um...I'll have a gin and tonic, how about you?
AMANDA: I think I'll just have a sparkling water.
WAITRESS: Oh, right, thank you.
AMANDA: Mm, let's have a look. Oh, I see they've got pizzas.
PAUL: Mm, I think I fancy some fish tonight actually.
AMANDA: Do you? Hey, Paul, what does a Greek salad consist of?
PAUL: Greek salad? Well, it's got cucumber, tomato, olives and...um...you know, that feta goat's cheese.
AMANDA: Oh, I don't like goat's cheese. Oh, what about...um...*Wiener Schnitzel*, what's that?
PAUL: I'm not sure. We could ask the waitress. Oh, hold on, do you know what Spanish omelette is?
AMANDA: Oh yeah, it's an omelette with chopped potatoes and onions in it.
PAUL: Mm, sounds good.
AMANDA: It is.
PAUL: What about *Lasagne al forno*?
AMANDA: Oh, well, I know it's some sort of pasta, but I'm not quite sure. Well, we'll have to ask the waitress . . .
WAITRESS: Um...are you ready to order?
AMANDA: Yeah...um...could you just tell me something: what is *Wiener Schnitzel*?
WAITRESS: It's a thin piece of veal coated in egg and breadcrumbs and then it's pan-fried.
PAUL: And what's *moules marinière*?
WAITRESS: That's...um...mussels cooked in wine with onions and a little cream. You can have those as a starter or as a main course.
PAUL: Mussels, mm, and what's...er...*Rosti*?
WAITRESS: Haha, *Rösti*, yeah, that's...um...grated potatoes, bacon and onions fried together. You can have it with two fried eggs on top as a main course, or you can have it with your main course instead of French fries, if you like.
AMANDA: And just one more thing: what's *Lasagne al forno*?
WAITRESS: Oh yes, that's...um...thin layers of pasta and meat sauce with a creamy sauce, baked in the oven with cheese on top.
AMANDA: Oh, well . . . Um...I'll have mussels as starter, please, and...um...then I'd like the Spanish omelette with a mixed salad . . . No, no, sorry, could you make that a green salad?
WAITRESS: Sure.
PAUL: Er...and I won't have a starter. If I could have the lasagne as a main course and a mixed salad to go with it.
WAITRESS: Right, so that's one *moules marinière* as a starter, a Spanish omelette, a lasagne and two mixed salads.

AMANDA: No...er...mine was a green salad.
PAUL: Er...can I have a Greek salad instead of mixed salad. But as a starter, is that all right?
WAITRESS: Yes, right, that's fine. Anything to drink?
PAUL: What do you fancy, red wine?
AMANDA: Oh, no, no, I won't have any wine, I'm driving. Have you got any apple juice?
WAITRESS: I'm afraid not, but we have got orange juice.
AMANDA: Oh, that'll be fine, thank you.
PAUL: Mm. Er...mm...can I have...er...half a bottle of the house red?
WAITRESS: Oh yes, fine.
PAUL: Thanks.

B 1

TRANSCRIPT *2 minutes*

FIRST WOMAN: Shall we have a look at the menu? I'm so hungry.
MAN: Yeah, OK. Boy, there are a few things here that I don't understand.
SECOND WOMAN: There's a lot of this stuff I don't understand. What's all this then?
FIRST WOMAN: Well, what about the starters? Hey, do you know what 'prawns' –
MAN: Appetisers.
FIRST WOMAN: Appetisers, oh. 'Prawns' are what?
MAN: They're like large shrimps.
SECOND WOMAN: Oh, they're delicious with avocado.
FIRST WOMAN: Really? Mind you, I like the sound of 'melon and orange salad'.
MAN: Hey, hey, look at the main courses. What is 'Lancashire hotpot'?
SECOND WOMAN: I've heard of that. That's sort of lamb and vegetables cooked in the oven sort of broiled and the potatoes are sliced on top and put in a layer. It's delicious.
FIRST WOMAN: It sounds good. And what's this one: 'steak and kidney pie', do you know what this is?
MAN: Yeah, that now is a typical English dish – it's made of beef which is cut up into pieces along with pieces of kidney in a rich brown sauce. It is lovely. And that is traditionally English.
FIRST WOMAN: Sounds delicious!
SECOND WOMAN: The one I don't understand is 'cottage pie'.
FIRST WOMAN: Now, I've come across that before. That's minced beef in gravy and it's got mashed potato on top. I don't know if that's going to be that good, although this does look like a good restaurant, don't you think?
SECOND WOMAN: OK. Now do either of you know what's this, what's 'nut and mushroom roast'?
MAN: Well, it's a vegetarian dish...er...hasn't got any meat in it – made of nuts, mushrooms and it's baked in the oven like a cake. Might be quite nice. Er...but the other one I don't know here is 'chicken Madras'. Anyone know that?
FIRST WOMAN: No.
SECOND WOMAN: Yes, that's an Indian dish. I can tell you that's...um...it's, I think it's pieces of chicken...

10.5 Compound words – 1
WORD STUDY

(A) 1

ANSWERS
3 He uses his left hand to write with.
4 with blue eyes and with red hair
5 list of wines
6 gadget to open cans
7 watch worn on the wrist

2

SUGGESTED ANSWERS

first	first floor first name first course (firsthand)
second	second-hand second-best second cousin (second floor) (second name)
high	high-class high-level
low	low-speed low-pressure
home	home-grown home-produced
middle	middle-aged middle-sized
self	self-respect self-discipline self-service
well	well-known well-off

3 📼 The recording has the correct answers and their correct pronunciation.

(B)

ANSWERS
2 old-fashioned   3 fast food
4 home-grown/home-produced   5 tin opener
6 food processor   7 self-service
8 mass-produced   9 first course
10 food poisoning   11 fruit juice
12 mineral water

10.6 On . . . and out of . . .
PREPOSITIONS

1

ANSWERS
1 on time   on business   2 out of order
3 on holiday/vacation   out of doors
4 on your own   5 on the house
6 on purpose
7 on the other hand/on the whole
8 out of reach   9 on duty   10 On the whole

The superfluous phrases were: *out of work, on the telephone* and *out of date.*

2 Example sentences:

He lost his job last year and he's been *out of work* ever since.
I spoke to her *on the telephone* last night.
Last year's diary is no use because it is *out of date.*

10.7 How do you make . . . ?
LISTENING AND WRITING

(A) 2 📼

ANSWERS
1 H   2 D   3 G   4 C   5 F   6 K
7 L   8 E   9 I   10 B   11 A
J is the superfluous instruction.

TRANSCRIPT   *1 minute 30 seconds*

JOAN: You know those potatoes you cooked for us the other evening?
NEIL: Mm.
JOAN: Well, you said you'd let me have the recipe.
NEIL: Yeah, here you are, I've written it out for you, w...a...at least I've written out the ingredients.
JOAN: Oh thanks...Oh yeah, I see. Um...but what do I have to do?
NEIL: Well it's quite easy . . . Um...right, this is what you do: Um...first of all you boil or steam the potatoes, but make sure you do it...er...in their skins, they've got to be in their skins and you've got to do it for ten minutes, so don't peel them first. Er...and then you drain them, then after you've done that you peel them, you might have to let them cool down a bit because they'll be very hot!
    Er...then you want to cut them into cubes, I'd say about...er...two centimetres square and...er...then let them...let them cool properly. Er...then you heat the...your oil in a frying pan, um...I use just ordinary vegetable oil, I usually find that's fine. And when the oil's hot you want to throw in...um...the sesame seeds. Mm...and then they'll start to pop and as soon as they do that you add the potatoes, and you want to fry them for about...er...I don't know about five minutes. Just keep stirring them, keep stirring all the time so they don't stick to the bottom. Then you add the cayenne pepper, and the salt...er...and...er...you squeeze on the lemon juice. And...um...just keep frying the...er...spuds till they're, you know, crisp and brown.
JOAN: Lovely.
NEIL: And...um...you can serve them with anything really...er...any meat dish, chicken, fish, whatever, or on their own, great.
JOAN: Brilliant, I can't wait to get home to try it.
NEIL: No, good luck.

(B)
Imagine that you're talking to a friend on the phone as you explain the recipe in Activity *55*. Then do the same with the recipe in *60*.

(C)

SUGGESTED ANSWERS
a letter to a friend: 2 and 5
a magazine article: 4 (and maybe 1 and 2)
a recipe book: 1
a story: 3

1 step-by-step impersonal instructions: 'removing only the rind'
2 personal references: 'our family'; informal language: 'that's the outside part'
3 past tenses
4 information and facts: 'available in cans and bottles'
5 personal references: 'you asked me to send' 'All you need'

Guidelines for evaluating your written work are given in Activity *61*.

MODEL COMPOSITION

Dear Les,

   You asked me to send you the recipe for a typical national dish. The one I've chosen is something I'm sure you'll enjoy cooking and eating, but it's one you've probably never tried before. It's called:

Blackberry Fool
To make it you need:

$\frac{1}{2}$ kilo fresh blackberries (frozen ones
   will do)
200 g sugar
3 eggs
$\frac{1}{2}$ litre milk
$\frac{1}{4}$ litre cream

Cook the fruit on a low heat with half of the sugar until soft (about 15 mins). Meanwhile, beat the eggs with the rest of the sugar in a bowl. Heat the milk to just below boiling point and pour it slowly onto the eggs and sugar, stirring all the time. Then put the bowl into a pan of almost boiling water and keep stirring until the mixture thickens (about 5 mins). Then remove the bowl and put the custard you have made in the fridge.

Rub the cooked fruit through a sieve and put the purée you have made in the fridge.

When everything is cold, whip the cream. Then fold the cold custard into the purée and then fold in the cream too.

Serve in a large glass bowl or individual glass dishes.

It's quite tricky to make but you'll find it's absolutely delicious!

Best wishes,

Education   Schools, colleges and universities

You never stop learning

 Education
VOCABULARY

A   Here is some useful vocabulary:

*active   chemistry   college   discover   experiment
globe   goggles   group work   hands-on   high school
information technology (IT)   involved   knowledge
lecture   lecturer   lesson   maths/mathematics   overall
passive   physics   primary school   pupil   school uniform
science   secondary school   skill   taking notes   tutor
tutorial   university*

B   **1**

ANSWERS
1 state   2 co-educational   3 primary
4 comprehensive   5 curriculum   6 pupils
7 head teacher   8 timetable   9 staff
10 exams   11 subjects   12 courses
13 compulsory   14 optional   15 sixth form
16 higher   17 university   18 eighteen

 If . . . sentences – 2
GRAMMAR REVIEW

A

ANSWERS
1 I would have been able to do my homework (*yesterday*) if I hadn't had a headache (*yesterday*).
2 I would be able to do my homework (*now*) if I didn't have a headache (*now*).
3 I'll be able to do my homework (*tomorrow*) if I don't have a headache (*tomorrow*).
4 I'm not doing my homework (*now*) because I've got a headache (*now*).
5 I won't be able to do my homework (*tomorrow*) unless my headache has gone (*tomorrow*).
6 I would be able to do my homework (*now/tomorrow*) if I hadn't missed the lesson (*yesterday*).

B   **1**

ANSWERS (Some variations, particularly in the use of contractions, are possible.)
2 If ***I had known where you lived, I could have got*** in touch with you.
3 He ***would have got a higher mark if he had studied*** harder.
4 If she ***had been less lucky/had not been so lucky, she would/might have done badly*** in the test.
5 If they ***hadn't had so much studying to do during the vacation, they could have gone*** on holiday.

2

ANSWERS

6 I *would have remembered to post the letter if I hadn't been* so busy with my work.

7 If she *had done more/some work at school, she wouldn't feel sorry* now.

8 I *couldn't have finished the work on time without your* help.

9 If he *had been learning English for longer he would/might be able* to speak it better.

C 1

SUGGESTED ANSWERS

2 would have been   3 wouldn't have
4 would have been   5 would have passed
6 wouldn't have   7 had taken up
8 would have learned   9 would be
10 might not be   11 was   12 would be
13 would be   14 would get   15 might feel
16 might not like   17 would be   18 were
19 am

11.3 Happy days?
READING AND LISTENING

A 1

ANSWERS

1 b   2 c   3 b   4 c   5 b   6 c
7 d   8 b

2 It's a matter of opinion which answers seemed unfair. But, in the exam always choose the best answer. Other answers may be partly correct, but the best one is completely correct.

B

ANSWERS

¶1 gym shoes   recklessly   slithered   abrupt
¶6 in (a bit of) a quandary
¶8 reluctant   conceal   obscure
¶10 from hearsay   ajar   trim

D 1

ANSWERS

1 Neil   2 Cecilia   3 Nick   4 No one
5 Kate   6 Adam

TRANSCRIPT *3 minutes*

NICK: Um...er...I remember actually getting on a bus to go to secondary school and I did something that was...um...completely against the rules, which was sitting on the back seat...er...where the prefects sit and the whole bus went quiet – actually they were quite nice about it – though they made us all sing a hymn going back...um...from school, back home, because that's what they made all the first years do.

KATE: Yes, I couldn't wait to get to school because my brother was there already, so I wasn't in the least bit unhappy about it. And my first teacher was Sister Francis of Assisi and...er...she was a sweet...sweet woman who squeezed my cheek so affectionately and so tightly it hurt me for the rest of the day.

ADAM: Well I kind of remember my first day at school, but it was a long time ago. It was in New York City and I remember taking a bus across town and...and I was going to a private school so I was wearing a uniform which was like little grey shorts and things, which in New York probably didn't make me too popular. I remember being stared at by the other kids when I was on the bus with my mother. And then we got to the school and my first teacher was called Mrs Norton and she was really really nice on the first day and then for the rest of the year she was just horrible. That's mostly what I remember about school is how nice that nasty teacher was when the parents were there.

CECILIA: Well, I don't really remember too much about the first day, the actual day, but I remember...um...the preparations in the morning, because I was going to school and I was only four and I thought, 'Yeah, I'm really clever, I'm going very early to school'. And...um...my mum made me this huge breakfast and I had everything I wanted that whole morning and I was just really spoilt. And...um...on the way to school we stopped and I said, 'Oh' – and I just felt I was in complete control, I remember that, my mum was doing anything I wanted – and we stopped and I had a cake in the morning. And I never forgot that because I was never allowed to do it again after that.

NEIL: I remember going to secondary school and...um... because it was down the road I went in with my friend Glyn Daley, who also lived sort of...he lived next door to me, and so we walked in together. And all I remember was the pair of us walking in and being surrounded by these *enormous* people...er...most of whom had crew cuts and sort of big bovver boots, and being absolutely terrified – and that was just the girls!

11.4 Compound words – 2
WORD STUDY

A 1 📼 (The correct answers to 1, 2 and 3 are recorded. Pay attention to the pronunciation.)

SUGGESTED ANSWERS

coffee break   computer program
exercise book   further education
general knowledge   high school
higher education   instant coffee
intelligence test   personal computer
railway station   restaurant owner
savings account   school teacher
sports ground   staff room   story telling
tea cup   television set   tennis court
university professor   wholemeal bread

There are many other possible answers:
general education   high ground
personal knowledge   sports teacher
university education etc.

2

SUGGESTED ANSWERS

breadcrumbs   chairman*   classroom
headache   homework   housekeeping
notebook   playground   postman*
schoolgirl   taxpayer   timetable   toothache
toothbrush   toothpaste

There are many other possible answers:
housework   schoolbook   schoolroom
taxman etc.

(*Many people prefer to use the terms *chairperson*
and *letter carrier* or *postal worker*.)

3

ANSWERS

blue-eyed   brand-new   curly-haired
good-looking   kind-hearted   last-minute
narrow-minded   old-fashioned   right-handed
short-sighted   sun-tanned   well-behaved

There are other possible answers:
good-hearted   short-haired etc.

11.5 In . . .
PREPOSITIONS

SUGGESTED ANSWERS

1 in other words   **2** in common   **3** in a hurry
4 in all   **5** In general   **6** in tears   in prison
7 in confidence   **8** in trouble
9 in public   in private   **10** in particular

11.6 Using your brain
LISTENING

ANSWERS

1 right-hand
2

LEFT (rational side)	RIGHT (irrational side)
language	rhythm
numbers	*colour*
linearity	*imagination*
analysis	*day-dreaming*
logic	space: three dimensions
lists	seeing *collections* of
sequencing	things as a whole

3 reversed
4 corpus callosum   successful thinking
5 12 multiplied by 137
6 directly above this chair in the room upstairs
7 look to the right   visual information
8 close their eyes
9 do not get worse
10 stimulation   exercise

11 fresh air/oxygen   lifestyle
12 Three Golden Rules:
   a) in an abstract, logical way   visually
   b) both halves
   c) you can't solve a problem   just as good

TRANSCRIPT   *5 minutes 50 seconds*

. . . so you see the human brain weighs about $1\frac{1}{2}$ kilos. It contains ten to fifteen thousand million nerve cells. Now, each nerve cell can connect with any number or combination of other neurons – that's what you call a nerve cell, a neuron – the total number of possible connections of course is enormous. Now, if you wanted to type that number so you'd have...get an idea of how many combinations there are, you'd have to start by typing a one, then follow that with ten million kilometres of zeros.

Every human brain has an unlimited potential – only a small fraction of neurons are used for...er...everyday routine tasks like eating, moving, routine work, etc. The rest are constantly available for thought.

Now, our brains consist of various parts, some of which control routine functions. But the important parts that make us into those marvellous thinking machines, we like to think we are, are the two hemispheres or the two sides of the brain: the left and the right. Now, the left hemisphere controls the right half of the body, that's right, the left controls the right, and the right controls the left half. Normally the left half of the brain is dominant.

Now, the left side, which is known as the rational side, controls the...these functions: language, numbers, linearity, analysis, logic, lists and sequencing.

The right side, which is known as the irrational side, sometimes people call it the artistic side of your brain, controls those things...er...which are...well, less specific perhaps: rhythm...er...er...colour, imagination, day-dreaming, space: spatial dimension, three-dimensional thought...erm...seeing collections of things as one, as a whole. One interesting thing is that left-handed people often have a dominant right hemisphere, and in this case the priorities of the things I've just mentioned are all reversed.

The corpus callosum is very important. That's corpus C O R P U S, callosum C A L L O S U M – you should make a note of that, it's very important – that's the link between the two hemispheres in the brain and it's the key to successful thinking, linking the two parts of the brain, so you don't use them independently.

By the way, you...you could try this experiment: you'll see the two halves being used. Ask someone two questions, one to do with numbers – er...you could say 'What's 12 multiplied by 137?', and the other one to do with space. For example, you could say, 'What piece of furniture is directly above this chair in the room upstairs?'. OK? Now, while they're trying to answer the first question, that was the...the numbers one, they'll probably look to the right to prevent being distracted by visual information, and while they're trying to answer the second, that's the spatial one about what's upstairs above the chair, they'll probably look to the left. But of course, some people just close their eyes and that ruins the whole test!

According to experts, as we get older our memories do not get worse. Er...that's just an old wives' tale. In fact, we forget things at all ages. If you *expect* your memory to be bad or to get worse, it probably will. Lack of stimulation, brain exercise and lack of interest can mean that you forget things more easily. Lack of concentration simply.

Ah, lack of fresh air can also lead to your brain being less efficient because it gets starved of oxygen, and an unhealthy lifestyle – take note – can also damage your brain: er...alcohol, smoke, um...pollutants in the air like lead, er...chemicals in food, they can all add to a generally deteriorating condition of the brain.

You've probably heard a lot of people say 'I'm not brainy' or 'That's too difficult for my brain' – but this is not true because everyone's brain has an equal potential.

There are a few rules, Golden Rules of brain power:
One: Use your senses: don't only think in an abstract, logical way. Try to imagine a problem visually.
Second rule: Use both halves of your brain. For example, if you're faced with...er...an abstract, logical problem, try thinking about it imaginative...er...try thinking about it imaginatively. Or if you're faced with a creative problem, try to analyse it. Think logically about it.

And don't ever say you *can't* solve a problem because your brain is just as good as anyone else's.

11.7 Use of English: Correcting errors
EXAM TECHNIQUES

A The wrong answer is 5, where the superfluous word is *much*, not *to*.

B 2

ANSWERS
6 on	7 still	8 the	9 ✔	10 ✔
11 we	12 so	13 it	14 with	15 to

11.8 Advantages and disadvantages
WRITING

B Here are some model notes – not all of which can be included in a 150-word article.

ADVANTAGES
Everyone gets a chance to speak – not just the more confident students
You don't feel so self-conscious
You can express yourself without feeling embarrassed
Not being corrected helps to develop fluency
It's more like real life
You're more active
You're more likely to remember things you've worked out for yourself

DISADVANTAGES
Your mistakes aren't corrected
Some students don't always talk in English
It can be noisy

C Activity *61* includes some questions which will help you check your written work.

---

12 What shall we do this evening?

12.1 Just for fun
VOCABULARY AND LISTENING

A Here is some useful vocabulary:

*accident   action   adventure   affair   chase   comedy
drama   fall off   fight   get into trouble   motorbike
seduce   sexual harassment   thriller*

B 1 🔲

ANSWERS

	Joan	Chris	Bob
action films	✗	✗	✔
old black and white films	✔		✔ (*westerns?*)
cartoons	✗		
horror films	✗		✔
romantic comedies	✔	✗	✗
thrillers	✗		✔
westerns		✗	✔
dubbed foreign films		✗	✔
foreign-language films with subtitles	✔	✔	✗

TRANSCRIPT   *3 minutes*

1 CHRIS: So, Joan, what films do you like?
  JOAN: Mm, quite gentle sort of slow-moving films, I like, such as romantic comedies...um...the old black and white films I like very much and some European films that are subtitled I like very much. Um...I don't like thrillers, I really don't like being frightened in the cinema, I know it's not for real, but I don't like thrillers. I don't like action films as well, for the same reason. Um . . .
  CHRIS: Do you like horror films?
  JOAN: No, not at all and I...and I don't like cartoons either.

  JOAN: Now, Chris, tell me: what sort of films do you like?
2 CHRIS: Well, I...I prefer foreign films, by and large, although not dubbed films. I...I can't bear dubbed films, I think dubbing is a ridiculous thing to do to a film. I only really go and see foreign films...er...they have to have subtitles, although I...I'm very fluent in French so I prefer to try and ignore the subtitles if possible and just listen to the...er...the language. Um...other than that really I can't bear action films or sort of those horrible American romantic comedies, I can't stand. Um...same is true of westerns, I'm afraid, they again leave me very cold, I don't like those at all.

  JOAN: So Bob, tell me, what sort of films do you like?
3 BOB: I like action films me, yeah, big ones, the bigger the better...er...you know, specially if they've got special effects because I do like special effects. I do like lots of sparks, lots of things blowing up, lots of things going up in flames, up in smoke, and...er...yeah, that's great, I love that. And I also like...er...westerns, er...er...you know, because it's so great actually: big feel to it and great scenery usually, specially in, you know, in the old ones. And...er...I like...er...what else do I like? I like thrillers, I like...I like a good cop

chase, I do with police things and lots of suspenseful things, which is the same reason I like...er...I like the horror films.

JOAN: Could you tell me what sort of films you don't like?

BOB: Well, I'm not keen on foreign films on the whole. No, I don't...it's just...I don't mind them...it's just if they've got those subtitles, I don't like them. Er...I don't mind them so much if they're dubbed because at least I can follow the action. But...er...what else? Erm...and I don't like, I get a bit bored if they're you know too romantic, because I don't really like that much, because I like action.

ANSWERS

Ritz Film Centre				
5 screens all with Dolby Stereo Surround Sound				
DUMB AND DUMBER 12	12:30	3:30	**5:20**	9:00
TIMECOP 12	11:20	3:35	5:55	8:10
I LIKE IT LIKE THAT 15	**1:15**	3:45	5:55	**8:50**
DISCLOSURE 18	1:05	3:25	5:40	8:35
Movie Classics: CASABLANCA U			6:30	9:00
recorded information 774112		credit card bookings 774422		

TRANSCRIPT *2 minutes 20 seconds*

WOMAN: Thank you for calling the Ritz Film Centre. Here is information about films showing from today until Thursday next.

Screen One is showing *Dumb and Dumber* starring Jim Carrey and Jeff Daniels, certificate 12. Performances begin at 12.30, 3.30, 5.20 and 9 pm.

Screen Two is showing *Timecop* starring Jean-Claude van Damme, certificate 12. Performances begin at 11.20, 3.35, 5.55 and 8.10 pm.

Screen Three is showing *I Like It Like That* starring Lauren Velez and Jon Seda, certificate 15. Performances begin at 1.15, 3.45, 5.55 and 8.50.

Screen Four is showing *Disclosure* starring Michael Douglas and Demi Moore, certificate 18. Performances begin at 1.05, 3.25, 5.40 and 8.35.

And in our Movie Classics season Screen Five is showing *Casablanca* starring Humphrey Bogart and Ingrid Bergman, certificate U. Performances begin at 6.30 and 9 pm.

All seats may be booked and paid for in advance by calling this number 774422 with your credit card details. Thank you for calling the Ritz Film Centre.

12.2 Groundhog Day
READING

 1

ANSWERS
1 romantic comedy
2 He starts the same day again.
3 He's a weather forecaster and he reports from Punxsatawney on the festival.

B The answers depend on the questions that you noted down.

ANSWERS
True: 2 6
False: 1 3 4 (*at least not in the long run – he gets no satisfaction*) 5

ANSWERS
¶2 predicament   loathsome   dead-end career
¶3 ingenious   it dawns on him
¶4 be back to square one
¶5 fluffs it   rebuffed   jerk
¶6 reeling
¶7 churlish   dazzling

12.3 -ing and to . . . – 2
GRAMMAR REVIEW

ANSWERS
Verbs followed by *-ing*:
   imagine   stop   leave   spend time

Imagine having to live your life . . .
you can stop worrying . . .
The horror of Murray's situation leaves you reeling.
and spend his time in the local library, studying Western philosophy

Verbs followed by *to . . .*:
   wake up   try   have   forced

you wake up . . . to discover . . .
if you're trying to make Andie MacDowell fall in love with you . . .
you'll have to start again.
Yet he is forced to live . . .

B **1**

SUGGESTED ANSWERS
2 sneezing   3 to stop talking   talking
4 to help her (to carry them)   5 to do it
6 to be ill   7 to make the speech
8 to rain/raining

ANSWERS (Some variations are possible.)
2 I'm **not used to dressing up** when I go out for the evening.
3 Would **you prefer to go** to the cinema or theatre?
4 I can't afford **to go to/to eat at such an** expensive restaurant.
5 They didn't **stop smoking** all through the meal.

6 The drive was so *tiring that we stopped to* have a break.

7 I'll always *remember going to (see)* Walt Disney's *Pinocchio* when I was little.

8 Oh no, I *didn't remember to* phone my uncle!

12.4 **Rewriting sentences**
EXAM TECHNIQUES

 In 3 both answers have changed the word, and the second also has too many words. In 4 the first answer has changed the meaning, and the second has changed the word. (In the exam a contracted form, such as *she's* or *haven't*, counts as two words. However, using or not using a contraction would never bring the total number of words below two or above five in an exam question, as this would be unfair.)

ANSWERS
1 I*'d rather not* go out this evening.
2 You'll find *it impossible to* get a ticket for the show unless you book in advance.
3 I *don't approve of* violent films.
4 *Some Like It Hot is supposed to be* a really funny film.

B

ANSWERS
5 If I *were/was/felt more energetic I would/might* feel like going out for a walk.
6 When the film *was over we went* to have a pizza.
7 We *arrived early so* that we didn't have to queue.
8 There is a *big difference between* watching a film on video and at the cinema.
9 After *reading the reviews of* the film I decided not to go and see it.
10 You laughed at all the jokes, *so you must have enjoyed* the show.

12.5 **Words + prepositions – 1**
PREPOSITIONS

A

ANSWERS
1 for   2 with   3 for   4 of
5 with   about   6 in   7 from   8 for
9 about   10 from   11 of   12 on
13 of   14 for   15 of

12.6 **Using suffixes – 1: Adjectives**
WORD STUDY

A 1

ANSWERS
1 showing care   not showing care
2 not giving pain   giving pain
3 unable to help   willing to help
4 showing tact   not showing tact

2

ANSWERS
delightful   endless   hopeful/hopeless
powerful/powerless   restful/restless
speechless   successful   thoughtful/thoughtless
useful/useless

B

ANSWERS
-able   comfortable   enjoyable   fashionable
preferable
-al   educational   emotional   traditional
-ical   geographical   philosophical
-ish   foolish   oldish   smallish   tallish
youngish
-y   bloody   cloudy   dirty   noisy   rainy
sleepy

 The answers are recorded, as well as the *-ible* words in the note.

C

ANSWERS
2 thoughtful   3 musical   4 childish
5 sunny   6 readable   7 geographical
8 reddish   9 unreliable   10 unforgettable

12.7 **Short sentences? Or long ones?**
WRITING

A Although the first paragraph is probably the most interesting to read, perhaps the second is more the kind of paragraph that you should aim to write – long complex sentences often lead to pitfalls and errors.

Instead of repeating *he* and *she* so much, giving the person a name would reduce the dullness of the second and even the third paragraphs.

C MODEL REVIEW

'Barcelona' is an American film set in Spain. It was made on a small budget and there are no famous stars in it – apart from the two main characters all the actors are Spanish, talking English most of the time.

It's about two male cousins who grew up disliking each other. Now, in their twenties, they meet up again. One cousin works for a company in Barcelona and the other, who is an officer in the US Navy, arrives unexpectedly to stay in his flat – and share his life. The story is about how they get on each other's nerves, their involvements with local girls, and the local pro- and anti-American attitudes.

The most enjoyable thing about the film is the dialogue: it's a film full of words and without any violence or anything shocking. You have to listen carefully to catch all the jokes, because the actors are sometimes hard to understand, but it's worth the effort.

The only fault I can find is that the film is rather too long. There are times when you wonder what's going on and where things are leading.

It's an intelligent, witty film which I heartily recommend. The ending will certainly take you by surprise. See it if you can!

Books and magazines   Prescribed books

Read any good books?

 13.1 ## A good read
VOCABULARY

 B

ANSWERS
1 literature   2 characters   3 glossary
4 chapters   5 index   6 publisher
7 message   8 well-written   9 favourite
10 put it down   11 minor   12 borrow

C

ANSWERS
1 central   main   principal
2 entertaining   readable   true-to-life
3 amusing   believable   likeable
4 convincing   realistic   true-to-life
5 biographies   textbooks   non-fiction
6 bear   enjoy   stand

Look at all the wrong answers in B and C because there's a lot of useful vocabulary there too.

D

ANSWERS
1 library   bookshop/bookstore   2 author
3 paperback   4 title   cover   5 biography

E Here's more information about each book:

500 Mile Walkies is an amusing account of the author's walk around England's South-West Peninsula Coastal Path with his dog – it's all about the people he meets and the conversations he has with them.

Alaska is a very long novel about Eskimos and Russian and American explorers and colonists trying to survive in a hostile environment. The action spans thousands of years and it's a blend of historical fact with fictional narrative.

Empire of the Sun is the story of an English boy living in China, who is separated from his parents during the Second World War. He is imprisoned in a Japanese internment camp, where he has many exciting and amusing experiences. It's a semi-autobiographical story, based on J.G. Ballard's own boyhood experiences. (Made into a movie by Steven Spielberg.)

13.2 The Great Gatsby
READING

B The simplified version omits a great deal of detail, some difficult words and similes:

came and went like moths
scampered like a brisk yellow bug

but there are also some additions:

water-skiing
a dance floor was laid down on the lawn
with dozens of waiters to serve it
I remember the sense of excitement at the beginning of the party.
The party has begun.

C The main points of the description are given in both versions – though the details may be different. Questions 5 and 6 refer to information that's only given in one of the versions.

ANSWERS

2 They swam, lay in the sun or water-skied – *simplified version*
They dived, took the sun (or took motor-boat rides) – *original version*
3 His big open car – *simplified version*
His Rolls-Royce – *original version*
4 Eight – *both versions*
5 With a special machine – *original version*
6 On a special dance floor laid down on the lawn – *simplified version*
7 In the main hall – *both versions*
8 A big group of musicians – *simplified version*
No thin five-piece affair but a whole pitful of all kinds of instruments – *original version*

13.3 Reading habits
LISTENING

A 1&2 📼

ANSWERS

1 85 electronic noise
2 inexpensive/cheap portable
3 bookmark
4 one airport plane beach
5 best-selling/established authors
6 John Grisham – *The Pelican Brief* (1c) Barbara Vine – *Gallowglass* (2e) John Le Carré – *The Night Manager* (3a) Judith Krantz – *Dazzle* (4b) Michael Crichton – *Rising Sun* (5d)

TRANSCRIPT *4 minutes 40 seconds*

PRESENTER: According to a recent survey, 85 per cent of American adolescents quote: 'can no longer take in a printed page if their act of reading does not have an accompanying background of electronic noise' end of quote. And many students nowadays seem to need a background noise of music on headphones to cut out outside distractions. But are we reading less these days? Will the days of books soon be over? I have with me Jason Marshall from the Booksellers' Association.

JASON: Well, there are two questions really. First, will other entertainments – computer games, videos, TV and so on – stop people reading, and second will the new technology – that's CD-ROMs, laptop computers and books recorded on cassettes and so on – will these things provide substitutes for the printed page?
Well, the main advantage that books have over all these media is that they're relatively inexpensive and they're very portable. I mean, you can take a book with you wherever you go, it doesn't break down if you get sand inside it, you don't need batteries and you can put it down and pick it up whenever you like – the only equipment you need is a bookmark.

PRESENTER: Haha, yes – a very good point!

JASON: Now, according to the survey, many people only buy one book a year – as holiday reading. They probably buy it at the airport on their way to the sun and they read it in the airport (while their flight is delayed), on the plane and on the beach of course.
Nevertheless, books by best-selling authors are selling more and more copies every year not fewer.

PRESENTER: That's good, isn't it?

JASON: Mm. All the signs are that people are spending more and more money on books. The most popular books are books by *established* authors – that's writers who've developed a product that their readers know they'll enjoy and whose books they'll 'collect'.

PRESENTER: Who do you mean by 'established authors'?

JASON: Well, for example, John Grisham. He's an American lawyer and the main character in his books is usually a lawyer. Many of his books have been filmed. One of his best sellers was *The Pelican Brief* . . .

PRESENTER: Oh, what was that about?

JASON: It's about a beautiful young law student who is trying to find out why two judges have been murdered.
Another established author whose books are always best sellers is Ruth Rendell. Her books are also about crimes and about strange people who commit crimes or who find it hard to live in society – her characters are never glamorous.

PRESENTER: Yes, she's very popular, isn't she?

JASON: Mm. She writes books under her own name and also under the name...um...Barbara Vine as pen name. For example *Gallowglass*, which is about a clever young man's plan to kidnap a rich young woman. The story teller is rather pathetic, a stupid young man, who becomes the clever one's partner – or more like his servant really.

PRESENTER: Anyone else?

JASON: Yeah, John Le Carré: he's British and his books are mostly about spies – he used to be a spy himself. For example, *The Night Manager* is about a man who used to be a spy who now works as a hotel manager. He has to catch the world's most dangerous arms dealer. Now . . .

PRESENTER: Mm, sounds interesting.

JASON: Mm, yes, it's a great book, a great book. Judith Krantz i...er...completely different, is another established writer. Now, she lives in California, is married to a movie producer and used to be a fashion editor. All her books are best sellers. *Dazzle* is about a rich and beautiful woman. She's a world-famous photographer and three different men are in love with her. Her enemies are the members of her own family.

PRESENTER: So those people are really writing from their own experience?

JASON: Well, partly yes. Or they're using it as a background, you know, I'm not saying it's all completely accurate.

Then there's Michael Crichton, who used to be a doctor. Now, his books are thrillers, many of which have been made into films. For example, um...*Rising Sun?*

PRESENTER: No, I don't know it.

JASON: It's about a man who is trying to find out why a young woman has been murdered in an office in a Japanese company.

Now, apart from making their authors millionaires, the one thing that all these books have in common is that they're all 300 to 700 pages long, which is fine if you're used to reading . . . But the problem is that many people aren't. Now, reading tends to be something you enjoy more as you get older – but if you don't develop a taste for it when you're young, you may never discover the pleasures of getting involved in a good book.

PRESENTER: Mm, that's right.

JASON: Now, technology and its influence on reading is, as I said, another question. Will people who study need to buy textbooks in the future? Or will they just sit in front of computer screens and get all the information they need on the Internet? . . .

13.4 Joining sentences – 1: Relative clauses GRAMMAR REVIEW

ANSWERS

2 Agatha Christie, *who wrote detective stories*, died in 1976 when she was 86.
3 Her books, *some of which have been made into films*, have all been best sellers.
4 Hercule Poirot, *who is Belgian*, is Agatha Christie's most famous creation.
5 ✓
6 ✓
7 The victim's elder brother, *who lived in Paris*, was an accountant.
8 ✓

ANSWERS (Several variations are possible.)

2 New York, *which is a wonderful city, is a place I'd love to go to one day.*
New York *is a wonderful city, which I'd love to go to one day.*
3 Ms Fortune, *who was a writer, was found dead in the cellar.*
Ms Fortune, *who was found dead in the cellar, was a writer.*
4 My friend, *who is a great reader, told me all about a book he'd just read.*
My friend, *who told me all about the book he'd just read, is a great reader.*
5 The car *which was stolen was found at the airport.*
The car *which was found at the airport was stolen.*

6 Science fiction, *which is about the future and space travel, is loved by some people and hated by others.*
Science fiction, *which some people love and others hate, is about the future and space travel.*
7 The book *(which/that) you recommended to me was very good.*
The book *was very good which/that you recommended to me.*
8 A simplified edition, *which is easier to read than the original, is shorter.*
A simplified edition, *which is shorter than the original, is easier to read.*

ANSWERS

1 which	2 about	3 whose	4 who
5 who	6 whose	7 After	8 who
9 but	10 During	11 between	
12 but	13 until	14 When	15 after

13.5 Using suffixes – 2: Actions and people WORD STUDY

ANSWERS

1 very loud, loud enough to make you deaf
2 a person who is an expert in psychology (the study of how the mind works and human behaviour)   a doctor who is an expert in psychiatry (the study of mental illness), or who treats mentally ill patients
3 made simple
4 person who invented
5 given a subsidy (money to support)
6 person who takes photographs   person who creates works of art

ANSWERS

-ise/-ize	generalise memorise personalise summarise
-en	deafen loosen straighten weaken
-ify	intensify simplify

ANSWERS

-er	driver painter reporter speaker
-or	collector director editor inspector supervisor visitor
-ant	accountant assistant
-ent	correspondent
-ist	artist guitarist novelist pianist scientist violinist

D

ANSWERS
1 scientist(s)   assistants   2 widened   motorist
3 pianist   violinist   4 sharpening
5 rider   cyclist   6 inhabitants   immigrants
descendants   7 narrator   writer   8 classify

13.6 Words + prepositions – 2
PREPOSITIONS

ANSWERS
1 (introduce you) to   (involved) in
   (hope) for   (confidence) in   (lack) of
   (deal) with
2 (engaged) to   (married) to
   (forgive Bill) for
3 (depends) on   (exchange it) for
   (borrowed it) from
4 (insisted) on   (interfering) with

13.7 Writing against the clock
EXAM TECHNIQUES

If you are reading one of the set books, look at
Activity *19*.

MODEL LETTER

Dear Peter,

I felt I simply had to write to you
about the enclosed book, which I'm
sure you'll enjoy reading.

As you'll see from the cover it's by
David Lodge and it's called 'Nice
Work'. It's all about two people who
live close to each other in the same
city. One is a female university
teacher who lectures about English
literature, the other is the male
managing director of a factory. They
have nothing in common but they are
thrown together when the teacher
becomes the industrialist's 'shadow'
and spends one day each week with
him as part of a scheme to increase
co-operation between the university
and local companies. I won't spoil it
by telling you what happens in the
end!

You'll enjoy the humour of the
relationship and the contrast between
the world of the university and real
life in the factory.

When you've read it, let me know
what you think.

Best wishes,

All in a day's work

14.1 Earning a living
VOCABULARY

ANSWERS
1 profession   2 career   3 in
4 employee   5 permanent   6 promoted
7 training   8 pension   9 a salary
10 routine

C

ANSWERS
1 company   firm   organisation
2 makes   manufactures   produces
3 dismissed   fired   sacked
4 experience   personality   qualifications
5 department   staff   team

14.2 Paper 5: Speaking
EXAM TECHNIQUES

A This section can be done with a partner, but
it's better with a group of four. You can't do
it on your own.

14.3 Joining sentences – 2: Conjunctions
GRAMMAR REVIEW

ANSWERS (Some variations are possible.)
1 She's been looking for work
   since leaving university.
2 She sent in her application
   as soon as she saw the advertisement.
3 She felt very nervous
   before the interview.
4 She didn't do well in the interview
   even though she is intelligent and charming.
(5 She didn't think she'd get the job
   after the interview had gone so badly.)
6 The other candidates were well qualified
   so she wasn't very optimistic.
7 She was amazed that they offered her the job
   before she had even left the building.
8 She got the job
   because she had such good qualifications.

B 1

ANSWERS

2 I've brought my dictionary with me *even though it is (very/so)* heavy.

3 I phoned the office *to let them know* my time of arrival.

4 My friends were *having fun while* I was working.

5 If I *have enough time, I'll* go for a swim at lunchtime.

6 I'm going to try to get to work *despite the bus drivers' strike* tomorrow.

2

SUGGESTED ANSWERS (Many variations are possible.)

1 Getting *a part-time job would help you to pay for your course besides giving you useful experience.*

2 She can't *decide what kind of job she wants to do until she has finished her studies and got her degree.*

3 Although *some school subjects such as history seem irrelevant to the world of work, other subjects such as languages have a direct relevance and are likely to be useful in work.*

4 He's probably going to take *the new job that he has been offered in another city because, even though moving there would mean leaving his family, the job itself sounds really interesting and living in another city would be interesting too.*

C

SUGGESTED ANSWERS (There are lots of possible variations.)

2 A teacher who saved a kitten from drowning has been given a reward by its grateful owner.

3 Although the liner sank all the passengers and crew were rescued and there were no casualties.

4 After heavy rain in the mountains a landslide might destroy several villages.

5 A huge victory for the ruling party in the forthcoming general election is predicted because the President has promised to reduce taxes.

6 Due to a fall in the value of the pound sterling and a rise in the value of the US dollar, exports have risen during the past month.

7 The teachers have called off their threatened strike because the government has agreed to give them a pay rise.

8 Five hundred new jobs have been created now that a new factory has opened.

14.4 **First jobs**

LISTENING

A

ANSWERS

1 b	2 a	3 c	4 c	5 b	6 c
7 b	8 a	9 a	10 c		

TRANSCRIPT *4 minutes*

DAVID: Do you remember the...er very first job you ever had?

JILL: Yes, I certainly do. I wasn't very good at it actually. Um...it was as a secretary, I was supposed to be a secretary but I hadn't done very much secretarial training, and I went along – it was a design studio – and in fact I wanted to be a designer, so I used to sit around doing drawings all the time when I should have been typing letters, shorthand and typing. And...er...my boss went away for three weeks' holiday and there was...um...a horrible woman put in charge and she was very very nasty and got me into terrible trouble with my boss, who came back and gave me a big lecture and I ran home in tears and then I didn't go back and then several...several weeks later I had a letter from him saying: 'Please come back because the...' – now what did he call her? Something horrible, anyway, haha – 'She's gone' he said.

DAVID: So you went back?

JILL: 'And would you like to come back?' – No, I didn't. Tell me about yours.

DAVID: Oh mine, oh, straight out of school I worked in a library for six months, which was so boring it was untrue and the...the only excitement we got out of the day was seeing people come in the door which was at the far end and we would all decide between ourselves what sort of book they were going to take out, right? So they'd come up to the desk and you'd...you'd sort of say: 'Oh, she's going to get an Agatha Christie.' 'No, no, no she's into cars,' you know. And then of course it would turn out to be something totally different. We...we used to have a point system, you know, you'd score points according to... But apart from that I would never ever go back to work for a library, but what I do know now is how to get...how to find my way round in a library. So if you find yourself in a library you don't know, you can find your way around. That's the only part I enjoyed about it.

RICHARD: Well, the first job I had and certainly one of the best was straight after school and before I went to university, I had some months off, and I was fixed up with a job in Berlin as a postman in...in a...a quarter of Berlin called Spandau...Spandau. Er...and it was a lovely job. I find postmen the world over tend to be very friendly sort of people and the...there were a group of us Englishmen in there and the German postmen were wonderful, they sorted all our mail for us and everything, and took us round, got drunk with us after the round and... And...er...it was strange for me because I'm not used to getting up quite that early but I lived about an hour and a half away, the other side of the city, I had to get up at five in order to be there for half past six, do the round and I was back in bed by about one o'clock in the afternoon. Haha.

JOSCELYN: Was it well paid?

RICHARD: Well, it...for someone who had just left school it was quite well paid, yes. Er...it was...um...a German postman has to do far more than an English postman. They have to take the old-age pensions round and hand them out and collect various moneys and things, so it's a much more responsible job and I was amazed that they were giving me all this responsibility – an English schoolkid, basically, carrying thousands of pounds around with me, accountable for it in theory. But it was great fun.

JOSCELYN: My first job was about the same time really, I suppose, I was leaving school, but I made a lot of money but it was an awful job: it was selling encyclopedias door-to-door in the United States and the pressure to sell was incredible. I mean, you had to go back every night and...and...and produce the goods and I found that I just used to burst into tears. They would drive you into an area that...where you didn't know the streets, you didn't know where you were, and they said: 'Well, we'll pick you up in four or five hours,' and there was no sort of steady wage, you had to sell in order to make any kind of money at all. And at first I was so timid I'd, you know, ring the doorbell and I'd expect them to slam the door in my face and of course they did. And after a while I thought: 'The only thing that's going to save me is a sense of humour here'. So I would make jokes, I would run through the sprinklers on the lawn and this seemed to....um...interest them. Haha. So I found myself getting asked in and I would spend the evening talking about everything else other than encyclopedias and then sort of towards the end I'd say: 'Oh by the way...' And they would buy them. It would be...yeah...

RICHARD: So you made a living out of it?

JOSCELYN: Yeah, I did, I did. Well, I put myself through college on it.

RICHARD: Fantastic!

B Four possible questions are:

* What did you have to do?
* What was enjoyable/dull about the work?
* How hard did you have to work?
* Would you like to do the same work again? Why/Why not?

14.5 Words + prepositions – 3
PREPOSITIONS

A

> **ANSWERS**
> 1 (preparations) for (suffering) from
>   (thank them) for
> 2 (reminds me) of (related) to
> 3 (rely) on (provide you) with (tired) of
>   (waiting) for
> 4 (suspected the man) of
>   (stealing the goods) from (paid) for
> 5 (share them) with
> 6 (welcome you) to
> 7 (succeed) in (revise) for
> 8 (worked) for (responsible) for
>   (complaints) from (resigned) from

14.6 How to create a good impression . . . READING

A 2

> **ANSWERS**
> DOs   1 3 4 5 6 7 8 9
> DON'Ts   2 10

3

> **ANSWERS**
> DOs   12 15 16 18 19 20
> DON'Ts   11 13 14 17

B 1

> **ANSWERS**
> 1 b 2 b 3 c 4 b 5 a 6 b

2

> **ANSWERS**
> 1 c 2 a 3 c 4 c 5 a 6 b

4 The article was written for school-leavers who are going to attend their first interview, not for experienced job-seekers.

Some more DOs:
* Look your best
* Send a good photo of yourself
* Appear to be confident: body language and good eye contact

Some more DON'Ts:
* Move your chair closer to the interviewer
* Offer the interviewer a cigarette
* Stand up and start walking around the room

C In the FCE Speaking paper you don't need to take your certificates with you (point 7) – but you do need to take your identity card or passport to prove you are who you say you are, and that someone else isn't impersonating you.

The other DOs that are relevant to the FCE Speaking paper are probably: 5, 6, 8, 9, 12 and 18.
And DON'Ts 2, 10, 13 and 14.

The other points are probably irrelevant, but if an examiner holds out her hand to shake yours, it's a good idea to be polite and respond!

14.7 Using suffixes – 3: Abstract nouns
WORD STUDY

A 1 & 2

> **ANSWERS**
> -ment agreement astonishment employment
>   encouragement entertainment
>   improvement replacement
>   retirement
> -ance insurance resistance
> -ence insistence preference
> -ion   collection creation decision
>   direction protection
> -tion production
> -ation imagination
> -al   approval proposal survival

B 1 & 2

ANSWERS

-ness	carelessness happiness loneliness nervousness politeness rudeness selfishness
-ance	importance significance
-ence	patience presence
-ity	formality popularity possibility reality security simplicity
-cy	efficiency fluency privacy proficiency

3

ANSWERS

anxious   free   strong   wise   bored   proud   hungry   thirsty

C

ANSWERS

1 difficulties   2 modernisation   3 useful
4 retrained   5 computerisation
6 knowledge   7 employment   8 awareness
9 recognition   10 replacement

14.8 Including relevant information
WRITING

A 2

SUGGESTED ANSWERS

Missing information in Letter 1:
– previous experience
– languages

Irrelevant information in Letter 1:
– height
– missing lectures and attendance record
– the question about working hours is answered in the advertisement itself

Other faults in Letter 1:
– the writer isn't 'selling' him/herself hard enough: 'I wonder if I might be suitable', 'my typing is quite good', etc.

Missing information in Letter 2:
– perhaps a bit more detail of previous experience?

Irrelevant information in Letter 2:
– 'at top of page 13'

15
How things work   Technology and science

Can you explain?

15.1 Science and technology
VOCABULARY

A   The photos show:

1 a remote control (or 'zapper')   **2** the sticky part of a Post-it™ Note, seen under a microscope
3 a computer keyboard   **4** a TV satellite dish on the roof of a house

B

ANSWERS

1 hydrogen   oxygen   **2** chemistry   physics   biology   **3** practical   **4** experiments   laboratory   **5** practice   **6** hardware   software   disk/hard disk/floppy disk
7 adjust/lower/increase/control   button   instructions/manual   **8** serviced   break down   repaired/fixed/mended   **9** carpenter   chisel/screwdriver/drill/plane/sander, etc.
10 screws/nails/glue – and various tools, presumably

15.2 Using the passive
GRAMMAR REVIEW

A

ANSWERS

It *was done* yesterday.
It *was being done* last week.
It *has already been done*.
It *will be done* eventually.
It *will have been done* before long.
It *had been done* earlier.
It *had to be done* at once.
It *may not have been done* yet.

B   Generally, the information given at the **beginning** and **end** of a sentence is the important or emphasised information. The last thing mentioned (at the **end** of the sentence) is usually more important.
However, in conversation, if you place a stress on information **within** the sentence you can emphasise that instead:

Camcorders were marketed by _Sony_ in 1982.
   (stress on _Sony_)
Camcorders were _first_ marketed by Sony in 1982.
   (stress on _first_)
. . . and so on!

SUGGESTED ANSWERS

1 Emphasis on *by an expert*.
2 Emphasis on *be repaired*.
3 Emphasis on *camcorders*.
4 Emphasis on *the year* (and Sony is unimportant).
5 Emphasis on *New York*.
6 Emphasis on *restaurants*.

C

ANSWERS (Some variations are possible.)

2 These particles **can't be seen without** a microscope.
3 Computers **are being used everywhere** nowadays.
4 Dangerous **chemicals must be kept** in a secure place.
5 Both Scotch Tape and Post-it™ Notes **are made by 3M**.
6 Intelligent life **will probably not be discovered** on other planets.
7 This room **hasn't yet been** cleaned.
8 No one is sure who **President Kennedy was shot** by.

D For your interest, these are the correct dates:

ANSWERS

aeroplane (1903)	bicycle (1840)
camcorder (1982)	computer (1943)
compact disc (1982)	light bulb (1878)
margarine (1869)	Post-it™ Notes (1980)
telephone (1876)	television (1926)
thermometer (1593)	

15.3 Paper 4: Listening
EXAM TECHNIQUES

A For further information on this paper consult *Cambridge Practice Tests for First Certificate* Teacher's Book and *Specifications and Sample Papers for the Revised FCE Examination*, available from UCLES.

B   These are the first two parts of a mock exam paper. Parts 3 and 4 are in 16.4.

1 Allow yourself 60 seconds to read the questions for Part 1.
2 Play each of the eight short situations **twice** in turn – don't play all eight all the way through non-stop. (In the exam, each situation is heard twice on the tape, but here we have only recorded each situation once, so you'll have to rewind each one to play it again.)
3 Allow yourself 45 seconds to read the questions for Part 2; play Part 2.
4 Rewind Part 2 and play it again.

ANSWERS

Part 1 1 B 2 C 3 C 4 B 5 B
  6 B 7 A 8 C
Part 2 9 ships 10 aircraft 11 weapon
  12 cooling systems 13 by-product
  14 substitute for rubber 15 stick
  properly/permanently 16 more sticky
  17 less sticky/leave a mark
  18 sang in a (church) choir

TRANSCRIPTS *11 minutes 20 seconds* – but if you play each part twice and pause for the specified time between playings, the whole sequence will take about *25 minutes*

PART 1

NARRATOR: These are the instructions that you will hear in the exam.

ANNOUNCER: Hello. I'm going to give you the instructions for this test and tell you about what you are going to hear. I'll introduce each part of the test and give you time to look at the questions.

Remember, while you're listening, write down your answers on the question paper. You'll have time at the end of the test to copy your answers onto the separate answer sheet.

The tape will now be stopped. Please ask any questions now, because you must not speak during the test.

NARRATOR: Then you'll be told to open your question paper and look at Part 1. Each piece is played twice.

ANNOUNCER: Look at Part 1. You'll hear people talking in eight different situations. For questions 1 to 8 choose the best answer: A, B or C.

NARRATOR: In the exam you'll hear each question and the three possible answers read out in full. (But we won't bother reading all the possible answers out now.)

ANNOUNCER: One. Listen to this woman talking to a friend. Why was she angry?

WOMAN: Well, they said that they'd send someone round on Monday, which was OK because...um...I don't work on Mondays. The only trouble was it was a beautiful day, really sunny and...er...I could have gone out for a walk, or gone shopping or something. Anyway, I waited in until 5.30 and nobody came, so I telephoned them and all I got was a recorded message telling me to call during office hours. And there was this programme I really wanted to see that evening. But the doorbell rang, and would you believe it, it was him. And I tell you I really gave him a piece of my mind!

ANNOUNCER: Two. You've taken your camera to a shop for repair. When is it going to be ready?

MAN: Mm, well, let's see, five days from today is Monday the 27th – ah ah ah, but that's a public holiday so...er...the workshop will be closed over the weekend. So...ah...let's say a week tomorrow, no no a week on Wednesday, but you'd better phone us on the Tuesday...um...just to make sure, I...I wouldn't want you to have a wasted journey.

ANNOUNCER: Three. Listen to this woman talking to a colleague. Why is she upset?

WOMAN: Well, you see, I left it on my desk during the lunch-hour and...er...and then when I got back it had gone. Well, to be honest actually I didn't notice it had gone till...er...Max brought it back later that day. Well, he said he'd just borrowed it for an hour or so. Er...he said he would have asked me but he couldn't find me. Anyway, he said he bought his own tape to use and that he took it out in the park to film his girlfriend and...er...and then when it started raining he...he said he put it back in the bag and it couldn't have got wet. Well that's what he said anyway. Well, I used it myself at the weekend and...and now the tape keeps going slow.

ANNOUNCER: Four. Listen to a man talking about a gadget. Why do the batteries need replacing?

MAN: No it'll probably be all right for a while but before too long it'll stop working. What's worse is that if you go on using it you may do permanent damage to the motor and replacing that will cost a lot of money. Did they put these batteries in for you in the shop?

WOMAN: Mm.

MAN: Well in that case it's their fault, they should have known they were wrong. My advice is to take it back to them and tell them that rechargeable batteries shouldn't be used – as it says in the instructions here, look.

WOMAN: Mm.

ANNOUNCER: Five. You're in the kitchen at a friend's flat. What does he want you to do?

MAN: Um...could you give me a hand please? Er...look I've tried opening it using this but it's stuck now. I think there must be some kind of special trick or knack you have to know – I've already made all this mess, look, and now I've cut my finger too. Ow. Could you take over and see if you can do it please? I should have asked you in the first place but...um...because you're much stronger than me.

ANNOUNCER: Six. Listen to a man talking to a colleague. What is he talking about?

MAN: Well, this red light keeps coming on and it makes a sort of buzzing noise. It was working all right earlier today. I...I've had it for a couple of months and I've never had any problems with it before. Look. I...I'll show you. I...if I feed the document in it, well, it grips it all right, then when I dial the number the red light will come on and I won't be able to send it, then this light will come on and, well, it won't go off again till I press the red button . . .

ANNOUNCER: Seven. Listen to a woman talking to a man. She's an expert, but what is she an expert in?

MAN: So...er...what do you think I should do?

WOMAN: Let's see. Have you tried turning it off and on?

MAN: Yeah, yes, but it...it still prints out like this. Look, look at this document. I can't send this to a customer, can I?

WOMAN: No, I see what you mean. Well looks to me as if the cable connection may be loose . . .

MAN: No no no no, it's OK I've checked it.

WOMAN: Really? Then it must be the driver software. Could I just sit down and try it myself? It's probably corrupted or something . . .

ANNOUNCER: Eight. Listen to this man talking. Who is he talking to?

MAN: So you see all you have to do is put a very small amount of the liquid on a damp cloth – only this much, no more. And then you rub the surface ever so gently, like this. And after just a few seconds the whole surface is sparkling. Now this remarkable product is only on special offer . . .

ANNOUNCER: That's the end of Part 1.

PART 2

ANNOUNCER: Part 2. Now you're going to hear part of a radio programme. For questions 9 to 18, complete the notes which summarise what the speaker says.

PRESENTER: . . . and good luck plays a part in scientific research too. In this case it's often referred to as serendipity, which, according to my dictionary, is 'the natural talent that some people have for finding interesting or valuable things by chance'. Debbie Charles has been looking into this for us. Debbie.

DEBBIE: That's right, Jenny. In fact, you know, most important discoveries in the world of science and technology came about by some sort of lucky accident. Starting with the wheel, presumably.

Now let's just look at a few of these, starting with...er...penicillin. Now, Alexander Fleming found some mould growing on a laboratory dish which he'd...er...absent-mindedly left on a window-sill. Now, he found that this mould stopped the spread of bacteria, which as you know is the cause of illnesses like pneumonia. And modern antibiotic drugs based on penicillin save millions of lives every year.

And then there's radar. Now, all sea and air transport depends on radar for navigation and safety – and armies depend on it for defence as well, of course. Radar was discovered during the war while British military scientists were trying to find a death ray, which was...er...some sort of radio wave that could be used to kill people. They didn't find a death ray, but they did find a technique.

And then there's...er...Teflon, which is a substance which is used in non-stick frying pans. Now, this was discovered by accident in a laboratory by DuPont scientists, who were doing research into gases to use in refrigerators. Now, they discovered that a plastic coating had formed on their equipment and this was unaffected by heat and it was also very slippery. Now, no use was found for this until some time later a French researcher used it in a frying pan – and...er... Teflon's also used in space vehicles.

And then there's artificial sweeteners: now, from saccharine to the more modern sweeteners, all of these (for example...ah...Cyclamate, Nutrasweet, etc.) were discovered by accident. The usual pattern was that scientists were...were doing another experiment and they happened to taste one of the by-products, which they found to be sweet. Some of these sweeteners are thousands of times sweeter than sugar, you know.

And then there's chewing gum, which was discovered while scientists were looking for a substitute for rubber. And again there seemed at the time to be no apparent use for this product of the...er...Mexican Sapodilla tree! But serendipity made this product – there's no country in the world where chewing gum isn't available...

PRESENTER: Haha, no, but...er...I'm not sure that that is quite as beneficial to mankind as the others you've talked about!

DEBBIE: Oh, maybe not. But here's one more very useful product. You know those...er...little yellow stick-on notes we use in the office and...er...for leaving phone messages and so on? Um...Post-it™ Notes, they're called I think. Well, a researcher at 3M (which is the firm that makes Scotch Tape) was doing research into adhesives and glue, and...er...he discovered a substance that seemed to be completely useless. I mean, it was...was quite sticky but it wouldn't stick permanently to anything. You know, that's what adhesives obviously are supposed to do. And in fact, however long he left the adhesive sticking to various surfaces, it didn't make a mark on the surface and the bond became no more and no less effective. All other adhesives either get more sticky or less sticky with age, you know. Now, he was a member of a church choir and he always had to use slips of paper to mark the place where each of the hymns was in his hymn-book – and the slips of paper kept falling on the floor. So he used these bits of sticky paper with this...er...'useless' adhesive on to mark his place in the hymn-book. And then he realised that other people could find a similar use . . .

PRESENTER: Brilliant!
DEBBIE: No, just serendipity!
PRESENTER: Haha. Yah. Thank you, Debbie.

15.4 Effortless cycling
READING

A

ANSWERS
1 F   2 E   3 G   4 H   5 B   6 A
7 I   8 C   (D is the odd one out.)

15.5 How do they do that?
LISTENING AND SPEAKING

A 1 The correct sequences are shown here:

How to juggle

You will need:
three bean bags, balls or any other small evenly-shaped objects of the same size

Facing a bare wall, imagine two spots about 30cms away, in front of your forehead. Keep concentrating on them at all times.

1d Practise tossing one ball from your right hand so that it passes through the imaginary spot on the left and is caught by your left hand.

2c Then toss it back to the right hand, making sure it passes through the spot on the right. Repeat this until you can toss one ball in an even figure-of-eight.

3b With a ball in each hand, start as before. When the first ball reaches the spot on the left, toss the second ball. Repeat this until both balls move evenly and you catch them every time.

4a Hold two balls in your right hand and one in your left. Begin as for two balls, but toss the third ball when the second one passes through the spot on the right as it makes its way to your right hand. Do not worry about catching the third ball at first. It is more important to learn when to toss it, aiming for the spot on the left when it leaves your right hand. Keep practising and you will improve.

TRANSCRIPT   *2 minutes 30 seconds*

JULIET: OK, now imagine that you've got two spots...er...about 30 centimetres away from your eyes...Yeah?
NICK: What, straight out in front?
JULIET: Straight out in front of you, yeah. Now I want you to con...keep concentrating on them at all times. OK, is that clear?
NICK: Right...yeah yeah.
JULIET: Right, now take one ball in your right hand and just practise throwing it from your right hand to your left hand, passing through that imaginary spot.
NICK: Wh...which one? The one on the –
JULIET: The one on the left-hand side.
NICK: So with the right hand through the –
JULIET: Through the left-hand spot...OK.
NICK: OK, like that...yeah...and then back.
JULIET: Now, take...the...the ball is now in your right hand, yeah? And you throw it back to the...um...left hand.
NICK: To the right hand.
JULIET: Oh, sorry, it's in the left –
NICK: It's in the left hand now, yeah.
JULIET: Oh right, it's in the left hand. So you throw it back to the right hand making sure it passes through the spot on the right...
NICK: On the right-hand side, OK, I see.
JULIET: Right, OK so far?...Now you repeat this until you can...you can toss the ball from one hand to the other in a...in a figure-of-eight, in an even figure-of-eight...Just keep doing that for a bit.
NICK: Is that right?
JULIET: That's good, yeah. That's OK so far. Right, now take the other ball...so you've got one ball in each hand now and then what you have to do is, when the first ball reaches the spot on the left, you then throw the second ball up.
NICK: Right, so I throw the right hand first, when it reaches the spot on the left, then I throw the left-hand ball and it's got to go through the spot on the right.
JULIET: Exactly, exactly, and you just repeat that until you've got both balls moving evenly and you catch them every time.
NICK: One, two...They've both got to go up, haven't they?
JULIET: Yeah. So when that one hits that point over there, at that point the other ball...yeah...but you want that one to go up as well.
NICK: One of them's going straight across, isn't it?...Hm...that was better, wasn't it?
JULIET: That was much better, yeah. You've got it, haven't you?...OK, that's great, great. Now, with two balls in your right hand...and one ball in your left...now what you're going to do is . . .

B Record your explanations on a blank cassette.

15.6 Opposites
WORD STUDY

A 1

ANSWERS
dishonest   unkind   illegal   unlucky
immature   unnecessary   impersonal
unpleasant   impolite   irregular   irrelevant
unsafe   untrue   invisible   unwilling

2

> **ANSWERS** (Many variations are possible.)
>
> modest   ugly   expensive   kind   safe
> empty   well/healthy/fit   confident
> quiet/silent   modern/up-to-date   polite
> hard/rough   fresh   loose   fast asleep
> right/correct

3

> **ANSWERS**
>
> lose   lower   fall   lie   lose   break
> finish/end   turn off

B

> **ANSWERS**
>
> **2** wet/rainy   **3** easy   **4** soft   **5** heavy
> **6** dark   **7** calm   **8** smooth   **9** pass
> **10** succeeded   **11** rich/wealthy/well-off
> **12** good   **13** Lucky   won   **14** found
> **15** gained

15.7 Coming and going
VERBS AND IDIOMS

A

> **ANSWERS**
>
> **1** come   **2** go   **3** take   **4** Come   bring
> **5** take (*or* bring)   **6** delivered
> (*or* taken/brought)   **7** fetch   **8** carry
> (*or* deliver/take/bring)

B

> **ANSWERS**
>
> **2** came across   **3** go with   **4** comes in   goes
> out   **5** gone off   **6** gone off   **7** went off
> **8** went in for   **9** Come on   **10** go on
> go over

15.8 Describing a process
WRITING

A   The first paragraph lacks detail and the second has rather too much irrelevant detail. These faults are ones to avoid when writing the composition in B.

B   MODEL EXPLANATION

> ### MICROWAVE OVENS
>
> Microwaves are a type of short-wave radiation, rather like radio waves. They are produced by a device called a magnetron which is housed inside the oven. The microwaves are reflected by metal surfaces but absorbed by food. They cause the molecules of the food to vibrate billions of times a second, making the food heat up and cook. Larger amounts of food take longer to cook so microwaves are especially effective when cooking small portions.
>
> The advantages of microwave cooking are that it is both quicker and cleaner than conventional cooking. Food that has already been cooked can be re-heated at any time without loss of flavour or juices, and frozen food can be defrosted and cooked very easily.
>
> Microwave ovens use less energy than conventional methods of cooking and are very safe. As soon as the door is opened, they automatically switch off and microwaves cannot normally leak out of the door while they are operating – despite some frightening stories about this!

16

Current affairs   Politics   Newspapers and the media

Keeping up to date

16.1 The press, politics and crime
VOCABULARY

B

ANSWERS
2 article   report   3 editorial   leader column
4 hostages   people   5 civil war   revolution
6 earthquake   explosion   7 election
referendum   8 PM   prime minister
9 arrested   caught   10 seized   stolen
11 gaol   jail   12 convicted   found guilty

16.2 What happened?
WRITING

A The stories these headlines are from can be found in Activities *3, 8* and *12*.

B & **C**

MODEL STORY

> We received this fax from St Lucia:
> 'One of our workers dropped her wedding ring in one of the boxes. Please can you find it?'
> When the shipment arrived it was my job to open up the crate and start searching. Just laying the bananas out on the floor took all morning. Then I had to pick up each bunch, shake it and then put it back into the box. By 6 o'clock there was just one more bunch to check.
> I picked up the bananas and shook them hard. There was a little ringing noise on the concrete floor. Success! I went straight to the office and sent a fax with the good news.
> The next morning, when I got to work, there was a fax waiting for me: 'Thank you! As a reward, we'd like to invite you to come to St Lucia for a free holiday.'

16.3 Shoplifting in America
READING

A 2

ANSWERS
A matches paragraph 3
B matches paragraph 4
(C matches paragraph 1)
D matches paragraph 7

E matches paragraph 6
F matches paragraph 2
G has no match
H matches paragraph 8
I matches paragraph 5

B

ANSWERS
¶1 bust   euphemism
¶4 merchandise   policing   weird
¶5 gimmicks   bonus   snatch
¶6 communal   collude
¶7 stunts   mock   sticky-fingered villain

C The 'right answers' are in Activity *56*.

16.4 Paper 4: Listening
EXAM TECHNIQUES

A Play the whole of Part 3 through, then rewind it and after a ten-second pause, play it again. Then, after a pause of 30 seconds, play the whole of Part 4 twice with a pause of ten seconds between each playing.

ANSWERS
Part 3
19 C   20 A   21 E   22 D   23 B

Part 4
24 BB   25 MM   26 MM   27 MM
28 TT   29 BB   30 MM

TRANSCRIPT   *4 minutes 20 seconds (not including pauses)*

PART 3

NARRATOR: You're going to practise Parts 3 and 4 of the Listening paper.

ANNOUNCER: Part 3. For questions 19 to 23, choose from the list A to F the best summary of what each speaker says. Use the letters once only. There is one extra letter which you do not need to use. You have 30 seconds to look at Part 3.

SPEAKER 1 (WOMAN): . . . Well, um...I...I...came back in the...er...er...in the middle of the afternoon and I saw a...a red Ford Fiesta it was, um...parked outside the building. I...I didn't recognise the car at all but the only reason I noticed it was because it was...er...because it was parked...um...at quite an unusual angle, you know, as if it had been abandoned or something. Anyway I...er...I called the lift and when it came these two young men got out, each of them was...was carrying a shopping bag. Well, I...I got upstairs and I...I opened my front door and everything was...was upside down. I...it was a real mess and...er...it took quite a long time to work out exactly what was missing. But...um...at least they didn't get away with the video.

SPEAKER 2 (MAN): . . . I was on my way to town and I stopped outside the bank to get some money. There was a parking space just outside, which was lucky, but...er...when I got into the bank this shopkeeper was in front of me paying in all his takings – thousands of pounds. And it all had to be counted. Well, I only wanted to cash a cheque. And while I was waiting, I...I couldn't help noticing this, well, rather dirty-looking man with long hair reading a newspaper, standing away from the queue. And, when the shopkeeper had finished, this man sort of looked around him and followed him out. Well, I...I cashed my cheque and went outside. And there was another car in the space where I'd left mine and I didn't realise at first what had happened because . . .

SPEAKER 3 (WOMAN):   . . . got away with a hundred thousand pounds, which is an incredible amount, I mean, more than most people earn in a lifetime. I mean, when I think of that man i...it makes my blood boil. And all the publicity he's got in the papers make...makes him out to be some kind of hero, wh...when in fact he's committed a terrible crime. I mean the trouble is with people like that i...if they go to prison, when they come out they've invested all the money somewhere and i...it earns interest while they're inside, and . . . Still people like that can pay for the best lawyers and they usually get away with it, don't they? I mean it's just not really very fair . . .

SPEAKER 4 (MAN):   . . . and I mean that's a really dreadful thing. A man's car is...is something special, you know. To do that to it and...and for no reason! I...I don't usually leave it in the street and...er...never again, I can tell you, but this time I did. I mean, I should have realised when I heard these guys outside in the night. I...I opened the curtains and I looked out to see what was going on and...and they must have seen the light from the window and th...they ran off. But it wasn't until I...er...went out the next morning to drive to work that I noticed the mark all down the side – I mean, they must have used a key or something. Honestly, if I catch those guys, I . . .

SPEAKER 5 (WOMAN):   He was driving down the road when this car overtook him, then it braked so suddenly that he nearly crashed into the back of it. Well, he jumped out and he was going to start swearing at the driver when this really glamorous young woman got out of the driver's seat and smiled at him so sweetly. Well, all his anger sort of vanished. She walked towards him and took hold of his arm and pushed him down onto the ground. Then she bent down, kicked him hard and put her hand in his pocket and grabbed his wallet. Then she drove off. He was so shocked he didn't even get the number of the car.

ANNOUNCER: That's the end of Part 3.

TRANSCRIPT   *3 minutes 30 seconds (not including pauses)*

PART 4

ANNOUNCER: Part 4. For questions 24 to 30, write 'TT', 'BB' or 'MM' in the boxes provided. You have 30 seconds to look through Part 4.

PRESENTER (KATHY):   The resignation of the Minister for the Family has raised again the topic of the press and what their role is in telling the world about the private lives of the rich and famous. I have with me Tony Towers, editor of the *Sunday Globe*, Bill Brown editor of the *Daily Echo* and Mary Matthews editor of *Hi!* magazine. First of all, Tony, good morning.

TONY TOWERS: Hello, Kathy. Yes, well it seems to me that there's absolutely nothing wrong with what we've been doing. The Minister was having an affair with his secretary, his marriage was about to break up and this is the man who was standing up in public talking about the importance of family and threatening to reduce benefits to single-parent families. He deserved what he got.

PRESENTER: Mary Matthews.

MARY MATTHEWS: Well, ...er...it seems to me that people who are in the public eye and who are making their living from appearing in public can't start making a fuss when...um...a magazine publishes photos of them lying by their swimming pools or...er...kissing the people they love. Well, after all in the end it's the public who are paying them and I...they don't really have the right to say when the public are allowed to see them and when they aren't. I believe that public figures can't really expect to live private lives.

PRESENTER: Bill Brown.

BILL BROWN: Y...yes, well I can't agree with Tony or Mary. First of all, the Minister's private life was his own affair . . . No, no, there's no reason, there is no reason why the things he does in private should affect his work. He was doing a perfectly good job and I don't see . . . I don't see why he shouldn't still be in office – in countries like...like France or Italy he still would be.

But...um...now as I see it you have to separate people's lives into a public side and a private side, whoever they are – famous people or members of the public. And, I mean, how famous do you have to be to...er...to forgo the right to privacy? Do *slightly* famous people like soap opera actors or...or newspaper editors lose their right to privacy? Now, I...I assume that even Tony would agree he himself has a right to privacy?

PRESENTER: Mm. Tony?

TONY TOWERS: Not if the public are interested, no . . . No! We don't publish details of Mr Jones having an affair with Mrs Smith next-door, simply because that wouldn't sell papers . . . Nobody would be interested (except Mrs Jones and Mr Smith!) . . . Ha. We try to report what our readers want to know about. They do want to know about soap opera characters and film stars, they don't want to know about my private life.

PRESENTER: Mary Matthews.

MARY MATTHEWS: Well, I...I don't actually agree there. People *are* interested in how other people live however ordinary they are. You know, one of our best-selling issues was the one where we interviewed the man who won the...er...lottery jackpot of £20 million and...er...didn't·want anyone to know who he was or where he lived. But...er...he was happy to talk to my magazine and...er...let us photograph him and his family in their new villa in Spain. And, you know, our readers really loved that article, and...er...he...he was pretty pleased too. Th...the point is that every person likes to be treated with respect, and...er...well, they have every right to object if they aren't.

ANNOUNCER: That's the end of Part 4.

16.5   The past – 3: Reported speech
GRAMMAR REVIEW

SUGGESTED ANSWERS

2 What's the time? / Do you know what the time is? / Could you tell me the time?

3 Have you had lunch yet (by any chance)?

4 Would you like to come for a walk with us? / Do you feel like coming for a walk with us? / How about coming for a walk with us?

5 Don't forget to make the/that phone call. / Remember you've got to make a phone call.

6 I've just got back from holiday.
7 Can you meet me here tomorrow? / Please meet me here tomorrow.
8 Do you think you could possibly help me with my work? / Would you mind giving me a hand with my work?

B

SUGGESTED ANSWERS

2 He asked her when she had set off.
3 He wondered how she felt now that she was home again.
4 He asked her what the worst moment of her voyage had been.
5 He asked her if she was pleased to be home.
6 He wondered if she would like to sail round the world again.

8 She told him (that) she had said goodbye to her family on 1 April and (that) she hadn't seen them again until that day.
9 She admitted (that) she felt very tired, but she was proud of what she had achieved.
10 She told him (that) the worst moment had been when the sails were torn in a storm.
11 She said (that) she was delighted to be back home because she had missed everyone terribly.
12 She told him (that) if she did it again, she would take her family with her on the trip.

14 She advised them not to spend so long on their own as she had just done.
15 She warned them not to expect her to be the same person she used to be.
16 She invited them to/She offered to take them to a fancy restaurant to celebrate her return.
17 She asked them to lend her some money and promised to pay them back the next day.
18 She told them to open the champagne because she wanted to celebrate.

16.6 Pauses and stress
SPEAKING

 A There is no single correct way to read any sentence. The pauses and stresses in the recordings are model readings. Moreover, some syllables are more strongly stressed than others.

B Record your readings on a blank cassette. Then compare your readings with the model versions.

16.7 *Put*
VERBS AND IDIOMS

 A

ANSWERS
(1 put on = switch on)
2 put out/off = switch off
3 put up = provide accommodation
4 put off = distract
5 put off = postpone
6 put up = raised
7 put on = gained
8 put down = write down
9 putting back = replacing
10 put away = remove to proper place
11 put forward   put back = change to later/earlier time
12 put through = connect to phone extension
13 put up with = tolerate
14 put off = discouraged

16.8 Paper 1: Reading
EXAM TECHNIQUES

A For more information about the Reading paper see *Cambridge Practice Tests for First Certificate* Teacher's Book and *Specifications and Sample Papers for the Revised FCE Examination*, available from UCLES.

B Choose a suitable test paper to do. Check your answers in the Teacher's Book.

16.9 Giving your opinions
WRITING

Ask someone to mark your composition. Ask them to point out what particular points you should be careful about in the exam.

What are **your** typical 'careless mistakes' of spelling and grammar, that you should notice when checking your work?

Different countries   Regions and people
Geography

17 It's a small world

17.1 Other countries
VOCABULARY

A Here are some adjectives that can be used to describe each photograph:

1 *comfortable   domestic   harmonious   uncomfortable traditional*
2 *busy   colourful   crowded   lonely   urban*
3 *intimate   kind   polite   private   thoughtful*
4 *active   independent   happy   lighthearted uninhibited*

B 1

ANSWERS

(top row, left to right) Portugal, Turkey, Japan, Spain, Poland, Germany, Australia
(bottom row, left to right) Italy, China, Switzerland, Ireland, Canada and Greece.
The two largest countries are Canada and China.
The two smallest countries are Ireland and Switzerland.

2

ANSWERS

Japanese	Spanish	Polish	German
Australian	Italian	Chinese	Swiss Irish
Canadian	Greek		

C 1

ANSWERS

1 important   2 century   3 image
4 employed   5 modern   6 blocks   7 cities
8 thinking   9 become   10 whether
11 safety   12 problems   13 understanding
14 chance   15 unique

2 & 3

ANSWERS

1 what   2 where   3 For   4 with
5 found   6 by   7 what/which/how/that
8 as   9 on/about   10 what
11 country/place   12 for   13 as
14 need/want/require   15 language

17.2 Comparing and contrasting
GRAMMAR REVIEW

A Here are two examples:

In 1950 there were far fewer retired people in Britain than now.
In 2025 there will be over twice as many retired people in Japan as there are now.

B

ANSWERS (with errors underlined and corrected)

2 The daytime temperature in Tokyo in July is the same <u>than</u> New York.
  as
3 There <u>are not much differences</u> between the weather in New York and Warsaw.
  is not much difference
4 The weather in Athens in July is <u>more warmer</u> than London.
  warmer
5 New York is <u>more cold</u> in winter <u>as</u> London.
  colder   than
6 There are <u>much less</u> wet days in Tokyo than in Warsaw.
  far fewer

C

ANSWERS

2 There isn't **as much rain in** Buenos Aires as in New York.
3 More **rain falls in Athens than** in Tokyo in January.
4 In July Buenos Aires **is much cooler than** New York.
5 About the same amount **of rain falls in London** as in New York.
6 Summer nights in London are **not as hot as in** Cairo.
7 Warsaw **is a colder place than** New York in winter.
8 New York and London **have the same number of** rainy days as each other.

17.3 A nice place
READING

A

ANSWERS

1 a   2 c   3 d   4 d   5 d   6 c

B

ANSWERS

¶2 courteous   ¶7 needless to say
¶3 squeezing   ¶8 citizens
¶4 agents   ¶9 consolation
¶5 award   ¶10 reasonably
¶6 manners

17.4 Not such a nice place
READING

A The original headline was: 'How to visit Miami and survive'.

B

ANSWERS

1 G 2 F 3 D 4 C 5 I 6 E 7 A
8 H (Sentence B doesn't fit anywhere.)

17.5 Stressing the right syllable
WORD STUDY

A 1

ANSWERS

verbs and *-ing* forms	nouns and adjectives
(They expórted the goods to the USA.	Tourism is an invisible éxport.)
(These bananas are impórted.	Ímports have risen this month.)
He insúlted me.	That was a terrible ínsult.
They perfécted a new method.	Your work is not quite pérfect.
Smoking is not permítted.	You need a pérmit to fish in the river.
His work is progréssing well.	New Prógress to First Certificate.
They protésted about the situation.	They held a prótest meeting.
Listen to the recórding.	Have you heard their new récord?
He is suspécted of the crime.	He is the main súspect.

B 1

ANSWERS

(emplóy   emplóyer   emplóyee
emplóyment   applý   applicátion)
ádvertising   advértisement   attráction
certíficate   cómfortable   communicátion
députy   désert   dessért   desírable   détails
devélopment   expérience   gírlfriend
informátion   intélligence   machíne
pérmanent   phótograph   photógraphy
qualificátion   recéptionist   reservátion
secretárial   sécretary   télephone
teléphonist   témporary   themsélves
tóothache   végetable   yoursélf

C 1

ANSWERS AND TRANSCRIPT

2 It takes móst péople a lóng tíme to perféct their pronunciátion in Énglish.
3 Nórwich is pléased to púll óff a níce óne.
4 We fóund Nórwich to be a cíty with a smíle.
5 We're réasonably níce to éach óther, but I'm súre that mány óther tówns are équally as níce.
6 Sáve the gréen Bermúda shórts and yéllow pólo shírts for Orlándo.
7 Hów to vísit Miámi and survíve.
8 Tínted wíndows would be níce. Só wóuld a cár phóne.

17.6 Bring, call and cut
VERBS AND IDIOMS

ANSWERS

1 brought about   2 brought up
3 bring (them) down   4 bring (them) back
5 called off   6 call in   7 call (it) off
8 call for   9 call (me) back   10 cut down
11 cut out   12 cut off

17.7 When in Rome . . .
LISTENING

ANSWERS

1 D   2 F   3 A   4 B   5 C
(Sentence E is not used.)

TRANSCRIPT   *3 minutes 30 seconds*

NICK: (*talking about Uganda*): Well, I was amazed, I don't know, I think I was expecting somewhere very dry and barren for some reason and in fact it's the most incredibly lush and rich place. And it...the soil is a deep red and it looks as if you threw a seed in the ground it would grow into a tree by the next day. And the people are incredibly friendly...er...very welcoming.

SUSANNA: (*talking about Switzerland*): Well, I know it quite well because my grandparents live there, so as a child I used to go there every year. And it's very clean and there are a lot of flowers, but all the same flower: geraniums, red geraniums. And they're in every window box on every house so wherever you go you see these flowers, bright red. Um...there's cows in the mountains and you hear...you hear the cow bells going and...and the grass is very green, and little tiny chalets sort of nestling. Um...it's kind of too good to be true, and the people are a bit like that too.

NEIL: (*talking about Poland*): . . . and I couldn't get anywhere because they have their own code of politeness and behaviour, you have to understand it and I...I couldn't make myself understood, I would go to a canteen and I would ask for...like...a piece of lemon to go in my tea and I wouldn't get it. And I asked my friend...um...who came from...came from the local place...um...what I should do about this because it was driving me nuts. And he said, 'Ah you must remember,' he said, 'We do things differently in this country, you must . . . everything's done with charm, between man and woman is charm.' So the next day I went into the canteen and I said to this enormous woman, who must have been at least 90 years old, 'Could I please have a bit of lemon?' And she gave me a bit with a big smile on her face and she kissed me and it was great.

GERTRUD: (*talking about Japan*): Well, it's quite extraordinary because...um...it's really like a different planet, it's so alien to everything you know when you come from the West...er...so it's quite overwhelming. Apparently it takes eight years to learn the basic rules of behaviour, which is a bit daunting really. And everything's just so different: the smells, the colours, um...the food, the taste, the music even. And...um...everything is very aesthetic, they're very aesthetic people, and so the way the food is arranged is very beautiful, and...um...for instance you can apparently even give someone a glass marble but it's got to be beautifully wrapped and you can give that as a present to your boss.

NIGEL: (*talking about the USA*): One of the things that struck me really was the portions of the food when you go into a restaurant. You get this huge quantity of food that everybody seems to manage to finish. And when you look at some of the people, most of the people, they're either very thin and terribly health-conscious or they're grossly overweight, obviously from eating these huge portions of food.

17.8 Paper 2: Writing
EXAM TECHNIQUES

B MODEL LETTER

Dear Yoshi,

Thank you for the lovely postcard.

I'm afraid that there's a slight problem because I'll be away when you arrive.

So what I've done is book a room for you in a nice hotel called the Hotel Comfort. I'm sending you the brochure so you can see what it's like. Then, when I get back on Monday 16th, you can come and stay with me.

From the airport take the bus which says CITY CENTRE on it. It goes non-stop to the railway station, and the Hotel Comfort is directly opposite.

But it would be better if you could change your flight date – is it possible to do that, or is it too late?

Now for your questions. The same clothes you'd wear at home will be fine here. And about £200 spending money will be plenty – if you do run out, I can lend you some.

And some great news! My brother is free during your second week. He's offered to drive us around in his car so that you can see some of our lovely mountains, beaches and historic buildings.

I'm really looking forward to seeing you!

Best wishes

---

18 The arts   Culture   Music
Yes, but is it art?

18.1 The arts
VOCABULARY AND SPEAKING

A **1 & 2** Here are some suitable adjectives to describe the pictures:

1 *calm   massive   monumental   puzzling   serene*
2 *beautiful   classical   harmonious   lyrical   melodic   quiet*
3 *deafening   exciting   exhilarating   loud   modern   noisy   tuneful*
4 *colourful   jolly   rhythmic   traditional   festive*

3 & 4 The instruments heard on the recording are:

1 a violin, 2 a saxophone, 3 an acoustic guitar, 4 an electric guitar, 5 a piano, 6 a flute, 7 a trumpet, 8 an organ, 9 drums, 10 a clarinet.

B **1**

> **ANSWERS**
> 1 actor/actress/dancer/performer
> 2 pianist/piano player   3 guitarist/guitar player   4 violinist   5 conductor
> 6 soloist   7 potter   8 sculptor
> 9 dramatist/playwright   10 genius

C The styles illustrated are:

Murnau with Church (1910) by Wassily Kandinsky – abstract, 20th century
The Morning Walk (1785) by Thomas Gainsborough – portrait
Dance at Bougival (1883) by Pierre-Auguste Renoir – French impressionist
The Poppy Field (1873) by Claude Monet – French impressionist, landscape
Playing chess (c 1400) by Elwes? – medieval
Self portrait (1669) by Jan Rembrandt van Rijn – great master, portrait
The Wizard (1951) by René Magritte – surrealist, 20th century

18.2 Mozart
READING

A

> **ANSWERS**
> 2 3   3 5   4 5   5 7   6 0   7 7   8 5
> 9 2½   10 1   11 0   12 14   13 1791

B Record your answers to the questions.

18.3 The future
GRAMMAR REVIEW

A

SUGGESTED ANSWERS
1 will pass   2 is going to   3 are coming
4 rises/will rise   5 arrive   will have been
6 get   'll make
7 are you going to tidy/clean it
8 will pay back   can

B

ANSWERS

2 *If the telephone rings, I'll answer it.*	✓
3 *After the floor will have been cleaned, I'll polish the furniture.*	has
4 *By the time you get home we will finish dinner.*	will have finished
5 *We'll be waiting for you when your plane is going to land at the airport.*	lands
6 *Liz has a baby next month.*	is going to have/ is having
7 *The new bypass shall be finished in the spring.*	will
8 *You won't be able to unlock the door if you won't remember your key.*	don't remember/ haven't remembered

C

ANSWERS (Many variations are possible.)
2 This weekend the weather ***'s going to get worse and it's going to*** snow.
3 Nobody seems to know ***why there aren't going to be*** any lessons next week.
4 They ***'re holding an exhibition*** of students' work in the main hall next week.
5 We ***won't find out the*** exam results until the end of September.
6 The performance ***is going to start in*** five minutes' time.

18.4 Art in New York
READING

A

ANSWERS (Many variations are possible.)
A 4   B 2, 4 and 6   C 5   D 5   E 1
F 6   G 3 and 6   H 2   I 5   J d   K b

B If you don't know anything about local museums, you might prefer to write about local clubs, discos, or maybe cinemas.

18.5 Joining up words
SPEAKING

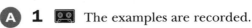

A 1 🔲 The examples are recorded.

2 & 3 MODEL VERSION 🔲

These are the consonant-to-vowel catenations that the two readers made in the recording. Alternative readings are possible.

SOUND_OF MUZAK SOOTHES PATIENTS

IT'S heard_in supermarkets, cinemas, lifts and_on the telephone_as callers wait to be connected. But – muzak_in the doctor's consulting room?

A family doctor trainee has found that background music relaxed patients, allowing them to absorb more information during_a consultation.

Dr Jonathan Kabler, of St Helier, Jersey, played continuous music during consultations with_a hundred_and two patients. He chose Mozart's piano concertos seven_and twenty-one.

Sixteen patients reported not hearing the music. Of the rest, one felt the music_interfered with the consultation, eighty-three per cent found_it relaxing, and sixty-seven per cent said_it helped the consultation.

'The result_appears to be a more_enjoyable surgery with lower levels_of stress for patients,' Dr Kabler writes_in_a letter to the British Journal_of General Practice.

18.6 *Fall* and *hold*
VERBS AND IDIOMS

ANSWERS
1 falls for (= is attracted to)
2 fell out with (= quarrelled)
3 fell over (= fell on the ground)
4 fallen through (= failed before completion)
5 fell in (= fell in the water)
6 held up (= robbed)
7 hold on (= hold firmly)
8 hold on (= wait)
9 held up (= delayed)
10 hold against (= allow a bad opinion to influence a decision) – there is a famous old play on words: 'If I say you have a beautiful body will you hold it against me?'

18.7 Works of art?

LISTENING AND SPEAKING

A The illustrations show two of Christo's works: *Surrounded Islands* (1983) and *Pont Neuf* (1985).

B

ANSWERS (Some variations are possible.)

1 1935   2 $23 million   3 1995   4 trivial and dull   5 14   6 40 km   7 temporary/ephemeral/not permanent   8 discussing it/arguing about it   9 next projects   10 take things for granted/be cynical

---

TRANSCRIPT   *5 minutes*

PRESENTER: Christo Javatcheff is the Bulgarian artist who is famous for wrapping things – not small things like birthday presents but huge things like buildings and islands. Although they stay wrapped for only two weeks these creations are hugely expensive and take years to plan. Julian Morris has been looking at his work.

JULIAN: Actually, it's *their* work, um...Christo is actually two people: Mr Javatcheff and his French wife Jeanne-Claude have been working together since...ooh...since the 1960s. They...in fact they were born on the very same day in 1935.

Their most expensive project so far was called *The Umbrellas*, which was in 1991, and that cost $23 million. There were 1,340 yellow umbrellas, which were stuck in the ground in California, and then 1,760 blue ones in Japan. And the umbrellas were opened simultaneously by 810 workers.

PRESENTER: That's amazing. Now the wrapped buildings are what he's best known for, aren't they?

JULIAN: Yes. Perhaps most famous of all is the *Wrapped Reichstag*, um...when Christo wrapped the Reichstag in Berlin in 1995. The idea was first developed in 1972, but it wasn't until 1994 that they finally actually got permission. And that project cost $7 million.

And another famous landmark they wrapped was the Pont Neuf across the River Seine in Paris – this was covered in 40,000 square metres of a very beautiful gold fabric, which was tied down with 13,000 metres of rope. Even the lamps and statues along the bridge were wrapped. Millions of people came to see it in 1985 and to discuss it. And it was...it was a marvellous sight. For 14 days the bridge remained wrapped, and...um...during those days, well, everything around the bridge looked somehow trivial and...and dull. The bridge was the focus of everyone's attention – it was a wonderful sight.

PRESENTER: I've always admired his . . . their work with coastlines and landscapes.

JULIAN: Yes, yes, well, their wrapped landscapes are famous: *Surrounded Islands* (which was...um...actually Jeanne-Claude's idea in the first place) um...consisted of 14 islands in Florida surrounded by sheets of bright pink nylon. That was in 1983 – it...it was a wonderful sight and the islands seen from the air looked like...um...tropical flowers floating in...in a blue sea.

And the *Running Fence*, which was a 40-kilometre long fence in Northern California running down in wonderful curves, following the curves of the hills to the Pacific Ocean. And the fence was made of...of sheets of fabric, over five metres high and supported by thousands of steel poles.

PRESENTER: Now, what inspired him, do you think?

JULIAN: Well, in 1920 the surrealist artist Man Ray wrapped a sewing machine in a blanket, gave it a title, and created a new work of art and this may have been Christo's original inspiration. His first works, which now are worth a small fortune, were wrapped bottles and cans, but nobody wanted them when he created them in Paris in the sixties.

PRESENTER: Now, most people judge works of art by whether or not they stand the test of time and are still considered to be works of art by future generations. Christo's work isn't like that, is it?

JULIAN: No, the Christos say that their art is all about challenging the immortality of art – the whole point is that the creation is temporary. They borrow a space for a couple of weeks and create a...well, a gentle disturbance. Their works are ephemeral, not permanent. And yet for years before, while the project is being planned, people all over the world are discussing it, disagreeing about whether it's a beautiful idea or a terrible one. And then the public take an active part in the Christos' creations in a way that...that visitors to an art gallery looking at a painting or a...or a statue can't do.

And the other thing is that the Christos' works don't *belong* to anyone – they aren't paid for by businessmen or millionaires – they're for everyone and no one has to pay to go and see them. They raise the money themselves and...and pay for the works by selling their sketches and models and plans. And all the money they make is used to pay for their next projects.

PRESENTER: So, why do they do it?

JULIAN: To make people think, to make people discuss them, to make people see things in a new way, to make them aware of the...the shapes and textures of buildings or...or landscapes they might otherwise take for granted or simply not notice at all. To persuade people not to be cynical, I suppose and encourage them not to take things for granted. To make them wonder – to remind everyone of something we tend to forget nowadays: 'If you don't wonder at the wonderful, it stops being a wonder.'

PRESENTER: Julian Morris, thank you very much.

18.8 We all make mistakes

EXAM TECHNIQUES

A

SUGGESTED ANSWERS
(Several variations are possible.)

I enjoy **visiting** galleries **because** I'm really interested **in** art. My favourite paintings are modern **ones, (delete 'painted')** by painters like Picasso and Matisse. Whenever I visit another city I **always** try to find time to **spend** an afternoon looking **at** paintings in an art museum. Some quite small cities have an art gallery, which may not contain any really famous or **valuable** works of art, **but** every museum has **its** surprises and there are often **fascinating** things to see – especially works by local artists who are unknown in **other** countries.

But I must confess that sometimes it's the people **(no comma)** who are more interesting **than** the paintings. As you wander round a museum it's wonderful to watch different people looking at the exhibits and reacting in different ways. It's a bit like sitting in a pavement café because you can watch other people without feeling **embarrassed** about **staring** at them.

So, I'd recommend a visit to a museum next time **you have nothing** else to do on a **rainy** day!

19 Describing people   Personalities and behaviour

Other people

19.1 It takes all sorts . . .
VOCABULARY

The signs of the zodiac are: Capricorn, Aquarius, Pisces, Aries, Taurus, Gemini, Cancer, Leo, Virgo, Libra, Scorpio and Sagittarius.

 Some more derogatory adjectives are: *arrogant, fussy, lazy, touchy, miserable, intolerant, unsociable, unreliable* and *mean*. And some more complimentary adjectives are: *sincere, reliable, practical, modest, cheerful, tolerant, loyal, sociable* and *generous*

ANSWERS
1 cheerful   2 bad-tempered   3 sensitive
4 likeable   5 sympathetic (= *showing sympathy to people who have problems*)   6 jealous
7 naughty   8 generous   9 self-confident
10 spoilt

19.2 Adverbs and word order
GRAMMAR REVIEW

ANSWERS
2 ✓
3 ✓
4 He ran into the room very suddenly.
5 I had toothache really badly yesterday.
6 She tripped over the cat and nearly fell over.
7 He had completely misunderstood what I told him to do.
8 ✓

 B 1

ANSWERS
1 position c for all adverbs
2 position b for all adverbs

2

SUGGESTED ANSWERS
In both sentences **all** the adverbs can be used in position **a** at the beginning of the sentence. The other 'comfortable' positions are as follows:
as usual 1d 2d   *certainly* 1c 2b
definitely 1c 2b   *maybe* (only a)
normally 1b or c or d 2b or d   *obviously* 1c 2b
often 1c 2b   *on Friday* 1d 2d   *one day* 1d 2d
perhaps 1c or d 2b or d   *possibly* 1c 2b
probably 1c 2b   *really* 1b or c 2b   *still* 1c 2b
surely 1c or d 2b or d   *usually* 1c or d 2b or d
yesterday 1d 2d

 C

SUGGESTED ANSWERS
2 You *hardly ever meet such* charming people.
3 The task *took an unexpectedly long* time to finish.
4 130 km of spaghetti *is eaten annually by* the average Italian.
5 She *rarely loses her* temper.
6 By now you *(will) have probably* already done some FCE practice tests.
By now you *(will) probably have* already done some FCE practice tests.
By now you *probably (will) have* already done some FCE practice tests.
7 You *definitely must/must definitely do some thorough* revision before the exams.
8 You *will certainly/certainly will* do well in your exams.

19.3 Use of English: Tricky questions
EXAM TECHNIQUES

 A

ANSWERS
1 You *had/'d better be* more careful.
2 I *wish I wasn't/weren't* so unhappy.
3 I *would/'d like you to* use a dictionary.
4 It *was Tony who* told me to do that.
5 I *suggest (that) you* arrive a few minutes early.
6 It *is time to do/you did* the work.

 B

ANSWERS
Sentences 1, 3, 5, 6, 9, 10, 11, 12, 13 and 15 are correct. These contain errors:

2	*You had better <u>to do</u> some revision.*	do
4	*I suggest <u>you to read</u> the questions very carefully.*	(that) you read
7	*Would you rather <u>being</u> healthy or rich?*	be
8	*I would rather <u>to wear</u> a sweater than a jacket.*	wear
14	*He wishes he <u>is</u> more intelligent.*	was/were
16	*If only I <u>have</u> worked harder.*	had

 C

ANSWERS
1 I'd *rather you didn't* interrupt me when I'm speaking.
2 I *suggest (that) you* phone and ask for information.
3 It's *better to be tactful than* frank.

4 I'd *prefer you to tell/give* me your decision now.
5 I *would/'d like you to* fill in this questionnaire.
6 It *is/'s time we found out/to find out* how much it's going to cost.
7 I *wish I didn't have* so much to do today.
8 If *only you had/'d told* me earlier.

19.4 First impressions
READING

A

ANSWERS

¶1 scared   startled   instinctively   pace
¶2 collided   reassure him
¶4 conveyed   agitation
¶6 delicately   disclosed
¶13 atmosphere   exaggerated   respective
doubtful   foresaw   utter

B

ANSWERS

1 a	2 c	3 c	4 b	5 c	6 c	7 a
8 a	9 c	10 d				

C   A description of the stranger:

The stranger seems very nervous, as though he is scared of the narrator. He is wrapped up in his own thoughts and rather unwilling to talk. He is smartly dressed, has small, pale, well-manicured hands and a charming smile. His teeth are 'like broken rocks'.

19.5 People talking . . .
LISTENING

To simulate what will happen in the exam, listen to each situation twice.

ANSWERS

1 b	2 c	3 c	4 c	5 a	6 c	7 b	8 a

TRANSCRIPT   *6 minutes*

NARRATOR: One. Listen to these two friends talking. What kind of document is the man filling in?

WOMAN: You're not really going to fill that in, are you?

MAN: Yes, why not?

WOMAN: Well, I think it's a waste of time.

MAN: It may be, but it doesn't cost anything, look. Anyway, as you're here you can help me. Right, now the first bits are name and address and so on, so I'll do those later. Right, now what about personality? How would you describe me? Serious? Reliable?

WOMAN: Serious and reliable? Hardly! Put down 'silly and unreliable'.

MAN: I can't do that, those aren't the alternatives. What about 'fashionable'?

WOMAN: In those shoes? Haha!

NARRATOR: Two. Listen to this woman talking about a man called Bill. Why can't she describe him?

WOMAN: Well everyone says he's a really nice guy, you know, intelligent, friendly. But even though I've been doing work for him since, what, November, I've only met him once. The problem is that the...the first time I met him I hardly paid him any attention because he'd just joined the company and my meeting was with Laura – w...we were introduced but I thought he was just one of Laura's very many assistants, you know? Um...then Laura left and...er...he took over. And then for months we only ever communicated by...by letter or fax – and...um...you know, the odd phone call. And on Tuesday I'm due to meet him again about six months after that first meeting and, do you know, I can't even remember what he looks like!

NARRATOR: Three. Listen to this man talking about a friend called Jane. What is Jane's greatest fault?

MAN: Oh, yeah, we go way back, I've known Jane for years. We've fallen out from time to time – that...that's not surprising because we're both quite strong characters. She has her views and I have mine – and we don't usually agree! But still we do get on surprisingly well. The problem is that she goes on trying to convince you, even though it's obvious that you're never going to agree with her. I mean, her...her frankness I don't mind, that's reasonable most of the time. Er...and there used to be times when she wouldn't talk to me for days when she thought I'd won one of our arguments.

NARRATOR: Four. Listen to this woman talking. When must the work be finished?

WOMAN: You told me it would be ready on Friday, but it's now Monday and you still haven't finished.

MAN: Well, I'm sorry but there have been other calls on my time, you know.

WOMAN: All right, but you did promise. Look the point is that the deadline is in two days' time and if everything isn't ready by then, then, well, I'm the one that's going to be in trouble.

MAN: I'm sorry. It'll be on your desk first thing tomorrow. I promise.

NARRATOR: Five. Listen to this man talking. Who is he speaking to?

MAN: It's very nice, very good. Who's that person on the right? It looks like me – oh it is me! I don't have such a long nose surely? Well, even if you think I do, I...I don't mind. I'm really quite flattered that you've included me. Um...listen, what I'd love to do is show it to Mrs Maycock – if you don't mind me borrowing it for a day or two. Would that be...um...would that be OK?

NARRATOR: Six. Listen to this man talking to a friend. Why is he late?

WOMAN: Here you are! You said you'd be here at half past.

MAN: I'm sorry I'm so late. I was running late all afternoon and then I...well, then I had this call just as I was leaving. It was Gary and he went on and on and I couldn't get him to stop. Anyway, by the time he did stop it was...well, it was already half past and it takes at least ten minutes to get here. I'm sorry, I would have been here earlier if it hadn't been for Gary.

NARRATOR: Seven. You're staying at a friend's flat. What does she want you to do?

WOMAN: Oh, hello, you're up already. Sleep well? I'm just going out to the supermarket. I've left the breakfast things on the table, there's coffee in the flask and the milk's in the fridge. I should be back in an hour or so. See you later . . . Oh, um...I nearly forgot. Tony may phone – he wanted me to give

him Chris's phone number, which is on a yellow
Post-it™ Note next to the phone. So if he calls, can
you let him have it? See you!

NARRATOR: Eight. You're sitting in a restaurant when you
overhear this conversation. How many pizzas are
ordered?
WAITRESS: Are you ready to order?
ALAN: Er...yes, I'd like a pizza with ham and mushrooms.
BRENDA: Um...I...I'll have one with tuna and anchovies,
please.
CHARLIE: Just a plain one for me, please.
DEBBIE: Um...I don't feel like pizza. What kind of fresh
pasta do you have today?
WAITRESS: Er...today's special is home-made spaghetti with
tomato and mushroom sauce.
DEBBIE: Oh that sounds nice. I'll have that please.
ALAN: Um...I'm going to change my mind . . . C...can I
have the same as her instead please?
CHARLIE: Yes, me too. Sorry.
WAITRESS: That's all right. So that's...um . . .

19.6 Synonyms
WORD STUDY

 2

SUGGESTED ANSWERS

nice	pleasant attractive satisfying friendly likeable agreeable
good	splendid excellent terrific perfect fine great marvellous wonderful
bad	terrible dreadful awful
thing	object topic article item subject
like	love appreciate enjoy value
dislike	hate loathe detest dread despise

3

large	big enormous huge immense great
small	little tiny unimportant
important	serious vital essential
intelligent	clever bright brainy smart
interesting	exciting entertaining fascinating
strange	unusual unfamiliar odd
unpleasant	nasty disgusting annoying terrible frightening
beautiful	attractive good-looking pretty

B

ANSWERS

3 plants
4 animals/mammals
5 meat
6 vehicles
7 buildings/dwellings
8 birds
9 metals
10 meals
11 seasons
12 clothes/garments
13 food
14 currencies
15 sports equipment
16 sports/games
17 hobbies
18 professions
19 pets
20 cereals
21 flowers
22 insects
23 publications
24 (musical) instruments

19.7 Leave, let, pull and run
VERBS AND IDIOMS

ANSWERS

1 let   2 pulling   3 pull   4 leave   5 leave
6 let   7 leave/run   8 ran/runs   9 left
10 run   11 let   12 runs/ran

B

ANSWERS

1 leave out (= omit)   2 left over (= remaining)
3 left behind (= forget)   4 let down
(= disappointed)   5 let in (= admit)
6 let off (= allow to explode)   7 pulls up/is
pulling up (= stops)   8 pulled out (= removed)
9 pulled down (= demolished)   10 running
over (= killing or injuring)   ran into (= collided
with)   11 run out of (= have no more)
12 run after (= chase)   13 ran into (= met by
chance)   14 run off with (= left secretly or
unexpectedly)

19.8 Describing people
WRITING

SUGGESTED ANSWERS

1 He is a slightly overweight man in his mid-30s.
He is terribly selfish and even dishonest but
his worst feature is that he loses his temper
whenever people disagree with him.
2 She is a very thin lady in her late 50s. She does
tend to be rather absent-minded but she has a
delightful sense of humour and is always ready
to help other people with their problems.
3 He is 18 years old and very athletic. He really
loves sport and his favourite game is football.
In his spare time he enjoys going out with his
friends and particularly going to the cinema.
4 She is 16 years old and a very studious young
woman who enjoys reading. She has four
brothers and two sisters. When she leaves
school, she hopes to go to university, where
she wants to study engineering.

B THREE MODEL COMPOSITIONS

1

The two people I admire most are my aunt and uncle. They are my mother's sister and her husband and they have a small farm in the country about 200 km from where I live.

My aunt is quite tall, she has wavy black hair and wears glasses. She has a round, friendly face and smiles quietly to herself while she's working – even when she's cooking or washing up! She has two children who are two and four years old. Amazingly, she is able to look after them and do all her work in the home and on the farm and she never, never loses patience or gets cross. That's what I admire in her.

Her husband is quite a short man with attractive brown eyes who always behaves charmingly even when people are not pleasant to him. He's busy every day of the week from morning till evening. Whenever I go to visit them he encourages me to help with the work, and with him even routine jobs seem fun. That's what I admire about him – he makes work seem a pleasure.

2

I'll never forget the first time I met Chris. He was sitting on a bench in the park, looking very depressed and cold. He had no coat on and it had started to rain quite heavily.

Normally, I wouldn't have dreamt of stopping to talk to a complete stranger who looked like that – not that he looked like a tramp or anything: his shoes were well polished and his clothes were quite smart. But on an impulse I stopped walking and said to him, 'Are you OK?' in a sympathetic voice.

He said he was but I sat down beside him and he started telling me how his wife had just locked him out of the house after a row and so he was sitting in the rain waiting for her to calm down and let him in again. I suggested that we went somewhere warm and dry, so we found a nearby café and continued our conversation.

And that was how I met Chris – the man who was later to become my worst enemy.

3

Dear Maria,

As this is my first letter to you, let me begin by introducing myself: my name is Susan Underwood and I live with my parents in Brompton, which is a little town about 40 km north of London.

I have curly fair hair, blue eyes and a round freckled face. I'm quite tall and a bit overweight at the moment! I enjoy listening to classical music and going to the cinema. Of course, I also watch television and I particularly enjoy watching old movies.

I'm still at college and I'm studying for a diploma in hotel management at Brompton College. If I pass my final exams next summer, I hope to get a job somewhere abroad for a year to get experience of foreign hotels, and also learn a foreign language. I'm really looking forward to starting work, even though the course I'm doing is excellent.

That's about all I can think of to tell you about myself. Do write back and tell me all about yourself. I'll write again soon.

Yours truly,

20
Memories

 20.1

Paper 1: Reading
EXAM TECHNIQUES

A For the answers to these questions, see 16.8 in the Student's Book.

B

ANSWERS

1 E   2 D   3 G   4 B   5 F   6 A
(Sentence C is not used.)

 20.2

Paper 2: Writing
EXAM TECHNIQUES

A

ANSWERS

Careless mistakes and slips of the pen:

1 *The castle <u>contain</u> many <u>treasure</u> und <u>painting</u>.*
contains   treasures   paintings

2 *Spelling mistakes are not serious but they do <u>lost</u> you marks.*   lose

3 *My brother has brown eyes and so <u>do</u> my sister.*
does

4 *Could you tell me what time <u>does</u> the museum opens?*   ~~does~~

5 *Which one of you <u>payed</u> for the tickets?*   paid

Mistakes that may be harder to notice:

6 *After visiting the museum he <u>had not</u> very much time left.*   did not have

7 *His hair is very long, it's time for him to have <u>cut it</u>.*
it cut

8 *I <u>am</u> waiting for you <u>since</u> four hours.*
have been   for

9 *They <u>never visited</u> Rome before their first visit in 1987.*   had never visited

10 *She <u>never wrote</u> a letter by hand since she <u>has</u> bought a computer.*   has never written   ~~has~~

11 *I <u>am</u> learning English <u>during</u> five years.*
have been   for

12 *A <u>suspicious</u> is <u>questioning</u> by the police.*
suspect/suspicious person   being questioned

13 *Before they <u>had gone</u> out they <u>had been watched</u> the news on TV.*
went   had been watching/watched

B For the answers to these questions, see 17.8 in the Student's Book.

C MODEL COMPOSITION FOR PART 1

Dear Bob,

Thanks for your letter. Given a choice between York and Cambridge, I think I'd recommend Cambridge. The main reason is that the two-hour journey to York would take four hours out of your day. I know this will disappoint Richard, but never mind.

In Cambridge Helen would enjoy looking at the paintings in the Fitzwilliam Museum and Kettle's Yard. But because this wouldn't appeal to you, Bob, I think Helen and Mary should concentrate on the museums before lunch. Meanwhile, Richard and you could go for a walk beside the river and explore the old colleges. You could all meet for lunch, perhaps in a pub by the river – the money you'd save by not going to York could be spent on a really good lunch.

Then after lunch why don't you hire a boat on the river before going together to admire King's College Chapel. By that time you'll be ready to catch the train to London, and you'll be back there in an hour or so.

Hope you enjoy your day! Send me a postcard!

Best wishes,

20.3

Paper 3: Use of English
EXAM TECHNIQUES

PART 1 ANSWERS

1 A   2 D   3 C   4 B   5 A   6 B
7 A   8 C   9 B   10 B   11 D   12 B
13 B   14 A   15 B

PART 2 SUGGESTED ANSWERS

16 experience   17 than   18 seats
19 hour   20 sell/rent   21 from
22 many/most/some   23 instance/example
24 century   25 sport/game
26 living/livelihood   27 paid
28 children/sons/daughters   29 rather
30 between

PART 3 ANSWERS

31 It's *ages since I last saw/met* my old school friend.
32 The questions *were (too) hard to* answer.
33 I *had never visited/been to* North America before.
34 The *Pyramids were built by* the ancient Egyptians.
35 She *will/'ll soon have to* give up her job.
36 We *found that the shop* was closed due to illness.
37 The hill *was easy to climb* despite the heat.
38 You *shouldn't have put so* much salt in the soup.
39 It *is/'s too salty to* eat.
40 We *ran out of time so* we didn't finish the exercise.

PART 4 ANSWERS

41 ✓   42 so   43 as   44 if   45 it   46 ✓
47 an   48 end   49 ✓   50 with   51 ✓
52 so   53 ✓   54 ✓   55 about

PART 5 ANSWERS

56 industrial   57 production   58 employees
59 purchasers   60 marketing
61 manufacturers   62 advertisements
63 descriptions   64 satisfaction
65 enjoyment

20.4 Paper 4: Listening

EXAM TECHNIQUES

A For the answers to these questions, see 15.3 in the Student's Book.

B 📼

ANSWERS   (Questions 1–10)

1 about three or four   2 playground/park
3 alone   4 (her) teddy
5 bite/get her teddy   6 ran away/off
7 empty/deserted   8 fetch help/their father
9 their father   10 liked/trusted dogs

TRANSCRIPT   *2 minutes*

LIZ: I remember when I was very little, about three or four, my brother used to take me to the local playground. He was a bit older than me. And he used to look after me while I went on the swings and, you know, the slide and things. Well, one afternoon I went out with him after tea and I was sitting on one of the swings with my teddy bear and I was swinging away and talking to Teddy, you see, when it gradually dawned on me that I was all alone and that my brother had left me by myself and there was no one else in the playground at all. And it was starting to get dark. Then – ooh, I can remember it, it sends shivers down my spine even now – I saw this big fierce dog sniffing around the swings a...and as I was going backwards and forwards it started to bark at me. Well, first I sort of, you know, tried to be terribly brave and I wanted to make it go away so I shouted at it and it took no notice and started, you know, jumping up at me and trying to bite, well not me, but I think it was my teddy bear. Well, I started to cry and scream and got in a terrible state sort of trying to climb up the swing and...and no one came and it was getting darker and darker. And...er...oh, I was in such a state. Well, eventually I saw my Dad running towards me waving a big stick and shouting at the dog and he chased the dog away and took me in his arms and I...I clung onto him and he held...held me and I cried and cried and cried until eventually I suppose I stopped. Well, I never saw the dog again but I always made sure that, you know, after that there were other people in the playground when I went. And well, of course, later I realised that my brother hadn't abandoned me to be eaten by this dog. I suppose he must have run back home to fetch my father and...and er...I suppose he must have been very frightened too. But he obviously felt very responsible for me and he ran home to get help. But since then...whew...I've always been so careful with dogs and I've never trusted them.

ANSWERS   (Questions 11–15)

11 D   12 C   13 E   14 F   15 A
(Sentence B is not used.)

TRANSCRIPT   *5 minutes*

SPEAKER 1: I'll...um...I'll never forget the time, it was when my kid was quite young, he must have been about two I think...um...and I was working in the sitting room and he was going up the stairs and then suddenly there was this enormous crash, the biggest...er...loudest bang you've ever heard and things falling down and then one single scream and I rushed out of the sitting room and...to see Joe, my child, lying face down on the floor. And I rushed over to him and...um...shake...shook him and said 'Are you all right? Are you OK?' and couldn't rouse him, he was...he had his eyes closed, absolutely nothing. So I rushed to the phone, picked up the phone, dialled 999 and said 'You've got to come round here immediately. You've got to come round, this is happening', manic, you know, mad panic and everything. And I was just at a pause in what I was saying to the person on the other end of the phone and there was this little giggle and laugh and he'd been having me on all the time.

SPEAKER 2: Well, I'll never forget the time that I flew over the Grand Canyon. I was staying in Las Vegas and decided to go over in...in a plane because they do these sort of little flights in these tiny little planes, about 20 people can go at a time, you get a little commentary in your ears with these headphones on and you've got these great big windows that come up. And I remember...er...thinking 'Oh, this is nice, this is nice' as we approached it, 'Oh this is really rather amazing'. And then we approached it again, and approached it from all sorts of different angles, and kept flying over it. It was the most awe-inspiring experience, and I remember bursting into tears, quite unexpectedly at the...um..astou...just incredible vastness and beauty of the whole thing.

SPEAKER 3: . . . I'd been at work all day and I got off the train, went to the road where I'd actually parked my car and in its place was another red car, and I walked around this car, which was a Mini and was much smaller than my car and I don't know what I expected it to do, whether I expected it to change back into my car, but I was completely flabbergasted because there was no glass on the floor, there was no sign that anybody had forced entry into my car, and then of course it dawned on me that my car had gone, and was nowhere to be seen, so I had to then go and phone the police and...um...it...it was the most frustrating experience because I was actually about to move house.

SPEAKER 4: . . . it was last year, we'd been away on holiday and...er...we'd just arrived back from the airport. And...um...I went to open the front door and couldn't get in, it was locked and I...I kept thinking 'This is very strange' but my mind wouldn't really accept the fact that I couldn't open the door and so I kept thinking 'Well, perhaps somebody's in there who we'd sort of let stay in there while we were away and they've locked the door and they're asleep and they can't hear us' even though I knew that there wasn't anybody and that we hadn't let anybody sleep in the house. Anyway so we went round the back...um...and sure enough there was a window open, so I had to be brave and climb through the window. I sort of went around the house stomping loudly and shouting to see if anybody was there but there wasn't, and of course all the hi-fi and things and televisions and whatever had been stolen.

SPEAKER 5: I'll never forget the time I was inside my house and I heard bang-bang-bang from outside. And I thought, 'My gosh, that's either somebody making a hell of a noise or that's a gunshot'. So I opened my front door and looked outside and saw two men rush past me in rather a hurry...ha...so I rushed to phone the police, I didn't really know what had happened but I assumed that they had shot somebody. Phoned the police, came back outside, went along the corridor – we live along a corridor of flats – um...saw some people making a lot of commotion, saying 'He's been shot, he's been shot'. Anyway, what had happened was somebody had shot somebody else through the shoulder, narrowly missing the child that was standing behind him. And...um...er...it turned out that had I opened my front door just a second earlier, I would have been shot too because there were three shots and two of them went into that house and one went down the corridor right next to our front door and there's still a mark on the wall to this day the police have marked up and that would have been me, gone.

NARRATOR: That's the end of 20.4 and now you've come to the end of the listening exercises in New Progress to First Certificate. We hope you've enjoyed them and found them useful. Good luck with your exam!

C Parts 1 and 4 have not been practised.

20.5 Paper 5: Speaking
EXAM TECHNIQUES

A For the answers to these questions, see 14.2 in the Student's Book.

B If possible, do this activity with another student, not on your own.

20.6 Good luck!

During the exam:

Don't . . .
- spend too long on any one question
- get flustered if time seems to be short.

Do . . .
- make notes
- write legibly
- leave room to put in further ideas or make corrections later.

It would be a good idea to do a complete practice test from *Cambridge Practice Tests for First Certificate* now.

FCE at a glance

The UCLES (University of Cambridge Local Examinations Syndicate) FCE (First Certificate in English) exam is held in June and in December each year. The exam assesses general proficiency in English through the testing of the candidates' abilities in reading, writing, speaking and listening and their knowledge of vocabulary and grammar.

PAPER 1: READING   *1 hour 15 minutes*

Part	Task Type	Focus	Number of Questions	Task Format
1	Multiple matching	Understanding the gist, the main points, detail, the structure of the text, specific information, or deducing the meaning	6–7	A text preceded by multiple matching questions. Candidates have to match an item from one list with an item in another list, or match items to elements within the text itself.
2	Multiple choice	as Part 1	7–8	A text followed by four-option multiple choice questions.
3	Gapped text	Understanding the gist, main points, detail and text structure	6–7	A text from which paragraphs or sentences have been removed followed by the removed items in jumbled order. Candidates have to decide where in the text the items were removed from.
4	Multiple matching or multiple choice	as Part 1	13–15	as Part 1

- One part may contain one text, or two or more shorter texts.
- The texts may come from any of these sources: advertisements, correspondence, fiction, brochures, guide books, manuals, messages, newspaper articles, magazine articles or reports.
- In all, candidates have to read 1,900–2,300 words (about 350–700 words per text).
- Candidates indicate their answers by shading the correct lozenges on the special answer sheet (see page 283). The total number of marks is 40 (20% of the total).

Part	Task Type and Focus	Number of Tasks and Length	Task Format
1	Question 1 Writing a transactional letter	1 compulsory task 120–180 words	The candidate is guided by 1–3 short texts and sometimes visual prompts as well as by the rubric (instructions).
2	Questions 2–4 Writing one of the following: – an article – an informal or non-transactional letter – a discursive composition – a descriptive or narrative composition or short story	4 tasks from which candidates choose 1 120–180 words	The task or composition is explained in the rubric.
	Question 5 Writing one of the above on a prescribed background reading text	2 options	The task is explained in the rubric.

- Part 1 (Question 1) is compulsory.
- For Part 2, Candidates choose ONE question from Questions 2–5.
- Candidates may be asked to write any of the following task types: letters, articles, reports, compositions or essays – all written for a given purpose and target reader.
- Candidates write in a special answer booklet which is read and marked by an examiner. The total number of marks is 40 (20% of the total).
- The examiners have followed standardised induction, training and co-ordination procedures and use criterion-referenced assessment scales. The scales assess such language features as: range of vocabulary and structure; accuracy of vocabulary, structures, spelling and punctuation; appropriacy; organisation and cohesion; task achievement.

PAPER 3: USE OF ENGLISH   *1 hour 15 minutes*

Part	Task Type	Focus	Number of Questions	Task Format
1	Multiple choice cloze	Emphasis on vocabulary	15	A 'modified cloze' text with 15 gaps, followed by 15 four-option multiple choice questions.
2	Open cloze	Grammar and vocabulary	15	A 'modified cloze' text with 15 gaps.
3	Key word transformations	Grammar and vocabulary	10	Sentences with gaps. The gaps must be filled using the given word and other words which are necessary, but without changing the meaning of the sentence.
4	Error correction	Emphasis on grammar	15	A text containing errors. Some lines are correct, some lines contain an extra unnecessary word which must be identified.
5	Word formation	Vocabulary	10	A text with 10 gaps. Each gap must be filled with a word formed from the 'stem' word which is given beside the text.

- Candidates write their answers on the special answer sheet (see pages 284–285). The total number of marks is 65, which is 'scaled down' to 40 (20% of the total).

Part	Task Type	Focus	Number of Questions	Task Format
1	Multiple choice	Understanding gist, main points, function, location, roles and relationships, mood, attitude, intention, feeling or opinion	8	A series of short unrelated extracts (about 30 seconds each) from monologues or interacting speakers. The multiple choice questions have three options.
2	Note taking or blank filling	Understanding gist, main points, detail or specific information, or deducing meaning	10	A monologue or interacting speakers (about 3 minutes).
3	Multiple matching	as Part 1	5	A series of short related extracts (about 30 seconds each) from monologues or interacting speakers. In the multiple matching questions candidates have to select the correct items from a list.
4	Selection from 2 or 3 possible answers	as Part 2	7	A monologue or interacting speakers (about 3 minutes). Candidates have to select between 2 or 3 possible answers: true/false, yes/no, three-option multiple choice, which speaker said what, etc.

- Each text is heard twice.
- The recordings contain a variety of accents.
- The monologues may include the following text types: answerphone messages, commentaries, documentaries, instructions, lectures, news, public announcements, advertisements, reports, speeches, talks, stories or anecdotes.
- The interacting speakers may be taking part in: chats, conversations, discussions, interviews, quizzes, radio drama or transactions.
- Candidates indicate their answers by shading the correct lozenges or by writing the correct word or words on the special answer sheet (see page 286). The total number of marks is 30, which is 'scaled up' to 40 (20% of the total).

PAPER 5: SPEAKING   *14 minutes approximately*

Part	Task Type	Focus	Length	Task Format
1	Short exchanges between each candidate and the interlocutor	Giving personal information and socialising	3 minutes	The candidates give personal information about themselves.
2	Long turn from each candidate with brief response from the other candidate	Exchanging personal and factual information, expressing attitudes and opinions, using discourse functions related to managing a long turn	4 minutes	The candidates are in turn given two colour photographs. They each talk about their photographs for about a minute. They are also asked to comment briefly on each other's photographs.
3	Candidates talk with each other	Exchanging information, expressing attitudes and opinions	3 minutes	The candidates are given visual prompts (photographs, line drawings, diagrams, etc.) which generate a discussion while they take part in tasks such as planning, problem solving, decision making, prioritising, speculating, etc.
4	Candidates talk with each other and with the interlocutor	Exchanging and justifying opinions	4 minutes	The interlocutor encourages the candidates to discuss other aspects of the topic of Part 3.

- Parts 2–4 are based on the same general theme.
- There are usually two candidates together with two examiners. One examiner acts mainly as interlocutor and manages the interaction by asking questions or giving the candidates cues. The other acts as assessor and does not join in the conversation.
- The examiners have followed standardised induction, training and co-ordination procedures and use criterion-referenced assessment scales. The scales assess such language features as: use of grammar; use of vocabulary; pronunciation; interactive communication and task achievement.
- This paper contributes 20% of the total marks.

RESULTS

Candidates are given semi-profiled results on their result slips. These show them in which particular papers their performance was very good or very weak. Pass certificates are issued to candidates who gain grades A, B or C. Certificates are not issued to candidates with failing grades: D, E or U (unclassified).

Sample answer sheets

CAMBRIDGE
EXAMINATIONS, CERTIFICATES AND DIPLOMAS
ENGLISH AS A FOREIGN LANGUAGE

University of Cambridge
Local Examinations Syndicate
International Examinations

For Supervisor's use only

Shade here if the candidate is
ABSENT or has WITHDRAWN

↳ — ↵

Examination Details	9999/01	99/D99
Examination Title	First Certificate in English	
Centre/Candidate No.	AA999/9999	
Candidate Name	A.N. EXAMPLE	

• Sign here if the details above are correct

⊠

• Tell the Supervisor now if the details above
  are not correct

Candidate Answer Sheet: FCE Paper 1 Reading

Use a pencil

Mark ONE letter for each question.

For example, if you think **B** is the right answer to the question, mark your answer sheet like this:

| 0 | A B C D |

Change your answer like this:

| 0 | A C D |

1	A B C D E F G H I
2	A B C D E F G H I
3	A B C D E F G H I
4	A B C D E F G H I
5	A B C D E F G H I

6	A B C D E F G H I
7	A B C D E F G H I
8	A B C D E F G H I
9	A B C D E F G H I
10	A B C D E F G H I
11	A B C D E F G H I
12	A B C D E F G H I
13	A B C D E F G H I
14	A B C D E F G H I
15	A B C D E F G H I
16	A B C D E F G H I
17	A B C D E F G H I
18	A B C D E F G H I
19	A B C D E F G H I
20	A B C D E F G H I

21	A B C D E F G H I
22	A B C D E F G H I
	B C D E F G H I
24	C D E F G H I
	A B C D E F G H I
26	A B C D E F G H I
27	A B C D E F G H I
28	A B C D E F G H I
29	A B C D E F G H I
30	A B C D E F G H I
31	A B C D E F G H I
32	A B C D E F G H I
33	A B C D E F G H I
34	A B C D E F G H I
35	A B C D E F G H I

SAMPLE

CAMBRIDGE
EXAMINATIONS, CERTIFICATES AND DIPLOMAS
ENGLISH AS A FOREIGN LANGUAGE

University of Cambridge
Local Examinations Syndicate
International Examinations

For Supervisor's use only

Shade here if the candidate is
ABSENT or has WITHDRAWN

➡ ▭ ↩

Examination Details	9999/03
Examination Title	First Certificate in English
Centre/Candidate No.	AA999/9999
Candidate Name	A.N. EXAMPLE

99/D99

• Sign here if the details above are correct

X

• Tell the Supervisor now if the details above
  are not correct

Candidate Answer Sheet: FCE Paper 3 Use of English

Use a pencil

For **Part 1**: Mark ONE letter for each question.

For example, if you think **C** is the
right answer to the question,
mark your answer sheet like this:

0	A B C D

For **Parts 2, 3, 4** and **5**: Write your
answers in the spaces next to the
numbers like this:

0	example

Part 1				
1	A	B	C	D
2	A	B	C	D
3	A	B	C	D
4	A	B	C	D
5	A	B	C	D
6	A	B	C	D
7	A	B	C	D
8	A	B	C	D
9	A	B	C	D
10	A	B	C	D
11	A	B	C	D
12	A	B	C	D
13	A	B	C	D
14	A	B	C	D
15	A	B	C	D

Part 2	Do not rite here
16	16
17	17
18	18
19	19
20	20
21	21
	22
	23
24	24
25	25
26	26
27	27
28	28
29	29
30	30

Turn
over
for
Parts
3 - 5

➡

Part 3		Do not write here
31		31 0 1 2
32		32 0 1 2
33		33 0 1 2
34		34 0 1 2
35		35 0 1 2
36		36 0 1 2
37		37 0 1 2
38		38 0 1 2
39		39 0 1 2
40		40 0 1 2

Part 4		Do not write here
41		
42		
43		43
44		44
45		45
46		46
47		47
48		48
49		49
50		50
51		51
52		52
53		53
54		54
55		55

Part 5		Do not write here
56		56
57		57
58		58
59		59
60		60
61		61
62		62
63		63
64		64
65		65

© **UCLES K&J** *You may photocopy this page.*

CAMBRIDGE
EXAMINATIONS, CERTIFICATES AND DIPLOMAS
ENGLISH AS A FOREIGN LANGUAGE

**University of Cambridge
Local Examinations Syndicate
International Examinations**

For Supervisor's use only

Shade here if the candidate is
ABSENT or has WITHDRAWN

➡ ▭ ⬅

Examination Details	9999/04	99/D99
Examination Title	First Certificate in English	
Centre/Candidate No.	AA999/9999	
Candidate Name	A.N. EXAMPLE	

• Sign here if the details above are correct

☒

• Tell the Supervisor now if the details above
  are not correct

Candidate Answer Sheet: FCE Paper 4 Listening

Mark test version below

A	B	C	D	E
▭	▭	▭	▭	▭

Use a pencil

For **Parts 1** and **3**:
Mark ONE letter for
each question.

For example, if you
think **B** is the right
answer to the
question, mark your
answer sheet like this:

0	A	B	C
	▭	▬	▭

For **Parts 2** and **4**:
Write your answer in
the spaces next to the
numbers like this:

0	*example*

Part 1

1	A	B	C
2	A	B	C
3	A	B	C
4	A	B	C
5	A	B	C
6	A	B	C
7	A	B	C
8	A	B	C

Part 2

		Do not write here
9		▭ 9 ▭
10		▭ 10 ▭
11		▭ 11 ▭
12		▭ 12 ▭
13		▭ 13 ▭
14		▭ 14 ▭
15		▭ 15 ▭
16		▭ 16 ▭
17		▭ 17 ▭
18		▭ 18 ▭

Part 3

	A	B	C	D	E	F
		B	C	D	E	F
20	A	B	C	D	E	F
21	A	B	C	D	E	F
22	A	B	C	D	E	F
23	A	B	C	D	E	F

Part 4

		Do not write here
24		▭ 24 ▭
25		▭ 25 ▭
26		▭ 26 ▭
27		▭ 27 ▭
28		▭ 28 ▭
29		▭ 29 ▭
30		▭ 30 ▭

Index

Exam techniques

Grammar review

Prepositions

Verbs and idioms

Word study

Writing